This volume is inspired by recent developments in two strands of economic theorising. The first one consists of various lines of research on structural economic dynamics that are based principally on three sources: John Hicks's work on traverse analysis, Luigi Pasinetti's on disproportional growth and Richard Goodwin's on methods of dynamic decomposition and economic fluctuations. The other strand goes back to Nicholas Georgescu-Roegen's development of an organisational theory of production based upon the interrelationship between tasks, fund factors and material transformations.

This volume proposes a new approach in the analysis of structural dynamics, in which a comprehensive view of the dynamics of the whole economic system is associated with the decomposition of the latter into subunits (such as processes, industries, vertically integrated sectors, eigensectors) in order to represent the disaggregated dynamics of structural adaptation and compositional change. On the other hand, a detailed representation of micro-organisational features leads to the analysis of networks and networking processes within and amongst such subunits.

In both cases, methods of decomposition feature prominently and play a critical role in the analytical representation of structural dynamics.

Production and economic dynamics

Production and economic dynamics

EDITED BY

MICHAEL LANDESMANN

Johannes Kepler University, Linz
Jesus College, Cambridge

ROBERTO SCAZZIERI

University of Bologna
Clare Hall, Cambridge

CAMBRIDGE UNIVERSITY PRESS
Cambridge, New York, Melbourne, Madrid, Cape Town, Singapore, São Paulo, Delhi

Cambridge University Press
The Edinburgh Building, Cambridge CB2 8RU, UK

Published in the United States of America by Cambridge University Press, New York

www.cambridge.org
Information on this title: www.cambridge.org/9780521114257

First published 1996
This digitally printed version 2009

A catalogue record for this publication is available from the British Library

Library of Congress Cataloguing in Publication data

Production and economic dynamics / edited by Michael A. Landesmann and
Roberto Scazzieri.
        p.   cm.
    ISBN 0-521-46251-7
    1. Production (Economic theory)   I. Landesmann, Michael A.
    II. Scazzieri, Roberto.
    HB241.P728   1996   95-39212
                                                                    CIP

ISBN 978-0-521-46251-8 hardback
ISBN 978-0-521-11425-7 paperback

Contents

Part II Production organisation and economic dynamics

Figures

Tables

Contributors

SALVATORE BALDONE Professor of Economics, Polytechnic University of Milan

BERNARD BELLOC Professor of Economics, University of the Social Sciences, Toulouse

MARIO FALIVA Professor of Econometrics, Catholic University of Milan

CHRISTIAN GEHRKE Assistant Professor of Economics, University of Graz

RICHARD M. GOODWIN Emeritus Professor of Economics, University of Siena; formerly Reader of Economics, University of Cambridge; Fellow of Peterhouse, Cambridge

HARALD HAGEMANN Professor of Economics, University Hohenheim, Stuttgart; Life Member of Clare Hall, Cambridge

MICHAEL LANDESMANN Professor of Economics, Johannes Kepler University, Linz; Research Director, Vienna Institute for Comparative Economic Studies; formerly Fellow of Jesus College, Cambridge

CARLO FELICE MANARA Professor Emeritus of Geometry, State University of Milan; formerly Lecturer of Logic, Catholic University of Milan

ALBERTO QUADRIO CURZIO Professor of Economics, Catholic University of Milan; Chairman of the Faculty of Political Sciences, Catholic University of Milan

ALESSANDRO ROMAGNOLI Professor of Economics, University of Bologna; formerly Professor of Agricultural Economics, University of Florence

ROBERTO SCAZZIERI Professor of Economics, University of Bologna; Life Member of Clare Hall, Cambridge

Preface

The conception of this volume was inspired by recent developments in two strands of economic theorising. The first one consists of various lines of research on *structural economic dynamics*. Here, early work by John R. Hicks on traverse analysis, by Luigi L. Pasinetti on disproportional growth and by Richard M. Goodwin on methods of dynamic decomposition and economic fluctuations lay the basis upon which further contributions in the theory of structural change analysis were made. The other strand goes back to Nicholas Georgescu-Roegen who, in a number of contributions, pointed towards an *organisational theory of production activity* (based upon the interrelationships between tasks, fund factors and material transformations) which has inspired us in our own work.

What emerges from these two strands is that structural change can be approached in two ways: one way is 'macro to micro' analysis where the focus is to keep a comprehensive view of the dynamics of the economic system as a whole while decomposing the latter into sub-units (such as processes, industries, vertically integrated sectors, eigensectors, and so on) so that the disaggregated dynamics of structural adaptation and compositional change can be represented. The other way is 'micro to macro' in which the starting point is a richer representation of micro-organisational features of micro-units leading to the analysis of 'network' relationships within and amongst such sub-units. In both these two types of approaches, methods of decomposition (of a static and dynamic kind) feature prominently and seem to play a crucial role in the analytical representation of structural change processes.

The focus on production rather than on other types of economic activity in this volume is largely the result of the traditional emphasis of work in this area. The analytical tools presented in this volume could be applied to other types of economic activity but, for a number of reasons which will be discussed later on in the volume, they emerge in a very direct way when production activity is taken as the starting point. This volume aims at providing a comprehensive presentation of current research in the area of structural economic dynamics and at demonstrating how the above mentioned two strands can fruitfully complement each other.

We worked on this volume for a number of years in a number of places. We are grateful to the Department of Applied Economics at the University of Cambridge as well as the Faculty of Economics and the Economics Department at Bologna University where the bulk of the work was done. We here gratefully acknowledge a grant by the Italian Research Council ('Dynamics of Production Systems'), which was essential in the start-up phase of this project. We are also grateful to Jesus College, Cambridge, where Michael Landesmann was a Fellow until recently, as well as Clare Hall, Cambridge, where Roberto Scazzieri was a Visiting Fellow during a critical stage in the preparation of the manuscript, for research facilities and intellectual stimulation. The Faculty of Statistics of the University of Padua and the Department of Economics of the Johannes Kepler University in Linz also provided support for our cooperation and research.

We dedicate this book to our parents, our wives, Ayesha and Cristina, and our children, Luigi and Raphael, who, at various stages of our lives, gave us the support, space and, finally, the sense of urgency to complete this project.

MICHAEL LANDESMANN
ROBERTO SCAZZIERI

Introduction
Production and economic dynamics

MICHAEL LANDESMANN AND ROBERTO SCAZZIERI

1 The production process and economic dynamics

The aim of this volume is to develop a new conceptual framework for the analysis of the interrelationship between productive structures and economic dynamics. This will be done by investigating the relationship between sectoral representations of the dynamics of economic systems and more detailed analyses of productive organisations and economic change.

The theory of economic dynamics is by now an established tradition in the discipline. In extreme synthesis, a number of distinct approaches to economic dynamics may be identified. One approach considers the relationships between elements of an economic system within a given time interval, and exposes them to the impact of certain 'impulses', such as changes in exogenous variables or parameters. (Stability analysis in a general equilibrium framework of the neoclassical or classical type is an example of this approach to dynamic theory). Another approach, which is characteristically pursued by multisectoral analysis, concentrates upon the evolution over time in the composition of macroeconomic variables such as overall employment or investment. A third approach views dynamic processes in terms of relationships between the rates of change of economic variables (for instance employment growth, technical progress, rate of accumulation). This approach has its roots in Harrodian macrodynamics and has received considerable attention in the recent literature on economic dynamics.

A common, if seldom explicitly acknowledged, feature of all three approaches is the relevance of *structural constraints*, and of their evolution over time, in determining the dynamic paths followed by the economic system. Thus particular restrictions on the distribution of characteristics of economic agents (Hildenbrand, 1983), or on the specification of productive activities (Kirman, 1989), have been found important sources of constraints on the patterns of interactive behaviour leading to stability. On the other hand, the lack of coordination between the movements over time of different components of a given economic system (differential growth of

1

different industries/activities) combined with certain structural rigidities may be a major source of aggregate economic fluctuations or macro-economic disequilibria (see Hawkins, 1948; Hawkins and Simon, 1949; Pasinetti, 1981 and 1993; Baumol, 1967). Finally, within the framework of dynamic systems analysis, different speeds of adjustment of different but interrelated behavioural relationships will provide a 'structure' within which an overall process of change takes place (see, e.g., Medio, 1984; Silverberg, 1984).

The analysis of the organisational features of productive structures also lends itself to a considerable variety of approaches. For example, productive activity may be described by focusing upon the operations or tasks into which a complex process may be decomposed, thus following an approach that goes back at least to Smith's analysis of division of labour (Smith, 1776). Alternatively, production phenomena may be primarily related to the active elements (agents) in a productive transformation, such as human beings or machines. In this case, the issue of agents' capabilities, and of their utilisation over time, emerges as a critical organisational feature, which may interact with the subdivision of a process into tasks and sets of tasks (see, in particular, Babbage, 1835; Georgescu-Roegen, 1969). Finally, production has to do with the transformation of certain materials, which are carried over from one fabrication stage to another until a finished product is obtained. This last point may be associated with economists such as Böhm-Bawerk (1889), Menger (1981 [1st edn 1871] and 1888) and Lowe (1976).

Productive activities are a major source of differentiated and uneven change and, in general, of the complex dynamics of advanced industrial economies. Different sources and patterns of transformation are associated with productive activities, linked to the interaction over time among three fundamental *networks* of productive elements: (i) the *tasks* being performed; (ii) the *agents* participating in the process; (iii) the *materials* that enter the process and undergo a transformation in the course of productive activity. Each one of these three networks is associated with the *time* dimension in terms of either *durability* or the *sequential character* of process structures: tasks have to be completed and sequenced, often within given time intervals; agents may exert one or more capabilities to different degrees in different time intervals; materials may be carried through a sequence of fabrication stages in a continuous or intermittent way. The state of a productive process at any given time reflects the coordination pattern among productive elements within each network, and the coordination of the different networks with each other. As a result, the evolution of the economic system over time depends to an important degree on the internal structure of productive processes (made up of the three elements above) and their pattern of coordination over time. The detailed consideration of productive processes calls attention to a number of important issues in the analysis of economic dynamics.

The 'real time' dimension in characterising productive activity is of particular relevance for the study of *change* in economic systems: the reason is that production processes which have inherent features of *persistence* tend to constrain the feasible range of dynamic paths which the economic system may follow. The relationship between production processes and economic dynamics makes specification of the above features of durability a critical issue when the transformation of economic systems is considered. The notions of durability and 'complementarities over time' (Hicks, 1939; see also below) point towards a more general phenomenon, that of *relative structural invariance*. By this we mean that processes of transformation affecting any set of productive activities have to cope with inherent features of persistence, which may relate to a number of the analytical dimensions of the production process (such as material transformation flows, the utilisation of the capabilities of productive agents, and forms of sequencing and organisation of productive tasks; see also Landesmann and Scazzieri, 1990).

Structural economic dynamics may be defined as the analysis of economic transformations that explicitly account for the *relative persistence* of certain elements or relationships of economic structure while other elements or relationships are subject to change. This definition is of a general kind, for it encompasses changes at different levels of the economic structure and of different origins. For example, one may observe structural dynamics at the level of the overall economic system, as in Ricardo's macroeconomic analysis of decreasing returns (see, in particular, Ricardo, 1817, chapter 2 'On Rent'). But structural dynamics may also take place within smaller units, such as individual establishments and networks of establishments, as in Dahmén's 'development blocks' (Dahmén, 1955), or at the level of individual industries, as in Lowe's analysis of structural change *within* one particular sector (the sector producing machine tools; see Lowe, 1976, part I and chapter 12).

The special linkage between structural change and relative invariance points to the importance of production activities when structural dynamics are considered. The reason is that production processes are generally characterised by the co-existence of features of persistence and features of change: the dynamic element is primarily associated with the transformation of materials (essentially, the transformation of raw materials into finished products), whereas the 'persistence' element is associated with the productive apparatus, and with the organisational set-up that 'survives' from one production period to another and ensures that a certain productive potential is maintained over time. The latter feature is of critical importance, for it entails that any given productive apparatus (or productive unit) maintains its identity independently of the particular materials that are being processed at any given time.

The analysis of the internal dynamics of production processes (or sets of production processes) is thus an essential feature in investigations concerning the structural dynamics of economic systems, particularly in the presence of sustained technical progress and organisational change.

2 The three analytical dimensions of productive activity

At one level of analysis, a production process may be decomposed into primitive elements such as human actions, mechanical operations, chemical reactions and so on. In this way, the purely 'praxeological' dimension of productive activity (tasks and processes) comes to the fore, whilst the structural analysis of capabilities (of human beings or machines) and the 'transformational' analysis of the materials-in-process may be overlooked on a first approximation.[1] Another level of analysis focuses upon *skills* (according to which a given agent *knows how* a certain task or function may be performed) and *capabilities* (according to which a given agent can actually perform a certain operation given the scale at which it must be executed). In this case, the analysis of the production process establishes a relationship between the virtual set of actions that could be undertaken (the actions that are feasible with certain skills or capabilities) and the set of actions that are executed under particular circumstances. The emphasis upon skills and capabilities highlights the fact that productive activities require the existence of a certain 'fund' of formal and informal knowledge, which may then be used in a variety of ways depending upon the production programme adopted. Skills and capabilities point to the importance of the immaterial side of production, that is, of the complex network of cognitive rules and practices, customs, and social norms from which production is made possible.[2]

The third level of analysis of production processes considers production activity from the point of view of the *materials* entering it, or leaving it as products or residuals. In this case, the production process appears as a network of stocks and flows of finished commodities and work-in-process materials. Here, *time dependence* emerges as the most critical feature of production activity, for any given material is significantly related to production on condition that a certain *sequence* of transformation stages takes place. It follows that consideration of the production process as one of the transformation of materials poses most starkly the issue of synchronisation in time and quantity in dynamic processes. Materials 'bear the mark' of the transformation processes that have previously operated upon them, so that, at any given time, a certain range of future transformations is possible, whereas other transformations are 'blocked' by the very fact that, in general, previous transformations cannot be undone.

3 Structural economic dynamics

The economic history of major economies since the first industrial revolution shows that periods of high growth rates of production and national income are generally associated with compositional and qualitative changes of national production, as well as with changes in the dynamic characteristics of productive sectors (see, for instance, Deane and Cole, 1967; Landes, 1969; North, 1981; Baumol et al., 1989; Baumol, 1992; Rosenberg et al., 1992; Pasinetti and Solow, 1994). Similarly, phases of relative stagnation (or decelerated growth) are also characterised by changes in the relative weight of the various sectors, in their qualitative features (types of commodities produced, productive methods used) and in their dynamic behaviour.

The connection between economic dynamics and structural change was well known to the classical economists, whose growth theories (such as those of Smith and Ricardo) are inherently structural in the sense that growth is necessarily associated with the change of economic structure. In Smith, the division of labour may be extended in different sectors at different rates, thereby modifying the relative contribution of each sector to the overall increase of productivity and total output (Smith, 1776). In Ricardo, the existence of non-producible resources (land, mines) brings about a connection between growth and structural change that is based upon diminishing returns (Ricardo, 1817). In the classical theories, the relationship between economic dynamics and structural transformation is reinforced by the belief that an economic system whose structure is unchanging is bound to enter a zero-growth phase (Ricardo's stationary state, Smith's situation in which a 'full complement of riches' is attained).

Until recently modern economic theory has generally withdrawn from a comprehensive reformulation of the classical contributions on growth and structural change. Most analytical research has considered the 'engine of growth' in terms of proportional dynamics at a given rate, whereas structural change has often been described by a particular selection of facts (such as Hoffmann's ratio of capital goods to consumers goods, or Kaldor's share of manufacturing output) without attempting its general interpretation in terms of a theoretical model (see Hoffmann, 1958; Kaldor, 1966). In this book, we will consider a number of recent theoretical contributions (see particularly the chapters in part I) which have investigated structural change using a variety of analytical formulations.

3.1 Structural specification and relative structural invariance

In recent economic literature, the economic theory of structural change has attempted the formulation of a rigorous analytical framework by considering a variety of stylised facts and by adopting a variety of structural specifications. In general, it has proceeded from a limited selection of facts to the construction of analytical models capable of explaining certain critical features of structural dynamics.

One aim of this volume is to present an up-to-date assessment of the theory of structural economic dynamics and to consider the linkage between a purely analytical treatment of structural change and a more realistic analytical reconstruction of organisational features of productive activities and of their evolution through time. In this connection, *structural specification* emerges as a critical feature of dynamic models. Structural specification, extracting a limited set of analytical components and analysing their interrelationships, is always a restricted representation of reality as only a limited number of features are included. The careful examination of structural specification thus permits us to identify the descriptive basis of each model, that is, the range of historical situations to which it may be applied. A particular structural specification is generally associated with a definite pattern of *structural dynamics*, for the stylised historical features end up constraining the evolution of the model economy through logical time. It is associated with a particular range of feasible transformation paths that derive from the existence, within the given structure, of elements characterised by *different degrees of persistence*. The evolution of structures is thus regulated by a *principle of relative structural invariance*. In this way, structural dynamics is a process in which different elements or relationships of the existing structure are changing at different speeds (a special case would be that of elements that do not change at all). As a result, the relative position (or weight) of each element would get modified through time, and the evolution of the economic structure will be characterised by different degrees of resilience with respect to particular factors of change (such as technical innovation or population growth).

Analytical models of structural change introduce relative structural invariance in a variety of ways. For example, Hicks's traverse analysis considers the relative persistence of production processes due to 'complementarities over time', that is, due to the inherently sequential pattern of fabrication stages (see Hicks, 1973). Another example is Pasinetti's relationship between rising per-capita incomes and the law of the changing composition of the consumers' basket (Engel's Law) (see Pasinetti, 1981, 1993). This law is considered as a 'structural invariant', and structural change is analysed as the adjustment process ensuring the long-run consistency between producers' and consumers' learning. Richard Goodwin's contributions to dynamic analysis provide a third example of the workings of relative structural invariance in analytical models. Here, technical progress acts as a growth factor while distributional relationships/structures impose constraints on the dynamic utilisation of the growth potential (see Goodwin, 1982, 1990; Goodwin and Punzo, 1987).

Historical processes bring about the formation of relatively persistent structures, and a primary role of economic theory would be that of identifying a conceptual framework making sense of emergent structures, even if their generation is the outcome of independent and unrelated subprocesses (see Arthur, Landesmann and Scazzieri, 1991).

Structural change cannot be considered as a deterministic process regulated by precisely identified structural invariances. It is rather a probabilistic process generated through history but constrained by the relative persistence of certain coordination mechanisms. Such mechanisms can accommodate certain transformations but not others, so that structures of productive organisation may be an important factor in orienting the course of historical processes. For example, a given sequence of technical innovations may be associated with different paths of structural change depending upon the effectiveness of coordination devices within each form of productive organisation. As a result, a probabilistic 'generation of novelties' may be associated with precisely identifiable constraints and reinforcing mechanisms due to the relative persistence of institutional set-ups.

Organisational features of production processes may influence economic dynamics in an important way. In this context, productive structures may be described as *forms of productive organisation*, that is, as combinations of historical features that have acquired some degree of cohesion and persistence quite independently of the process by which they came about. In this way, we will attempt to show that analytical models of 'system-wide' processes of structural change (i.e., the contributions in part I) are compatible with approaches which discuss the analytical set-up of historical forms of productive organisations; this allows for a coordination of 'macro' and 'micro' perspectives in the analysis of economic dynamics. In particular, 'micro-to-macro' relationships call attention to the factors of change that emerge from processes at the level of individual productive units, or networks of such units, which may then affect the overall economic system. On the other hand, 'macro-to-micro' relationships focus on the opposite 'chain' of influences, in which a given impulse (or force) first modifies certain general (or 'aggregate') features of the economic system (such as macrodistributional relationships) which then start deeper processes of transformation at the level of microunits and of their networks. In this context, we will attempt to show that the specification of subsystems (i.e., ways of decomposing the overall economic system) plays an important role in this linkage of macro and micro perspectives of economic dynamics.

3.2 Stability, temporary equilibrium and adjustment processes

One important research tradition addresses the question of changes in the equilibrium values of certain endogenous variables (such as prices and quantities) if the so-called 'fundamentals' of the economic system (such as preferences, resource endowments, expectations) are being changed (see Hicks, 1939; Lindahl, 1939 [1st edn 1929]; La Volpe, 1993 [1st edn 1936]; see also Hahn, 1982).

Much of the literature following this approach is concerned with the problem of stability (tendency of a given equilibrium state to maintain itself through time independently of perturbations) and structural change is virtually reduced to the (unexplained) process by which the fundamentals of the economic system are varied over time. A distinction within the above line of research concerns whether the economic system adjusts instantaneously to parameter changes, or some lag is introduced between the original impulse and the completion of the adjustment process. The former approach, which was originally introduced by La Volpe (1993 [1st edn 1936]), is characteristic of many subsequent contributions on stability of general equilibrium (see, for example, Smale, 1981). The latter approach, which was originally followed by Lindahl (1939 [1st edn 1929]) and Hicks (1939), is rooted in the concept of 'temporary equilibrium', that is, of an equilibrium set of prices established at the beginning of one time interval which remains unchanged until the beginning of the next interval (on the assumption that no revision of expectations may take place during the period).

Temporary equilibrium leads to the idea that adjustment to an exogenous parameter change may take some time before it is completed. For example, a change in fundamentals may not always entail an immediate revision of expectations; information may be gathered and expectations may be revised at discrete points of time, say every Monday, so that it will only be after a certain sequence of weeks that the original impulse (or perturbation) will be fully absorbed.

The role of the adjustment lag in a temporary equilibrium framework suggests a treatment of structural change quite different from the comparative statics (or the comparative dynamics) approach. For in this case a perturbation leads to a sequence of changes connected with each other in a systematic way, so that 'complementarities over time' (i.e., causal linkages of adjustment processes across periods) are bound to emerge.

The temporary equilibrium approach suggests a number of ways in which a *process* of structural change may be accounted for.[3] First, full equilibrium is considered as the outcome of a sequence of changes. Second, the changes are teleologically connected (this is implied by the consideration of an adjustment process). Third, some notion of 'relative invariance' may be introduced.

3.3 Traverse analysis

The full implications of the temporary equilibrium approach for structural change analysis may only be considered if the original formulation of temporary equilibrium is dropped, and attention is shifted to the analysis of the traverse, which is a *transition path* joining two successive equilibrium growth trajectories (see Hicks, 1973). It may be worth noting that the connection between temporary equilibrium and traverse is due to the fact that a *sequence* of temporary equilibria may be a suitable representation of a traverse path on which the economic system gradually adjusts to a certain initial perturbation. Given Hicks's original treatment of temporary equilibria, and his emphasis upon 'complementarities over time', only a small step is necessary in order to explicitly consider the adjustment of economic structure over time.

Nonetheless, the shift from temporary equilibria to traverses is a fundamental one from a methodological point of view, for in traverse analysis structural change appears to be to a large extent an endogenous process, rather than an exogenous parameter change to which the economic system has to adjust. The approach adopted by traverse analysis is that of distinguishing distinct phases in which structural change processes take place. Take the case of, for example, the introduction of a new technique of production. If this new technique is of an 'embodied' type, i.e., requires the construction of new machines and the training of work forces with new skills to operate these machines, then there will be a 'construction' (training) phase prior to the actual utilisation of the new technique in production. This construction phase is the first phase of a 'traverse'. The characteristic of this phase – both in terms of microeconomic consequences, such as the profitability of firms, as well as in terms of macroeconomic consequences, such as the impact upon the overall employment level, aggregate consumption–investment relations, etc. – are quite distinct from the subsequent phase in which the new technique is actually introduced and when it accounts for a gradually growing proportion of output. It is important to recognise that traverse analysis considers the changeover from one technique to another as a gradual process (due, for example, to capacity constraints in the sector producing new machines or in training facilities) so that the middle phase of the traverse is characterised by a side-by-side co-existence of (and competition between) new and old techniques of production.

From our adopted analytical perspective, the changeover processes analysed by traverse analysis describe the emergence of new subsystems and the dynamic interrelationships between old and new subsystems (new and old processes and networks of activities related to the introduction and sustenance of these processes). The overall dynamic is thus one of shifting weights of different subsystems in the course of a traverse. Such shifts have important macroeconomic consequences for the overall growth rate, for aggregate distributional relationships, for the division of expenditure into consumption and savings, etc. These implications for macro-dynamics are the traditional focus of traverse analysis (see the contributions by Belloc and Baldone in this volume).

3.4 Non-proportional dynamics of an equilibrium growth path

Endogenous structural change is also considered in the theoretical formulation proposed by Luigi Pasinetti (1981, 1993). In this case, the productive structure of the economic system is analytically represented by a certain number of sectors corresponding to the different final consumption goods, and structural change is considered as a continuous process that the economic system undergoes if equilibrium, full-employment growth has to be consistent with continuous changes of technical coefficients (technical progress) and consumption coefficients (consumers' learning).

The particular decomposition technique adopted by Pasinetti makes it possible to 'assign' all original factors (such as labour) and intermediate inputs to the production of the different components of the final demand vector. In the simplest case considered by Pasinetti (a 'pure labour' economy, in which commodities are produced by means of labour only, without having recourse to natural resources or produced inputs), overall employment at time t may unambiguously be decomposed into the different quantities of 'direct' labour (that is, labour at time t) used in producing the different consumption goods delivered by the economic system (see, in particular, Pasinetti, 1965, 1986, 1993).

A more 'realistic' representation of economic structure is the one obtained by means of the vertical integration of interindustry flows. Here (following Pasinetti's notation), column vector $x(t)$ denotes the physical quantities of commodities produced in the accounting period t within each industry, column vector $c(t)$ denotes the commodities entering final consumption, column vector $s(t)$ the commodities required as intermediate goods (Pasinetti's 'capital stocks'), while $L(t)$ denotes total employment. Vertical integration decomposes the above set of magnitudes into the following elements

$$x^{(i)}(t) = [B - (1+r_i)A]^1 C^{(i)}(t)$$

$$l_i(t) = \alpha_n [B - (1+r_i)A]^{-1} C^{(i)}(t)$$

$$s^{(i)}(t) = A[B - (1+r_i)A]^{-1} C^{(i)}(t)$$

$$\Sigma C^{(i)}(t) = c(t), \ \Sigma x^{(i)}(t) = x(t)$$

$$\Sigma s^{(i)}(t) = s(t)$$

$$\Sigma l_i(t) = L(t)$$

where $x^{(i)}(t)$, $l_i(t)$, $s^{(i)}(t)$ denote, respectively, the vector of physical quantities produced, the labour employed (a scalar) and the vector of stocks of intermediate inputs in the vertically integrated sector corresponding to final good i, while r^i is the rate of demand growth for that good, matrices A and B are the matrices of input and output coefficients respectively and the variables with the bracketed superscripts (i) refer to vectors with only the ith element containing non-zero entries.

The analytical purpose of the vertical integration of interindustry flows is that complicated technologies (in particular technologies characterised by much roundaboutness, circular interdependencies and so on) may be made analytically equivalent to a *pure labour* economy. This allows Pasinetti to examine some important cases of structural dynamics by considering a simplified model. In particular, the above approach shows that an economic system cannot maintain itself on a path of equilibrium, full-employment growth unless technological progress and consumers' learning are matched by continuous changes in the proportions of vertically integrated sectors (*disproportional growth*) (see, in particular, Pasinetti, 1981, pp. 91–7; and Pasinetti, 1993, pp. 36–59). The analytical approach to structural economic dynamics in Pasinetti is thus again one of analytical specification of subsystems (i.e., a particular decomposition of the overall system) and of tracking the dynamic movements of these subsystems (which amounts to a decomposition of the overall dynamics) and studying the macroeconomic implications of such movements.

In Pasinetti, structural change is endogenously generated but cannot be taken to describe a real process of transformation of the economic structure. For it is a sequence of *virtual* changes in the relative proportions between vertically integrated sectors on the assumption that economic growth follows an equilibrium, full-employment path.

3.5 Non-proportional dynamics and maximal growth

Another view of structural change is taken if the endogenous transformation of economic structure derives from the consideration of the 'maximal growth' path (i.e., of the dynamic path permitting maximum utilisation of the investible surplus (see Quadrio Curzio, 1975, 1986; Quadrio Curzio and Pellizzari, 1991, 1996)). In this case, it has been shown that bottlenecks on the supply side (due to natural resource scarcity or technical progress) may generate non-investible residuals and uneven growth.

A description of the above dynamic has been obtained by Quadrio Curzio with a particular decomposition of the productive structure, based on the so-called 'composite technology' description (see Quadrio Curzio, 1986). Here, the economic system comes to be represented by a set of vertically integrated subsystems using specific non-produced resources (of which Ricardian lands may be an example).

Quadrio Curzio's 'composite technology' model may be briefly presented as follows.

The overall economy is split into a number of self-contained subsystems $A(h)$, ($A(h)$ being a matrix of technical coefficients) such that no subsystem needs inputs produced from other subsystems as far as the self-replacement of each subsystem is concerned; h refers to a technological subsystem but also to the natural resource base specific to that subsystem.

Each subsystem $A(I)$, $A(II)$, ..., $A(K)$ shows a one-to-one correspondence between commodities and production processes, and identifies a 'viable' technology. As a result, each subsystem could provide the technological basis for the indefinite expansion of the economic system, provided there are no bottlenecks on the supply side. The internal growth potential of each subsystem may be identified with its maximum von Neumann growth rate $g^*(h)$.

Here the relationship between the maximum *internal* growth rates of the various subsystems and the maximum *feasible* growth rate of the whole economic system depends on the historical linkages connecting different time periods. As a result, a simple aggregation of subsystems does not lead to the identification of the dynamic properties of the economic system as a whole. The reason for this is that, once the economic system is no longer able to expand along a von Neumann ray (on which commodity growth rates coincide with each other and with the maximum growth rate of the whole system), the production growth rates of individual commodities g_i start to be different from each other and from the system's maximum rate of expansion. In Quadrio Curzio's analysis, natural resource constraints lead to patterns of unbalanced growth which can be represented as the uneven expansion of subsystems. The emerging pattern of disproportional growth is, furthermore, itself changing over time as the result of the impact of a spectrum of natural resource constraints and of technological responses to these.

The existence of rigidities due to the limited 'substitutability' between technologies brings about the formation of 'residuals' (inputs produced within a certain subsystem and not completely usable by other subsystems). Once residuals are formed (which may be the result of resource constraints, as in Ricardo's analysis, but may also follow from technical progress), the growth potential of any given economic system is best described by considering *commodity* growth rates rather than system or subsystem growth rates. In particular, if a commodity i is produced by subsystems $A(\mathrm{I})$ and $A(\mathrm{II})$, the corresponding growth rate g_i (I, II, t) is a weighted average of the internal growth rates of these subsystems, which depends on the degree to which the net products of $A(\mathrm{I})$ can be accumulated in $A(\mathrm{II})$ (see Quadrio Curzio, 1986, p. 331).

Vertical integration of economic structure allows Quadrio Curzio to identify what may be called the 'growth poles' of the economic system, that is, the analytically independent subsystems on which the growth potential of the whole system depends. As time unfolds, historical linkages between subsystems (i.e., their historical 'order of activation') determine particular composition effects, due to the fact that 'the dynamics of the economic system depend not only on the net products of the techniques in activity, but also on the *structural compatibility* between *techniques* successively activated' (Quadrio Curzio and Pellizzari, 1991, p. 486; our italics). In this way, the actual dynamic path followed by the output of individual commodities takes place within bounds set by the existing (and slowly changing) technological structure. Quadrio Curzio's approach may be considered an attempt to tackle, from a theoretical point of view, certain important features of historical processes of economic transition, which are characterised by bottlenecks, lack of coordination and uneven change. The model is not fully 'realistic' in a descriptive sense, for the investigation concerns the properties of maximum feasible growth, rather than those of actual growth paths.

3.6 Hierarchy of sectors and the time phasing of structural change

A similar approach is followed by Adolph Lowe (Lowe, 1976) in his analysis of real capital formation and structural change (see, in this volume, chapter 4 by Christian Gehrke and Harald Hagemann). Lowe shares

Quadrio Curzio's idea that processes of economic transition may be considered by directly examining the circular interdependencies within the economic system, and by following the 'instrumental' approach to economic dynamics, that is, by setting a certain goal for the overall system (such as maximum growth) and then investigating the structural (or behavioural) conditions for that goal to be achieved.

There is, however, one important difference between Lowe and Quadrio Curzio. That is the analytical representation of production technology, which Lowe bases upon a three-sector description of interindustry flows: the consumer-goods sector (sector III), the capital-goods sector delivering intermediate inputs to the consumer-goods sector (sector II), the capital-goods sector delivering intermediate inputs to the former capital-goods sector and to itself (sector I). There is thus only one sector (sector I, which may be identified with the sector producing machine tools) that is capable of self-reproduction, in the sense that its rate of expansion only reflects the quantities of its own output that it is able to use for its own gross investment. As shown in the matrix of technical coefficients that describes the utilisation of the three commodities in Lowe's model, Lowe considers a definite hierarchy of sectors

$$\begin{bmatrix} \alpha_{11} & \alpha_{12} & 0 \\ 0 & 0 & \alpha_{23} \end{bmatrix}$$

The above input–output structure entails that structural change (a reproportioning due to natural resource bottlenecks, technical progress or the shift to a different overall rate of growth) should follow a precise *temporal sequence*, so that the formation of new consumer goods or new intermediate goods and machines has to be preceded by the formation of new machine tools (machines producing machines). Differently from Quadrio Curzio, Lowe considers circular economies (that is, economies capable of self reproduction) in which the productive structure, for any given technology, is differentiated into subsystems that are not completely interlinked. (This feature derives from the asymmetric position of productive sectors with respect to each other.) As a result, complementarities over time emerge in this case not because of residuals connecting different time periods (as in Quadrio Curzio) but because the analytical representation of production technology is by itself sequential and conducive to the consideration of adjustment processes in historical time (see also the chapter by Gehrke and Hagemann in this volume, particularly section 2).

Structural change is thus considered as an endogenous process, which may be induced by external impulses but then takes shape largely as a result of internal 'thwarting' or 'focusing' structures.

4 Methods of decomposition, structural specification and economic dynamics: the contributions in this volume

The contributions in this volume apply the notion of relative structural invariance to the analysis of economic dynamics in a number of different ways. In this connection, the distinction between different *methods of decomposition* of an economic system is crucial (see also Baranzini and Scazzieri, 1990; Landesmann and Scazzieri, 1990, 1993). The reason is that one feature of structural economic dynamics deals with changes in the relationship of components of an economic system to each other. Such components may either be individual units (households, individual production processes, etc.) or 'networks' of such units. The identification of such networks or, as we shall also call them, '*subsystems*', determines in a fundamental way the type of decomposition adopted and, therefore, the type of structural change analysis which can be attempted. In this volume, we shall consider a variety of subsystem definitions and analyse their implications for the analysis of economic dynamics. In particular, we will show that subsystem definitions are closely linked to the ways in which production processes are being analysed. For example, the specification of a subsystem might primarily focus upon the common utilisation of particular durable instruments of production, or upon the degree of interdependence of material-in-process flows, or upon the similarity of productive tasks. The contributions in this volume thus discuss a variety of approaches to the analysis of economic dynamics using decomposition techniques. In the following, we shall review these and also explore potential extensions involving the perspective of a more detailed production-analytical framework adopted in the book.

The contributions in part I (Decomposition of economies and structural dynamics) consider from a number of different perspectives the modelling of production economies that are undergoing processes of structural transformation at the level of the economic system as a whole. The chapter by Bernard Belloc (Traverse analysis in a neo-Austrian framework) presents the formal structure of a 'longitudinal' model of a production economy, in which production processes are considered along the time dimension. 'Longitudinal' models are contrasted to 'transversal' models in which the set of existing and interdependent production processes is considered as taking place within a given time interval. In this way Belloc considers 'a superposition of elementary processes which have begun at different past dates' (Belloc, p. 33).

The chapter presents a formulation of the longitudinal model that avoids the vertical integration of productive activities, and shows that the vertically integrated model discussed in Hicks's *Capital and Time* is a particular case of the non-integrated longitudinal model. In this latter case, production processes are considered as sequences of fabrication stages leading from primary resources to finished goods and, differently from the vertically integrated model, the interrelationships among processes that started at different points of time are explicitly examined. The chapter then assesses the role of prices in guiding individual choices along efficient paths, and finds that longitudinal and transversal approaches are not significantly different in this respect. Subsequently, the evolution of an economic system along the traverse path between two steady states is considered by using a non-integrated longitudinal model in which it is possible to keep track of the complex interrelationships among the different activities in the productive system, and a number of apparently paradoxical features may be detected. For example, 'the introduction of more mechanised processes in a particular branch can increase the employment in this branch because the demand for the good produced in this branch increases and because the negative relative profitability effect in other branches leads to a shift of the available resources to start new processes in the branches where mechanisation takes place' (Belloc, p. 64 of this volume).

Finally, the chapter shows how the particular use of traverse considered in Hicks's *Capital and Time* may be derived within the more general framework of the non-integrated model. It argues that the results concerning convergence to a new steady state that may be obtained within the simple 'neo-Austrian' vertically integrated model can be extended to a general model without vertical integration of productive activities.

One feature of this chapter which deserves further consideration is the fact that complementarities (and substitutabilities) over time are explicitly investigated. Belloc's model (as well as the theoretical framework presented in Hicks's *Capital and Time* that provides its starting point) analyses the 'materials-in-process' dimension of production activity and discusses a number of propositions dealing with the form of traverse when the transformation of the networks of materials in process is considered. Possible extensions (and reformulations) of this model may involve the investigation of other dimensions of productive activity as well. For example, analysis of the capability dimension could lead to an explicit consideration of issues such as the versatility of the productive structure, the pattern of capabilities' utilisation, and the possibility of using 'slack resources'. Similarly, analysis of the 'task-process' dimension may suggest ways in which a traverse may be made less (or more) difficult by exploiting similarities in process design (or, respectively, by increasing the differences between the patterns according to which the processes are organised).

The time structure of a set of interrelated production processes is also considered in the chapter by Salvatore Baldone on 'Vertical integration, the temporal structure of production processes and transition between techniques'. In particular, this chapter emphasises the role of the composition of the vector of means of production available at the beginning of each traverse in determining the characteristics of the transitional path. Baldone shows that the assumption of full utilisation of means of production along a traverse (the 'full performance' assumption made in Hicks's *Capital and Time*) may be incompatible with the introduction of new processes when a multisectoral (rather than vertically integrated) representation of the economic system is adopted. The above consideration leads the author to suggest a new concept of 'full performance' as 'that situation where . . . the number of starts of any process cannot be increased without reducing that of some other process' (Baldone, pp. 90–1). Such an assumption, while making incomplete utilisation of existing means of production possible on the traverse path, implies that the traverse itself may be not fully determined, due to the fact that different levels of operation of the various new processes are possible. The chapter then explicitly examines a number of cases in which the co-existence over time of incompatible production techniques may influence the actual course of the traverse. In particular, it is shown that the transfer from one time period to another of 'residuals' (commodities delivered by old processes and not immediately used up in starting new processes) may significantly influence the structure of the economic system at any given time. On the other hand, it is also argued that 'new' basic commodities (commodities that are basic with the new technique but not with the old one) may be introduced on condition that sufficient amounts of the 'new' basics are produced as *non-basic* commodities by pilot processes using the old production technique.

The chapter explores, from the materials-in-process point of view, a set of situations that may also present themselves if attention is focused upon the role of capabilities or process design. For example, we may conjecture that incomplete utilisation refers not only to produced means of production, but also to the range of capabilities associated with certain agents (such as workers or machines). This comes to reinforce Baldone's result on the indeterminacy of the traverse due to the possibility of incomplete utilisation of means of production. Also, the emergence of residuals may find an analogue in the existence of capabilities that are forcibly idle, or only partially utilised, due to a lack of compatibility between old and new processes. In other cases, lack of compatibility may be due to differences in the 'task-process' structures of old and new processes, quite independently of the actual commodities being produced. Finally, we may conjecture that the possibility of pilot processes introducing new basic commodities is enhanced by the existence of underutilised (or idle) capabilities, as well as by the possibility of identifying complementarities in design between old and new processes.

The chapter by Alberto Quadrio Curzio, with Appendices by Carlo Felice Manara and Mario Faliva (Production and efficiency with global technologies), considers a situation in which the utilisation of limited non-produced resources (such as land) brings about a complex technological set-up, such that two or more processes may be used at the same time for the production of each commodity requiring non-produced resources. The chapter suggests that the above situation may be analytically represented in terms of 'global technologies', that is, by considering technology matrices such that different processes delivering the same commodity may be joined together as components of the same economic system, and then separated again by means of particular coefficients (the 'splitting supply coefficients'), which allow identification of the shares of different processes in the overall supply of any given commodity. The general case in which k different processes are used to produce the same type of commodity (for example, k different types of land are used to produce corn) suggests an analytical simplification by means of which the first $k-1$ processes, which are all operated at their respective maximum intensities compatible with the existing availability of resources, are aggregated into a single process, whereas the remaining kth process is separately considered. It is argued that changes in the overall scale of the economic system are reflected in a changing weight of the $(k-1)$ 'maximum intensity' processes (aggregated into a single process) relative to the weight of the remaining kth process, whose intensity of operation may be varied depending on the overall scale requirements.

The chapter considers the patterns of structural dynamics that may emerge when it is assumed that a change in activity levels is associated with a continuous, or discontinuous, change of productive efficiency. In particular, a specific set of 'cost-of-production' prices is introduced, to allow for a synthetic evaluation of changes in productive efficiency, as expressed by the changing weight of the less efficient process k with respect to the more efficient set of the 'maximum intensity' $(k-1)$ processes. Finally, it is argued that changes in productive efficiency may be associated with an apparently paradoxical behaviour in the output levels of 'industrial' commodities, that is, of commodities that do not directly require non-produced resources as their inputs. In particular, it is shown that, within certain limits, a decrease in productive efficiency is compatible with increasing output levels of the 'industrial' commodities, until the type of production process that is last operated is so inefficient that it generates a negative net product rate.

A number of conceptual and analytical issues raised in this chapter may also be relevant if one moves to the consideration of capabilities and of the 'task-process' structure of production activity. For example, the utilisation of limited non-produced resources may have an analogue in the existence of a pool of formal and informal knowledge, which may be conceived as the outcome of historical processes to be considered as 'given' when the present situation is analysed. It may be conjectured that in this case as well an increase in activity level could lead to the utilisation of different 'grades' of knowledge, even if a grade of knowledge that comes to be relevant only after other grades are fully used is not necessarily knowledge of an inferior type. Here, we may rather have a transition from formal to informal knowledge, which may entail either a decrease *or* an increase of productive efficiency, depending on the type of informal knowledge that is being considered.

More generally, this chapter suggests an analytical framework useful in the investigation of paths of structural dynamics constrained by the *limited speed* at which elements of technology in use may be changed (quite independently of the existence of non-producible and essential means of production).

The interplay between the relative degree of rigidity associated with existing economic systems, and the flexibility that is often required in order to achieve certain forms and speeds of structural change is considered in the contribution by Christian Gehrke and Harald Hagemann (Efficient traverses and bottlenecks: a structural approach). In particular, the authors examine the type of traverse analysis that may be undertaken by adopting an analytical representation of the economic system that combines features of the circular approach à la Quesnay–Leontief with features related to the time structure of productive activity. This is done by considering Lowe's tripartite representation of productive activity, in which the investment-goods sector is split into a subsector delivering investment goods to the production of consumption goods, and another subsector that produces the physical capital goods required in the investment-goods sector itself. Such a decomposition makes it possible to analyse physical bottlenecks (capital constraints), their influence upon the sequence of transformation stages followed by any given economic system, and the speed at which the bottlenecks due to the inherited structure of capital goods may be overcome.

The authors call attention to the existence of a definite 'hierarchy of sectors' in Lowe's schema of industrial production and point to the critical role of the machine tool sector, which is capable of physical self-reproduction and provides an economic system of the industrial type with a unique means for overcoming shortages in the supply of certain means of production thus making structural change possible. At the same time, the production of machine tools is itself a 'bottleneck which any process of accelerated growth must overcome' (Gehrke and Hagemann, p. 8).

The above analytical representation of the economic system points to a combination of flexible and rigid features, and suggests that the analysis of traverse should be carried out by distinguishing between the feasible efficient path of structural transformation (the one on which, as Lowe points out, it is possible to achieve the 'maximum speed of adjustment constrained by the condition that malinvestment must be avoided' (Lowe, 1976, p. 124)) and the actual behavioural pattern that will set the economic system on a goal-adequate trajectory. In the contributions examined above, decomposition of an economic system calls attention to the existence of rigidities and differences in the degree to which different parts of the economic system are adjusted to given factors of change. However, disaggregated economies also lend themselves to the analysis of long-run trends and of the different ways in which long-run factors may affect different parts of the economic system independently of the consideration of adjustment processes.

One possible extension of the analysis of this chapter may be emphasised. This is the identification of a 'hierarchy of sectors' relevant to the investigation of economic dynamics. For it may be conjectured that a hierarchy of sectors may be identified by looking not only (as in Lowe's model) at the network of input–output flows, but also at the network of capabilities and at that of tasks and processes.

The relationship between structural change and cyclical movements of an economic system is taken up in the chapter by Richard Goodwin and Michael Landesmann (Structural change and macroeconomic stability in disaggregated models). This contribution gives an overview of the evolution of formal, disaggregated models of the business cycle, as developed by Goodwin himself and other authors. The paper first discusses a number of early contributions in which the focus of analysis is the impact of the degree of interconnectedness between sectors and industries on the dynamics/stability of the overall macroeconomic system. This analysis is limited to linear disaggregated representations of economic interdependencies. There follows a discussion of lower dimensional, nonlinear formulations in which the 'dynamic coupling' of different cyclical mechanisms (e.g. the differential dynamics of inventory and fixed capital accumulation and decumulation), as well as of interdependent discrete lag-structures, generates complex dynamical patterns. In the review of these early contributions, it is also recalled that the analytical device of diagonalising the coefficients matrix of the economic system could be the basis for identifying distinct modes of dynamic behaviour in a linear system of interdependencies (so that the actual dynamics of each original sector appears as a particular linear combination of such distinct modes or dynamic behaviour). In particular, the cyclical behaviour of sectors or industries may in this way be explained in terms of the behaviour of the different dynamic subsystems (eigensectors) and of their interaction at an aggregate level (through the impact of aggregate variables, such as the aggregate wage rate, profit rate, the level of total final demand, etc.). On the other hand, it is realistic to assume that dynamic impulses (such as technical progress) affect the economic system at first via the original sectors or industries. The chapter also contains a discussion of early and more recent formulations of synergetic approaches in which a hierarchy in the dynamics of different sub-systemic structures is identified. This produces an analytically tractable system in which a Marshall-type dynamics emerges (i.e. long-term dynamics constrains medium-term dynamics which, in turn, constrains short-term dynamics). From the perspective of the methodology adopted in the book, this chapter points: firstly, to the yet incompletely understood set of relationships between macroeconomic dynamics and disaggregated structures of an interdependent economic system; secondly, to the importance of the contributions which various techniques of decomposition have made and could make in the future to understanding the formal complexity of structural economic dynamics.

The contributions in part II (Production organisation and economic dynamics) consider structural change of an economy from a point of view that is distinct but complementary with respect to the one adopted in part I. For part II considers economies that are undergoing processes of transformation originating at the level of individual productive units or sets of interrelated productive units, such as those arising from the various patterns of interaction between productive activities, or from patterns of technical progress which result from mutual learning processes within an industrial district.

The aim of part II is to provide a conceptual framework for the analysis of structural changes as phenomena originating within the organisational structure of a productive system; these then lead to changes occurring at the level of individual sectors which affect the dynamics of the economic system as a whole.

The first contribution by Michael Landesmann and Roberto Scazzieri (The production process: description and analysis) starts with a heuristic approach to the analysis of production processes and identifies three fundamental levels at which a production process may be considered. One is the level of tasks to be performed; the other is that of agents participating in the production process; the third is that of materials that enter the process and undergo a sequence of fabrication stages. It is argued that the structure of the production process derives from the introduction of coordination devices operating at each one of these three levels. As a result, any process requires the execution of a number of tasks according to a definite precedence pattern (even if sometimes the production process is not rigid in the sequencing of fabrication stages). In addition, the productive agents responsible for the actual transformation of the material in process have to be coordinated with one another, so that the pattern by which tasks are executed by particular productive agents ensures at the same time a satisfactory performance of tasks, utilisation of existing capabilities and the movement of material in process (throughput) from one stage of fabrication to another.

The chapter argues that a heuristic representation of productive activity should include all the above features of a production process. However, the analytical investigation of a production economy often proceeds by selecting a subset of the above features and by considering the interrelationships that may be detected on that basis. As a result, the above view of productive activity lends itself to the consideration of alternative ways in which 'subsystems' may be identified, depending on whether a production economy is considered as a set of interrelated tasks and task performances, as a network of productive agents that are coordinating their operations with one another or as a system of flows and stocks of different materials in process. It is also argued that the actual structure of real production processes (and of patterns of interrelationships among such processes) reflects the particular way in which the above classes of coordination problems are dealt with. Furthermore, it is argued that it is generally possible to identify a certain degree of structural permanence with respect to the coordination devices implemented over a particular period of time. In this connection, the consideration of forms of production organisation (defined as repeated patterns of coordination determining the identity of the production process over time) is an essential prerequisite for the analysis of the particular modes of dynamic behaviour that characterise the evolution of the different parts of any given economic system.

The second contribution in part II is by Alessandro Romagnoli (Agrarian forms of production organisation). This chapter outlines a conceptual framework for the analysis of agricultural production whose distinctive features are: (i) the emphasis on the similarity of agricultural tasks (in spite of different crops) and on the strong time constraints upon the execution of such tasks, as important factors explaining the lower subdivision of tasks in agricultural activities as compared with manufacturing activities; (ii) the consideration of the division of labour as a process reflecting differences in workers' capabilities rather than the subdivision of tasks, (iii) the identification of 'crop-growing techniques' (agronomic recipes) as technological constraints determining the useful period in which each agricultural operation has to be executed if a given 'crop-growing path' is to be followed; (iv) the consideration of a typical farm-organisational problem as one in which productive funds (plots of land, machinery) are allocated to different 'competing crops' so as to achieve the maximum degree of utilisation over time.

Romagnoli then moves to the consideration of the most important forms of agrarian production in modern history, that is, (i) mixed farming (in which crops and live-stock are produced), (ii) mechanised agriculture, (iii) protected crops. It is argued that each form of agrarian production should be analysed by considering the pattern of utilisation of fund elements (most importantly, land) in the production process, the characteristics of the tasks to be executed and the pattern of coordination of tasks within each process. The different ways in which different forms of agrarian production lend themselves to the introduction of specific types of technical change (for example, intensive utilisation of machinery at peak times, greenhouses, etc.) are also considered.

The third contribution in part II is by Michael Landesmann and Roberto Scazzieri (Forms of production organisation: the case of manufacturing processes). This chapter studies different forms of production organisation in manufacturing. In particular, an attempt is made to derive general organisational principles from the consideration of a number of historical forms of production organisation.

In this connection, the chapter starts with an analysis of the 'job-shop' form of manufacturing, which is considered to be characteristic of early craft production (even if instances of job-shop organisation may also be found in contemporary manufacturing). It is argued that distinct features of the job shop are the utilisation of multiskilled fund inputs executing in an interlocking way tasks belonging to different fabrication processes, and the existence of stop-and-go phases of the material in process to allow different consumers' orders to be processed within reasonable waiting times. The job shop is a flexible form of production organisation, for it allows for some readjustment of the product mix in each productive unit without upsetting the organisational pattern according to which workers' capabilities are utilised and flows of materials in process are coordinated with each other. However, the interlocking mode of coordination among the flows of materials in process makes the job shop especially sensitive to the time structure of the different fabrication processes. As a result, the job-shop organisation is compatible with moderate changes of the product mix but not with sudden shifts of product composition from one type of 'large-scale' production to another.

The specialisation of tasks is a common feature of the forms of production organisation which substituted the job shop organisation when output levels of specific commodities increased above a certain upper bound, or when technical devices reducing the length of particular tasks would have led to excessive waste within the job shop.

The 'putting out' system and the factory are the two most important forms of production organisation in which the different fabrication stages of a production process are carried out by splitting the process into subgroups of constituent tasks. However, the putting out and the factory differ from each other in the way in which the coordination between different fabrication stages is obtained. As a matter of fact, the putting out form of production organisation leads to a process of 'craft differentiation', so that each fabrication stage leads to a separate set of tasks executed in specialised productive units. However, each task (or set of tasks) is still identified in terms of the corresponding fabrication stage of the materials in process, and no attempt is made of splitting complex tasks into simpler constituent operations. On the other hand, the factory form of production organisation is characterised by a detailed subdivision of complex tasks into elementary tasks, their efficient allocation to specialised productive agents (workers or machines) and the precise time coordination of different material flows within each productive unit.

The putting out system is characterised by the existence of flexible linkages among different stages of a fabrication process, with inventories of semi-finished products providing buffers between such stages. This makes the fabrication of large quantities of particular commodities possible, without upsetting the utilisation pattern of productive agents within particular workshops. On the other hand, the putting out system implies that the 'just-in-time' delivery of finished (or semi-finished) commodities may be difficult, as it may be difficult to introduce technical devices requiring standardisation of component parts of products or precise time coordination among different material flows.

It may be argued that the transition from 'dispersed' to 'concentrated' forms of production organisation (say, from the putting out to the manufacture or the factory) is due to the need to achieve a better 'just-in-time' coordination of tasks and material flows, so that customers' wants could be satisfied almost without delay. However, the factory system embodies a high degree of rigidity, since the coordination of tasks, the allocation of productive agents to tasks, and the organisation of the system of material flows is based upon the full-utilisation requirements for indivisible units of productive agents. As a result, it may be difficult, within the factory form of production, to adjust to changes in the composition of demand or in productive agents' capabilities (learning) without violating the full-utilisation condition.

The concluding section of the chapter examines recent attempts to deal with the above drawbacks of the factory system by introducing flexible coordination devices, such as those associated with the flexible manufacturing system (FMS). In this connection, it is argued that an important feature of flexible manufacturing systems is the relative decomposability of the production process into 'cells' of interacting and multiskilled productive agents. An advantage of this system is its capability to react in a flexible (albeit 'imperfect') way to changing production programmes. For example, higher utilisation of plants may be achieved by allowing the formation of inventories at the juncture between different cells, or the implementation of a new system of task execution and task coordination may require a period in which learning and adjustment processes substantially bring down the efficiency of the productive system.

Another important feature of new forms of manufacturing organisation is the just-in-time pattern of material flows coordination. A characteristic feature of just-in-time manufacturing is the attempt to achieve the highest possible degree of continuity in the flows of materials in process, while at the same time allowing for changes in the production programmes and in the patterns of allocation of productive agents to tasks. This continuity is not primarily the result of inventory control techniques; rather the emphasis on materials-in-process continuity serves as a 'focusing device' (Rosenberg) that calls attention to the parts of the productive system in which changes in the coordination mechanism are called for. The final section of this chapter suggests a conceptual framework for assessing the impact of different forms of production organisation upon the formation of networks among different productive units.

The final chapter in part II by Michael Landesmann and Roberto Scazzieri (Coordination of production processes, subsystem dynamics and structural change) draws the volume to a close by explicitly analysing various types of economic change within the production-analytical framework set up in the previous chapters of part II and also by considering the relationships between the contributions of part I and part II.

As regards the analysis of economic change, the authors emphasise the role which decomposition plays in analysing the process of economic adaptation to a given impulse (such as technological innovation, differentiation in consumers' demand, material resource constraints, etc.). They attempt an explicit analysis of what they call 'dynamic network' formation in the wake of such an impulse. Thereby they exploit the notions of networks (productive interrelationships) previously explored in chapters 6 and 8 on the basis of 'neighbourhood' and 'similarity' relationships at the level of tasks, fund inputs and materials-in-process flows. Economic change involves the activation of a sequence of such networks and one can thus speak of an endogenisation of the process of economic change. In such a process, 'relative rigidities' play a role leading to a clear hierarchy in the adjustment ability of different networks (these rigidities depend upon the time horizon considered and on the nature of the impulse); also 'buffers' (i.e., underutilised capacities and inventories) play a role in 'dynamic network' specification in that they determine whether the impact of a particular impulse could – again, within a given time horizon – be contained within a particular region of the economic system. The notion of 'decomposable dynamics' is thus distinctly related to the analysis of the relative rigidities (structural invariances) of different networks/subsystems and to the organisational or conjunctural availability of buffers.

Both the 'macro-to-micro' and the 'micro-to-macro' approaches to the study of structural change, as represented by the contributions to parts I and II respectively, utilise concepts of decomposition and of network or subsystem specification. The contributions of part I (which represent a cross-section of the current state of the art of disaggregated modelling in economic theory) have the advantage of clearly representing an economic system in its entirety, embedding the dynamics of subsystems within a framework which keeps track of fundamental macroeconomic relationships. On the other hand, the representation of productive processes and the organisation of such processes is rather impoverished and this leads to a loss in the analytical ability to analyse the different sources and the impact of economic change. In the contributions of part II, on the other hand, emphasis is laid on the detailed representation of qualitatively distinct organisational and coordination patterns in productive systems. This allows a representation of qualitative differences in the organisational issues involved in the different sectors of an economy (such as those involved in agriculture, manufacturing and tertiary activities) – while the analytical representation of different sectors in the top–down approaches is rather uniform – and of the persistence of *heterogeneity within the sectors*. Of course, the richness in microanalytical description in this approach does divert attention from issues of coherence and dynamics at the macroeconomic level which are left unexplored in the contributions of part II. The relative strengths and weaknesses of the two branches of disaggregated modelling (the 'top–down' and the 'bottom–up' approaches) indicate that they will, also in the future, form complementary components of an important line of research on structural economic dynamics.

Notes

1 The above approach to production analysis, as mentioned in the text, has its roots in the Smithian analysis of the division of labour, as well as in the other numerous contributions of the eighteenth and nineteenth centuries in which the 'advantages' of division of labour had been considered (see, for example, Beccaria, 1771; Gioja, 1815–17; Hermann, 1832; Babbage, 1835; Dunoyer, 1845; Leroy-Beaulieu, 1896). The rich literature on 'time and motion' studies produced mainly in the United States around the beginning of this century made an important contribution to the analysis of the operational structure of productive activity. However, it also considerably narrowed the scope of production analysis by shifting attention away from other dimensions of the production process, and away from a full acknowledgement of the variety of organisational set-ups within which productive activities may take place (see, for example, Taylor, 1911; Gantt, 1912).

2 The role of technical knowledge and learning plays an important role in the classical theory of division of labour. Smith assigns much importance to the cognitive side of production activity in his analysis of the linkage between the division of labour and the effectiveness with which certain work steps are executed (Smith, 1776, chapters 1–3). In Smith's view, capabilities may be improved as a complex job is divided up into more elementary components, but no explicit mention is made of the 'best' way in which a certain mix of skills (or capabilities) may be used. Gioja (1815–17) and Babbage (1835), on the other hand, emphasised the allocative side of the utilisation of capabilities, by investigating into the 'best' pattern of utilisation compatible with a given set of skills and capabilities. In this way they implicitly assumed that skills and capabilities are given from the point of view of production organisation.

3 The possible utilisation of certain features of temporary equilibria for the analysis of structural change is already suggested in the final chapters of part IV of Hicks's *Value and Capital* (Hicks, 1939, pp. 283–302).

References

Anderson, P. W., Arrow, K. J. and Pines, D. (eds.) (1988) *The Economy as an Evolving Complex System. The Proceedings of the Evolutionary Paths of the Global Economy Workshop*, New York, Addison Wesley.

Arthur, B. W., Landesmann, M. and Scazzieri, R. (1991) 'Dynamics and Structures', *Structural Change and Economic Dynamics*, 2(1): 1–7.

Babbage, C. (1835) *On the Economy of Machinery and Manufactures*, London, Charles Knight, 4th edition.

Baranzini, M. and Scazzieri, R. (1990) 'Economic Structure: Analytical Perspectives', in M. Baranzini and R. Scazzieri (eds.), *The Economic Theory of Structure and Change*, Cambridge, Cambridge University Press, pp. 227–333.

Baumol, W. J. (1967) 'Macroeconomics of Unbalanced Growth', *American Economic Review*, 57 (June): 415–26.

(1992) *Growth, the Market and Dissemination of Technology*, Dublin, Economic and Social Research Institute.

Baumol, W. J., Batey Blackman, S. A. and Wolff, E. H. (1989) *Productivity and American Leadership: The Long View*, Cambridge, Mass: and London, MIT Press.

Beccaria, C. (1771) *Elementi di economia pubblica*, in S. Romagnoli (ed.) *Cesare Beccaria. Opere*, Florence, Sansoni, 1958.

Böhm-Bawerk, E. von (1889) *Kapital und Kapitalzins*, vol. II: *Positive Theorie des Kapitales*, Innsbruck, Wagner.

Dahmén, E. (1955) 'Technology, Innovation and International Industrial Transformation', in L. H. Dupriez (ed.), *Economic Progress: Papers and Proceedings of a Round Table held by the International Economic Association*, Louvain, Institut de Recherches Economiques et Sociales, pp. 293–306.

Deane, P. M. and Cole, W. A. (1967) *The British Economic Growth 1688–1959: Trends and Structure*, Cambridge, Cambridge University Press, 2nd edition.

Dunoyer, C. (1845) *De la liberté de travail*, Paris, Guillaumin.

Gantt, H. L. (1912) 'The Task and the Day's Work', in *Addresses and Discussions at the Conference on Scientific Management held October 12–13–14, 1911*, The Amos Tuck School of Administration and Finance, Dartmouth College, Hannover, New Haven.

Georgescu-Roegen, N. (1969) 'Process in Farming versus Process in Manufacturing: a Problem of Balanced Development', in G. U. Papi and C. Nunn (eds.), *Economic Problems of Agriculture in Industrial Societies*, New York, St Martin's Press, pp. 497–528.

Gioja, M. (1815–17) *Nuovo Prospetto delle Scienze Economiche*, Milan, Pirotta.

Goodwin, R. (1990) *Chaotic Economic Dynamics*, Oxford, Clarendon Press.

(1982) *Essays in Economic Dynamics*, London, Macmillan.

Goodwin, R. and Punzo, L. (1987) *The Dynamics of a Capitalist Economy: A Multi-sectoral Approach*, Cambridge, Polity Press and Basil Blackwell.

Hahn, F. H. (1982) 'Stability', in K. Arrow and M. D. Intriligator (eds.), *Handbook of Mathematical Economics*, Amsterdam, North-Holland, vol. II, pp. 745–93.

Hawkins, D. (1948) 'Some Conditions of Macroeconomic Stability', *Econometrica*, 15 (October): 309–22.

Hawkins, D. and Simon, H. A. (1949) 'Note: Some Conditions of Macroeconomic Stability', *Econometrica*, 17 (July–October): 245–8.

Hermann, F. B. W. von (1832) *Staatswirtschaftliche Untersuchungen*, Munich.

Hicks, J. (1939) *Value and Capital. An Inquiry into Some Fundamental Principles of Economic Theory*, Oxford, Clarendon Press.

(1973) *Capital and Time. A Neo-Austrian Theory*, Oxford, Clarendon Press.

Hildenbrand, W. (1983) 'Introduction', in G. Debreu, *Mathematical Economics*, Cambridge, Cambridge Universtiy Press, pp. 1–19.

Hoffmann, W. G. (1958) *The Growth of Industrial Economies*, translated by W. O. Henderson and W. H. Chaloner, Manchester, Manchester University Press.

Kaldor, N. (1966) *Causes of the Slow Rate of Economic Growth of the United Kingdom: an Inaugural Lecture*, Cambridge, Cambridge University Press.

Kirman, A. (1989) 'The Intrinsic Limits of Modern Economic Theory: The Emperor has no Clothes', *The Economic Journal*, 99: 126–39.

Landes, D. S. (1969) *The Unbound Prometheus: Technical Change and Industrial Development in Western Europe from 1750 to the Present*, Cambridge, Cambridge University Press.

Landesmann, M. and Scazzieri, R. (1990) 'Specification of Structure and Economic Dynamics', in M. Baranzini and R. Scazzieri (eds.), *The Economic Theory of Structure and Change*, Cambridge, Cambridge University Press, pp. 95–121.

(1993) 'Commodity Flows and Productive Subsystems: an Essay in the Analysis of Structural Change', in M. Baranzini and G. Harcourt (eds.), *The Dynamics of the Wealth of Nations. Growth, Distribution and Structural Change (Essays in Honour of Luigi Pasinetti)*, London, Macmillan, pp. 209–45.

La Volpe, G. (1993) *Studies on the Theory of General Dynamic Economic Equilibrium* (Italian original 1936), London and Basingstoke, Macmillan.

Leroy-Beaulieu, P. P. (1896) *Traité théorique et pratique d'économie politique*, Paris, Guillaumin.

Lindahl, E. (1939) *Studies in the Theory of Money and Capital* (Swedish original 1929), London, Allen and Unwin.

Lowe, A. (1976) *The Path of Economic Growth*, Cambridge, Cambridge University Press.

Marshall, A. (1890) *Principles of Economics*, London, Macmillan.

Medio, A. (1984) 'Synergetics and Dynamic Economic Models', in R. M. Goodwin, M. Krüger and A. Vercelli (eds.), *Nonlinear Models of Fluctuating Growth*, Berlin, Heidelberg, Springer-Verlag, pp. 166–91.

Menger, C. (1981 [1871]) *Principles of Economics*, Translated by James Dingwall and Bert F. Hoselitz; with an introduction by F. A. Hayek, New York and London, New York University Press.

(1888) 'Zur Theorie des Kapitales', *Conrad's Jahrbücher für Nationalökonomie und Statistik*, 17: 1–49.

North, D. C. (1981) *Structure and Change in Economic History*, New York and London, W. W. Norton and Company.

Pasinetti, L. L. (1965) *A New Theoretical Approach to the Problems of Economic Growth*, Vatican City, Pontificiae Academiae Scientiarum Scripta Varia.

(1981) *Structural Change and Economic Dynamics. A Theoretical Essay on the Dynamics of the Wealth of Nations*, Cambridge, Cambridge University Press.

(1986) 'Theory of Value – A Source of Alternative Paradigms in Economic Analysis', in M. Baranzini and R. Scazzieri (eds.), *Foundations of Economics. Structures of Inquiry and Economic Theory*, Oxford and New York, Basil Blackwell, pp. 409–31.

(1993) *Structural Economic Dynamics. A Theory of the Economic Consequences of Human Learning*, Cambridge, Cambridge University Press.

Pasinetti, L. L. and Solow, R. M. (eds.) (1994) *Economic Growth and the Structure of Long-Term Development*, Basingstoke, Macmillan in association with the International Economic Association.

Quadrio Curzio, A. (1975) *Accumulazione del capitale e rendita*, Bologna, Il Mulino.

(1986) 'Technological Scarcity: an Essay on Production and Structural Change', in M. Baranzini and R. Scazzieri (eds.), *Foundations of Economics. Structures of Inquiry and Economic Theory*, Oxford and New York, Basil Blackwell, pp. 311–38.

Quadrio Curzio, A. and Pellizzari, F. (1991) 'Structural Rigidities and Dynamic Choice of Technologies', *Rivista internazionale di scienze economiche e commerciali*, 38 (6–7, June–July): 481–517.

(1996) *Risorse, tecnologie, rendita*, Bologna, Il Mulino.

'Structural Rigidities and Dynamic Choice of Technologies', *Rivista internazionale di scienze economiche e commerciali*, 38 (6–7, June–July): 481–517.

Ricardo, D. (1817) *On the Principles of Political Economy and Taxation*, London, Murray.

Rosenberg, N., Landau, R. and Mowery, D. C. (eds.) (1992) *Technology and the Wealth of Nations*, Stanford, Stanford University Press.

Silverberg, G. (1984) 'Embodied Technical Progress in a Dynamic Model: The Self-Organisation Paradigm', in R. M. Goodwin, M. Krüger and A. Vercelli (eds.), *Nonlinear Models of Fluctuating Growth*, Berlin, Springer-Verlag, pp. 192–208.

(1988) 'Modelling Economic Dynamics and Technical Change: Mathematical Approaches to Self-Organisation and Evolution', in G. Dosi, C. Freeman, R. Nelson, G. Silverberg and L. Soete (eds.), *Technical Change and Economic Theory*, London and New York, Pinter Publishers, pp. 531–59.

Smale, S. (1981) *Global Analysis and Economics*, in K. J. Arrow and M. D. Intriligator, (eds.), *Handbook of Mathematical Economics*, Amsterdam, North Holland, vol. I, pp. 331–70.

Smith, A. (1776) *An Inquiry into the Nature and Causes of the Wealth of Nations*, London, A. Strahan and T. Cadell.

Taylor, F. W. (1911) 'The Principles of Scientific Management', in F. W. Taylor, *Scientific Management*, London, Harper and Row, 1964.

I Decomposition of economies and structural dynamics

1   Traverse analysis in a neo-Austrian framework

BERNARD BELLOC

1 The neo-Austrian framework

Any denomination is unsatisfying and it is not really convincing to call the neo-Austrian the Hicksian *Capital and Time* model. Our aim in this first part is to show that the so-called neo-Austrian framework is simply another way to look at production activities. We can gain in intuition by thinking of an analogy with demography. It is well known that, in this discipline, there is place for two approaches. The first one considers all the individuals of different ages, at a given date, and the second considers each generation all along their life time, at different dates. But the important events have the same significance: births, deaths, marriages, etc. . . . mean the same things in the two approaches.

As in demography, we may imagine two approaches in order to represent production activities. It is possible to interpret the standard von Neumann–Leontief–Sraffa model as a transversal approach: at a given date, we look at the productive system of an economy as a superposition of elementary processes which have begun at different past dates. So there is a place for a longitudinal approach; we may look at each different elementary process all along its economic lifetime. The neo-Austrian approach is a longitudinal approach of the productive system.

Clearly, in the two approaches, the modelling of production activities amounts fundamentally to represent the way by which goods are produced by other goods. But it is the manner of looking at this which matters when we distinguish between standard and neo-Austrian approaches. In the standard transversal approach, an elementary operation is simply an application from an input set into an output set, and the production function is defined by the set of efficient elementary operations. It is fundamentally the same idea if we consider the linear models, or the activity analysis models. In all these cases, it is only the form of the production function which differs. In a longitudinal neo-Austrian approach, we consider a set of input sequences over time and a set of output sequences over time. An elementary process is then defined by a mapping from the first set into the second one.

Clearly, the two approaches consist of looking at the same scenery from two different places. So, fundamental concepts are pertinent in the two approaches: goods, prices, rates of profit, employment, saving, etc. . . . Of course the analogy with demography is not complete. Indeed, it is often possible to transform an old elementary neo-Austrian production process into a younger one by modernising it. Unfortunately, that is not possible for people!

So we may not consider an exhaustive distinction between the transversal and longitudinal approaches in economics. In fact it is certainly not realistic to assume that at a given date it would be possible to distinguish the different elementary processes in a productive system. But exactly in the same way it is certainly not always easy to identify the von Neumann production activities or to estimate a production function.

In section 2 we consider a standard general linear model which corresponds to a transversal approach and we look at this model from a longitudinal viewpoint. This allows us to obtain a quite general neo-Austrian model (we call it the non-integrated model) and to show that the Hicksian *Capital and Time* model is a particular case of this non-integrated model.

In section 3 we analyse the role of prices in the general neo-Austrian model to guide the microeconomic choices along efficient paths. More precisely we use a model similar to the one of Malinvaud in his pioneering approach (Malinvaud, 1953 and 1962) and we translate it into a longitudinal approach. Then it is possible to show that the simultaneous consideration of the two approaches allows us to relate the usual microeconomic investment decisions to the standard theory of efficient allocation of resources. In this section our goal is to show that the prices play exactly the same role in the transversal and longitudinal approaches. Lastly, we discuss briefly the dynamic of prices in a neo-Austrian context. In fact we find again the traditional debate about the explanation of the dynamic of prices in an economy and the choice of a relevant concept of equilibrium to analyse this dynamic. We argue that the neo-Austrian models have no particular advantage nor disadvantage in this field.

2   The neo-Austrian production models

2.1   *A particular interpretation of the general linear model*

Let us consider a linear model in which inputs are transformed into outputs by m elementary operations. The elementary operation r, ($r=1$, ..., m), transforms a vector A_r of n inputs, $A_r=(a_{ir})_{i=1, ..., n}$ into a vector of n outputs $B_r=(b_{ir})_{i=1, ..., n}$.[1] Classically, as in the von Neumann or the Malinvaud models, the used fixed capital goods are simultaneously inputs and outputs for each elementary operation. We assume constant returns to scale. Labour is the only primary factor[2] and a_{or} is the quantity of labour needed by the elementary operation r.

Let us present as following our standard model. First we obtain a matrix of primary factor and input coefficients

$$
\begin{bmatrix}
a_{01} & \cdots & a_{02} & \cdots & a_{0j} & & a_{0j+1} & \cdots & a_{0n} & \cdots & a_{0l} & \cdots & a_{0m} \\
\hdotsfor{13} \\
a_{11} & \cdots & a_{12} & \cdots & a_{1j} & & a_{1j+1} & \cdots & a_{1h} & \cdots & a_{1l} & \cdots & a_{1m} \\
\vdots & \vdots & \vdots & \vdots & \vdots & \vdots & \vdots & \vdots & \vdots & \vdots & \vdots & \vdots & \vdots \\
a_{21} & \cdots & \cdots & \cdots & \cdots & \cdots & \cdots & \cdots & \cdots & \cdots & \cdots & \cdots & a_{2m} \\
\vdots & \vdots & \vdots & \vdots & \vdots & \vdots & \vdots & \vdots & \vdots & \vdots & \vdots & \vdots & \vdots \\
a_{n1} & & a_{n2} & & a_{nj} & & a_{nj+1} & \cdots & a_{nh} & \cdots & a_{nl} & \cdots & a_{nm}
\end{bmatrix}
$$

A second matrix describes the different ways to obtain the outputs

$$
\begin{bmatrix}
b_{11} & \cdots\cdots\cdots & b_{1j} & b_{1j+1} & \cdots\cdots & b_{1h} & \cdots\cdots & b_{1l} & \cdots\cdots & b_{1m} \\
\vdots & & \vdots & \vdots & & \vdots & & \vdots & & \vdots \\
b_{n1} & \cdots\cdots\cdots & b_{nj} & b_{nj+1} & \cdots\cdots & b_{nh} & \cdots\cdots & b_{nl} & \cdots\cdots & b_{nm}
\end{bmatrix}
$$

If we adopt the viewpoint of an individual producer, clearly he/she will not recognise his/her usual categories. Indeed, when an individual producer begins a new production, it is more realistic to consider the following sequence:

first he/she buys a fixed capital equipment (it is the investment necessary to start the operation);

secondly he/she works this equipment with other produced inputs and primary factors in order to obtain the finished products that he/she expects to sell. The working of the fixed capital equipment extends over several time periods.

It is not very clear how this succession of operations is represented in the preceding model. We have the same difficulty when we study the demography of human populations at a given date – the observation of all living generations does not provide any information, without additional assumptions about the behaviour of a particular generation all along its lifetime.

In the previous model, if we are interested in the time profile of the operations, we must consider that each elementary operation is a step in an investment which started at some date in the past. We can then interpret the m elementary operations in the preceding model in the following way:

$\begin{bmatrix} a_{01} \\ \hline A_1 \end{bmatrix}$ are the quantities of labour and produced goods needed for the initial investment. In fact these quantities are essentially fixed capital goods;

$\begin{bmatrix} a_{02} \\ \hline A_2 \end{bmatrix}$ are the quantities of inputs needed by the same investment one unit of time after its beginning;

$\begin{bmatrix} a_{0j} \\ \hline A_j \end{bmatrix}$ are the quantities of inputs needed by this investment over the last period of its life (we can think for example, of the inputs which are used to dismantle an industrial installation).

What are the productions obtained when this investment works?
We pursue our interpretation:

B_1 are the quantities of outputs produced when the investment is done (likely to be identically zero)

$B_2, ..., B_j$ are the quantities of outputs produced by the investment when it works since $1, 2, ..., j-1$ units of time.

Finally, we can summarise as follows the reinterpretation of the first j elementary operations: they represent the j steps during which a given investment project works and their input–output vectors indicate the goods needed and produced by this investment project, at different ages, all along its economic or technical[3] life. Thus we have

Age 0: inputs $= \begin{bmatrix} a_{01} \\ \hline A_1 \end{bmatrix}$, outputs $= B_1$;

Age 1: inputs $= \begin{bmatrix} a_{02} \\ \hline A_2 \end{bmatrix}$, outputs $= B_2$;

Age $j-1$: inputs $= \begin{bmatrix} a_{0j} \\ \hline A_j \end{bmatrix}$, outputs $= B_j$.

The same interpretation prevails for the other elementary operations. The operations $j+1, ..., h$ correspond to a second possible investment project, with the following time profile

Age 0: inputs $= \begin{bmatrix} a_{0j+1} \\ \hline A_{j+1} \end{bmatrix}$, outputs $= B_{j+1}$;

Age $h-j-1$: inputs $= \begin{bmatrix} a_{0h} \\ \hline A_h \end{bmatrix}$, outputs $= B_n$.

We have several possible investment projects which are in fact represented by a succession of input–output vectors of our standard elementary operations.

The last investment project in the list is constituted by the sequence of input–output vectors $1, ..., m$ and for this project, we have

Age 0: inputs $= \begin{bmatrix} a_{01} \\ \hline A_1 \end{bmatrix}$, outputs $= B_1$;

Age $m-1$: inputs $= \begin{bmatrix} a_{0m} \\ \hline A_m \end{bmatrix}$, outputs $= B_m$.

Clearly we have not constructed a new, different, model. It is only a different representation of the same phenomena, a longitudinal one.

At a given date, we observe potentially the simultaneous working of all these investment projects. In the standard model, we would introduce a vector of activity levels which would describe the intensity with which each elementary operation would be used. How can we interpret this point in a longitudinal approach? At each date, several investment projects of each type are started. Thus the intensity level of each elementary operation is simply the number of corresponding investment projects which have been started. For example, at a given date t, if λ_1 is the intensity level of the first elementary operation, we must consider that λ_1 investment projects of the first type have been started at date t. Each of these projects needs a_{01} units of labour, A_1 units of goods and produces B_1. At the same date t, if λ_2 is the intensity level of the second elementary operation, that means that λ_2 investment projects of the first type have been started one unit of time sooner, at date $t-1$. Today, at date t, each of these projects needs a_{02} units of labour, A_2 units of goods and produces B_2. More generally, the intensity level λ_j of the jth elementary operation is the number of the corresponding investment projects started at some date in the past. Finally, λ_m is the number of investment projects of the last type which have been started at date $t-m+1$.

Now we have almost a neo-Austrian model of the productive system of an economy. Before normalising precisely this neo-Austrian model, we may observe that we have no more restrictive assumptions than in a usual approach. In particular, we consider a multigood economy with, possibly, several primary factors.

Next, following our reinterpretation of our standard model, we construct a general neo-Austrian model, by defining appropriate concepts and notations.

2.2 The general neo-Austrian model (the non-integrated model)

In order to obtain a model formally similar to the Hicksian *Capital and Time* model, we shall adapt our notations and concepts. Previously, we interpreted each standard elementary operation as a step in an investment project. Let us denote by s the number of projects of each type which can be used in an economy.

The first of these projects is technically characterised by the pair of sequences $[a^1(u); b^1(u)]$ for $u=0, \ldots, j-1$. Of course $a^1(u)$ and $b^1(u)$ are vectors and we have $a^1(u)=\begin{bmatrix} a_{0u+1} \\ A_{u+1} \end{bmatrix}$ and $b^1(u)=B_{u+1}$ for $u=0, \ldots, j-1$. Similarly, the second of these projects is characterised by the pair of sequences $[a^2(u); b^2(u)]$, with $a^2(u)=\begin{bmatrix} a_{0j+1+u} \\ A_{j+1+u} \end{bmatrix}$ and $b^2(u)=B_{j+1+u}$ for $u=0, 1, \ldots, h-j-1$. And so forth for any element of the preceding input–output matrix. Thus all these elements are parts of an investment project and we assume that we have N such projects. Let us denote by $[a^k(u); b^k(u)]$, $u=0, 1, \ldots, D^k$, the characteristic sequences of the kth project whose lifetime is D^k units of time. Each pair of such vector sequences represents the technical characteristics of an investment project and we call elementary production process k the pair $[a^k(u); b^k(u)]$, $u=0, 1, \ldots, D^k$. For symmetry, we put zero as the first element of each $b^k(u)$, in order that $a^k(u)$ and $b^k(u)$ have the same dimension. The vector $a^k(u)$ is a $(n+1)$ dimensional vector. The first element of $a^k(u)$, denoted $a_0^k(u)$, is the quantity of labour used by a process k started u units of time ago, $u=0, 1, \ldots, D^k$. The n other elements, $a_j^k(u)$, $j=1, \ldots, n$ are the quantities of the different produced goods used by this process. Among these goods we have circulating and fixed capital goods, and also, in the von Neumann manner, used fixed capital goods. The last n elements $b_i^k(u)$, $i=2, \ldots, n$, of $b^k(u)$ are the quantities of all the goods produced by a process which had started u units of time ago. These goods can be production goods, final consumption goods and used fixed capital goods. We assume that for any used fixed capital good, the corresponding elements of $a^k(u)$ and $b^k(u)$ are equal, for any k and u, except for $u=D^k$. Indeed, at the end of a process, used capital goods can be produced, but no more such inputs are needed to pursue the process. In other words, we assume that each process produces all along its lifetime exactly the quantity of used capital goods that it needs to go on. This assumption excludes the possibility to transform a process that has already started, i.e., the minor switches in the terminology of Hicks (1973, p. 61).

Of course, the constant returns to scale imply that if a process $[a^k(u); b^k(u)]$, $u=0, \ldots, D^k$, is feasible, the process $[\lambda a^k(u); \lambda b^k(u)]$ is also feasible for the same duration, $\forall \lambda \geq 0$.

The set of the N production processes constitutes the general neo-Austrian model of an economy. We will call it the non-integrated model because it does not suppose any degree of vertical integration, and this is a major difference with the *Capital and Time* model. We will expose later the additional assumption necessary to obtain the *Capital and Time* model. In our opinion, the non-integrated model is the natural extension of Hicks's model, in order to take account of the multiplicity of goods and, possibly, of primary factors.

Now we must introduce the calendar time. At a given date t, in an economy different generations of production processes are simultaneously working, started at different dates in the past. Let us denote by $x^k(u)$ the number of processes k started at the date u, with $u < t$. At time t, each of these processes needs a vector of $a^k(t-u)$ units of inputs and produces a vector of $b^k(t-u)$ units of goods. For all the processes k of this generation, we obtain inputs equal to $a^k(t-u)x^k(u)$ and outputs equal to $b^k(t-u)x^k(u)$. Finally the vector of inputs for the whole economy is

$$\sum_{k-1}^{N} \sum_{u-t-D^k}^{t} a^k(t-u)x^k(u)=A(t)$$

and the vector of outputs is

$$\sum_{k-1}^{N} \sum_{u-t-D^k}^{t} b^k(t-u)x^k(u)=B(t)$$

The duration D^k of a process k can be technically or economically determined. So we shall assume that truncation of a process is possible before its technical death.[4] But if D^k is economically fixed, there is no reason to assume D^k constant over time for any process k. We will analyse later (see 3.2) how this parameter is fixed by economic considerations. But here we shall introduce appropriate notations to take account of this economic determination of D^k. More precisely, the lifetime will not be generally the same for all the generations of a given process k. Similarly, there is no reason to assume that all the generations of a process, belonging between the oldest and the youngest, are operating at a given date t: some generations of a given process may be missing, at a date t, whereas some older generations of the same process are still used.

Let us denote by $D^k(t)$ the age of the oldest process k living at time t, and $x^k(t, u)$ the number of processes of type k started at time u, and still working at time $t(u < t)$, with $x^k(t, u) \leq x^k(u)$. The vectors $A(t)$ and $B(t)$ may be written as follows

$$A(t)=\sum_{k=1}^{N} \sum_{u=t-D^k(t)}^{t} a^k(t-u)x^k(t, u)$$

$$B(t)=\sum_{k=1}^{N} \sum_{u=t-D^k(t)}^{t} b^k(t-u)x^k(t, u)$$

Henceforth, D^k will be used only to specify the technical duration of a process k. The functions $D^k(t)$ and $x^k(t, u)$ describe the effective life of a generation of processes. They are backward-looking functions.

Clearly, it is also necessary to define forward-looking concepts in order to represent, at a given date, the expected lifetime of any process. Let us define $D^k(t, u)$ as the lifetime, expected at time t, for a process k started at time u. Note that $D^k(u, u)$ is the anticipated lifetime of a process k when it starts at time u. So, if the anticipation of producers are correct, we have

$$x^k(t, u) = \begin{cases} x^k(u) \text{ for } u \leq t \leq D^k(u, u) \\ 0 \text{ elsewhere} \end{cases}$$

It is important to notice that with this definition of $x^k(t, u)$, $A(t)$ and $B(t)$ could be written by summing for all the values of u in the interval $[t-D; t]$ where D could be in fact any number larger than $D^k(t)$.

Consequently, we have

$$D^k(t, u) = \begin{cases} u + D^k(u, u) - t \text{ if } u - t + D^k(u, u) \geq 0 \\ 0 \text{ elsewhere} \end{cases}$$

If the anticipations are not correct over time, some unexpected adjustment will take place and we will have

$$x^k(t, u) \leq x^k(u)$$

with strict inequality for some dates t and

$$D^k(t, u) \neq u + D^k(u, u) - t$$

2.3 The Capital and Time model as a particular case of the general neo-Austrian model

The basic idea of Hicks's model in *Capital and Time* is that a temporal flow of primary input produces a temporal flow of final consumption.

Each process is a black box with a flow of labour as input and a flow of final consumption as output. Such a model assumes a complete vertical integration of production. No intermediate good appears. As soon as a production good is produced, it is used. Thus only primary factors and final consumption goods are observable in this approach. Therefore we refer to the *Capital and Time* model as the integrated model. It is interesting to examine what are the connections between these two classes of neo-Austrian models. Trivially, the *Capital and Time* model is a particular case of a non-integrated model whose processes are characterised by pairs of scalar sequences $[a^k(u); b^k(u)]_{u=0, \ldots, D^k}$. Inputs are only labour, and outputs final consumption goods. A much richer analysis consists in looking at the difference between integrated and non-integrated models through the restriction they imply when they are interpreted transversally as linear models. Burmeister (1974) examines such restrictions.[5] Let us assume that only one good, the nth good, is a final consumption good. Then we can introduce a slightly modified version of Burmeister's analysis with our notation.

He assumes that the input and output coefficients matrices have the following structure

$$
\begin{bmatrix}
0 & a_{12} & 0 & 0 & & 0 \\
\vdots & \vdots & a_{23} & 0 & & \vdots \\
& 0 & & & & \\
& \vdots & \vdots & a_{n-1,\,j-1} & & \\
0 & & \cdots & & & 0
\end{bmatrix}
$$

$$
\begin{bmatrix}
0 & a_{12} & \cdots & 0 & & 0 \\
\vdots & \vdots & a_{23} & \vdots & & \vdots \\
& 0 & & & & \\
& \vdots & & a_{n-1,\,j-1} & 0 & \\
0 & 0 & b_{n3} & \cdots & & b_{nj}
\end{bmatrix}
$$

The labour coefficient vector is

$$[a_{01}\ a_{02},\ \ldots,\ a_{0j}]$$

These coefficients must be read as following:

a_{01} units of labour produces a_{12} units of new capital good one period later;

a_{02} units of labour and a_{12} units of new capital good produces jointly a_{23} units of one year old durable equipment and b_{n3} units of final consumption good, etc. . . .;

a_{0j-1} units of labour and $a_{n-1,\,j-1}$ units of $n-1$ year old durable equipment produce finally b_{nj} units of final consumption good.

This sequence constitutes a neo-Austrian elementary process which is perfectly integrated since the only net input is labour and the only output is final consumption.[6]

Of course, in this version, we consider that only one neo-Austrian elementary process can be used. If several processes are available, other linear elementary operations must be considered simultaneously with the preceding one. Indeed, each neo-Austrian process corresponds to a particular input–output matrix and a labour vector. The global matrix representation of all these processes is obtained by the juxtaposition of these input–output matrices with the previously described structure, and by positioning the zeros in the right places. The global labour vector is the juxtaposition of all the labour vectors corresponding to the different processes.

This matrix representation of the neo-Austrian processes is a little more restrictive than necessary. Elsewhere we have proposed a more general version than Burmeister's one.[7] In fact that important feature in a matrix representation of an integrated neo-Austrian process is the utilisation of durable capital goods only to produce jointly used capital goods and final consumption. But it is always possible to consider that circulating capital goods can be used, jointly with labour, in order to produce circulating capital, etc. . . . and finally make possible the production of new durable equipment, which itself produces final consumption and older durable equipment when it is used with labour and circulating capital. Thus following Sraffa (1960), it is possible to construct the sequence of dated labour quantities which result in the production of new fixed capital goods. Following this argument, it is easy to see that each neo-Austrian process is perfectly integrated: each process is fully characterised by a sequence of labour quantities and a sequence of final consumption quantities. The sequence of labour quantities is first the sequence of the quantities of labour used to obtain the new durable equipment, then the sums of the quantities of labour directly used to work upon this durable equipment and indirectly necessary to produce the circulating capital needed to use durable equipment. Thus it is possible to consider an interpretation more general than the Burmeister one. Indeed our analysis shows that the integrated neo-Austrian model is compatible with the utilisation of circulating capital in order to produce durable equipment and to work upon it.

But we must admit that a restrictive condition subsists. In order to consider integrated processes with a finite duration, we must indeed assume the possibility to produce some good with labour only as an input.[8] In any case, the model of *Capital and Time* corresponds to a particular case of von Neumann's model, but the restrictions imposed on the input–output matrix are not as severe as Burmeister claims it. On the other hand, the non-integrated neo-Austrian model does not impose such restrictions. In particular, any production good can be produced by means of any production good and labour, and the possibility to obtain something with labour only may be excluded.

As a result, potentially at least, when a non-integrated model is used, traverse analysis may be carried out within a rather general framework, as we shall later see.

3 Prices and investment decisions in the non-integrated model

In this section, we first analyse the relationship between prices and efficiency in the non-integrated model, following Malinvaud's approach (Malinvaud, 1953 and 1962). Secondly, we examine the consequences of this relationship on producers' investment decisions. In particular, we shall see how the usual rules for truncation emerge naturally in this type of model. Lastly, we conclude with some remarks on the dynamic of prices.

3.1 Prices and efficient programmes

On the basis of the particular interpretation of the Malinvaud–von Neumann model we gave in the first section, it is not very difficult to reinterpret the analysis and the results of Malinvaud (Malinvaud, 1953, 1962). We shall not formally recall Malinvaud's work, nor its systematic interpretation in terms of the general neo-Austrian model.[9]

Let us indicate the essential points only. First, a programme in our model is simply a pair of sequences $[A(z); B(z)]$, $z=t$, $t+1$, ..., describing the sequence of global inputs and outputs from now, the date t, to infinity, if we consider infinite programmes. Of course, only possible programmes may be considered which correspond to sequences of vectors $A(z)$, $B(z)$ constructed, for any z, by possible elementary processes, including their eventual truncations.

Among possible programmes, an efficient programme $[\bar{A}(z); \bar{B}(z)]$, $z=t$, $t+1$, ..., is such that no other possible programme $[A(z); B(z)]$ exists with $B(z)-A(z) \geq \bar{B}(z)-\bar{A}(z)$, for $z=t$, $t+1$, ...[10] The difference between the output and input vectors describes, for each date z, the net production of each type of goods. With our presentation, the terms of these difference are non-negative, except for the first, which is always strictly negative, because our model is not a closed model and labour is not a produced good. In other words, it is not possible to do as well as with an efficient programme and strictly better for any date and for any good.

Now prices must be introduced. In this section, we take into consideration only the prices associated with efficient programmes, that is, shadow prices. This rules out useless debate about the choice of the relevant equilibrium concept and enlightens unambiguously the role of prices in the choice of processes and in the decision concerning their economic truncation. We denote by $P(z)$ the price vector, at date z, including the wage rate as its first component. Such prices are non-actualised prices, so that a normalisation rule (or a *numéraire*) is defined for each date. This choice does not matter for our purpose. If $R(t, z)$ is the discount factor from date t to date z, with $z>t$, the present value, at time t, of $P(z)$ is $R(t, z)\cdot P(z)$.[11] Conventionally, we set $R(t, t)=1$.

Then, following Malinvaud's teaching, we know that associated with any infinite efficient programme there exists a sequence of prices for which the profits are maximum all along the programme under consideration. Of course, because of the infinite horizon, supplementary conditions are necessary for this result to hold. For instance, Malinvaud uses a non-tightness assumption in his original paper. We assume that such a condition holds also in our general neo-Austrian model. Thus, associated with any infinite efficient programme there exists a non-negative non-null sequence $R(t, z)\cdot P(z)$, $z=t, t+1, \ldots$, such that

$$\sum_{z=t}^{+\infty} R(t, z)\cdot P(z)[B(z)-A(z)] \tag{3.1}$$

is maximum for the programme $[A(z); B(z)]$, $z=t, t+1, \ldots$ among all the possible programmes.[12]

We may note that usually this result is given with actualised prices. Of course, such a presentation is logically more satisfying because it is clearly a direct generalisation of the general competitive equilibrium approach. This difference does not matter for our purpose.

Now, if we replace in (3.1) $A(z)$ and $B(z)$ by their definitions, expression (3.1) becomes

$$\sum_{k=1}^{N} \sum_{z=t}^{+\infty} \sum_{u=z-D^k(z)}^{z} R(t, z)\cdot P(z)[b^k(z-u)-a^k(z-u)]x^k(z, u)$$

Let us invert the order of the second and third sums. Recalling the definition of $D^k(t, u)$ and $x^k(z, u)$, it is possible to verify that (3.1) is equivalent to[13]

$$\sum_{k=1}^{N} \left\{ \sum_{u=t-D^k(t)}^{t-1} \sum_{z=t}^{t+D^k(t,u)} R(t, z)\cdot P(z)[b^k(z-u)-a^k(z-u)]x^k(z, u) \right.$$
$$\left. +\sum_{u=t}^{+\infty} \sum_{z=u}^{u+D^k(t,u)} R(t, z)\cdot P(z)[b^k(z-u)-a^k(z-u)]x^k(z, u) \right\} \tag{3.2}$$

What is the economic significance of this expression?

Denote by $V^k(t, u)$ the value, at time t, of the expected profits of a process k (in short, the present value of process k) started at time u, and evaluated along an efficient programme with the prices sustaining this programme.[14] By definition

$$V^k(t, u) = \begin{cases} \sum_{z=t}^{u+D^k(t,u)} R(t, z) \cdot P(z)[b^k(z-u) - a^k(z-u)] \\ \qquad\qquad\qquad\qquad\qquad \text{if } u < t \\ \sum_{z=u}^{u+D^k(t,u)} R(t, z) \cdot P(z)[b^k(z-u) - a^k(z-u)] \\ \qquad\qquad\qquad\qquad\qquad \text{if } u \geq t \end{cases}$$

Expression (3.2) may be rewritten as follows

$$\sum_{k=1}^{N} \left[\sum_{u=t-D^k(t)}^{t-1} V^k(t, u) x^k(z-u) + \sum_{u=t}^{+\infty} V^k(t, u) x^k(z, u) \right]$$

The first series within the brackets is the present value of the different processes k started in the past, before time t, and still in operation at this time. Similarly, each term of the second series is the actual value of the different processes k that will be started in the future along this programme.

Thus the prices sustaining an efficient programme are such that the present value of any process started along this programme is maximum for these prices.

The above property has simultaneously two implications: at first on the type of processes which are used, and also on their duration. Indeed the lifetime of these process, $D^k(t, u)$, must be adapted every time it is possible, in order to maximise their present values. If we follow a usual interpretation, we could simply say that in a decentralised economy where the producers choose their investment projects, including their duration, on the basis of maximised present value, some efficiency path could be obtained. Of course, we use conditional because this dynamic extension of the general equilibrium approach must be prudently considered if a concept of equilibrium is to be chosen. But assuming maximising present value behaviour seems clearly a reasonable assumption in order to determine how processes and their durations are actually chosen. Besides, the presentation of these classical results in a general neo-Austrian model allows us to synthesise different viewpoints that are usually independently presented.

At last, let us recall that proportional programmes, or steady states, constitute a special case of possible programmes. In such programmes, the rate of starts of the different processes has the particular form

$$x^k(t, u) = x^k(1+g)^u$$

where g is a constant and x^k, $k = 1, \ldots, N$, indicates the number of processes k started at some base date.

A price system sustaining an efficient steady state has a special property. Indeed, as Malinvaud has shown, all these prices (non-actualised prices) are constant over time (Malinvaud, 1953). Thus, for efficient proportional programmes, we have

$$\begin{cases} P(z)=P \ \forall z \\ R(t, u)=(1+r)^{t-u}, \ \forall t, \ \forall u \end{cases}$$

As a result, the whole usual analysis of steady states could be directly adapted to our general neo-Austrian model.[15]

3.2 Economic truncation of processes along efficient paths

This subsection presents a more precise characterisation of the truncation rules which prevail along efficient paths.

If the lifetime of a process is not imposed by technical considerations, it must be chosen so that the present value of the process cannot be greater. Thus, for any process k, there exists no other choice $D^k(t, u)$ for which the actual value of the process would be greater than $V^k(t, u)$.

Formally, $D^k(t, u)$ satisfies

$$\sum_{z=u+D^k(t-u)}^{v} P(z) \cdot R(t, z)[b^k(z-u)-a^k(z-u)]<0 \qquad (3.3)$$
$$\forall v>u+D^k(t, u)$$

Thus we necessarily have

$$P[u+D^k(t-u)] \ [b^k(D^k(u, u))-a^k(D^k(u, u))]\geq 0 \qquad (3.4)$$
$$P[u+D^k(t-u)+1] \ [b^k(D^k(u, u)+1)-a^k(D^k(u, u)+1)]\leq 0$$

Conditions (3.3) and (3.4)[16] are the classical conditions satisfied by the optimal lifetime of an investment project when its present value is maximised.[17]

The economic interpretation of (3.4) is immediate:

(i) If the value of the net product of a process was negative when it is stopped, it would be more profitable to stop it sooner (first inequality).
(ii) Any marginal increase of the duration beyond $D^k(t, u)$ is unprofitable (second inequality).

Of course, on a steady state, $D^k(t, u)$ is constant over time for each process: $D^k(t, u)=D^k, \ k=1, \ ..., \ N$.

Another interesting feature concerns a classical result in the theory of optimal replacement for durable equipments. It is known in the literature as the 'three-dates-equation'.[18] To see this point, suppose that in the succession of the different process along an efficient path stands a chain of processes k: at date $u+D^k(u, u)$ this process k is replaced by another process k, until the date $u+D^k(u, u)+D^k(u+D^k(u, u), u+D^k(u, u))$ etc. . . . .

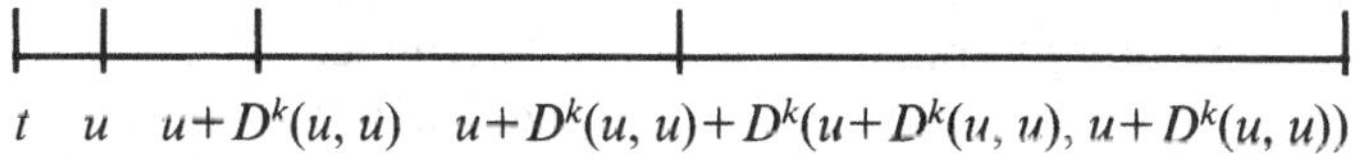

t u $u+D^k(u, u)$ $u+D^k(u, u)+D^k(u+D^k(u, u), u+D^k(u, u))$

Figure 1.1 Succession of processes and optimal replacement

Because expression (3.2) is maximum, the sum of present values of processes k in this chain is also maximum for the prices sustaining the efficient path. Thus any shift in a replacement date must produce a lower sum of present values for all these processes k.

In particular, shifting $D^k(u, u)$ into $D^k(u, u)+1$ or $D^k(u, u)-1$ must lower the present value of the entire chain. In order to formalise this point, let us denote by $V^k(t, u, D^k(t, u))$ the present value, at t, of a process k starting at time u for a duration $D^k(t, u)$. This present value is calculated for the prices associated with the efficient path under consideration.

After some manipulations, the following inequalities can be established

$$V^k(t, u, D^k(t, u))+V^k(t, u+D^k(t, u), D^k(t, u+D^k(t, u)))$$
$$> V^k(t, u, D^k(t, u)+\varepsilon)+V^k(t, u+D^k(t, u)+\varepsilon, D^k(t, u+D^k(t, u)))$$

for $\varepsilon=-1, 1$.

After rearranging the different terms we obtain

$$V^k(t, u, D^k(t, u))-V^k(t, u, D^k(t, u)+\varepsilon)$$
$$> V^k(t, u, D^k(t, u))+\varepsilon, D^k(t, u+D^k(t, u))$$
$$- V^k(t, u+D^k(t, u), D^k(t, u+D^k(t, u)))$$ (3.5)

for $\varepsilon=-1, 1$.

What is the economic interpretation of the above inequalities?

When the choice of processes maximises the present value of these processes, it is impossible to obtain some gain by changing the dates of replacement in a succession of processes. There is no net gain in advancing a replacement date (the first inequality, with $\varepsilon=1$) nor in putting it back (the second inequality with $\varepsilon=1$). For instance, if $\varepsilon=1$, the left-hand side of the inequality, is the gain (or the loss) obtained (or respectively, suffered) if the replacement date is shifted from $D^k(t, u)$ into $D^k(t, u)+1$. It is less than the loss (respectively the gain) suffered (respectively obtained) because putting back the replacement of process k of generation u is also putting back the beginning of the following processes. A similar interpretation holds for $\varepsilon=-1$.[19]

3.3 Equilibrium, prices and choice of processes

Before analysing the traverse problem, we must complete our neo-Austrian framework by some considerations about the equilibrium concepts we may choose. In other terms, how are prices determined? The neo-Austrian approach is a longitudinal one. Thus time and dynamic problems are at the heart of this approach. In a neo-Austrian framework, the choice of an equilibrium concept is the choice of a method for dynamic analysis. In *Capital and Growth* (1965) and *Methods of Dynamic Economics* (1985), J. R. Hicks considered the different possibilities. We do not pretend to add any complement to his masterly analysis.

Fundamentally, three possibilities arise: (i) full intertemporal equilibrium, which implies perfect anticipations and a complete system of future markets;[20] (ii) temporary equilibrium with markets only for the present time; (iii) disequilibrium, with no equilibrating markets, and persistent excess supply or demand on these markets.

In subsection 3.1, the properties of prices sustaining efficient paths were studied. In our general neo-Austrian model, some interesting features were emphasized. But we kept away from a market interpretation of these shadow prices. Indeed, with an additional transversality condition (due to infinite horizon), the usual interpretation is the following: an economy follows an efficient path if the agents, taking prices as given, maximise their profits when they choose the elementary processes and their durations. Of course this amounts to assuming that the prices $P(z)$ and the discount factors $R(t, z)$, for $z \geq t$, are perfectly anticipated. If the perfect anticipations hypothesis is relevant in a normative approach, it is a rather curious assumption in a descriptive approach. And, in our view, the neo-Austrian approach is typically a descriptive one. Thus we will reject the full intertemporal equilibrium approach as non-relevant for the situations in which the neo-Austrian approach is the adequate method of dynamic analysis.

An alternative choice is the temporary equilibrium method. This choice implies an assumption about anticipations, plus the flexibility of prices on the markets: at any date, prices adjust in order to make demand equal to supply on every market. In *Capital and Time*, J. R. Hicks uses a polar case of this situation. When he assumes perfect flexibility of prices, he also assumes completely static expectations. But the only full intertemporal equilibria to which Hicks refers are steady states. Thus the static expectations assumption considerably simplifies the analysis of price dynamics, because it allows for the use of the well-known properties of price systems associated with steady states. But if the conditions of a steady state are modified, the agents know that any steady state will no longer be possible for a long time, and it would be rather difficult to admit completely myopic expectations. Alternative assumptions about anticipations are as difficult to manage in a neo-Austrian approach as in a standard transversal approach if one seeks to describe the real path of an economy.

The last possibility consists in assuming entirely rigid prices with non-cleared markets. It is the fix-price method (the fix-wage method in the case of the integrated model of *Capital and Time*).

Unfortunately, it is not a more satisfying method to analyse a traverse than the two preceding ones. Indeed, the fix-price method is relevant for short-term analyses. With a short horizon, one can admit that quantity adjustments precede price adjustments. But, in the usual sense, the short-term excludes notable adjustments in the stock of capital. Thus the relevance of the fix-price method for traverse analysis is also questionable.

The above criticism is not addressed to Hicks and his neo-Austrian approach. The simplifications and the methods he employed in *Capital and Time* allowed great progress in many directions. Our criticism of the three fundamental methods of dynamic economies concerns rather economic theory itself. Indeed, there exists no theory simultaneously capturing the true dynamic of prices and the true dynamic of quantities in a satisfying manner. The great modesty of Malinvaud in his 1986 article reflects exactly this fact. The neo-Austrian approach is not the universal method to understanding all features of the dynamics of an economy. But in our opinion it certainly is one of the best ways to understand the consequence of adjustments in the structure of fixed capital.

Nevertheless, we need some assumptions in order to formulate precisely how the processes and their durations are chosen. In a decentralized economy, the most reasonable and natural assumption is to assume that the processes and the truncation rules are such that, at any time, the present value of these processes is maximum for the anticipated prices and interest rates. This is all we will assume, and we will not enter here into the debate on flex- or fix-prices, operating markets, and so on. There are present prices $P(t)$ and the agents anticipate $P(z)$ and $R(z, t)$ for $z > t$. That is all we need to know about economic choices in order to present the working of the neo-Austrian approach.

Another related problem concerns the determination of the rates of starts of the new processes and the truncation decisions of the old ones – that is, the level of activity intensities in a transversal approach. Indeed, if prices are completely flexible, markets are in equilibrium and thus the rates of starts of the new processes and the truncation of the old ones may be determined. Of course, if a complete system of future markets exists, this equilibrium is a general intertemporal equilibrium: all markets, both present and future, are equilibrated and anticipations are correct. If such a system of markets does not exist, the flexibility of prices can ensure equilibrium for present markets only and the rates of starts and truncation choices depend on the (generally false) anticipations. In this case, it is the concept of temporary equilibrium that is used.

In the fix-price approach, such flexibility of prices is not assumed and supply and demand are not equalised on the different markets. Thus, the rate of starts of the new processes and the truncation of the old ones correspond to some disequilibrium situation. We will not consider the details of such situations.

To understand how the neo-Austrian approach allows for the descriptive analysis of a traverse, it is sufficient to assume that the productive system works at full capacity. In other words, we assume that we are in full-performance situation: 'At full performance, the rate of starts is at its maximum – at the maximum permitted by the share of current output that is not absorbed by consumption of other kinds. The full performance path still shows the highest level of activity that can be maintained' (Hicks, 1973, p. 52).

We will assume full performance, without examining how this situation is attained. But it is not necessary here to choose between a flex- of a fix-price assumption. The concept of full intertemporal equilibrium must be, however, discarded. Indeed, the neo-Austrian approach is essentially a tool for traverse analysis. A traverse occurs only when the economy leaves a stable situation in order to evolve towards another stable situation. But, if the concept of full intertemporal equilibrium is retained, there is never a place for any traverse at all! With this concept of equilibrium we must associate a perfect foresight assumption, so that any change in the exogeneous parameters of the economy is perfectly anticipated and thus perfectly integrated within it: when this change takes place, all the structures of the economy are perfectly adapted to this one. Past, present and future are entirely confused and there is no place for a truly dynamic analysis.

As a result, in order to analyse traverse problems, something like a temporary equilibrium concept must be used: at any date, the type and number of the new processes that are started, and the type and number of the old processes that are stopped, are determined simultaneously by prices and by the expectations (generally false) of economic agents. Of course, full performance is an additional constraint, but full performance can clearly be attained even if anticipations are not correct.

4 Traverse - structural change of the fixed capital stock

In *Capital and Time*, Hicks studied specifically the evolution of an economy along a traverse path between two steady states. At a given date

(date O), a non-anticipated event occurs (a technical improvement, for example), and the conditions which made possible a given steady state hold no longer. The structure of the population of processes is not adapted to this unanticipated event, and some time will elapse before structural adaptations make possible the convergence towards a new steady state. That is, fundamentally, Hicks's problem in *Capital and Time*. But it is clearly a very particular traverse situation. It is a particular case of the general situation in which an economy leaves an equilibrium path because unanticipated events happened and move eventually towards another equilibrium path. In the next subsection, it is a somewhat general case which will be examined within a non-integrated neo-Austrian model. In subsection 4.5, we will consider a simplified traverse between two steady states as in Hicks's *Capital and Time*, except that we conduct our analysis in a general integrated neo-Austrian model without any restriction about the time-profile of processes.

4.1 Assumptions and notations

The general analysis of a traverse would be largely intractable without some simplifications. Thus we adopt the seven following assumptions.

Assumption 1
Each process produces only one type of finished good, either a consumption good or a production good. In particular, the first good is assumed to be the only consumption good.[21]

Assumption 1 amounts to supposing that the economy is subdivided into branches: in each branch only one type of finished good is produced and reciprocally each finished good is produced in one branch only.[22]

Assumption 2
In each branch, at each date, only one type of process is started.

Assumption 2 excludes the possibility that two processes have the same expected return at a given date. This assumption simplifies considerably the analysis and is the natural complement of assumption 1. Of course, the second assumption does not say that it is the same process which is started, at any date, in each branch of the economy.

Assumption 3
Time is a continuous variable.

This assumption is a technical one which allows to simplify considerably the mathematics of the traverse.

Clearly the three previous assumptions lead to another formalisation of the input–output sequences associated with each neo-Austrian process. Indeed, each generation of process specialising in the production of a given good includes only one type of process. Possibly this type differs from one generation to another. Thus we will denote by $a^k(t, u)$ the vector of input quantities used by a process k started at time u and still operating at time t. Similarly, $b^k(t, u)$ is the quantity (a scalar under assumption 1) of the kth finished good produced at time t by a process k of generation u. Of course, exactly as in the second part of this chapter, the functions $a^k(t, u)$ and $b^k(t, u)$ take strictly positive values for $t \in [u, u+D^k(u, u)]$ when the anticipations are correct, and, more generally, for any (t, u) such that $t \geq u$ and $D^k(t, u) \geq 0$. These functions vanish elsewhere. At last, these functions are assumed to be continuous and differentiable.

We need to characterise now saving-consumption behaviour:

Assumption 4
There is no saving out of wages, no consumption out of profit.

This assumption is a rather extreme one. But it allows us to concentrate upon the problems due to the structural adjustments along a traverse and not to some insufficient saving.

Assumption 5
No employment constraint is binding.

By this assumption, unemployment is possible along a traverse path. This seems quite natural because the reason for which full employment would be obtained along a traverse is not very clear. This last assumption is equally related to assumption 4. Indeed, these two assumptions can be interpreted like a perfectly inelastic labour supply assumption, with a wage rate at a subsistence level. Nevertheless we do not explicitly assume the rigidity of the wage rate.

Now we can write the fundamental relationships which hold along any full-performance path. Let us denote by $w(t)$ the wage rate, at time t, measured in units of good 1 (the consumption good). Under assumptions 1–5 we have

$$\int_{t-D^1(t)}^{t} \left[b^1(t, u)x^1(t, u) - w(t)\sum_{k=1}^{N} a_0^k(t, u)x^k(t, u) \right] du = 0 \qquad (4.1)$$

$$\int_{t-D^i(t)}^{t} \left[b^i(t, u)x^1(t, u) - \sum_{k=1}^{N} a_i^k(t, u)x^k(t, u) \right] du = 0 \qquad (4.2)$$

$$i = 2, \dots, N$$

In order to simplify the presentation, we adopt the following vector notations

$$Q_1(t, u)=[b^1(t, u)-w(t)a_0^1(t, u); -w(t)a_0^2(t, u) \ldots w(t)a_0^N(t, u)]$$

$$Q_i(t, u)=[- a_i^1(t, u) \ldots \underbrace{b^i(t, u)-a_i^i(t, u)}_{i\,th\text{ element}} \ldots -a_i^N(t, u)]$$

$i=2, \ldots, N$

$$x(t, u)= \begin{bmatrix} x^1(t, u) \\ \vdots \\ x^k(t, u) \\ \vdots \\ x^N(t, u) \end{bmatrix}$$

(4.1) and (4.2) may be rewritten as follows

$$\int_{t-D^1(t)}^{t} Q_1(t, u)x(t, u)du=0 \qquad\qquad (4.3)$$

$$\int_{t-D^i(t)}^{t} Q_i(t, u)x(t, u)du=0 \qquad\qquad (4.4)$$

$i=2, \ldots, N$

Under full performance, these N relationships hold because the produced quantity of a consumption good is entirely absorbed by wages (equation (4.3)) and because supply is equal to demand for any finished good (equation (4.4)).

At time t, the type and number of the new processes, and the truncation of the old ones, must be such that the N relationships (4.3) and (4.4) hold along any full-performance path.

What is the situation when an unforeseen event arises at time 0? What are the relations corresponding to (4.3) and (4.4) in this case? In order to understand the consequences of this unexpected change, it is clearly necessary to distinguish the effective (unexpected) path followed by the economy after date 0 from the expected path which would have been followed if the unforeseen change had not taken place at time 0. In order to do so, we introduce the following functions defined for every k such that $k\epsilon(1, \ldots, N)$

for $0 \leq u \leq t$, $a_i^{k*}(t, u)$, $k=1, 2, ..., N$ and $b^{k*}(t, u)$ are the input–output functions describing the process started at time u, and participating in the production of the finished good k.

$w^*(t)$ is the actual wage rate, for any date $t \geq 0$. In general $w^*(t) \neq w(t)$. That is, the actual (unexpected) wage rate $w^*(t)$ will differ from $w(t)$, the previously expected wage rate.

$Q_i^*(t, u)$ are vectors exactly like vectors $Q_i(t, u)$ but with the functions $b^{k*}(t, u)$, $a_i^{k*}(t, u)$, $w^*(t)$ instead of functions $b^k(t, u)$, $a_i^k(t, u)$, and $w(t)$ respectively.

$x^{k*}(u)$ is the rate of starts, at time u, $u \geq 0$, of the production process.

$x^{k*}(t, u)$ is the number of such processes still alive at time t.

$x^*(u)$ is the column vector $[x^{k*}(u)]$, $k=1, ..., N$.

$x^*(t, u)$ is the column vector $[x^{k*}(t, u)]$, $k=1, ..., N$.

$D^{i*}(t)$ is the age of the oldest process contributing, at time t, to the production of good i.

for any (t, u) such that $t \geq 0$ and $u \leq t$, $D^{i*}(t, u)$ is the expected remaining lifetime, at time t, of a process i, belonging to the generation u, still in operation at time t.

In other words, the notations without * concern the different elements that characterise the expected evolution of the economy which would have been the real evolution if unexpected change had not occurred at time 0, and the notations with * correspond to the actual values of these elements, after the unexpected change has taken place.

Of course, we have

$$\forall(t, u) \text{ such that } u < 0 \leq t, \; x^{k*}(t, u) = \begin{cases} x^k(u) \text{ if } D^{k*}(t, u) > 0 \\ 0 \text{ elsewhere} \end{cases}$$

$$\forall(t, u) \text{ such that } 0 \leq u \leq t, \; x^{k*}(t, u) = \begin{cases} x^{k*}(u) \text{ if } D^{k*}(t, u) > 0 \\ 0 \text{ elsewhere} \end{cases}$$

Now, for any date $t \geq 0$, we shall distinguish two successive periods. The first one elapses from 0 until no process started before 0 is working. It is the first phase of the traverse, during which some old processes, started at dates $u < 0$, are still operating, and co-exist with new processes, started after time 0. Following Hicks's terminology, this phase is the early phase of the traverse. Formally it corresponds to the period of time $[0; T]$ such that

$$\begin{cases} T - D^{i*}(T) = 0, \; \forall i \in (1, 2, ..., N) \\ t - D^{i*}(t) \leq 0, \; \forall i \in (1, ..., N), \; \forall t \in [0; T] \end{cases}$$

Finally in order to simplify our analysis, we suppose the following:

Assumption 6

$D^{i*}(t, u)$ and $D^i(t, u)$ are positive for any (t, u) such that $0 \leq u \leq t \leq T$.

This assumption implies that, during the early phase of the traverse, only the oldest processes of each generation are truncated. This assumption is not very compelling, but in general it could be the case that some processes belonging to old generations would still be alive at time t, whereas younger processes could have been stopped.

We adopt the following normalisation rule (*Assumption 7*)

$$b^k(t, u) = b^{k*}(t, u), \forall(t, u), u \leq t, k = 1, \dots, N$$

At any date during the early phase of a traverse, the equality between supply and demand for every finished good implies:[23]

$$\int_{t-D^{1*}(t)}^{0} \left[b^1(t, u)x^{1*}(t, u) - w^*(t) \sum_{k=1}^{N} a_0^k(t, u)x^{k*}(t, u) \right] du$$

$$+ \int_{0}^{t} Q_1^*(t, u)x^*(u)du = 0 \tag{4.5}$$

$$\int_{t-D^{1*}(t)}^{0} Q_i(t, u)x^*(t, u) \, du + \int_{0}^{t} Q_i^*(t, u)x^*(u)du = 0$$

$$i = 2, \dots, N \tag{4.6}$$

The second phase of the traverse begins when the last processes started before 0 are stopped. It corresponds to the late phase of a traverse in the Hicksian terminology. This late phase begins at time T, and we have $t - D^{i*}(t) > 0, \forall t \geq T$.

At any date during the late phase, we have

$$\int_{t-D^{1*}(t)}^{0} Q_1^*(t, u)x^*(t, u)du = 0$$

$$\int_{t-D^{i*}(t)}^{t} Q_i^*(t, u)x^*(t, u)du = 0$$

$$i = 2, \dots, N \tag{4.7}$$

In order to compare the actual (unexpected) path with the initially expected path, we shall proceed in two steps. First, we suppose that the stopping rules of the old processes, belonging to generations $u < 0$, are identical to those that would have been followed if no unexpected change had occurred at 0. In this first step, it is possible to isolate the pure effect of the change in the type of processes started after 0. We will call this the *pure substitution effect*. The trajectory of the economy when only this pure substitution effect is present is called the *fictive path*.

In a second step, we shall take into account the consequences of adapting the durations of processes started before 0. By so doing, we isolate, in the second step, the pure effect of the adjustment in the truncations of the old processes, induced by the unexpected change happening at 0. We call this the *truncation effect*.

Of course, the complete consequence of the change occurring at 0 is the combination of these two effects: pure substitution effect plus truncation effect.

In the general case, nothing may be said about the late phase of a traverse. Indeed, during this phase, it is the eventual convergence of the economy towards another equilibrium which should be analysed. It is somewhat like a convergence problem. But the problem is intractable when general cases are considered. It is only in the case of a traverse between two steady states that the problem of the late phase can be treated. We shall examine this problem later. Clearly, in the context of a general traverse, only the early phase can be analysed.

4.2 Traverse with truncations unchanged – the pure substitution effect during the early phase of a general traverse

If the durations of the old processes, started before 0, were not adapted to the new conditions prevailing after 0, we would have, for every i

$$D^{i*}(t) = D^i(t) \forall t \geq 0$$

$$D^{i*}(t, u) = D^i(t, u) \forall (t, u),\ u \leq 0 \leq t$$

The second equality involves

$$x^{i*}(t, u) = x^i(t, u) \forall (t, u),\ u \leq 0 \leq t$$

Then, if the truncations of the processes started before 0 are unchanged, the rate of starts of the processes after 0 along a full-performance path does not satisfy (4.5) and (4.6). Indeed, these relations hold only when the truncations of all the processes take account of the new conditions prevailing after 0. If this is not the case, the rate of starts of the processes after time 0 would be described by functions $\bar{x}^i(u)$, $i = 1, ..., N$, $0 \leq u \leq t$, different from the functions $x^{i*}(u)$. Denote $\bar{x}(u)$ the column vector $\begin{bmatrix} \bar{x}^1(u) \\ \vdots \\ \bar{x}^N(u) \end{bmatrix}$. The following relations hold

$$\int_{t-D^1(t)}^{0} \left[b^1(t, u)x^1(t, u) - w^*(t) \sum_{k=1}^{N} a_0^k(t, u)x^k(t, u) \right] du$$

$$+ \int_0^t Q_1^*(t, u)\bar{x}(u)du = 0 \tag{4.9}$$

$$\int_{t-D^i(t)}^{0} Q_i(t, u)x(t, u)du + \int_0^t Q_i^*(t, u)\bar{x}(u)du = 0$$

$$i = 2, \dots, N \tag{4.10}$$

Equations (4.9) and (4.10) are the same relations as (4.5) and (4.6), except for $D^1(t)$, $D^i(t)$, $x^k(t, u)$, $x(t, u)$ and $\bar{x}(u)$ instead of $D^{1*}(t)$, $D^{i*}(t)$, $x^{k*}(t, u)$, $x^*(t, u)$ and $x^*(u)$ respectively. Of course, if there were no truncation effect along this traverse, (4.9) and (4.10) would be the same as (4.5) and (4.6), and the functions $x^{i*}(u)$ and $\bar{x}^i(u)$ would be identical.

Now, by using assumption 7, it is clear that (4.3) and (4.9) have some identical terms, and similarly for (4.4) and (4.10). After some elementary manipulations, we obtain

$$\int_0^t Q_1^*(t, u)\bar{x}(u)du = \int_0^t Q_1(t, u)x(u)du$$

$$+ [w^*(t) - w(t)] \int_{t-D^1(t)}^{0} \sum_{k=1}^{N} a_0^k(t, u)x^k(t, u)du \tag{4.11}$$

$$\int_0^t Q_i^*(t, u)\bar{x}(u)du = \int_0^t Q_i(t, u)x(u)du$$

$$i = 2, \dots, N \tag{4.12}$$

The relations (4.11) and (4.12) constitute a system of N Volterra's equations of the first kind.[24] The unknowns are the N functions $\bar{x}^i(u)$ describing the path followed by the economy when only the pure substitution effect works.

Of course, we are interested here not in the formal solution of (4.11) and (4.12) but rather in comparing $\bar{x}(u)$ and $x(u)$, in order to obtain the sign of the pure substitution effect. Let us denote by $E_1(t)$ the second term of the right side of (4.11). It is the difference between the total wages paid on the old processes, started before 0, along the actual (unexpected) path and along the expected (initially expected) path. Thus (4.11) and (4.12) become

$$\int_0^t Q_i^*(t, u)[\bar{x}(u) - x(u)]du = E_1(t) + \int_0^t [Q_1(t, u) - \bar{Q}_i^*(t, u)]x(u)du$$

$$\int_0^t Q_i^*(t, u)[\bar{x}(u) - x(u)]du = \int_0^t [Q_i(t, u) - \bar{Q}_i^*(t, u)]x(u)du$$

$$i = 2, \ldots, N$$

By forming the $N \times N$ matrix $Q^*(t, u)$ such that $Q^*(t, u) = \begin{bmatrix} Q_1^*(t, u) \\ \vdots \\ Q_i^*(t, u) \\ \vdots \\ Q_n^*(t, u) \end{bmatrix}$

and the $N \times 1$ column vector $E(t)$ with the right hand of these equations, we can write in matrix form the relations (4.11) and (4.12).

$$\int_0^t Q^*(t, u)[\bar{x}(u) - x(u)]du = E(t) \tag{4.13}$$

Let us integrate the left-hand side of (4.13) and denote by $\bar{X}(t) - X(t)$ the integral $\int_0^t [\bar{x}(u) - x(u)]du$, and by $\dot{Q}_u^*(t, u)$ the vector of partial derivatives of $Q^*(t, u)$. We then obtain

$$Q^*(t, t)[\bar{X}(t) - X(t)] - \int_0^t \dot{Q}_u^*(t, u)[\bar{X}(u) - X(u)]du = E(t) \tag{4.14}$$

Of course, we assume that $Q_u^*(t, u)$ is well defined for all the relevant range of values of (t, u). In fact, each element of $Q(t, u)$ must only be differentiable almost everywhere, and not continuously. We will not insist here on these formal points.

Equations (4.14) are the fundamental equations that give the sign of the pure substitution effect. Indeed, this sign can in principle be obtained from the sign of the elements of $Q^*(t, t)[\bar{X}(t) - X(t)]$, the solution of (4.14).

When system (4.14) admits a solution, it is well known from Volterra's equation theory that it takes the form[25]

$$Q^*(t, t)[\bar{X}(t) - X(t)] = E(t) + \int_0^t S(t, u)E(u)du \tag{4.15}$$

The solvent kernel $S(t, u)$ is a $N \times N$ matrix constructed as the following

$$S(t, u) = \sum_{n=0}^{+\infty} (-1)^{n+1} [\dot{Q}_u^*(t, u) \cdot Q^*(u, u)^{-1}]^{(n)}$$

where $Q^*(t, t)^{-1}$ is the inverse of $Q(t, t)$

$$[\dot{Q}_0^*(t, u) \cdot Q^*(u, u)^{-1}]^{(0)} = \dot{Q}_u^*(t, u) \cdot Q^*(u, u)^{-1}$$

$$[\dot{Q}_0^*(t, u) \cdot Q^*(u, u)^{-1}]^{(n)} =$$

$$= \int_u^t [\dot{Q}_v^*(t, v) \cdot Q(v, v)^{-1}]^{(n-1)} \cdot [\dot{Q}_v^*(v, u) \cdot Q(u, u)^{-1}] dv$$

Observe that when the kernel of (4.14) is constituted by non-positive elements, that is, when the terms of $\dot{Q}_u^*(t, u) \cdot Q(u, u)^{-1}$ are non-negative, the solvent kernel, $S(t, u)$ is a non-negative matrix.

In this case, the comparison between $\bar{X}(t)$ and $X(t)$ is made easier because the sign of the solution of (4.14), $Q(t, t)[\bar{X}(t) - X(t)]$, is, at least for some interval after 0, the same as the one of $E(t)$. More precisely, if the vector $E(t)$ is positive (negative) for $t \in [0; \bar{t}]$, the vector $Q(t, t)[\bar{X}(t) - X(t)]$, solution of (4.14), is also positive (respectively, negative) for any $t \in [0; \bar{\bar{t}}]$, with $\bar{\bar{t}} > \bar{t}$.

What are the implications on the sign of $\bar{X}(t) - X(t)$? It is quite natural to suppose that $Q^*(t, t)$ contains only non-positive terms. Indeed, the matrix $Q^*(t, t)$ describes the net production of the different goods produced by processes just started at time t, and the quantities of these goods needed as inputs by the different processes. Clearly all these terms are non positive. This is obvious for all terms out of the principal diagonal of $Q^*(t, t)$, and, for these last elements, they are non-positive because an elementary process does not produce anything when it is started, whereas it needs some inputs in order to work. A machine does not produce anything during its installation, but it needs some inputs in order to be able to operate. Thus the signs of the terms in $\bar{X}(t) - X(t)$ are presumably the opposite of the sign of $Q^*(t, t)[\bar{X}(t) - X(t)]$. In any case, that is true at least for some elements of the vector $\bar{X}(t) - X(t)$ (we will discuss this point later).

Finally, if the solvent kernel of (4.14) is positive, we can presume that the number of processes started since time 0 will be greater or less than the one expected *ex ante*, according to the sign of the right-hand side of (4.14). It will be greater if this last vector is positive, and smaller if it is negative.

The economic interpretation of this result is simple: the elements of vector $E(t)$ represent exactly the difference between the needs in terms of different goods, if the rate of starts and the type of processes started after time 0 were the expected ones, and the real inputs of each good for any $t > 0$, when the type and the number of the started processes are the unexpected ones. This difference is positive if the type of the new processes allows to save some resources when they are started at the same rate as the old, expected ones, $x(t)$. These saved resources permit to start more processes of the new types. Of course, we have the symmetric interpretation when $E(t)$ is negative. This is the fundamental meaning of equations (4.14).

In economic terms, the interpretation of this pure substitution effect is that an unexpected increase (decrease) of the wage rate and the choice of new processes using more (respectively, less) resources than the old ones, brings about a reduction in the rate of starts of processes 0 compared with the level of the rate of starts if no unforeseen event occurs at 0.

Of course, if we look at the first element of $E(t)$, it is clear that an unexpected change in the wage rate can be compensated for by the choice of an appropriate type of process. Here, we are in the presence of a classical substitution effect: an increase (decrease) in the wage rate can be compensated for by the choice of processes using globally less (respectively, more) resources, at their beginning, than with the old ones, for a given rate of starts.

Fundamentally, the above treatment summarises the many results of Hicks's *Capital and Time*. But here we are considering the more general framework of a non-integrated neo-Austrian model, and a general traverse between an expected and an unexpected (or badly expected) path.

But reasoning within a more general framework involves some additional difficulties and also some limitations in the results. As can be observed from the previous comments, two types of difficulties arise from the analysis of the solution of (4.14). First, in order to have a non-negative solvent kernel for (4.14) we need apparently to impose some restrictions upon the elements of the kernel of this equation. We shall appreciate later the effectiveness of these restrictions. Second, it is clear that, even if the first type of difficulty is ruled out, we only have information about the sign of the elements of vector $Q^*(t, t)[\bar{X}(t) - X(t)]$ and not directly on those of the vector $\bar{X}(t) - X(t)$. More precisely, the problem is to deduce something about the sign of $\bar{X}(t) - X(t)$ from the sign of $Q^*(t, t) \cdot [\bar{X}(t) - X(t)]$.

We will treat these two problems in succession.

First, what are the effective economic restrictions imposed in order to obtain the non-negativity of $S(t, u)$, the solvent kernel of (4.14)? Because $Q^*(t, t) \leqq 0$, we have $\dot{Q}^*_u(t, u) \cdot Q^*(u, u)^{-1} \leqq 0 <=> \dot{Q}^*_u(t, u) \leqq 0$, or equivalently

$$\frac{\partial}{\partial u} [b^{*1}(t, u) - w(t)a_0^*(t, u)] \leq 0$$

$$\frac{\partial}{\partial u} [b^{*1}(t, u) - a_i^{*i}(t, u)] \leq 0, \ i = 2, ..., N$$

$$\frac{\partial}{\partial u} [a_j^{*i}(t, u)] \geq 0, \ i = 2, ..., N, j = 0, 2, ..., N, i \neq j \qquad (4.16)$$

The first N conditions mean that in each branch, at any date t, the youngest processes do not produce more net output than the oldest ones. Although the opposite situation would seem more natural, we can admit these N first conditions. Indeed, it would always be possible to choose a normalisation rule such that the net output produced by each process is first zero, then a constant. The other conditions (4.16) say that each process, at any time t, needs at least as much inputs as any older process. Clearly these conditions are very restrictive, since in practice we must admit that the quantities of inputs used by any process is not a decreasing function of the age of this process.

Let us observe that the conditions (4.16) are satisfied in particular if each elementary process has a temporal profile such that the input and output flows are constant functions of the age of the process, that is the case under the simple profile assumption used by Hicks in his *Capital and Time* integrated model.

Clearly we must consider the possibility that conditions (4.16) are not satisfied by the temporal profiles of the processes. In this case, it is not possible to deduce directly something about the sign on $Q^*(t, t)[\bar{X}(t) - X(t)]$ from the sign of $E(t)$. We must turn the difficulty by considering the following system

$$\int_0^t K(t, u)Z(u)du = E(t) \tag{4.17}$$

where $Z(u)$ is a $N \times 1$ vector, and $K(t, u)$ a $N \times N$ matrix. This matrix consists of non-negative functions, which are non-increasing in u, each of them being uniformly greater or smaller than the corresponding function of $Q^*(t, u)$ for any (t, u), $u \leq t$.

The functions used to construct $K(t, u)$ are assumed integrable and differentiable almost everywhere. Thus a possibility to construct $K(t, u)$ consists in selecting the intervals where the functions in $Q^*(t, u)$ are increasing in u, and in completing by constant functions elsewhere. We can transform (4.17) into

$$K(t, t) \cdot Z(t) - \int_0^t \dot{K}_u(t, u)Z(u)du = E(t)$$

so that $K(t, t)Z(t)$ is given by

$$K(t, t) \cdot Z(t) = E(t) + \int_0^t \bar{S}(t, u)Z(u)du$$

where the solvent kernel $\bar{S}(t, u)$ is non-negative, by construction of $K(t, u)$.

Exactly as we obtained (4.14) from (4.13), and because it is always possible to choose $K(t, t) = Q^*(t, t)$, we may write

$$Q^*(t, t)[Z(t) - \bar{X}(t)] - \int_0^t \dot{K}_u(t, u)[Z(u) - \bar{X}(u)]du$$

$$= \int_0^t [K(t, u) - Q^*(t, u)]\bar{x}(u)du \qquad (4.18)$$

By construction, the solvent kernel of (4.18) is non-negative. Thus $Q^*(t, t)[Z(t) - \bar{X}(t)]$ has the same sign as $K(t, u) - Q^*(t, u)$, that is, either positive or negative according to whether $K(t, u)$ is chosen uniformly greater or smaller than $Q^*(t, u)$.

Now it is clear that $Z(t)$ would be the sum of the total number of processes started since time 0 if the processes in each branch satisfy conditions analogous to (4.16). Thus, if $E(t)$ in (4.14) is non-positive, we can always find functions $Q^*(t, t)Z(t)$ such that $Q^*(t, t) \cdot Z(t) \leq Q^*(t, t)\bar{X}(t)$ at least for some interval of time after date 0. We may note, in this sense, that $Q^*(t, t) \cdot \bar{X}(t)$ is greater when (4.16) are not satisfied, than it would be if (4.16) hold.

Thus, in the case where $E(t) \geq 0$ for $t \epsilon [0; \tilde{t}]$, we may choose $K(t, u) \leq Q^*(t, u)$ in order to have

$$Q^*(t, t)[\bar{X}(t) - X(t)] \geq Q^*(t, t)[Z(t) - X(t)] \geq 0$$

at least for the interval $[0; \tilde{t}]$.

Of course, a symmetric argument holds for the case in which $E(t) \leq 0$, $\forall t \epsilon [0; \tilde{t}]$. In this case, $K(t, u)$ must be chosen such that $K(t, u) \geq Q^*(t, u)$, $\forall (t, u)$, $u \leq t$, in order to have $Q^*(t, t)Z(t) \geq Q^*(t, t)\bar{X}(t)$. In this case we can conclude $Q^*(t, t)[\bar{X}(t) - X(t)] \leq Q^*(t, t)[Z(t) - X(t)] \leq 0$, at least for $t \epsilon [0; \tilde{t}]$.

In any case, either (4.16) hold and there is no problem or they do not hold and it is always possible to find the solution of (4.14) by functions whose sign is directly obtained from those of the $E(t)$s one. As a result, we can consider that (4.16) are not too restrictive and we will suppose simply that (4.16) hold.

Finally, we recall our partial conclusion: an unexpected rise (decrease) in the wage rate and/or the choice of processes using more inputs at their beginning than the processes of the expected type reduces (or, respectively, increases) the total resources available to start new processes.

But this conclusion solves the first problem addressed by the qualitative analysis of the solution of (4.14): the sign of $Q^*(t, t)[\bar{X}(t) - X(t)]$ may be reasonably deduced from the sign of $E(t)$, the right-hand side of (4.14).

The second difficulty remains: is it possible to obtain the sign of the pure substitution effect, that is, the sign of $\bar{X}(t) - X(t)$, from the one of $Q^*(t, t)[\bar{X}(t) - X(t)]$? Clearly, if $Q^*(t, t)[\bar{X}(t) - X(t)]$ consists of non-negative (non-positive) functions, some differences $\bar{X}_i(t) - X_i(t)$ may be non-positive (or, respectively, non-negative). But are there cases in which all functions in $\bar{X}(t) - X(t)$ have the opposite sign of the functions $Q^*(t, t)[\bar{X}(t) - X(t)]$? There are two types of answer. First, a well-known theorem establishes that if it is impossible to find Z such that $Z \cdot [-Q^*(t, t)] \leq 0 (\geq 0)$, and

$$Z \cdot [E(t) + \int_{0}^{t} S(t, u)E(u)du] > 0 \text{ (or, respectively, } < 0), \text{ then it is possible to find}$$
a

vector $W(t)$ such that $W(t) \geq 0 (\text{serp.} \leq 0)$ and $-Q^*(t, t) \cdot W(t) = E(t) + \int_{0}^{t} S(t, u)E(u)du$.

Thus, in this case, the vector $\bar{X}(t) - X(t) = -W(t)$ is also non-positive (or, respectively, non-negative). This reasoning technically establishes the cases in which $\bar{X}(t) - X(t)$ have the same sign as $Q^*(t, t)[\bar{X}(t) - X(t)]$. In particular, we can use the previous theorem if the start of each process needs only one input, that is, if only one element of each column of $Q^*(t, t)$ is non-zero.

The second type of answer is less formal: if each process needs, in order to be started, one specific input, the matrix $Q^*(t, t)$, after rearranging its terms, can be put in a diagonal form. Thus the sign of each element $\bar{X}_i(t) - X_i(t)$ is directly the opposite of the sign of the corresponding element of $Q^*(t, t)[\bar{X}(t) - X(t)]$. This second argument is economically interesting because, for example, many equipments in new fixed capital are specific to the branch where they are used. This argument is also related to some non-transferability hypothesis about fixed capital.

As a matter of fact, as we shall see later, the difficulty in obtaining the sign of the pure substitution effect is really the specific difficulty with the non-integrated neo-Austrian model. When this difficulty is solved, we can finally conclude that the substitution effect is negative (positive) when an unexpected rise (or, respectively, reduction) in wage rates occurs and/or a new type of process using more inputs in its initial phase is chosen. Thus, our analysis generalises in some aspects the results obtained by Hicks in the special model of *Capital and Time*. These results extend to the general non-integrated neo-Austrian model, with multiplicity of production goods. But an important feature of analysis lies in the fact that if the sign of $\bar{X}(t) - X(t)$ cannot be deduced directly from the one of $Q^*(t, t)[\bar{X}(t) - X(t)]$, the substitution effect may have any sign. In particular, a rise in wage rate can accelerate the rate of starts of some processes, and the introduction of processes more intensive in inputs at their beginning can accelerate the rate of starts of the processes in the branch where these new processes are introduced. Of course, in this case, the effect upon employment for some branches may be surprising: a rise in the wage rate and the introduction of more mechanised processes (more intensive in inputs at their beginning) can increase the employment in the branches where these events occur. These paradoxical phenomena are not very difficult to understand. The non-integrated model takes account of all the relations between the different activities in the productive system. Thus, when an unexpected evolution in global available resources occurs, it is the global reallocation of these resources which is taken account of in the non-integrated neo-Austrian model. The introduction of more mechanised processes in a particular branch can increase the employment in this branch because the demand for the good produced in this branch increases and because the negative relative profitability effect in other branches leads to a shift of the available resources to start new processes in the branches where mechanisation takes place. At last, let us observe that in the preceding analysis of the substitution effect is independent of any saving behaviour, only because we assume that profits are entirely invested and wages fully consumed.

4.3 Truncation effect and substitution effect

The pure substitution effect concerns only the pure effect of an unexpected change in the type and the rate of starts of the new processes chosen after date 0. Of course, we must consider another effect induced by the adjustment of truncations of processes started before 0, and still used after this date. It is the pure truncation effect that we shall examine in this section. In order to isolate the pure truncation effect we shall analyse the sign of $X^*(t) - \bar{X}(t)$, where $X^*(t)$ is the actual total number of processes started since 0, and $\bar{X}(t)$ is the total number resulting form the pure substitution effect. The final effect induced by the unexpected change occurring at 0 is entirely described by the sign of $X^*(t) - X(t) = [X^*(t) - \bar{X}(t)] + [\bar{X}(t) - X(t)]$, that is, by the sum of the substitution effect and the truncation effect.

Let us rewrite the system (4.5), (4.6) as follows

$$\int_{t-D^{1*}(t)}^{0} Q_1(t,u)x^*(t,u)du + \int_0^t Q_1^*(t,u)x^*(u)du$$

$$= [w^*(t) - w(t)]\sum_{k=1}^{N} \int_{t-D^{1*}(t)}^{0} a_0^k(t,u)x^{k*}(t,u)du \qquad (4.5)'$$

$$\int_{t-D^{j*}(t)}^{0} Q_i(t,u)x^*(t,u)du + \int_0^t Q_i^*(t,u)x^*(u)du = 0$$

$$i = 2, ..., N \qquad (4.6)'$$

Similarly, (4.9) and (4.10) may be written as such

$$\int_{t-D^{1*}(t)}^{0} Q_1(t, u)x(t, u)du + \int_{0}^{t} Q_1^*(t, u)\bar{x}(u)du = E_1(t) \tag{4.9}'$$

$$\int_{t-D^{i*}(t)}^{0} Q_i(t, u)x(t, u)du + \int_{0}^{t} Q_i^*(t, u)\bar{x}(u)du = 0$$

$$i = 2, ..., N \tag{4.10}'$$

Observe that the right-hand side of (4.5)′ is similar to $E_1(t)$ except for the durations $D^{1*}(t)$ and the functions $x^{k*}(t, u)$. Let us denote by $E_1^*(t)$ the right-hand side of (4.5)′; if we subtract (4.9)′ from (4.5)′, and (4.10)′ from (4.6)′, we obtain

$$\int_{0}^{t} Q_1^*(t, u)[x^*(u) - \bar{x}(u)]du = E_1^*(t) - E_1(t)$$

$$+ \int_{t-D^{1*}(t)}^{0} Q_1(t, u)[x(t, u) - x^*(t, u)]du$$

$$+ \int_{t-D^1(t)}^{t-D^{1*}(t)} Q_1(t, u)x(t, u)du \tag{4.19}$$

$$\int_{0}^{t} Q_i^*(t, u)[x^*(u) - \bar{x}(u)]du = \int_{t-D^{1*}(t)}^{0} Q_i(t, u)[x(t, u) - x^*(t, u)]du$$

$$+ \int_{t-D^i(t)}^{t-D^{i*}(t)} Q_i(t, u)x(t, u)du$$

$$i = 2, ..., N \tag{4.20}$$

Let us denote by $F(t)$ the $N \times 1$ vector whose elements are the terms of the right-hand sides of (4.19) and (4.20). (Recall that in $F(t)$, if a generation u of processes has been stopped before t, $x^{k*}(t, u) = 0$.) Finally, we obtain the following system of N Volterra's equations, with functions $x^*(t) - \bar{x}(t)$ as unknowns

$$\int_{0}^{t} Q^*(t, u)[x^*(u) - \bar{x}(u)]du = F(t)$$

Or, by integration

$$Q^*(t, t)[X^*(t) - \bar{X}(t)] - \int_{0}^{t} \dot{Q}_u^*(t, u)[X^*(u) - \bar{X}(u)]du = F(t) \tag{4.21}$$

where $X^*(t) = \int_{0}^{t} x^*(u)du$.

The sign of the pure truncation effect can potentially be deduced from this system.

Formally, (4.21) is similar to system (4.14). Thus, it is not useful to repeat the discussion about the sign of the solvent kernel of (4.21) since we would find again the same type of difficulties. Thus, for simplicity, we consider that the sign of $Q^*(t, t)[X^*(t) - \bar{X}(t)]$ depends directly on the sign of $F(t)$.

The interpretation of the elements of $F(t)$ is very simple: they represent the difference between the quantities of goods globally released by the truncated processes and the quantities of inputs required by the processes maintained in operation.

The sign of $F(t)$ is difficult to appreciate. For $[x(t, u) - x^*(t, u)]$ is non-negative by definition, but the elements of $Q(t, u)$ can have any sign and the terms in $\int_{t-D^i(t)}^{t-D^{i*}(t)}$ may also have any sign.

In order to simplify the analysis, we will treat here only the case in which the truncation rules for the old processes are more stringent after 0 than along the expected path. In other words, we will only consider the case in which the old processes are more rapidly obsolete after the occurrence of an unforeseen event at date 0 (for example, we may think of the consequences of an acceleration of technical progress after 0, or an increase of the wage rates, etc.). In this case, we may reasonably suppose that for any i, $D^i(t) > D^{i*}(t)$, $\forall t \geq 0$.

Consequently, the first term of $F(t)$ has the sign of $[w^*(t) - w(t)]$. The other terms can have any sign.[26] We may adopt two positions. First we may consider that, for each good, the quantities required by the old generations of processes as inputs, are always greater than the quantities produced by the processes of the same generations. For example, it is clear that the energy required as an input by the oldest machines is largely greater than the production of energy by the oldest processes specialised in this type of production. If we adopt this position, the integral terms in $F(t)$ are non-positive. Thus we may conclude in this case that if $w^*(t) - w(t) \leq 0$, more interruptions of processes make $Q^*(t, t)[X^*(t) - \bar{X}(t)]$ non-positive. From the previous section, we know in what circumstances the sign of $X^*(t) - \bar{X}(t)$ can be deduced from the one of $Q^*(t, t)[X^*(t) - \bar{X}(t)]$. Finally, it appears that an acceleration in the obsolescence of the old processes may increase the number of processes started since date 0, compared with the situation where no truncation effect exists. Of course, this conclusion seems a rather natural one: the termination of more old processes releases more resources in order to start new processes. Except if a rise in the wage rate occurs, these supplementary resources make possible an increase in the rate of starts of new processes. And this phenomenon can last all along the early phase of the traverse. Observe that, similarly to what we have said in the previous section about the substitution effect, the truncation effect has not necessarily the same sign as $Q^*(t, t)[X^*(t) - \bar{X}(t)]$. Thus, the rate of starts of new processes is not necessarily increased in the branches where the obsolescence of old processes is the most rapid. This apparent paradox may be explained by the fact that, in the non-integrated model, a global reallocation of resources between all branches is taken into account.

But it is possible that the elements of $F(t)$ have any sign. Thus, we must adopt another point of view. Let us consider $P(t)$, the $1 \times N$ vector of prices at time t, in terms of good 1

$$P(t) = [1, P_2(t), P_3(t), ..., P_N(t)]$$

We know from the first part of this essay that, by necessity, the processes stopped after date 0 are processes with negative revenue flows. Thus $P(t) \cdot F(t)$ is necessarily negative for some interval of time, and becomes positive later. In the neighbourhood of 0, $P(t) \cdot Q(t, t)[X^*(t) - \bar{X}(t)] \leq 0$, and, by continuity, this will be the case at least as long as $P(t) \cdot F(t) < 0$. We may conclude that, even in this more complicated situation, the truncation effect will also be positive at least for some period of time at the beginning of the traverse. But the truncation effect can also become negative after some interval of time. Indeed, the termination of more old processes increases the quantities of resources available to start new processes, but after some time only. It may happen that more truncations entail such a great reduction in some output levels that the rate of starts of new processes will also decline, compared with its level if no truncation effect exists.

The analysis of the truncation effect is a complicated one, but we may draw two conclusions. First, we can presume that the truncation effect will be positive at least in a first period of the traverse because it corresponds to a rapid increase of the resources available to start new processes. In this sense, the truncation effect can be the opposite of the substitution effect when this last is negative. This explains perhaps why more mechanisation can be accompanied by an acceleration in the rate of starts of new processes and therefore by an apparently paradoxical rise in employment: more rapid obsolescence allows the release of more resources in order to start new and eventually more mechanised processes. The second conclusion is that, if we had some empirical information about the processes and the characteristics of the expected path followed by the economy, the neo-Austrian approach would permit us to describe precisely the truncation and substitution effects. It is this descriptive ability which is the strength of the neo-Austrian approach.

4.4 The simplified case of the integrated model

The adaptation of traverse analysis to the integrated neo-Austrian model is formally very simple. Indeed, it suffices to consider the particular non-integrated model with only one sector. All notations about goods and processes become useless: at each date, only one type of process is started, which produces the consumption good by using only one primary factor. Nevertheless, as we have shown in section 1, this interpretation of a neo-Austrian integrated model is a very formal one. In fact, a neo-Austrian integrated model is not a one-sector model. We must recall that such a model is a multisectoral model, in which a perfect vertical integration of all productive activities is assumed. All the matrix and vector relationships of sections 2.2 and 2.3 become simple relations between scalars, and only the first terms of vectors $Q_1(t, u)$, $Q_1^*(t, u)$, $x(t, u)$, $x^*(t, u)$, $\bar{X}(u)$ must be considered. Let us denote by $q(t, u)$, $q^*(t, u)$ the first terms in $Q_1(t, u)$ and $Q_1^*(t, u)$ respectively. We thus have

$$q(t, u) = b^1(t, u) - w(t) a_0^1(t, u)$$
$$q^*(t, u) = b^{1*}(t, u) - w^*(t) a_0^{1*}(t, u)$$

Thus, equations (4.3) and (4.4), which hold along any full-performance path may be rewritten simply as follows

$$\int_{t-D(t)}^{t} q(t, u) x^1(t, u) du = 0$$

where $D(t)$ stands for $D^1(t)$.

Similarly, the relationships describing the pure substitution effect are reduced to

$$\int_0^t q^*(t, u)[\bar{x}^1(u) - x^1(u)] du = E_1(t) + \int_0^t [q(t, u) - q^*(t, u)] x^1(u) du \quad (4.22)$$

where $E_1(t) = [w^*(t) - w(t)] \cdot \int_{t-D(t)}^{t} a_0^{1*}(t, u) x^1(t, u) du$

Finally, with some obvious change of notation, we may write the equation describing the truncation effect

$$\int_0^t q^*(t, u)[x^1(u) - \bar{x}^1(u)] du = E_1^*(t) - E_1(t)$$

$$+ \int_{t-D^*(t)}^{0} q(t, u)[x^1(t, u) - x^{1*}(t, u)] du$$

$$+ \int_{t-D(t)}^{t-D^*(t)} q(t, u) x^1(t, u) du \quad (4.23)$$

Let us denote by $X^{1*}(t)$, $X^1(t)$, $\bar{X}^1(t)$ the first terms of $X^*(t)$, $X(t)$, and $\bar{X}^1(t)$ respectively, by $q_u^*(t, u)$ the partial derivative of $q^*(t, u)$, and by $e(t)$ and $f(t)$ the right-hand sides of (4.22) and (4.23) respectively.

Thus, in the framework of an integrated model, the Volterra's equations giving the pure substitution effect and the truncation effect are respectively

$$q^*(t, t)[\bar{X}^1(t) - X^1(t)] - \int_0^t q_u^*(t, u)[\bar{X}^1(u) - X^1(u)]du = e(t) \qquad (4.24)$$

$$q^*(t, t)[X^{1*}(t) - \bar{X}^1(t)] - \int_0^t q_u(t, u)[X^{1*}(u) - \bar{X}^1(u)]du = f(t) \qquad (4.25)$$

What are the differences between these equations and the corresponding equations of the two previous sections?

First, we observe that the $q^*(t, t)$ is a scalar. Thus, contrary to the case of the non-integrated model, we may directly deduce the signs of the substitution effect and of the truncation effect from the signs of $q^*(t, t)[\bar{X}^1(t) - X^1(t)]$ and $q^*(t, t)[X^{1*}(t) - \bar{X}^1(t)]$ respectively.

Next, is it possible to deduce the signs of these two effects from the signs of the second members of (4.24) and (4.25)? On this point, the analysis is exactly identical to the one of section (2.2). Thus, either the kernel of (4.24) and (4.25) is non-negative, and the solutions of these equations have the same signs as $e(t)$ and $f(t)$ respectively, or these kernels have any sign and we can always bind the solutions of these equations by functions that have the same signs as $e(t)$ and $f(t)$. Exactly as in section 2.2, it is not very restrictive to assume that the kernel of (4.24) is non-negative, that is that $q_u^*(t, u) \leqq 0$.

It is easy to obtain results similar to those of Hicks about the substitution effect, but with more general profiles for the elementary processes.

Concerning the truncation effect, the analysis is identical to that of the previous section, and we may conclude that a more rapid truncation of the old processes allows for an increase in the number of young processes that are started. This acceleration will take place as long as the net production of the supplementary processes started by stopping old processes is less than the net production of these last processes; later it is possible that an inverse trend takes place at the end of the early phase, for more rapid truncation can bring about a decline in the rate of starts of the new processes.

The simplified case of the integrated neo-Austrian model does not change fundamentally the traverse analysis, compared with the case of the non-integrated model. Nevertheless, this simplification allows more precision on some points and it may be that this simplified approach could lead to more positive results under some circumstances.

4.5 The particular case of a traverse between two steady states

The simplest type of traverse is the one between two steady states: in an economic system, a steady state prevails as far as an unforeseen event occurs, which destroys the conditions of the steady state. From this moment, and if some special conditions are realised concerning in particular prices, their anticipations, the evolution of techniques and the development of primary factors, the economy will evolve through a traverse period towards a new steady state. This is precisely the scenario considered by Hicks in *Capital and Time*. Generally, this is also the type of traverse considered by economists when they use this term in dynamics: traverse between steady states.

Of course, this is a very particular situation which may be considered essentially to illustrate how the neo-Austrian approach may be useful in more general situations.

The traverse between two steady states has been extensively studied by Hicks in a neo-Austrian integrated model. This type of traverse analysis has essentially two advantages. First, it allows one to give structure to the reference equilibrium path along which the economy would continue to evolve if no unanticipated event would happen. Second, the analysis of a traverse between two steady states allows us to be more precise about the future equilibrium path to which the economy might converge in the long run, when all adjustments will have taken place. Clearly, it is only when a traverse between two steady states is analysed that the convergence problem has some meaning. Moreover, it is only in this perspective that we will treat, to end this essay – the case of a traverse between two steady states. Indeed, it is clear from the previous sections that this particular case does not add anything, except some simplifications to the analysis of the early phase of a traverse.

We will use the *simple neo-Austrian integrated model* in order to analyse the traverse between two steady states. All the following results concerning convergence in the long run can be extended to a general neo-Austrian *non-integrated* model.

In the first step, we will formalise the problem within the framework of an integrated model. Then we will consider the problem of convergence in the long-run towards a steady state.

We add four assumptions to the list given in section 4.1.

Assumption 8
Before time 0, the economy is under conditions of steady growth, with a rate of growth equal to r.

The following are the main consequences of such an assumption within the context of an integrated model:

(i) $x^1(t, u) = x^1 e^{r(t-u)}$, $u \leq t$ where x^1 is a constant. Of course, for any $u > 0$, $u < 0$ it may be the case that $x^{1*}(t, u) < x^1 e^{r(t-u)}$.

(ii) prices are constant before time 0. In an integrated model, the prices that explicitly appear are the wage rate w, and the interest rate r.

(iii) before time 0, at each instant, processes of the same type are started in the economy. Thus it is useless to describe a process in terms of the current date t and of its birth date u. In fact, when the same type of process is started at each instant, the age of this process is sufficient in order to locate precisely this process. Therefore we will denote by $q(t-u)$, rather than by $q(t, u)$, the net production of a process that is $(t-u)$ units of time old. Prices being constant and there not being any technical change, it does not matter if we do not know the birth date of this process – age only is important.

(iv) at any date, the age of the oldest processes still in operation is a constant under conditions of steady state: $D(t) = D$.

(v) the rate of growth is equal to the interest rate. This property comes from our particular assumption on saving. Under this assumption, the golden rule of accumulation holds.

Now, if we seek to examine convergence in the long run towards a new steady state, we must suppose that this new steady state can exist. This is the reason for the three following assumptions:

Assumption 9
Prices are constant

(This assumption implies that the wage rate is the same before and after the date 0.)

Assumption 10
Dating from 0, a new elementary process can be used. This possibility is not anticipated before it occurs. The new elementary process is more profitable than the old one at the prevailing wage rate. Let us note by $q^*(t, u)$ the net production of such a new process when it is $(t-u)$ units of time old.

Clearly these assumptions plus constant returns to scale imply that, after date 0, the interest rate r^* is equal to the internal rate of return of the investment project associated with the new elementary processes. Of course, the lifetime of these processes is optimally adjusted to prices (w, r^*), in the sense of the optimal truncation rules given in 3.2.[27] Formally, if we denote D^* the lifetime of the new processes, we have

$$\int_0^{D^*} q^*(u)e^{-rk_0}du = 0$$

Assumption 11
$D=D^*$

We adopt this assumption in order to simplify computations. It would not be very difficult to consider the case where $D \neq D^*$. The analysis would be formally more complex but the results about convergence would be exactly the same.

The rate of starts of new processes $x^{1*}(t)$ is given by the following relation

$\forall t \in [0; D]$:

$$\int_0^t q^*(t-u)x^{1*}(u)du = - \int_{t-D}^0 q(t, u)[x^{1*}(t, u)]du \qquad (4.26)$$

$\forall t > D$:

$$\int_{t-D}^t q^*(t-u)x^{1*}(u)du = 0 \qquad (4.27)$$

Strictly speaking, the function $x^{1*}(u)$ has some discontinuity point for $t=0$. This discontinuity is equal to

$$\Delta x^{1*}(0) = \frac{\int_{-D}^0 q(-u)x^{1*}(0, u)\, du}{q^*(0)}$$

Of course, this discontinuity comes from the discontinuity of the function $x^{1*}(t, u)$ for $t \to 0^*$. Indeed, at time 0, some old processes will be suddenly interrupted before their 'normal' death. It can be easily verified that this jump has some 'echo' at each period of D time units. But these 'echos' have an amplitude equal to a multiple of $| q^*(D)/q^*(0) |$. Either D has been perfectly adjusted to the new economic conditions, and $q^*(D)=0$, or it is natural to assume $q^*(D) < | q^*(0) |$. Thus the 'echo' of the initial jump will diminish as time goes on. Finally, the initial jump will disappear when time goes on to infinity. Thus, in order to analyse the convergence of the economy in the long run, we can neglect this discontinuity problem. The results would not be changed.

When a traverse between steady states is considered, the important formal simplification lies in the fact that we shall solve particular Volterra's equations which are convolution equations. A powerful approach is provided by symbolic calculus, that is, Laplace's transformation.[28] Let us denote by $h(t)$ the function defined, for the different intervals of t, by the right-hand sides of (4.26) and (4.27), and let Lg be the Laplace transformation of a function g. We then have, provided that the Laplace transform exists

$$Lx^{1*} = \frac{Lh}{Lq^*}$$

It is well known that the behaviour of $x^{1*}(t)$ when t goes to infinity is determined by the singular points of its Laplace transformation. In order to analyse these zeros, we shall analyse more precisely Lh. By construction of $h(t)$, we have

$$Lh = \int_0^D e^{-pt} \int_{t-D}^t q(t-u)x^{1*}(t,u)du\,dt$$

where p is a complex number.

Function $x^{1*}(t, u)$ describes the advanced truncations of the old processes started before time 0. This function is equal to 0 for all the generations of old processes interrupted between 0 and time t, and it is equal to $x^1 e^{r(t-u)}$ for all the generations of old processes still in operation at time t.

Let us call $[-\tilde{u}_1; -\tilde{u}_2]; [-\tilde{u}_3; -\tilde{u}_4] \dots [-\tilde{u}_{n-1}; -\tilde{u}_n]$ the time intervals to which the generations of processes started before 0 and still working at 0^+ belong, with n even. We have

$$x^{1*}(0, u) = \begin{cases} x^1 e^{-ru.} \forall u \in \cup[-\tilde{u}_i; -\tilde{u}_{i+1}] \\ \qquad i = 1, 3, \dots, n-1 \\ 0 \text{ elsewhere} \end{cases}$$

Of course, by considering the analysis of 3.2, if there is optimal adjustment of truncation for the old processes, we have

$$\int_{\tilde{u}_i}^{\tilde{u}_{i+1}} q(u)e^{-r^*u}du = 0$$

for $i = 1, 3, 5, \dots, n-1$

Let us now introduce $\alpha_i(t)$ which is defined in the following sense for $t \geq 0$

$$\alpha_i(t) = \begin{cases} t + \tilde{u}_i \text{ if } t < \tilde{u}_{i+1} - \tilde{u}_i \\ \tilde{u}_{i+1} \text{ elsewhere} \end{cases}$$
for $i = 1, 3, \dots, (n-1)$

The number of processes that belong to generation $u(u \leq 0)$ and are still operating at time $t(t \geq 0)$ may be written as

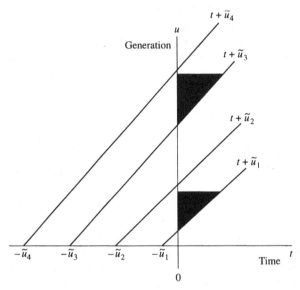

Figure 1.2   Generations of processes and the time dimension

$$x^{1*}(t, u)= \begin{cases} x^1 e^{r(t-u)} \cdot \forall u \in \cup[\alpha_i(t); -\tilde{u}_{i+1}] \\ \qquad\qquad i=1, 3, \dots, n-1 \\ 0 \text{ elsewhere} \end{cases}$$

The darkened areas in figure 1.2 illustrate the pairs (t, u) for which $x^1(t, u)=x^1 e^{r(t-u)}$. (This figure can be interpreted as a Lexis diagram in demography.)

At last, after some manipulations, we have

$$Lh=\int_0^D e^{-pt} \sum_{i=1,3}^{(n-1)} \int_{\alpha_i(t)}^{u_{i+1}} q(u)x^1 e^{r(t-u)}du\, dt$$

And, by using the definition of $\alpha_i(t)$

$$Lh=\sum_{i=1,3}^{n-1} \int_0^{\tilde{u}_{i+1}-\tilde{u}_i} e^{-pt} \int_{t+\tilde{u}_i}^{\tilde{u}_{i+1}} q(u)x^1 e^{r(t-u)}du\, dt$$

$$=\frac{x}{p-1} \sum_{i-1,3}^{n-1} \int_{\tilde{u}_i}^{\tilde{u}_{i+1}} q(u)[e^{(p-r)\tilde{u}_i-pu}-e^{-ru}]du$$

The term within brackets disappears for $p=r$, so that we have

$$Lh=\frac{x^1 H(p)\,(p-r)}{(p-r)}=x^1 H(p)$$

where $H(p)$ is a function of p, and finally

$$Lx^{1*} = \frac{x^1 H(p)}{Lq^*}$$

The zeros of Lq^* determine the behaviour of $x^{1*}(t)$ when t goes to infinity, that is, the numbers p are such that

$$\int_0^D q^*(u)e^{-pu}du = 0$$

Of course, $p = r^*$ satisfies this equation and r^* is in fact the only real number that is a solution of this equation when D is optimally chosen. Now, in general, this type of equation admits complex roots as well. Let $p_1, p_2, \ldots$ denote these complex solutions. We have

$$x_1^*(t) = \lambda_0 e^{r^* t} + \lambda_1 e^{p_1 t} + \lambda_2 e^{p_2 t} + \ldots$$

where $\lambda_0, \lambda_1, \lambda_2, \ldots$ are some real constants.

Thus we have to examine the real parts of complex numbers $p_1, p_2, \ldots$ and if such real parts are non-positive, the real number r^* would determine the evolution of $x^{1*}(t)$ when t goes to infinity. It is not very difficult to find sufficient conditions for which the real parts of all complex numbers $p_1, p_2, \ldots$ are non-positive. The simplest is that $q^*(u)$ is non-decreasing. In any case, it is always something like that: $q^*(u)$ is non-decreasing for u small and eventually 'not too' decreasing for u close to D, which is sufficient to ensure that $p_1, p_2, \ldots$ have non-positive real parts.

When the above conditions hold, we have

$$x_1^*(t) \to \lambda_0 e^{r^* t} \text{ when } t \to +\infty$$

In other words, if the economy converges in the long run towards a new steady state, this one has a rate of growth equal to r^* which is the internal rate of return of the new processes started after time 0. That is quite natural, because under our saving assumption, it is the golden rule of accumulation which applies. The economic interpretation is straightforward: as time goes on, the net resources released by the population of new processes increase at a rate r^*, the internal rate of return of these processes. When all perturbations are weakened, the economy will eventually grow at this rate, since all such resources are used to start new processes.

We obtain here a result somewhat different from the one obtained by Hicks in *Capital and Time*. The difference comes evidently from the fact that Hicks assumes that profits, that is, net resources, are partially consumed. Thus, in Hicks's analysis, it is only a mathematical equivalence between $x^{1*}(t)$ and $\lambda_0 e^{r^* t}$ which is proved and not an asymptotic convergence, as in our approach. Lastly, we insist on the fact that our approach is more general, since we do not assume that processes have simple profiles, as in Hicks's approach. This extension of the neo-Austrian approach is possible because the Laplace transformation is a powerful tool in order to analyse a traverse between steady states.

Notes

1 We refer to von Neumann (1945) and Malinvaud (1953, 1962) for a more precise discussion about this class of models. Strictly speaking, the model presented here is not a closed model. It differs from the usual von Neumann model and looks more like Malinvaud's 1953 model. For our purpose, this point does not matter.

2 For all the developments considered in this chapter, it would not be very difficult to consider several primary factors.

3 This point will be analysed later.

4 As Burmeister (1974) points out, the possibility of truncation is, in some cases, a restrictive assumption. But in many situations it is still more restrictive not to allow for this possibility.

5 For an analysis along the same lines, see also Craven (1975), Hagemann and Kurz (1976), Solow (1962), Van Schaik (1976), Van de Klundert and Van Schaik (1974).

6 In this presentation we ignore some problems that are not very difficult to be ruled out. For instance, if the construction of the new capital good takes more than one unit of time, it is trivial to break down the corresponding elementary operation into operations of unit duration. This is done by introducing eventually additional intermediate products. Equally it must be noticed that in our presentation we have necessarily $n=j-1$.

7 See Belloc (1980, chapter 1). It is possible to verify that all the analysis of Burmeister (1974) holds also in our more general presentation.

8 See Belloc (1980, chapter 1).

9 For such an interpretation, see Belloc (1978b).

10 Let us recall the $H \geq L$ means that no element of L is greater than the corresponding element of H and $H \neq L$.

11 Of course $R(t, z) = \prod_{i=t+1}^{z} [1+r(i)]^{-1}$, where $r(i)$ is the interest rate at time i.

12 It is well known that this result does not admit exactly an inverse one as in static welfare analysis because an infinite horizon is considered. A transversality condition is necessary in order to rule out infinite inefficient programmes along which profits are nevertheless maximised at each date. On this point, see Malinvaud's original papers and also Starrett (1970), Gale and Rockwell (1975) for the fundamental articles among an abundant literature.

13 See Belloc (1978b) for a detailed analysis.

14 This is a usual concept. In particular, when there are constant returns to scale, the present value of starting process is 0

$$V^*(u, u) = \sum_{z=u}^{u+D^k(u, u)} R(u, z) \cdot P(z)[b^k(z-u) - a^k(z-u)] = 0$$

The present value of a process also allows to value the fixed capital embodied in that process. $V^k(u, u)$ must be used to value the new fixed capital embodied in a process k starting at time u, and $V^k(t, u)$ for $u < t$ must be used to calculate the market value of the $(t-u)$ years old fixed capital goods used by the process.

This evaluation is quite intuitive but is not immediate in our non-integrated model. Indeed, some manipulations are necessary. The reasoning essentially consists in considering the maximisation of profit for the elementary linear operations whose succession constitutes a given neo-Austrian elementary process, and in converting this maximisation in terms of the present value of the expected profits for this elementary process. For a complete analysis, we refer to our previous research (Belloc, 1980).

15 In *Capital and Time*, J. R. Hicks presents an analysis of steady states within an integrated model. For an analysis of such programmes in a non-integrated model, see Belloc (1980). It may be noted that B. Schefold (1978) carried out a similar analysis with a model similar to our non-integrated model. Lastly, we may recall the fundamental contribution of M. Allais (1947) and (1962) to the analysis of steady states in models directly related to the Austrian tradition.

16 If we consider time as a continuous variable, condition (3.4) would be written, under some additional conditions of regularity, as follows

$$\begin{cases} P[u+D^k(t, u)][b^k(D^k(u, u)) - a^k(D^k(u, u))] = 0 \\ \dfrac{\partial P[u+D^k(t, u)][b^k(D^k(u, u)) - a^k(D^k(u, u))]}{\partial D^k(t, u)} \leq 0 \end{cases}$$

17 Similar conditions are implied in order to prove the uniqueness of the internal rate of return. On this point, see Arrow and Levhari (1959), Flemming and Wright (1971) and Hicks (1970, 1973).

18 We refer to the works of J. Desrousseaux (1963 and 1966). They are not very familiar to English-speaking economists. J. Desrousseaux is a French engineer who has extended some results established by M. Allais in the field of capital theory. He also systematically applied the approach of M. Allais to the actual management of industrial firms.

19 J. Desrousseaux calls relation (3.5) the 'three dates equation' because three dates, $u+D^k(t, u)-1$, $u+D^k(t, u)$ and $D^k(t, u)+1$ are concerned by this relation. The important point is that, in a replacement chain, a date of replacement is simultaneously the date of the beginning of the following process. J. Desrousseaux presents his result in continuous time. We translate his conclusion: 'At any date, we must truncate in such a way that the marginal cost of time towards the past equalises the marginal cost of time towards the future.' In other terms, with time as a continuous variable, when a process is being operated one unit of time later, the following process also starts one unit of time later, and in any case the variation of present value must be the same

$$\frac{\partial}{\partial D^k(t, u)} [V^k(t, u) + V^k(t, u + (D^k(t, u))] = 0$$

20 When a complete system of future markets cannot exist because of uncertainty, it is well known that rational expectations plus perfectly adapted markets at any date produce the same outcome as full intertemporal equilibrium. The rational expectation hypothesis is a skilful way of introducing the full-intertemporal equilibrium concept. As a matter of fact, the most important distinction between different equilibrium concepts concerns the flexibility of prices on markets.

21 Of course, 'good 1' can be a composite good, that is, a vector of consumption goods with a fixed composition.

22 Clearly, assumption 1 excludes joint production for finished goods. But it does not entail no joint production at all. Indeed, by construction, each elementary neo-Austrian process takes implicitly into account the presence of used fixed capital goods jointly produced in the different production activities.

23 Strictly speaking, we should write $dx^k(u)$ and $x^k(t, u)$ $d^k(t, u)$ in the integrals. Indeed, some discontinuities can appear after date 0 on the generations of processes still living. We neglect this possibility.

24 On Volterra's equations, see for example Volterra (1959). Of course, there exists an extensive mathematical literature about these equations, and, more generally, about integral equations. These integral equations are often solved by means of symbolic calculus. A good reference for this approach is R. Bellman and K.L. Cooke (1963). Some difficulties may also occur with this type of equation because they do not always have solutions in functional spaces. In this case the solutions, whenever they exist, are distributions. On these technical points, see Nardini (1990).

25 On the existence of solutions for Volterra's equations, see Volterra (1959). Of course, the existence of such solutions imply some regularity conditions that are not really compelling from an economic point of view.

We observe that equations (4.14) are not convolution equations. Thus the Laplace transformation is not useful to solve this system of equations. Nardini (1990) uses intensively the Laplace transformation but he analyses a traverse between two steady states. Clearly, in this particular case, as we shall see later, the equivalent of (4.14) will be a system of convolution equations. A difficulty may arise about (4.14) when the right-hand side is discontinuous at $t=0$. In this case, these equations admit only distributions as solutions. In his 1990 paper, Nardini considers this possibility, for the case of a traverse between two steady states, and obtains solutions in the class of Laplace transformable distributions. It is not our purpose in this essay to be more technical than necessary and we disregard these problems.

26 It is interesting to note that, even if we consider a very simple situation, this difficulty about the sign of $F(t)$ would subsist. Usually, when truncation effects are considered, it is assumed that only the oldest processes are stopped (see for example, Benassy, Fouquet and Malgrange (1975)). In this simple case, the

terms in $\int_{t-D^{1*}(t)}^{0}$ disappear and the last terms in $F(t)$ are non-null, but may have any sign. Hence the simplification is useless here.

27 We have not used prices with an integrated model. Clearly, the whole analysis of section 2 may be used in the simplified context of an integrated model. Simply the price system would be reduced to the real wage rate and formally one type of process is started at each date, for the global economy. This process is the one for which the present value of net production is maximal at the given price system. The truncation rules analysed in 2.2 are also valid in this simplified model.

28 The equations that would give the signs of the substitution and truncation effects during the early phase of the traverse would respectively be

$$\int_0^t q^*(t-u)[\bar{x}^1(u)-x^1e^{ru}]du$$

$$=\int_0^t [q(t-u)-q^*(t-u)]x^1e^{ru}du$$

and

$$\int_0^t q^*(t-u)[x^1(u)-\bar{x}^1(u)]du=\int_{t-D}^t q(t-u)[x^1e^{ru}-x^1(t,u)]du$$

Potentially, these equations may be solved by using symbolic calculations. See, for example, R. Bellman and K. L. Cooke (1963) for such an approach.

References

Allais, M. (1947) *Economie et Intéret*, Paris, Imprimerie nationale.
　(1962) 'The influence of the Capital–Output Ratio on Real National Income', *Econometrica*, 30: 700–28.
Arrow, K. and Levhari, D. (1959) 'Uniqueness of the Internal Rate of Return' *Economic Journal*, 79 (September): 560-6.
Bellman, R. and Cooke, K. L. (1963) *Differential Difference Equations. Mathematics in Science and Engineering*, Academic Press.
Belloc, B. (1978a) 'Equilibre et déséquilibre intertemporels dans la théorie de la production – généralisation de la méthode neo-autrichienne', Thesis, Université des Sciences Sociales de Toulouse, May 1978.
　(1978b) 'Programmes de production efficients, croissance équilibrée et analyse neo-autrichienne', Faculté des Sciences Economiques de l'Université des Sciences Sociales de Toulouse, n. 53.
　(1980) *Croissance économique et adaptation du capital productif*, Paris, Economica.
Benassy, J. P., Fouquet, D. and Malgrange, P. (1975) 'Estimation d'une fonction de production à générations de capital', *Annales de l'Insée* (May–August): 3–55.
Burmeister, E. (1974) 'Synthesizing the Neo-Austrian and Alternative Approaches

to Capital Theory: a Survey', *Journal of Economic Literature*, 12 (June): 413–56.

Craven, J. (1975) 'Capital Theory and the Process of Production', *Economica*, 42 (August): 283–91.

Desrousseaux, J. (1963) 'Théorie du déclassement et du prix de revient réel dans les industries capitalistiques', *Revue française de recherche opérationnelle*, no. 26, 1st quarter: 21–40.

(1966) *L'évolution économique et le comportement industriel*, Paris, Dunod.

Faber, M. (1979) *Introduction to Modern Austrian Theory*, Springer-Verlag, Berlin.

Flemming, J. and Wright, J. (1971) 'Uniqueness of the Internal Rate of Return: a Generalisation', *Economic Journal*, 81 (June): 256–63.

Gale, D. and Rockwell, R. (1975) 'On the Interest Rate Theorems of Malinvaud and Starrett', *Econometrica*, 43 (2): 347–60.

Hagemann, H. and Kurz, H. (1976) 'The Return of the Same Truncation Period and Reswitching of Techniques in Neo-Austrian and More General Models', *Kyklos*, 29 (4): 678–708.

Hicks, J. R. (1965) *Capital and Growth*, Oxford, Clarendon Press.

(1970) 'A Neo-Austrian Growth Theory', *Economic Journal*, 80 (June): 257–81.

(1973) *Capital and Time: A Neo-Austrian Theory*, Oxford, Clarendon Press.

(1985) *Methods of Dynamic Economics*, Oxford, Clarendon Press.

Malinvaud, E. (1953) 'Capital Accumulation and Efficient Allocation of Resources', *Econometrica*, 21: 233–68.

(1962) 'A Corrigendum', *Econometrica*, 30: 570–3.

(1986) 'Reflecting on the Theory of Capital and Growth', *Oxford Economic Papers*, 38 (November): 367–85.

Nardini, F. (1990) 'Cycle-Trend Dynamics in a Fixwage Neo-Austrian Model of Traverse', *Structural Change and Economic Dynamics*, 1 (1): 165–94.

Schefold, B. (1976) 'Reduction to Dated Quantities and Switches of Technique in Fixed Capital Systems', *Metroeconomica*, 28: 1–15.

(1978) 'Fixed Capital as a Joint Product', *Jahrbücher für Nationalökonomie und Statistik*, Band 192, Heft S. 5 (January): 415–39

Solow, R. (1962) 'Substitution and Fixed Proportions in the Theory of Capital', *Review of Economic Studies*, 29: 207–18.

Sraffa, P. (1960) *Production of Commodities by Means of Commodities*, Cambridge, Cambridge University Press.

Starrett, D. (1970) 'The Efficiency of Competitive Programs', *Econometrica* (September): 704–11.

Van de Klundert, Th. and Van Schaik, A. (1974) 'On Shift and Share of Durable Capital', mimeo, University of Tilburg.

Van Schaik, A. (1976) *Reproduction and Fixed Capital*, Tilburg, Tilburg University Press.

Volterra, V. (1959) *Theory of Functional and of Integral and Integro-Differential Equations*, Dower Publications Inc.

von Neumann, J. (1945) 'A Model of General Equilibrium', *Review of Economic Studies*, 9: 1–9 (German original 1935–7).

2 Vertical integration, the temporal structure of production processes and transition between techniques*

SALVATORE BALDONE

The interest in the temporal structure of production processes goes back, as is well known, to Ricardo (1817), Jevons (1871), and the Austrian theory of capital (Böhm-Bawerk, 1889; Wicksell, 1934; Hayek, 1941). According to this approach, in particular, the final output obtained at any given moment emerges as the result of the use of one or more original production factors at a moment, or in a series of moments, chronologically preceding the date at which the consumer good becomes available. An elementary production process is therefore defined as a process by which a succession of dated quantities of original inputs enables a unit of final product to be obtained.

The notion of production activity as a process of transformation of original factors into consumer goods obviously reduces the role of the means of production to that played by exclusively intermediate products, contained within the individual production processes.

Both the temporal sequencing of the production phases and the integration of the set of production instruments have seemed to represent characteristics which help to make the Austrian method the most suitable for an analysis of the dynamics of an economic system.

To be used for this kind of analysis, however, the Austrian representation of the production process has had to be modified. It goes without saying, in fact, that its vision of linking a sequence of original inputs to the emergence of the final product in a single instant is implicitly related to the idea of a productive configuration that only employs circulating capital. Durable means of production are, in fact, characterised by the fact that they participate in production for more than one period, and therefore contribute to the realisation of a production flow that extends over the whole working life of machines. The device which has allowed the difficulty of introducing durable means of production to be overcome within the original Austrian vision, has been to consider a single production process as a process which transforms a sequence of original inputs into a flow of final output.

This is, in fact, the configuration of the production process proposed by Hicks at the beginning of the 1970s as a neo-Austrian model[1] (Hicks, 1970, 1973a and b). Hicks, and, later, numerous other authors[2] have used this scheme in order to study particular stylisations of the process by which an economic system succeeds in moving from a growth equilibrium, adjusted to a given production technique, to another expanding situation, corresponding to more advanced technological set-ups.

It is precisely thanks to this contribution that the neo-Austrian model, a model based on the vision of production as a process which operates through a succession of causally connected phases, has been considered superior to interindustry analysis for studying problems of transition between production techniques and, more generally, non-proportional growth.[3]

When more attentively examined, however, the neo-Austrian method of representing the production process seems to be somewhat limited in scope and its superiority for studying 'traverse' problems seems to be only apparent and based on the analysis of particular cases.

In the following sections, some issues relating to the process of vertical integration of those production processes which employ durable means of production will be discussed first. Then, the meaning and limitations of the non-vertically integrated version of the Austrian model proposed by Belloc (1980) will be examined. Lastly, the general validity of a multi-sectoral approach of the Sraffa–von Neumann type for studying economic dynamics will be stressed.

Within this framework, a criterion for analysing the transition between techniques with different basic commodities will be suggested.

1 Production with fixed capital and vertical integration

As Sraffa[4] has demonstrated, it is always possible with a single-production system and, therefore, without fixed capital, to reduce every process of production of commodities by means of commodities to a profile of dated inputs of original factors terminating with the appearance of the corresponding output. This profile is obtained by vertically integrating the specific production process according to the production technique to which it belongs. Consider therefore a single-production economy with constant returns to scale in which n commodities are produced, with the last commodity being a pure consumption good, and supposing, for simplicity, that the only original factor is labour. Let A be the matrix of technical production coefficients and a_0 the vector of labour coefficients. Given our assumptions we have

$$A = \begin{bmatrix} A_{cc} & a_{c0} \\ 0 & 0 \end{bmatrix}$$

$$a_0 = [a_{0c} \quad a_{00}]$$

where A_{cc} is the square matrix, of dimension $n-1$, of the technical coefficients for the production of the means of production, and a_{c0} is a column vector the $n-1$ components of which measure their utilisation in the consumption-good sector at a unit level of production. The splitting carried out on the vector of labour coefficients can be read in a corresponding way. If we suppose that the net product is constituted by the unit of consumption good, then, in the current period, it will be necessary to employ a_{00} units of labour and a bundle of a_{c0} of means of production in order to obtain the final output. The quantities a_{c0} of means of production must, in turn, have been made available in the immediately preceding period through the utilisation of $a_{0c}a_{c0}$ units of labour and a bundle $A_{cc}a_{c0}$ of means of production previously obtained through the utilisation of $a_{0c}A_{cc}a_{c0}$ units of labour and $A_{cc}^2 a_{c0}$ units of means of production, and so on. The unit of final good obtained at time t can therefore be thought of in terms of a 'vertically integrated industry' corresponding to the consumption good produced, that is, by a sequence $a_{00}, a_{0c}a_{c0}, a_{0c}A_{cc}a_{c0}, a_{0c}A_{cc}^2 a_{c0}, \ldots$ of labour inputs at periods $t, t-1, t-2, \ldots$

The case of fixed capital can easily be incorporated into the example we are examining if it is supposed that a certain commodity, for example the $(n-1)$th, is a durable instrument of production and is used for the production of the consumption good. The consumption-good industry can then be subdivided into as many activities as there are possible utilisation periods for the machine. From each of these activities a certain quantity of consumption good will be obtained and, as a joint product, the machine aged by one period. Suppose the working life of the machine is k periods and denote, respectively, with m_i, b_i and a_{0i} ($i=1, 2, \ldots, k$) the machine i years old, the quantity of the consumption good produced by the activity which utilises this machine and the corresponding input of labour. If, moreover, we denote with the vectors a_{ci} ($i=0, 1, 2, \ldots, k$) the inputs of non-durable means of production and new machines, then the production technique can be represented as in table 2.1, where obviously m_0 is the last element in the vector a_{c0}.[5]

Considerations entirely analogous to those made for the single-production case allow us, in this case as well,[6] to carry out the vertical integration of the consumption-good industry. In order to obtain b_k units of consumption good at time t, utilising the machine during its last working year, a_{0k} units of labour and a_{ck} units of means of production will have to be utilised. In turn, the production of the bundle of commodities a_{ck} will have required the utilisation of $a_{0c}a_{ck}$ units of labour and of vector $A_{cc}a_{ck}$ of

Table 2.1. *Production technique with a mechanised consumption-good industry*

$$A=\begin{bmatrix} A_{cc} & a_{c0} & a_{c1} & a_{c2} & \cdots & a_{ck} \\ 0 & 0 & 0 & 0 & \cdots & 0 \\ 0 & 0 & m_1 & 0 & \cdots & 0 \\ 0 & 0 & 0 & m_2 & \cdots & 0 \\ & & & 0 & \ddots & \\ 0 & 0 & 0 & a_{02} & \cdots & m_k \end{bmatrix} \qquad B=\begin{bmatrix} I & 0 & 0 & 0 & \cdots & 0 \\ 0 & b_0 & b_1 & b_2 & \cdots & b_k \\ 0 & m_1 & 0 & 0 & \cdots & 0 \\ 0 & 0 & m_2 & 0 & \cdots & 0 \\ \vdots & & & & \ddots & \\ 0 & 0 & 0 & 0 & \cdots & 0 \end{bmatrix}$$

$$a_0=[a_{0c} \quad a_{00} \quad a_{01} \quad a_{02} \quad \cdots \quad a_{0k}]$$

Table 2.2. *Elementary process of the vertically integrated industry of the consumption good*

periods	t	$t-1$	$t-2$	...	$t-k$	$t-k-1$	...
consump. good output	b_k	b_{k-1}	b_{k-2}	...	b_0	0	...
labour inputs	a_{0k}	$a_{0c}a_{ck}$	$a_{0c}A_{cc}a_{ck}$	...	$a_{0c}A_{cc}^{k-1}a_{ck}$	$a_{0c}A_{cc}^{k}a_{ck}$	...
		$a_{0,k-1}$	$a_{0c}a_{c,k-1}$	...	$a_{0c}A_{cc}^{k-2}a_{c,k-1}$	$a_{0c}A_{cc}^{k-1}a_{c,k-1}$	...
				$\cdot\cdot\cdot\cdot\cdot$	$\vdots$	$\vdots$	
					a_{00}	$a_{0c}a_{c0}$	...
total	$l(t)$	$l(t-1)$	$l(t-2)$	...	$l(t-k)$	$l(t-k-1)$	...

means of production, and so on. A similar argument may be formulated for the production of b_{k-1} units of consumption good at time $t-1$ by employing the machine of age $t-1$ and so on until b_0 units of consumption goods are produced through the use of the machine when it is new.

The data in table 2.2 allow us, therefore, to associate the elementary process of the vertically integrated industry of the consumption good with the technique A, B, a_0. This process is represented by the two flows $l(t)$ and $b(t)$ of labour and the consumption good respectively. Here the production process appears to be split into two phases: one for the construction and the other for the utilisation of the machine; during the second phase, a positive final output flow emerges for as many periods as there are utilisation periods for the durable production instrument.

The possibility of carrying out, in terms of the neo-Austrian model, the vertical integration of the industry which utilises durable means of production depends, crucially, on having assumed that it produces a pure consumption good, that is to say, a commodity which is not used in production.[7]

In the event that the final good is reutilised in production within the interindustry scheme, its reduction to dated quantities of labour would require knowledge of its average conditions of production. This may in general be done through a process of 'temporal' integration of the activities which produce it using the machine over its working life, that is to say, by formally eliminating the temporal dimension of its utilisation period.[8]

This device is not without negative consequences for the vertical integration of the production process. This is formally represented, above all, as a flow-input/point-output process in which the 'coefficients' of the mechanised industry depend, in general, on the rate of profit. It follows, therefore, that also the 'dated requirements' of labour, related to the technique which incorporates the temporally integrated mechanised sector, depend on the rate of profit and not only on the technical characteristics of production. This is due to the fact that reference is made to the average technical characteristics of production of a final good whose gross output, in relation to the durable instrument utilised, is heterogeneous from the standpoint of the dates at which it is obtained.

A second drawback may be associated with the one already discussed above. The elimination of the temporal dimension of the utilisation period leads us, in fact, to neglect the specific characteristics of production within each of the activities which constitute the working life of the machine. Consequently, the labour input profile that is obtained from the vertical integration process ensures a correct economic measurement of the average content of labour directly and indirectly incorporated in each unit of final output, but it no longer ensures the synchronisation of the different stages of production, not even if the efficiency of the machine is constant over the whole length of its working life.

It should, however, be noted that these drawbacks go beyond the simple assumption of non-specialisation in commodity use. They arise, in fact, every time a means of production is produced with the utilisation of durable instruments. To allow for a correct representation of the production process in neo-Austrian terms, a mechanised production of non-consumption goods must therefore be excluded.

The Austrian school, and Carl Menger in particular, supposed that the production activity proceeded linearly, that is to say, with a sequential structure of production phases stretching from the first input of original factors to the emergence of the consumption good, in a finite number of stages.[9] For this to occur, the input matrix of circulating capital must have a particular structure. It must be of the upper triangular kind with all elements null along the main diagonal, or

$$
A_{cc} = \begin{bmatrix}
0 & a_{12} & a_{13} & \cdots & a_{1n} \\
0 & 0 & a_{23} & \cdots & a_{2n} \\
0 & 0 & 0 & \cdots & a_{3n} \\
 & & & \ddots & \vdots \\
0 & 0 & 0 & & 0
\end{bmatrix}
$$

This is a necessary and sufficient condition in order that, also in terms of vertical integration, the construction phase be exhausted after a maximum number of n periods.[10] For an elementary Austrian or neo-Austrian process to have, therefore, a finite duration, not only must there be no basic commodities, in Sraffa's sense, but also the slightest degree of circularity in the production processes has to be excluded. Production activity must be organised in a completely hierarchical way also when it is not vertically integrated.

Circularity in production, though not a problem for defining the average production period, at least in the case of single production,[11] does not allow the vertically integrated neo-Austrian model to be used for studying the problems of transition between techniques.

2 Neo-Austrian representation, vertical integration and the degree of 'linearity' in production activity

As is well known, even in the absence of technical improvements, it is advantageous to push the utilisation of machines to the limit of their physical life only if their efficiency is constant or increasing.[12] In general, the working life which is most advantageous depends on the value of the rate of profit: in the absence of disposal costs, the degree of profitability of the production process could be improved by truncating, at the right moment, the utilisation of the machine. It follows that the average technical inputs in the production of the final good depend, in general, on the effective length of time over which the machine is utilised, and therefore, on the distribution of income.

This difficulty arises not only in the case of completely general production structures, but also in the typically Austrian case of the complete absence of circularity.

By way of an example, consider the case in which labour, circulating capital (commodities 1 and 2) and a machine with a maximum working life of two years are used to produce a consumption good (commodity 4). The sector which produces the consumption good must consequently be regarded as being subdivided into two activities that produce b_0 and b_1

Table 2.3. *Time profile of labour inputs and final product output for the consumption-good industry*

Time period	-3	-2	-1	0	1
$l(t)$	$a_{01}a_{12}a_{23}$	$a_{01}a_{12}a_{24}+$ $+a_{01}a_{13}+a_{02}a_{23}$	$a_{03}+$ $+a_{01}a_{14}+a_{02}a_{24}+$ $+a_{01}a_{12}a_{25}$	$a_{04}+$ $+a_{01}a_{15}+a_{02}a_{25}$	a_{05}
$b(t)$	0	0	0	b_0	b_1
		construction period		utilisation period	

units of final product respectively according to whether the new machine m_0 or the already used machine m_1 is utilised. The new machine (commodity 3) is produced with the utilisation of labour and circulating capital which, in turn, is produced according to a Mengerian structure. The activities of the economic system may therefore be represented as follows

$$A = \begin{bmatrix} 0 & a_{12} & a_{13} & a_{14} & a_{15} \\ 0 & 0 & a_{23} & a_{24} & a_{25} \\ 0 & 0 & 0 & m_0 & 0 \\ 0 & 0 & 0 & 0 & 0 \\ 0 & 0 & 0 & 0 & m_1 \end{bmatrix} \quad B = \begin{bmatrix} 1 & 0 & 0 & 0 & 0 \\ 0 & 1 & 0 & 0 & 0 \\ 0 & 0 & m_0 & 0 & 0 \\ 0 & 0 & 0 & b_0 & b_1 \\ 0 & 0 & 0 & m_1 & 0 \end{bmatrix}$$

$$a_0 = [a_{01} \quad a_{02} \quad a_{03} \quad a_{04} \quad a_{05}]$$

The consumption-good industry may be vertically integrated by means of the procedure described in the preceding section, which gives rise to the profile of labour inputs and final product outputs of table 2.3.

As can be easily verified, if the machine were only used for one year, then there would not be all the required labour inputs for obtaining, at time 1, the circulating capital necessary for utilising the used machine. To prevent this interconnection between the profile of labour inputs and the length of time over which the machine is utilised from occurring, there must be no use of circulating capital during the utilisation phase. This is the only productive configuration which allows the neo-Austrian representation to be used with the characteristics attributed to it by Hicks.

For the same reasons, this representation is also the only one that lends itself to a reformulation in interindustrial terms which is not purely a formal translation. It is only in this case, in fact, that a Sraffa–von Neumann interpretation is possible,[13] with an internal structure of the activities which does not depend on the truncation period. On the other hand, the consideration of the activities which utilise the machine may be able to provide information on its efficiency trend, in relation to the number of years it has been working, only if it can be utilised in production without circulating capital. The labour inputs in the utilisation period would otherwise reflect not only the requirements for the mere functioning of the machine, but also those concerned with the reproduction of the non-durable means of production which are necessary for the sequential synchronisation of the production process.[14]

3 The non-integrated neo-Austrian model and the analysis of transition

The use of a non-vertically integrated neo-Austrian model has been suggested by Belloc (Belloc, 1980) in order to avoid the problems relating to the vertical integration of activities.

This solution allows an effective description of some significant characteristics of the production process, such as, for example, the mechanisation of intermediate phases of the production processes and the presence of assisted labour in all stages of production which are, as shown in the previous section, a source of trouble for a vertically integrated representation of technology. It is thus possible to associate with a flow of *finished commodity*[15] a temporal sequence of vectors whose elements denote the requirements for the commodities and the original factors necessary in order to obtain that particular finished product flow, even though, in general, it is not possible to associate a finite labour-input flow with a consumption-good flow. A similar representation will obviously be valid, in general, for each finished commodity produced in the economic system. The technology of the economic system may therefore be represented by a set of elementary processes. Each of these may be identified by a temporal sequence of commodity and labour-input vectors associated with a temporal sequence of output vectors for the finished commodity under consideration, as well as for the machines of different ages used to produce this commodity. If the finished commodities are n and joint production, other than that associated with the utilisation of machines, is excluded, a production technique will be formed by a set of n elementary processes, one for each commodity, as represented below

$$[A_k(u), B_k(u)] = [a_{ki}(u), b_{ki}(u)](u=0, 1, 2, ..., D_k)$$
$$k=1, 2, ..., n$$
$$i=0, 1, 2, ..., n$$

The vectors $A_k(u)$ and $B_k(u)$ have $n+1$ elements, of which the first, with index 0, measures the quantity of labour. We obviously have $b_{k0}(u)=0$. D_k

measures the maximum length of time for which the corresponding process can function.

With the inputs of labour and of means of production which are denoted by the elements of the vector $A_k(0)$, it will therefore be possible to produce, one period later, the vector $B_k(1)$ of commodities (commodity k and the machines installed at the beginning of the period and now one year old). Together with labour and any other means of production, the one-year-old machines constitute the inputs, measured by the elements of the vector $A_k(1)$, that allow the vector of commodities $B_k(2)$ to be produced, and so on. As a result we will obviously have $B_k(0)=0$, and, assuming that the truncation of the process has no disposal costs, $A_k(D_k)=0$.

Suppose, for the sake of simplicity, that the commodity n is the consumption good, and consider the conditions of reproduction of the economy along the balanced growth path at rate g. If we denote with $x_k(t)$ the number of starts of process k at time t, we have

$$x_k(t)=x_k(0)(1+g)^t (k=1, 2, \ldots, n)$$

Obviously, the realisation of a continuous flow of commodities requires all the processes to be synchronised. In each period, each single process will therefore display all its vintages. In equilibrium, the output of each commodity which is produced by activities of different ages will have to equal the quantities necessary to make all the processes function. Consequently, we must have

$$\sum_{k=1}^{n} x_k \sum_{u=t-T_k}^{t} a_{ki}(t-u)(1+g)^u = \sum_{u=t-T_k}^{t} x_i b_{ii}(t, u)(1+g)^u$$

$$(i=1, 2, \ldots, n-1) \tag{1}$$

were $T_k \leq D_k$ is the age of the oldest of the processes k operating at time t. In balanced growth, with both prices and rate of profit constant, T_k is constant and coincides with the most convenient length of time for maintaining in operation the process in question.

The labour employment at time t is given by

$$\sum_{k=1}^{n} x_k \sum_{u=t-T_k}^{t} a_{k0}(t-u)(1+g)^u$$

Suppose we adopt, for simplicity, a 'classical' consumption function where workers spend their entire income (wages) to acquire the consumption good, whereas capitalists reinvest the entire sum of their profits. If we denote with w^* the quantity of consumption good the wage can command in correspondence with the rate g of balanced growth, the balance between supply and demand for the consumption good will be expressed as follows

$$x_n \sum_{u=t-T_n}^{t} b_{nn}(t-u)(1+g)^u = w^* \sum_{k=1}^{n} x_k \sum_{u=t-T_k}^{t} a_{k0}(t-u)(1+g)^u \qquad (2)$$

The n homogeneous equations (1) and (2), and the condition of full employment of the labour force will allow us to determine the number of starts of the different processes at the beginning of the first time period, and consequently, assuming that the economy moves along a balanced growth path at rate g, the number of starts of the processes at time t.

Suppose now, at historical $t=0$ while the economy is moving along the path of balanced growth, that a more efficient production method, characterised by a different elementary process, becomes available for producing one or more finished commodities. Suppose that the resources available for starting new processes at time $t=0$ are utilised in order to start up the largest possible number of processes which will be of the new kind wherever they have become available. As time goes by, the economy will gradually move from the old to the new production technique.[16] It is reasonable to suppose that, for a remarkable length of time along the transition path, innovative entrepreneurs will enjoy a certain degree of legal or economic monopoly which will allow them to hold on to the benefits of innovation with their individual production units. By supposing that there are no variations in the real wage, the transition towards the new production technique can occur at constant prices with an increase in the rate of profit in the innovative sectors. In this way, the length of time for which old processes are utilised will remain unchanged, whereas for the new processes a decision will be made to truncate them so as to allow the maximum internal rate of return.

Even if we exclude, for the moment, a situation where the start-up of the processes belonging to the new technique requires the utilisation of some commodity which was not utilised for starting the initial activities of the processes belonging to the old technique,[17] the start-up of the transition path can present difficulties in an economy which is not vertically integrated. If, in fact, we suppose that the economy moves, during the transition phase, along a path of 'full performance',[18] characterised by the complete utilisation of all the available resources,[19] it is possible that the transition might not be started.

There are essentially two situations where this can occur. The first is when the vector of endowments, which become available due to the fact that the processes belonging to the old technique are no longer started up, is linearly independent of the n vectors which describe the initial activities of the processes which form the new production technique.[20] The most immediate economic example is provided by a situation in which there exists, among the initial available means of production, a commodity which was utilised in the 'start-up' activities of the old processes, but is no longer utilised in the initial activities of the new processes.

In this case there is, in fact, no way of absorbing the commodity in question at the beginning of the transition path.

The other case where the transition might not be started occurs when the complete absorption of the resources inherited from the past implies a negative level of starts for some process.

It would be absurd, however, to think that, in a similar situation, the economy would avoid altogether the start-up of new processes, since they could be initiated as long as the condition of utilising all available resources was given up. This kind of situation must obviously be distinguished from that which could occur in a more advanced stage of the transition process where the emergence of negative values in the number of starts of new processes indicates that current production is no longer able to maintain the processes already activated at full performance.

This is the only case which can be encountered in vertically integrated processes where the fixed wage transition path can be arrested, and represents the only situation where it is correct to say that it is impossible for the economy to move along a transition path.

It seems, therefore, suitable to redefine the state of full performance as that situation where, availability of commodities permitting and in relation to the starting of new processes, the level of starts of any process cannot be increased without reducing that of some other process. This is a modification which, if it allows us, on the one hand, to eliminate the above-mentioned problems thanks to its compatibility with an incomplete utilisation of all the resources, on the other hand, makes the transition path non-determinate since there will be, in general, more than one starting structure for the new processes which satisfies the requirement of full performance.[21]

If we denote with a star the quantities relating to the old technique in its equiproportional dynamics, and we suppose that the economy moves along a path of full performance during the transition path with the characteristics defined above, then the compatibility, at time t, between the requirements for and the availability of the $n-1$ means of production and the consumer good will be expressed by the following conditions

$$\left\{\begin{array}{l}
\displaystyle\sum_{k=1}^{n}[\sum_{u=t-min(t,T_k)}^{t}a_{ki}(t-u)x_k(u)+\sum_{u=t-T_k^{\cdot}}^{-1}a_{ki}^{*}(t-u)x_{k0}^{*}(1+g)^{u+1}]\leqslant \\[20pt]
\displaystyle\sum_{u=t-T_i^{\cdot}}^{-1}b_{ii}^{*}(t-u)x_{i0}(1+g)^{u+1}+\sum_{u=t-inf(t,T_i)}^{t}b_{ii}(t-u)x_{i0}(u) \\[20pt]
(i=1,2,...,n-1) \\[16pt]
\displaystyle W^{*}\sum_{k=1}^{n}[\sum_{u=t-min(t,T_k)}^{t}a_{k0}(t-u)x_k(u)+\sum_{u=t-T_k^{\cdot}}^{-1}a_{k0}^{*}(t-u)x_{k0}^{*}(1+g)^{u+1}]\leqslant \\[20pt]
\displaystyle\sum_{u=t-min(t,T_n)}^{t}b_{nn}(t-u)x_{n0}(u)+\sum_{u=t-T_n^{\cdot}}^{-1}b_{nn}^{*}(t-u)x_{n0}^{*}(1+g)^{u+1} \qquad (3)
\end{array}\right.$$

By utilising (1) and (2), which express the conditions of balanced growth, and by setting $q_{ki}(u)=b_{ki}(u)-a_{ki}(u)$ and $q_{ki}^{*}(u)=b_{ki}^{*}(u)-a_{ki}^{*}(u)$ $(i=1,2,...,n-1)$ with $b_{ki}(u), b_{ki}^{*}(u)=0$ for $k\neq i$, as well as $q_{kn}(u)=b_{kn}(u)-w^{*}a_{k0}(u)$ and $q_{kn}^{*}(u)=b_{kn}^{*}(u)-w^{*}a_{kn}^{*}(u)$ with $b_{kn}(u), b_{kn}^{*}(u)=0$ if $k\neq n$, (3) is reduced to the following system of relations

$$\sum_{k=1}^{n}\sum_{u=t-min(t,T_k)}^{t}q_{ki}(t-u)x_{k0}(u)\geqslant\sum_{k=1}^{n}\sum_{u=0}^{t}q_{ki}^{*}(t-u)x_{k0}^{*}(1+g)^{u+1}$$

$$(i=1,2,...,n)$$

which describes the possible transition path between the two techniques.[22]

4 Interindustrial analysis and transition between techniques

Let us now consider an economy consisting of three industries. In the first, the machine industry, a durable means of production is produced. Its production process is subdivided into a construction phase and a utilisation phase. The construction phase lasts two periods in which a specific durable instrument is produced with the utilisation of a non-durable means of production and labour and the reutilisation, in the second period, of the semi-manufactured product realised in the first year. In the utilisation period this machine can be used for two years in order to produce machines for the other sectors of the economy. The non-durable means of production is, in turn, produced by the second industry with the utilisation of machines produced by the first industry, of labour and with the reutilisation of the non-durable instrument itself. In this industry, the machines have a technical life of two years. In the third industry, that of the consumption good, production is carried out with the utilisation of labour, machines and the non-durable commodity. The machines employed in the production of the consumption good have a technical life of three years. It is worth noting how, within a context of production of commodities by means of commodities, the construction phase of the 'productive capacity' of a particular industry can be formally decomposed into as many activities as there are unit production periods which exhaust it. If the outputs of these activities are used in other phases of production or within other industries, they would have the characteristics of finished commodities and the corresponding activities would have the characteristics of autonomous industries. If, instead, we dealt with fictitious commodities which exclusively identify the corresponding state of progress of the work of construction, these would constitute specific stages of an industry integrated by a temporal dependence based on the production/utilisation relationship. In this case, it is formally convenient to represent these production activities not as autonomous industries, but as activities contained within the industry which produces the corresponding finished good.

If, with reference to the kth industry, we denote respectively with a $a_{ki}(j)$ and $a_{k0}(j)$ the inputs of the ith commodity and of labour per unit of machine in the jth activity, and with $b_k(j+1)$ the corresponding production,[23] the technique can be represented as in table 2.4.

Evidently, the technique is of the Sraffa–von Neumann type with single production and fixed capital. By denoting, with the elements of the vector $x(t)=[x_{kj}(t)]$, the activity level at time t of the jth activity of industry k, and with the elements of vector $c(t)$ the final demand of the corresponding commodities, the conditions of physical reproduction of the economic system can be written as follows

$$Ax(t+1)+c(t+1)=Bx(t) \qquad (4)$$

If the system is in a state of balanced growth at rate g, and we still assume that only the workers consume by spending all their wages to acquire commodity 3, and we suppose, for simplicity, that it is profitable to use the machines up to the limit of their technical life at the equilibrium real wage, (4) becomes

$$(1+g)Ax(0)+(1+g)w^*ea_0x(0)=Bx(0) \qquad (5)$$

where $e=[000\ ...1]$ is a unit vector of suitable dimension. By writing out the relations in full and by carrying out the integration of the temporally connected activities, (5) is reduced to

Table 2.4. *Technique with single production and fixed capital*

$$A = \begin{bmatrix} 0 & 1 & 0 & 0 & \vdots\,0 & 0 & \vdots\,0 & 0 & 0 \\ 0 & 0 & 1 & 0 & \vdots\,0 & 0 & \vdots\,0 & 0 & 0 \\ 0 & 0 & 0 & 0 & \vdots\,1 & 0 & \vdots\,1 & 0 & 0 \\ 0 & 0 & 0 & 1 & \vdots\,0 & 0 & \vdots\,0 & 0 & 0 \\ \hdashline a_{12}(0) & a_{12}(1) & a_{12}(2) & a_{12}(3) & \vdots\,a_{22}(0) & a_{22}(1) & \vdots\,a_{32}(0) & a_{32}(1) & a_{32}(2) \\ 0 & 0 & 0 & 0 & \vdots\,0 & 1 & \vdots\,0 & 0 & 0 \\ \hdashline 0 & 0 & 0 & 0 & \vdots\,0 & 0 & \vdots\,0 & 0 & 0 \\ 0 & 0 & 0 & 0 & \vdots\,0 & 0 & \vdots\,0 & 1 & 0 \\ 0 & 0 & 0 & 0 & \vdots\,0 & 0 & \vdots\,0 & 0 & 1 \end{bmatrix}$$

$$B = \begin{bmatrix} 1 & 0 & 0 & 0 & \vdots\,0 & 0 & \vdots\,0 & 0 & 0 \\ 0 & 1 & 0 & 0 & \vdots\,0 & 0 & \vdots\,0 & 0 & 0 \\ 0 & 0 & b_{11}(3) & b_{11}(4) & \vdots\,0 & 0 & \vdots\,0 & 0 & 0 \\ 0 & 0 & 1 & 0 & \vdots\,0 & 0 & \vdots\,0 & 0 & 0 \\ \hdashline 0 & 0 & 0 & 0 & \vdots\,b_{22}(1) & b_{22}(2) & \vdots\,0 & 0 & 0 \\ 0 & 0 & 0 & 0 & \vdots\,1 & 0 & \vdots\,0 & 0 & 0 \\ \hdashline 0 & 0 & 0 & 0 & \vdots\,0 & 0 & \vdots\,b_{33}(1) & b_{33}(2) & b_{33}(3) \\ 0 & 0 & 0 & 0 & \vdots\,0 & 0 & \vdots\,1 & 0 & 0 \\ 0 & 0 & 0 & 0 & \vdots\,0 & 0 & \vdots\,0 & 1 & 0 \end{bmatrix}$$

$$a_0 = \begin{bmatrix} a_{10}(0) & a_{10}(1) & a_{10}(2) & a_{10}(3) & \vdots\,a_{20}(0) & a_{20}(1) & \vdots\,a_{30}(0) & a_{30}(1) & a_{30}(2) \end{bmatrix}$$

$$\begin{cases} \displaystyle\sum_{k=1}^{3} x_{k0} \sum_{u=t-(T_k-1)}^{t} a_{k1}(t-u)(1+g)^u = x_{10} \sum_{u=t-T_1}^{t-1} b_{11}(t-u)(1+g)^u \\[2em] \displaystyle\sum_{k=1}^{3} x_{k0} \sum_{u=t-(T_k-1)}^{t} a_{k2}(t-u)(1+g)^u = x_{20} \sum_{u=t-T_2}^{t-1} b_{22}(t-u)(1+g)^u \\[2em] \displaystyle w^* \sum_{k=1}^{3} x_{k0} \sum_{u=t-(T_k-1)}^{t} a_{k0}(t-u)(1+g)^u = x_{30} \sum_{u=t-T_3}^{t-1} b_{33}(t-u)(1+g)^u \end{cases} \quad (6)$$

where T_k indicates the number of activities which constitutes the kth industry. As can be easily verified, these three relations reproduce, *mutatis mutandis*, relations (1) and (2) in the preceding section since in these we have

$$b_{ii}(0)=0, \quad a_{ki}(T_i)=0 \ (i, k=1, 2, 3)$$

In the present context, the transition process between two techniques is represented as the emergence of a sequence of mixed techniques, one for each period, beginning from the moment at which the introduction of new activities starts until the moment at which there will be no more activities of the old kind functioning. If we suppose that technical change begins to intervene in the economy at time $t=0$, and it has the same characteristics and modes of diffusion illustrated in the preceding section, then the input–output matrices in the period $t=0$, $A(0)$ and $B(0)$, will differ from the matrices of the old technique in the initial activities of the three industries which will be substituted for by the corresponding activities of the new technique. In period 1, the matrices $A(1)$ and $B(1)$ will also incorporate the activities corresponding to the second stages of the production processes of the new technique. In the tth transition period, the technique $A(t)$, $B(t)$, $a_0(t)$ will be formed by the first $t+1$ activities of the processes of the new technique and of those activities corresponding to the stages with an order higher than $t+1$ of the old technique. After a number of periods T^* equal to the maximum life of the old processes, only activities belonging to the new technique will be functioning and this will be completed in all its activities after a number of periods T equal to the maximum operational life of the new processes.[24] The transition path will therefore be governed by the following system of relations:

$$A(t+1)x(t+1)+w^*ea_0(t+1)x(t+1)\leq B(t)x(t)$$
$$t=0, 1, 2, ..., \max(T^*, T) \tag{7}$$

If, as usual, the elements relating to the old technique are marked with a star, and we continue to assume the full performance of the economic system, that is to say, the maximum activation of new processes which is compatible with maintaining the activity levels of those currently operating, (7) then becomes

$$
\begin{cases}
\sum_{k=1}^{3} [\sum_{u=t-min(t,T_i)}^{t} a_{ki}(t-u)x_{k0}(u)+ \sum_{u=t-(T_k^*-1)}^{-1} a_{ki}^*(t-u)x_{k0}^*(1+g)^{u+1}] \leq \\
\qquad \sum_{u=t-min(t,T_i)}^{t-1} b_{ii}(t-u)x_{i0}(u)+ \sum_{u=t-T_i^*}^{-1} b_{ii}^*(t-u)x_{i0}^*(1+g)^{u+1} \\
(i=1, 2) \\
w^*\sum_{k=1}^{3} [\sum_{u=t-min(t,T_k)}^{t} a_{k0}(t-u)x_{k0}(u)+ \sum_{u=t-(T_k^*-1)}^{-1} a_{k0}^*(t-u)x_{k0}^*(1+g)^{u+1}] \leq \\
\qquad \sum_{u=t-min(t,T_3)}^{t-1} b_{33}(t-u)x_{30}(u)+ \sum_{u=t-T_3^*}^{-1} b_{33}^*(t-u)x_{30}^*(1+g)^{u+1} \tag{8}
\end{cases}
$$

where x^*_{k0} measures the activity level of the old process in industry k, at the instant $t=-1$, that is to say at the beginning of the last period in which the economic system was still lying on its path of balanced growth, and T_k denotes the number of activities into which the kth industry is subdivided.[25]

The correspondence between (8) and (3) can also be easily verified by recalling that in the last set of relations, $b_{kk}(0)=0$, and $a_{ki}(T_k)=0$ $(i, k=1, 2, 3)$.

5 Reutilisation of residuals

Until now, it has been implicitly assumed that residuals deriving from a disproportion between availability and effective utilisation of commodities in starting up new processes did not survive the production period in which they appeared. If some commodities are characterised by a high degree of perishability, others possess, instead, a high degree of durability. If it is this last characteristic which is significant, the problem has to be considered of how to transfer residuals from one period to another so that they may be successively reutilised in production.

From a formal standpoint, the problem can be solved by introducing transfer activities for each of the commodities produced. In the event that the transfer from one period to another is costless and the commodities are not perishable, the production technique will be transformed by enlarging the input and output matrices with a unit matrix of the same dimension and the vector of labour coefficients with an equivalent number of zeros. We will then have

$$\tilde{A}(t)=[A(t) \vdots I], \; \tilde{B}(t)=[B(t) \vdots I], \; \tilde{a}_0(t)=[a_0(t) \vdots 0 \; 0 \; ... \; 0]$$

By also modifying, consequently, the vector $x(t)$ of the sectoral activity levels, the transition process, as far as the balance between utilisation and production is concerned, will be described by the following system of equations

$$\tilde{A}(t+1)\tilde{x}(t+1)+w^*e\tilde{a}_0(t+1)\tilde{x}(t+1)=\tilde{B}(t)\tilde{x}(t) \tag{9}$$

We will obviously have $\tilde{x}(-1)=[x^* \vdots 0 \; 0, ...,0]$.

If we continue to assume full performance, the unknown values of (9), in each period, will be start-up levels of the initial activities of the different industries as well as the volume of residuals. The transition process will be able to continue as long as it is possible to identify non-negative period solutions. The fact that it may be impossible for the solution of (9) to remain non-negative evidently indicates that the quantity of resources currently available is insufficient to keep the production apparatus operating at its full potential.

It goes without saying that the introduction of transfer activities, if it allows the problem of residuals to be studied in a formally correct way, does not allow the problem of the multiplicity of solutions to be solved.

If the transfer activity occurs, as supposed, without real costs, then the determination of the volume of non-utilised commodities is residual. If, instead, real costs have to be paid, the volume of residuals is determined at the same time as the start-up levels of new processes. In this case, however, the decision to transfer the residuals into the future is much more complex and cannot be determined on a purely technological basis. This decision must include an evaluation of economic convenience which depends, in a more or less complex way, on the relationship between transfer costs, the current price of the commodities and the state of expectations concerning future demand and future prices.

6 The introduction of new commodities

The appearance of new products is perhaps one of the most interesting and frequently encountered ways in which technical change manifests itself. Obviously, the features of novelty may take up different degrees of intensity, which extend from the purely qualitative aspects of the product to more significant aspects concerning the technical characteristics of the commodities as well as the way in which they can be utilised. The framework of analysis introduced in the previous sections can also be used, with a little adaptation, for studying this aspect of technical change.

The simplest case occurs when the new finished commodity is a pure consumption good produced with the use of labour and currently produced commodities. The sequence of transition techniques, obtained by adding one by one the activities of the new process, will give rise to the new technique which will differ from the old technique in terms of number of industries and activities. If no problems are posed from the standpoint of the technical representation, things become complicated when we consider the activity levels of the production processes. To assume that the economic system is operating at full performance is no longer sufficient to govern the new start-ups of the different processes.[26] The intensity with which the production of the new consumption good is started in relation to the start-up of new lines of production of the old consumption good, will depend not only on the volume of resources made available, but also on the degree of substitutability between the two consumption goods. From this standpoint, moreover, perhaps the very plausibility of assuming full performance may be questioned.

The introduction into the economy of a new non-basic commodity, in Sraffa's sense, as in the case examined above, is a situation whose interest extends beyond the specific problem here considered. It can be thought as the first phase in the technical process of transition towards a new technique characterised by the presence of a specific basic commodity. In this case, a direct transition from the old to the new technique can in no way be conceived given the impossibility of starting up new processes without the prior availability of the commodity in question. This must be produced, therefore, in sufficient quantities to allow the activities which utilise it to be started up by using a particular process – a pilot plant – which will be substituted or modified once the processes relating to the new technique have been started up.[27] The first phase of the transition between the two techniques is therefore a technical change consisting in the introduction of a new commodity which is non-basic in relation to the old production technique.

The entire transition path may be more or less determinable a priori due to problems associated with the extent to which the new product is present in the bundle of final consumption and with the process of diffusion of the new product in the economic system. We cannot rule out a situation where the new product is not only utilised in activities corresponding to the new technique but where it also, partially or completely, replaces some products previously used in those activities of the old technique which are still operating.[28]

It goes without saying that whenever basic commodities are utilised in the intermediate technique, the utilisation of vertically integrated neo-Austrian models prevents us from analysing the transition towards new techniques which utilise basic commodities, even if we used the device that has been illustrated above. Even if basic commodities were absent in the intermediate technique, we would not be able to employ the vertically integrated stylisation due to the lack of interconnection which it introduces among different types of processes.

7 Final remarks

The identification of a hierarchical structure among the different sectors of modern industrial economies by means of the so-called triangulation of interindustrial matrices has been used to back up a presumed unidirectionality, of the Austrian kind, of the production process.[29] Even if we suppose that an adequate level of disaggregation eliminates a large part of the so-called reutilisation by emptying the corresponding squares on the principal diagonal of the interindustrial tables, it is far from unrealistic to suppose that there is at least one basic sector, that of energy, operating within the economic system. In any case, it needs to be stressed how the triangulation of the tables has essentially a statistical value and does not at all exclude single significant transactions from downstream to upstream sectors within the hierarchical structure of intersectoral sales. From this standpoint, the 'basicness' of commodities, and hence the circularity of the production structure, represents a fact which is more qualitative than quantitative in nature. A finite dimension could always be attributed to the length of vertically integrated production processes by truncating the reduction to dated quantities of labour, when this reduction is possible, to a stage which would assure the desired degree of approximation.[30]

Even if a tendency towards a greater integration of production activities, in terms of an increasing complementarity between temporally differentiated inputs and outputs, has been observed in modern industrial systems, a complete transposition of the production processes into neo-Austrian profiles will not be logically possible as long as 'lathes' are used to produce 'lathes'.

If we take for granted, however, the general representability of production processes in neo-Austrian terms, or we limit the analysis to those cases in which it is technically possible, it is necessary to underline how the successful application of such a method to the problems of transition between techniques is essentially related to the assumption, usually introduced in this case, of an economic system at full performance. This means, as seen above, the full utilisation of the existing productive capacity and the complete exploitation of the growth potential of the economy to the extent that this is compatible with the institutional framework. It is this assumption in its first aspect, which allows us to determine the whole dynamics of the economic system in terms of labour requirements and final production flows once the initial activity level of each process is known.

That things stand in this way is proved by the fact that the assumption formulated in a different analytical context with non-vertically integrated activities, allows us to obtain results for the problem of transition which can be considered equally significant. The stylisation of the consumer-good industry in vertically integrated terms merely has the function of limiting the analysis of transition to a particular simple case which, other conditions being equal, allows the trajectory of the economic system to be made determinate.

The representation of the product structure of the economy in terms of activities not only avoids all the problems of vertically integrating the production processes, but, when combined with the assumption of full performance, allows an analysis of the transition in terms which are more general than those allowed by the vertically integrated stylisation. The possible plurality of trajectories which characterises the non-vertically integrated case does not, however, represent a drawback of inter-industrial analysis. This plurality in fact occurs even if the analysis is conducted in vertically integrated terms whenever it is supposed that many consumption goods are produced in the economic system and the demand for them is not of fixed proportions.[31]

Notes

* I would like to thank C. D'Adda, G. Pegoretti, R. Scazzieri, P. Varri and S. Zamagni for having read and commented on the text. The author, however, obviously takes full responsibility. Research leading to this chapter was supported by the Italian Ministry of Education.

1 Hayek (1941, chapter VI) already underlined how durable goods gave rise to a 'continuous output' representation of the production process.

2 See, for example, Amendola (1976), Magnan de Bornier (1980), Belloc (1980), Gozzi and Zamagni (1982) and Zamagni (1973).

3 See, for example, Belloc (1980, pp. 24 ff.), Gozzi and Zamagni (1982), Zamagni (1973).

4 See Sraffa (1960, chapter VI).

5 Obviously, the difference between the $m_i(i=0,1, ..., k)$ is purely qualitative or reducible to purely qualitative terms. Once the machines have been installed, the number of them which are utilised over the years is always the same even if they are qualitatively different commodities.

6 See Belloc (1980, p. 20).

7 The good produced by the machine is, therefore, a non-basic commodity in Sraffa's sense. It should be noted, however, that this property does not necessarily imply that the commodity in question is a pure consumption good. The assumption that a good has a unique specialised utilisation might not be immediately self-evident, especially if more than one final good is being produced. There are, in fact, some commodities that can be used both in consumption and in reproduction, as Menger himself observes (Menger, 1923, chapter 2, section 3).

8 On this point, see Sraffa (1960, section 76). The device consists in substituting for the complex of activities into which the final-good industry is subdivided, a composite industry which, by utilising all the means of production and labour of the individual activities, produces the total output. Obviously, all the machines used, appearing both as inputs as well as outputs in the same industry, can be eliminated. If inputs are expressed in terms of one 'unit of output' the technology of the temporally integrated economy can be described as denoted below, where the elements of the vector C_{cc} and the scalars C_{ci} measure the inputs of the final good in production

$$A = \begin{bmatrix} A_{cc} \sum_{i=0}^{k} a_{ci}(1+r)^{k-i} / \sum_{i=0}^{k} b_i(1+r)^{k-i} \\[2em] C_{cc} \sum_{i=0}^{k} C_{ci}(1+r)^{k-i} / \sum_{i=0}^{k} b_i(1+r)^{k-i} \end{bmatrix} \quad B = \begin{bmatrix} I & 0 \\ 0 & 1 \end{bmatrix}$$

$$a_0 = \begin{bmatrix} a_{0c} \sum_{i=0}^{k} a_{0i}(1+r)^{k-i} / \sum_{i=0}^{k} b_i(1+r)^{k-i} \end{bmatrix}$$

The durable instrument is thus eliminated and the economic system formally transformed into a single-production system. The reduction to dated quantities of labour can be carried out in the traditional way since the length of the utilisation period has been formally eliminated. It should be observed that if we exclude the case in which the efficiency of the machines is definable in physical terms as constant with the ageing of the instrument, then the 'technical coefficients' of the temporally integrated industry depend on the rate of profit.

9 The stages of the production process also formed the basis on which to define the hierarchical structure of the commodities, starting with those of a higher order (non-reproducible commodities or original factors of production) and finishing with those of a lower order (commodities that do not enter production or consumer goods) through a complete ranking.

10 Sufficiency immediately follows by recalling that a matrix A of dimensions $n \times n$ with the structure shown in the main text is such that $A^n = 0$. The $(n-1)$th stage of the reduction of the construction period involves therefore the use of labour alone. Necessity can also be easily proved by observing that, if the stages of the reduction process must be finite, there cannot be basic commodities in the system. If this were not the case, the increased powers of A, which measure the more and more indirect requirements of commodities in production, would produce commodity requirements which would always be positive. The matrix A must therefore be reducible and can therefore be written as follows

$$A = \begin{bmatrix} A_{11} & A_{12} & \cdots & A_{1s} \\ 0 & A_{22} & \cdots & A_{2s} \\ \vdots & & & \vdots \\ 0 & 0 & \cdots & A_{ss} \end{bmatrix}$$

where $A_{11}, A_{22}, ..., A_{ss}$ are irreducible square matrices. The powers of a matrix with a structure of this type are matrices with the same structure and with the main diagonal formed by the blocks A_{ii} which are correspondingly raised in power. This contradicts the assumption that the reduction process is finite. There cannot, therefore, be irreducible blocks A_{ii} and, consequently, it must be possible to write A as an upper triangular matrix with zero elements along the main diagonal.

11 See, for example, Weizsäcker (1971, pp. 32 ff).

12 See, for example, Baldone (1974), Schefold (1974) and Varri (1974).

13 See Burmeister (1974, section XX).

14 Obviously, this interpretative difficulty remains whenever it is supposed that more than one non-durable means of production is used in some activity of the construction period. In this case, a one-to-one correspondence between commodities (semi-manufactured) and labour input stages cannot be identified. Each labour input identifies, in fact, not so much the stage reached in the production of a commodity, but the sequential formation of the productive capacity of the process in question. The two interpretations coincide only when each activity of the construction period requires the input of labour assisted only by the semi-manufactured product delivered from the immediately preceding working stage.

15 By finished commodities we mean consumer goods and those commodities which are objects of interindustrial transactions.

16 Obviously, technical change will not necessarily affect all industries. It could, moreover, be limited only to some of the activities which constitute each industry.

17 It should be noted that this kind of situation includes, as a particular case, that which assumes the utilisation of a new basic commodity in the new technique.

18 See Hicks (1973a and b, chapter V). In the vertically integrated case, the number of starts of new processes, with full performance, is the maximum permitted by the quota of current production which is absorbed neither by wages paid to the workers employed in the old processes, nor by capitalistic consumption.

19 This is the definition adopted by Belloc (1980, p. 136).

20 If there are n finished commodities and n processes, the input vectors of the starting activities of the different processes form a square matrix of order n. Only if this matrix has full rank will there always be at time $t=0$ a vector of rate of starts for the processes belonging to the new technique (possibly with negative elements) which permit whatever quantities of commodities are initially available to be absorbed. If the rank is not full, there might not be a solution.

21 One way of solving this kind of indeterminacy could be to determine the structure of the new activity levels in such a way as to reproduce, for example, the structure of the balanced growth path of the new technique. This is, for example, the solution indirectly followed by Solow (1967), even though in a context which is different in terms of issues considered and technological stylisation (interindustrial representation with circulating capital only).

22 If we assume, as in Belloc (1980), that the elementary production processes can be described as continuous input and output flows and that the balance between these inputs and outputs along the transition path can be identified in terms of equalities, then the relation given here is interpretable as a Volterra system of integral equations of the first order. See Belloc (1980, pp. 136 ff) for an analysis of the transition path when these assumptions are made.

23 The difference of one period in the activity index between inputs and outputs allows us to make the interindustrial representation correspond to the neo-Austrian model where the production of period $t+1$ corresponds to the inputs of period t.

24 Evidently, the two phases may or may not last the same length of time: this will depend on how technical change influences the length of time for which the new processes are utilised with respect to the old processes.

25 The summations of the inputs and outputs of the old activities are obviously defined for $t \leq T_k$ ($k = 1, 2, 3$).

26 This indeterminacy would also appear in the vertically integrated version of the model and is typical of all those situations in which more than one consumer good is produced, with each good being produced by utilising a specific vertically integrated process, and where the final demand is not of fixed proportions. In the non-vertically integrated case, this indeterminacy supplements the one which may be due to the presence of a plurality of produced commodities.

27 This is a case where the introduction of a new technique could be justified even if it were not, at current prices, in itself convenient. It is, in fact, a necessary step for enabling the successive starting of more profitable processes to take place.

28 Think of the trivial case in which a new material for the production of gaskets is utilised which will not only be used in the production of new kinds of plants and in their productive utilisation, but also in those old plants which are still operating through the normal operations of maintenance and repair.

29 See, for example, Helmstädter (1965). On triangulation, see also Leontief (1966, chapter IV).

30 It is obviously a question of a quantitative approximation, concerning the size of the residual of the commodities, which does not solve the conceptual difficulties relating to the presence of basic commodities.

31 The presence of several vertically integrated processes, each producing a particular consumer good, can pose some problems of compatibility for the theory of value and distribution. On this point, see Hagemann and Kurz (1976, section iv).

References

Amendola, M. (1976) *Macchine, produttività, progresso tecnico*, Milan, Isedi.

Baldone, S. (1974) 'Il capitale fisso nello schema teorico di Piero Sraffa', *Studi Economici* (Engl. trans. 'Fixed Capital in Sraffa's Theoretical Scheme', in Pasinetti (1980)).

Belloc, B. (1980) *Croissance économique et adaptation du capital productif*, Paris, Economica.

Böhm-Bawerk, E. von (1889) *Positive Theorie des Kapitales*, Innsbruck, Wagner.

Burmeister, E. (1974) 'Synthesizing the Neo-Austrian and Alternative Approaches to Capital Theory: A Survey', *Journal of Economic Literature*, 12 (2, June): 413–57.

Gozzi, G. and Zamagni, S. (1982) 'Crescita non uniforme e struttura produttiva: un modello di traversa a salario fisso', *Giornale degli Economisti e Annali di Economia*, 41 (5–6, May–June): 305–45.

Hagemann, H. and Kurz, H. D. (1976) 'The Return of the Same Truncation Period and Reswitching of Techniques in Neo-Austrian and More General Models', *Kyklos*, 29 (4): 678–708.

Hayek, F. A. von (1941) *The Pure Theory of Capital*, London, Routledge.

Helmstädter, E. (1965) 'Linearität und Zirkularität des Volkswirtschaftlichen Kreislaufs', *Weltwirtschaftliches Archiv*, 94: 234–59.

Hicks, J. R. (1970) 'A Neo-Austrian Growth Theory', *Economic Journal*, 80 (June): 257–81.

(1973a) *Capital and Time. A Neo-Austrian Theory*, Oxford, Clarendon Press.

(1973b) *Capitale e tempo. Una teoria Neo-Austriaca*, Milan, Etas libri (It. trans. of Hicks (1973a)).

Jevons, W. S. (1871) *The Theory of Political Economy*, London, Macmillan.

Leontief, W. (1966) *Input–Output Economics*, Oxford, Oxford University Press.

Magnan de Bornier, J. (1980) *Capital et déséquilibre de la croissance*, Paris, Economica.

Menger, C. (1923) *Grundsätze der Volkswirtschaftslehre* Wien, Braumüller, 2nd edition.

Pasinetti, L. L. (ed.) (1980) *Essays on the Theory of Joint Production*, London, Macmillan.

Ricardo, D. (1817) *On the Principles of Political Economy and Taxation*, vol. I of *The Works and Correspondence of David Ricardo*, edited by P. Sraffa with the collaboration of M. H. Dobb, Cambridge, Cambridge University Press, 1951–73.

Schefold, B. (1974) 'Fixed Capital as a Joint Product and the Analysis of Accumulation with Different Forms of Technical Progress', published with modifications in Pasinetti (1980), pp. 138–217.

Solow, R. (1967) 'The Interest Rate and Transition between Techniques', in C. H. Feinstein (ed.), *Socialism, Capitalism and Economic Growth. Essays Presented to Maurice Dobb*, Cambridge, Cambridge University Press, pp. 30–9.

Sraffa, P. (1960) *Production of Commodities by Means of Commodities*, Cambridge, Cambridge University Press.

Varri, P. (1974) 'Prezzi, saggio del profitto e durata del capitale fisso nello schema teorico di Piero Sraffa', *Studi Economici* (Engl. trans., 'Prices, Rate of Profit and Life of Machines in Sraffa's Fixed-Capital Model', in Pasinetti (1980)).

Weizsäcker, C. C. (1971) *Steady State Capital Theory*, Berlin, Springer-Verlag.

Wicksell, K. (1934) *Lectures on Political Economy*, vol. I, London, Routledge (Engl. trans. of K. Wicksell, *Föreläsningar i Nationalekonomi. Första delen: Teoretisk Nationalekonomi*, Lund, 1901).

Zamagni, S. (1973) 'Struttura del capitale e crescita non uniforme', Appendix to Hicks (1973b), pp. 247–86.

3   Production and efficiency with global technologies*

ALBERTO QUADRIO CURZIO

WITH APPENDICES BY

CARLO FELICE MANARA AND MARIO FALIVA

1 Introduction

This chapter considers the problems of production and technology when natural resources or, more generally, non-produced means of production have a relevant role.

The theory of resources, technologies and production, on the one hand, and that of rent, distribution and prices, on the other, both founded on multisectoral structural schemes, have been a constant line of research for me. Firstly, the role of the relative scarcities due to land, natural resources, primary commodities, crops and raw material is analysed (Quadrio Curzio, 1967). This scheme is subsequently enlarged in various directions, examining also a wider category of non-produced means of production, in uniperiodical, comparative uniperiodical and dynamic contexts (Quadrio Curzio, 1975, 1977, 1986; Quadrio Curzio, Manara and Faliva, 1987; Quadrio Curzio and Pellizzari, 1991). In these analyses the original approaches have been improved through the use of more powerful mathematical tools applied also to the new problems. Some of the most important results have been already published in English (Quadrio Curzio, 1980, 1986; Quadrio Curzio and Pellizzari, 1991). Finally, a more general model on resources, technology and rent has recently been published (Quadrio Curzio and Pellizzari, 1996).

The nature and positioning of my approach within general economic theory has been explained in a survey of mine on 'land rent' (Quadrio Curzio, 1987). This category is for me the basis of any kind of rent deriving from 'technological scarcities' due to natural resources or to other 'scarcities'. In that essay the three more important theories of rent are examined (the surplus approach, the marginal productivity approach, the intersectoral approach), pointing out how my theory is a generalisation of the intersectoral rent approach.

The intersectoral rent approach can be linked back, in the history of economic thought, economic history and economic theory, to well-known and fundamental contributions, from Ricardo (1817–21) to Sraffa (1960).

Ricardo's contribution was rather strictly connected to the historical circumstances of the beginning of the last century. Sraffa's contribution, while wide and modern for the structural theory of prices, distribution and technology, was rather limited relative to the analysis of scarce natural resources. This is not only because Sraffa considered mainly 'land', 'corn' and 'crops' but especially because the interconnection between changes in distribution and changes in production were practically neglected both in uniperiodical and in dynamic situations. However, little help in these directions comes from many modern and fundamental dynamic multisectoral theories (see for instance von Neumann, 1945–6; Leontief, 1941, 1951; Pasinetti, 1981) which totally neglect the role of natural resources and technically similar non-produced means of production.

For these reasons I believe that my theoretical contribution, uniperiodical and dynamic, has a high degree of autonomy in the analysis of natural resources, of the non-produced means of production and of technologies in their interconnection with rent, distribution and prices.

As mentioned above, in the present chapter our attention is devoted to the problems of production, changes in activity levels, changes in techniques and in the efficiency of techniques. In the past I approached these problems by means of two theoretical schemes.

The first scheme is based on 'joint' techniques, which give rise to a 'global' technology of the economic system. Particularly important in this case is the use of 'splitting coefficients' and procedures of aggregation and disaggregation of all the processes which employ non-produced means of production. In the present chapter we will take up and widen this scheme.

The second scheme is based on 'disjoint' techniques, with each technique making use of one single non-produced means of production. More than one technique gives rise to 'composite' technologies of the economic system.

There are several reasons for choosing here and widening the global technology approach.

First, it is possible to extend the validity of representations of global multisectoral technology based on 'splitting coefficients' (as well as on technological coefficients) which allow us to examine changes in efficiency when the number of the activated production processes remain unchanged or when the number changes. More generally, three cases can be described: the 'Ricardian' case (diminishing efficiency); the neutral case (constant efficiency); the progressive case (increasing efficiency).

Second, it is possible to highlight further how the nature of 'technological scarcities' is similar, even if not completely identical, to that of 'natural resources scarcities'. In other words, we can maintain that the model takes us well beyond the traditional example of 'land' and 'corn', providing a representation of technologies which adequately fits the situation of contemporary economic systems.

Last but not least, it is possible to formulate a model, which is analytically very complex, in a more compact and synthetic but at the same time more general form. In fact the mathematical treatment with regard to the existence of solutions elaborates a set of instruments that is unusual in multisectoral schemes, which are often limited to the first version of Perron–Frobenius theorems.

This contribution is therefore divided into two parts: in the first part, Quadrio Curzio elaborates the model and the economic line of thought; in the appendices (second part), Manara (appendix 1) and Faliva (appendix 2) carry out the mathematical demonstrations.

2 Data, definitions and hypotheses

In presenting the data, definitions and hypotheses which lie behind this model, we assume that the reader is acquainted with the terminology of linear algebra.[1]

1 Basic commodities In the economic system $m+1$ commodities are produced, which are also the means of production. These basic commodities are of two kinds.

Commodity 1 (RMC1, raw material or commodity 1, an abbreviation we will often use) is a raw material and the quantity in which it is produced is denoted by $q_1(\ldots)$. In its production, non-produced means of production are also utilized in a number, quantity and quality to be determined.

The other m commodities whose quantities are denoted by q_j, for $j=2, \ldots, m+1$, are produced without any direct utilisation of the non-produced means of production.

2 Non-produced means of production (NPMP) and production processes which utilize them. The RMC1 is also produced by NPMP of different qualities up to a maximum number of k. The processes which produce RMC1 can therefore vary in number from 1 to k, and are represented by the vector of technical coefficients

$$[a_1'(h), l_1(h), t_1(h)], h=1, 2, \ldots, k \tag{1}$$

with

$$a_1'(h)=[a_{11}(h), \ldots, a_{m+1, 1}(h)], h=1, \ldots, k$$

The vector of technical coefficients $a_1(h)$ represents the inputs of $m+1$ commodities for producing the RMC1 through the utilisation of NPMP of type h. These coefficients also include quantities of 'necessary consumption' for each commodity (see the following point 4); $l_1(h)$ are the technical labour coefficients; $t_1(h)$ are the technical coefficients of NPMP of type h. Each vector $a_1(h)$ is such as to permit the viability, to the extent to which it concerns, of the technique of the successive type (4). With $T_1(h)$ denoting the available quantities of NPMP of type h, the quantity of RMC1 of process h is subject to the constraint

$$q_1(h)t_1(h) \leq T_1(h) \tag{2a}$$

From (2a), it follows that the maximum quantity of $q_1(h)$ which can be produced is equal to

$$\bar{q}_1(h) = T_1(h)/t_1(h) \tag{2b}$$

3 Processes of production for commodities j, that is, those which do not directly utilise NPMP. Each of these is produced by a single process

$$[a_j'; l_j]$$

with

$$a_j' = [a_{1j}, \ldots, a_{m+1j}], j = 2, \ldots, m+1 \tag{3}$$

the vector of the usual input–output coefficients, augmented by quotas of necessary consumption. These processes give rise to viable techniques (of the following type (4)).

4 Technical coefficients and levels of necessary consumption Each coefficient of the vectors $a_1(h)$ and a_j is augmented with respect to those of Leontief by levels of necessary consumption, that is, by amounts of each single commodity included in a conventional bundle of necessary consumption. In this way, every reference to final consumption demand can be avoided, if necessary, when a process of growth is analysed.

5 Production techniques Since the $m+1$ commodities are of a basic kind, all the processes (3) and at least one process (1) must be utilised to produce them. Since there are k viable processes of type (1), k distinct production techniques can be identified which differ only in terms of the process which produces commodity 1. Formally, each technique is represented by the matrix

$$A(h) = [a_1(h); a_2, \ldots, a_{m+1}] \geq O \tag{4}$$

together with the vector

$$L'(h) = [l_1(h); l_2, \ldots, l_{m+1}] \geq O$$

and with the constraints

$$t_1(h) \leq T_1(h)/q_1(h)$$

with $h = 1, \ldots, k$.

6 Viability of the techniques Each technique (matrix) $A(h)$ is non-negative, indecomposable and viable; it admits therefore a uniform rate of positive net product, or a maximum rate of positive profit (or an eigenvalue which is maximum, real, positive, not repeated and less than 1).

7 Scale constraints of the techniques Because of the limited quantities available of each NPMP of type h, and therefore because of constraint (2a) on $q_1(h)$, each technique (4) cannot produce more than a certain quantity of all the $m+1$ commodities since these are all basic.

8 Production technology The constraints of scale imposed on each technique by the limited quantities available of NPMP of type h may demand the activation of more techniques $A(h)$ in order to satisfy certain production goals. The simultaneous operation of several $A(h)$ techniques can be analysed by two distinct analytical methods: that of 'global technologies' in which the techniques $A(h)$ are 'joined' in a particular manner, and that of 'composite technologies' in which the $A(h)$ techniques remain 'disjointed', but nevertheless connected. As mentioned above, here we will utilise global technologies.

9 Orders of efficiency between techniques and non-produced means of production The differences between techniques (4) are caused solely by the process which produces RMC1. To establish an order of efficiency between the techniques (4) means, therefore, establishing an order of efficiency between the k non-produced means of production which cannot be compared in terms of 'corn per hectare', given the complexity of the processes in which they are contained.

For each technique (4), a price-distribution 'economic subsystem' (thus defined because the name 'economic system' is reserved for those technologies which contain several processes with NPMP) can be constructed as follows

$$[1 + \pi(h)]A(h)p(h) + L(h)w(h) = p(h), \quad h = 1, \ldots, k \qquad (5)$$

where $\pi(h)$ is the rate of profit, $w(h)$ the unitary wage (both uniform for each process) and $p(h)$ the price vector of the $m+1$ commodities.

For w, fixed exogenously, the order of efficiency of the k subsystem and therefore of the k non-produced means of production is given by the succession

$$\pi(1) > \pi(2) > \ldots > \pi(k) \tag{6a}$$

with the h indexes suitably permuted.

If $w=0$, the order of efficiency (6a) coincides with that given by the succession of the uniform rate of net product of each technique $A(h)$.

$$s(1) > s(2) > \ldots > s(k) \tag{6b}$$

If $w>0$, the succession (6a) and (6b) might not coincide, and, in fact, might even be reversed. In this case, the indices h of (6b) have been opportunely permuted with respect to those of (6a). The order (6a) can be called the 'price-distribution or uniperiodal' order since, by following it, there is no guarantee that the techniques $A(h)$ will be activated according to a succession of maximum growth potential. This is assured, instead, for each technique by following the order (6b) which can consequently be called the 'order of physical or dynamic efficiency'.

10 Succession of the eigencoefficients Let us assume, without losing anything in generality, that

$$a_{11}(1) \leq a_{11}(2) \leq \ldots < a_{11}(k) \tag{7}$$

since this is one condition sufficient for the existence of solutions when moving from aggregated to disaggregated matrices (see the following section 8, and appendix 1).

This assumption is not particularly restrictive. If the physical efficiency order is followed, it is a reasonably obvious assumption, even if it is not necessary. This does not imply, on the other hand, that the price-distribution order of efficiency coincides with the physical order.

11 Dimensions of the economic system These can be identified in various ways and on the basis of various criteria. One of these is the dimension of the technology, or the number of processes operating with NPMP. In this sense, it can be said that an economic system with one NPMP is 'smaller' than a system operating with two or more kinds of NPMP.

3 The problems

Our aim is to analyse:

1 The activity levels of the economic system and changes in these levels. This means determining the number of NPMP which are operating, the production processes and employment.
2 The technology of the economic system. When more than one process with NPMP is started up, the technology becomes a complex entity since it consists of more than one technique of type (4).

3 The changes in the technologies which can vary from changes in the activity levels, from the choice of techniques and from technical progress.
4 The changes in the uniperiodical physical efficiency of the economic system.

4 The economic system with one technique

Let us consider the smallest economic system in which there is only one technique operating, in other words, that system which includes the most efficient technique, on the basis of any one of the two orders of efficiency described above, among the k processes with NPMP. The production system which corresponds to a uniform rate of net product is given by

$$[(1+s(1))A(1)-I]q(1)=O \tag{8a}$$

$$[A(1)-\tilde{\lambda}(1)I]q(1)=O \tag{8b}$$

with

$$0<\tilde{\lambda}(1)=1/(1+s(1))<1 \tag{9}$$

$$q_1(1)\leq\bar{q}_1(1)=T_1(1)/t_1(1) \tag{10}$$

$$L'(1)q(1)=L\leq\bar{L} \tag{11}$$

With $s(1)$ we denote the uniform rate of net product; with $\tilde{\lambda}(1)$ the maximum eigenvalue of $A(1)$; with $q(1)$ the eigenvector of the production processes related to $\tilde{\lambda}(1)$; with $\bar{L}$ the existing labour force. Since $A(1)$ is non-negative, indecomposable and viable, the eigenvalue $\tilde{\lambda}(1)$ is real, positive, not repeated and less than one; the eigenvector $q(1)$ is strictly positive and structurally defined while its scale is determined on the basis of (10) (as an equality) or of (11).

Given that h can assume the values $1, ..., k$, by substituting in $A(1)$ the vector $a_1(h)$ for the vector $a_1(1)$, other $k-1$ subsystems or techniques (8), (9) and (10) can be constructed. Each of these is autonomous, apart from (11), with a maximum limit of production given by (10). Each of these techniques taken individually can grow at a maximum rate $s(h)$ within the limits given by (10) or (11). The problems of changes in the activity levels and of dynamics become, however, more complex when the techniques must be 'chained' due to the constraints of the NPMP.

Let us go back to the relations (8), (9) and (11) and consider (11) as an equality. If the resulting vector of the production processes, that is, the vector which gives full employment of labour violates (10), then NPMP of type 1 is insufficient to allow the full utilisation of labour. If we suppose that this is the case, then it will be necessary also to start up the process 2 which utilises NPMP of type 2.

5 Global technologies and splitting coefficients

The economic system must therefore utilise two processes with NPMP, as well as all the other m processes. The global technology which represents this situation is given by the matrix

$$A_\alpha(1,2)=\begin{bmatrix} a_{11}(1) & 0 & \alpha_{12}(1) & \vdots & \alpha_{1,m+1}(1) \\ 0 & a_{11}(2) & \alpha_{12}(2) & \vdots & \alpha_{1,m+1}(2) \\ a_{21}(1) & a_{21}(2) & a_{22} & \vdots & a_{2,m+1} \\ \vdots & \vdots & \vdots & \vdots & \vdots \\ a_{m+1,1}(1) & a_{m+1,1}(2) & a_{m,+1,2} & \vdots & a_{m+1,m+1} \end{bmatrix} \qquad (12)$$

The two processes $a_1(1)$ and $a_1(2)$ are now *jointed* in the production of RMC1 which is required by the whole economic system. The 'splitting or splitted supply coefficients' (α) identify the extent to which processes 1 and 2, respectively, supply RMC1 to every other process of the economic system. Elaborating them we therefore have

$$\alpha_{1j}(1)+\alpha_{1j}(2)=a_{1j}$$

The increase of $\alpha_{1j}(2)$ with respect to $\alpha_{1j}(1)$, which correspondingly falls, therefore indicates that process $a_1(2)$ assumes a greater relative weight in the economic system as it increasingly replaces process $a_1(1)$ in the supply of RMC1 compared with all the other processes in the economic system. In turn, the relative weight of this process in the economic system is reduced, even if it remains activated at its maximum level, which corresponds to the full utilisation of $T_1(1)$ (see (10) above).

It should be noted that in $A_\alpha(1, 2)$ those coefficients which could be defined as 'reciprocal splitting coefficients', that is, those which refer to the outputs supplied by process 1 to process 2, and vice versa, have not been inserted. The reason is evident: if the activity level of the economic system was so high that all the $\alpha_{1j}(1)$ were reduced to almost zero, process 1 would still produce a quantity of $q_1(1)$ sufficient for its own utilisation, given that $a_{11}(1)<1$. Supplying process 1 with RMC1 coming from process 2, that is, introducing $\alpha_{11}(2)>0$, means that an amount of RMC1 produced and already utilised by process 1 is released and allocated for utilisation in one or more of the j processes. Compensation (and not a substitution) would therefore occur which would prevent the operation from having any influence on the activity levels. The same reasoning can be carried out for the reciprocal splitting coefficients of process 1 with respect to 2.

The global technology $A_\alpha(1, 2)$ changes when there are changes in the α coefficients, is different, in part, from the leontievian matrices and represents, in our opinion, an innovation in the representation of production systems by including in the same matrix more than one process which produces the same commodity and other processes which produce different commodities. The matrices of type $A_\alpha(1, 2)$ have the following properties:

(a) they are non-negative;
(b) they are indecomposable (except in extreme theoretical cases when they assume the values of the splitting coefficients);
(c) they are viable, that is, they admit a uniform rate of net positive product (9). This property derives from relation (9);
(d) they are non-singular. We exclude processes which are linearly dependent.

6 The economic system with two techniques

The unknown values of the economic system, that is, α, s, q and L are determined by resolving the system

$$[(1+s_\alpha(1, 2))A_\alpha(1, 2)-I]q_\alpha(1, 2)=O \tag{13}$$

with respect to the conditions

$$\alpha_{1j}(1)+\alpha_{1j}(2)=a_{1j}; \alpha_{1j}(1)>0, \alpha_{1j}(2)>0; j=2, ..., m+1 \tag{14}$$

$$\bar{q}_1(1)=T_1(1)/t_1(1) \tag{15}$$

$$q_1(1)=\bar{q}_1(1) \tag{16}$$

$$q_1(2)\leq\bar{q}_1(2)=T_1(2)/t_1(2) \tag{17}$$

$$L'(1, 2)q_\alpha(1, 2)=L\leq\bar{L} \tag{18}$$

given that

$$L'(1, 2)=[l_1(1), l_1(2), l_2, ..., l_{m+1}]$$
$$q'_\alpha(1, 2)=[q_1(1), q_1(2), q_2, ..., q_{m+1}] \tag{19}$$

The solution can be found be increasing $\alpha_{1j}(2)$ in such a way that the constraint given by the full utilisation of NPMP of type 1, that is, by (16), does not prevent the production processes $q_\alpha(1, 2)$ from growing to that level at which (17) is satisfied as an equality, that is, up to the full utilisation of NPMP of type 2. At that level of $q_\alpha(1, 2)$, three alternatives can be given for the labour force:

(a) it is fully employed and (18) is therefore satisfied as an equality;

(b) it is insufficient for the full utilisation of NPMP of type 2, and (18) is, therefore, violated. In this case, by reducing the $\alpha_{1j}(2)$, $q_\alpha(1, 2)$ will be reduced so that (18) will become an equality;

(c) it is partially unutilised and (18) is therefore satisfied as an inequality. In this case, the economic system must expand by introducing a further NPMP, that of type 3.

We have required that the economy based on a joint technology has production processes which are structured in such a way as to generate a uniform rate of net production.

The meaning of $s_\alpha(1, 2)$ in this situation does not altogether coincide, however, with that of $s(h)$. Both $s_\alpha(1, 2)$ and $s(h)$ are indicators of the uniperiodal efficiency of the respective economic systems; $s(h)$ is also the maximum and constant growth rate of technique h; $s_\alpha(1, 2)$ is connected only to the growth rate of technology $A_\alpha(1, 2)$ and, moreover, is not constant.

The comparison between the two cases will become interesting for clarifying the differences between the dynamics with and without NPMP.

7 The economic system with k techniques

The number of processes operating with NPMP will depend, on the basis of what has been said, on the quantity constraints of the NPMP themselves and labour. The widest available global technology is that in which k processes with NPMP operate. This technology is given by the following matrix of order $(k+m)$ which has all the properties defined in section 2 above, and in which the processes from 1 to k produce RMC1, and the processes from 2 to $m+1$ produce the other m commodities. Such a technology will be employed, following the previously chosen order of efficiency, when the first $k-1$ processes with NPMP are utilised at their maximum level established by the quantity available of NPMP.

$$A_\alpha(1,\ldots,k) = \begin{bmatrix}
a_{11}(1) & 0 & 0 & \ldots & 0 & 0 & \alpha_{12}(1) & \alpha_{13}(1) & \ldots\alpha_{1,m+1}(1) \\
0 & a_{11}(2) & 0 & \ldots & 0 & 0 & \alpha_{12}(2) & \alpha_{13}(2) & \ldots\alpha_{1,m+1}(2) \\
\ldots & 0 & \ldots & \ldots & \ldots & & \ldots & \ldots & \ldots \\
0 & 0 & 0 & \ldots & a_{11}(k-1) & 0 & \alpha_{12}(k-1) & \alpha_{13}(k-1) & \ldots\alpha_{1,m+1}(k-1) \\
0 & 0 & 0 & \ldots & 0 & a_{11}(k) & \alpha_{12}(k) & \alpha_{13}(k) & \ldots\alpha_{1,m+1}(k) \\
a_{21}(1) & a_{21}(2) & \ldots & \ldots & a_{21}(k-1) & a_{21}(k) & a_{22} & a_{23} & \ldots a_{2,m+1} \\
\ldots & \ldots & \ldots\ldots & \ldots & \ldots & & \ldots & \ldots & \ldots \\
\ldots & \ldots & \ldots\ldots & \ldots & \ldots & & \ldots & \ldots & \ldots \\
\ldots & \ldots & \ldots\ldots & \ldots & \ldots & & \ldots & \ldots & \ldots \\
a_{m+1,1}(1) & a_{m+1,1}(2) & \ldots & \ldots & a_{m+1,1}(k-1) & a_{m+1,1}(k) & a_{m+1,2} & a_{m+1,3} & \ldots a_{m+1,1+1}
\end{bmatrix}$$

(20)

The economic system as a whole is described by the following relations

$$[(1+s_\alpha(1, ..., k))A_\alpha(1, ..., k)-I]q_\alpha(1, ..., k)=O \tag{21}$$

$$\sum_{h=1}^{k}\alpha_{1j}(h)=\alpha_{1j};$$

$$\alpha_{1j}(h)>0, j=2, ..., m+1; h=1, ..., k \tag{22}$$

$$\bar{q}_1(h)=T_1(h)/t_1(h) \tag{23}$$

$$q_1(h)=\bar{q}_1(h), h=1, ..., k-1 \tag{24}$$

$$q_1(k)\leq\bar{q}_1(k) \tag{25}$$

$$L'(1, ..., k)q_\alpha(1, ..., k)=\bar{L} \tag{26}$$

with

$$L'(1, ..., k)=[l_1(1), ..., l_1(k), l_2, ..., l_{m+1}]$$

$$q'_\alpha(1, ..., k)=[q_1(1), ..., q_1(k), q_2, ..., q_{m+1}]$$

Alternatively, instead of (25) and (26), the following relations can be considered

$$q_1(k)=\bar{q}_1(k) \tag{27}$$

$$L'(1, ..., k)q_\alpha(1, ..., k)=\bar{L} \tag{28}$$

There are three kinds of possible solution to this system.

(a) The solution of system (21)–(26) identifies the uniform rate of net product and the total production processes which correspond to the full utilisation of labour. The NPMP are completely utilised apart from the kth which cannot be completely utilised due to the labour constraint.

(b) The solution of system (21)–(24), (27) and (28) identifies instead the case in which NPMP are completely utilised, whereas, due to the constraints imposed by the availability of NPMP, labour is not completely utilised.

(c) The solution of system (21)–(24), (26) and (27) identifies the case of full employment of both the NPMP and labour.

This approach makes it possible, therefore, to establish how technology changes when there are two categories of limited means of production: 'labour' and 'land'. In turn, in the absence of technical progress, changes in technology can be of two kinds.

The first are those linked to an increase in the weight of the last process with NPMP activated, necessitated by an increase in the available labour force. In this case, the net product rate and outputs change, but not the processes.

The other changes are those which lead to an increase in the number of processes with NPMP activated. In this situation, changes in the dimensions of the global technology are also added to the changes occurring in the first case.

8 The aggregated and disaggregated economic system

The solution of system (21)–(26), or of system (21)–(24), (27) and (28), or of system (21)–(24), (26) and (27), as formulated, is not always easy with the usual procedures for calculating eigenvectors and eigenvalues. Constraints on the vector are at least $k-1$, as can be seen from (23) and (24), whereas the eigenvector of quantities can be defined, in most normal cases, by means of only one constraint.

However, having taken into account the economic significance of the problem, the first $k-1$ processes – activated at the maximum level – can be aggregated into one unique process. This approach consists precisely in introducing first the splitting coefficients as well as the disaggregated global technologies, and then passing to aggregated technologies (and vice versa), as can be immediately seen by defining

$$(a_1^*(k-1))' = [a_{21}^*(k-1), \ldots, a_{m+1,1}^*(k-1)] \qquad (29)$$

$$a_{i1}^*(k-1) = \sum_{v=1}^{k-1} a_{i1}(v)\beta(v), \ i=1, \ldots, m+1$$

$$l_1^*(k-1) = \sum_{v=1}^{k-1} l_1(v)\beta(v) \qquad (30)$$

$$\beta(v) = \bar{q}_1(v)/\bar{q}_1^*(k-1), \ \sum_{v=1}^{k-1}\beta(v) = 1 \qquad (31)$$

$$\bar{q}_1^*(k-1) = \sum_{v=1}^{k-1} \bar{q}_1(v) \qquad (32)$$

The problem of the production scale of the economy depends, therefore, on the relative weight of the $k-1$ aggregated processes with respect to the weight of process k, with all processes utilising NPMP.

The determination of the splitting coefficient can be related, therefore, on the one hand, to the process obtained through an aggregation of the first $k-1$ processes, and , on the other hand, to the kth process. The splitting coefficients shown in the same column can be summed in that they are multiplied by the same quantity and concern the same commodity. At this point, it is opportune, especially for the elaborations which follow, to introduce the following notations.

$$(\alpha^*(k-1))'=[\alpha^*_{12}(k-1), \ldots, \alpha^*_{1,m+1}(k-1)]$$

$$\alpha^*_{1j}(k-1)=\sum_{v=1}^{k-1}\alpha_{1j}(v), j=2, \ldots, m+1$$

$$\alpha'=[\alpha_1, \alpha_2, \ldots, \alpha_m]$$

$$\alpha_i=\alpha_{1,i+1}(k), i=1, 2, \ldots, m$$

$$a^*_1=\alpha^*(k-1)+\alpha \tag{33}$$

By means of these aggregations, the global technology can once again be described by a matrix of order $m+2$, as in the case of the economic system with only two techniques. The aggregated global technology is therefore given by

$$A^*_\alpha(k-1, k)=\left[\begin{array}{ccc|cccc} a^*_{11}(k-1) & 0 & \alpha^*_{12}(k-1) & \alpha^*_{13}(k-1) \ldots \alpha^*_{1,m+1}(k-1) \\ 0 & a_{11}(k) & \alpha_{12}(k) & \alpha_{13}(k) & \cdots & \alpha_{2,m+1}(k) \\ a^*_{21}(k-1) & a_{21}(k) & a_{22} & a_{23} & \cdots & a_{2,m+1} \\ a^*_{31}(k-1) & a_{31}(k) & a_{32} & a_{33} & \cdots & a_{3,m+1} \\ \cdots & \cdots & \cdots & \cdots & \cdots\cdots \\ \cdots & \cdots & \cdots & \cdots & \cdots\cdots \\ \cdots & \cdots & \cdots & \cdots & \cdots\cdots \\ a^*_{m+1,1}(k-1) & a_{m+1,1}(k) & a_{m+1,2} & a_{m+1,3} & \cdots & a_{m+1,m+1} \end{array}\right]$$

$$\tag{34a}$$

In order to analyse the changes in efficiency of the activity levels of the economic system in the following sections, it is opportune to rewrite immediately the above matrix also in a compact form

$$A^*_\alpha(k-1, k)=\left[\begin{array}{ccc} a^*_{11}(k-1) & 0 & (a^*_1-\alpha)' \\ 0 & a_{11}(k-1) & \alpha' \\ a^*_1(k-1) & a_1(k) & A(m) \end{array}\right] \tag{34b}$$

Having denoted the submatrix formed by the last m rows and columns of (34a) with $A(m)$, and denoted the vector formed by the elements of (34a) in the last m rows of the second column with $a_1(k)$.

The aggregated economic system is therefore given by

$$[(1+s_\alpha)A^*_\alpha(k-1, k)-I]q^*_\alpha(k-1, k)=O$$

$$[A^*_\alpha(k-1, k)-\tilde{\lambda}_\alpha I]q^*_\alpha(k-1, k)=O \tag{35}$$

with

$$s_\alpha=(1/\tilde{\lambda}_\alpha)-1; 0<\tilde{\lambda}_\alpha<1$$

$$(L^*(k-1, k))' = [l_1^*(k-1), l_1(k), l_2, ..., l_{m+1}] \tag{36}$$

subordinated to the constraints (22), (25), (27) and (32) and to the constraint

$$(L^*(k-1, k)), q_\alpha^*(k-1, k) \leq \bar{L} \tag{37}$$

In the formulation there are also three alternative kinds of solution:

(a) The first solution allows us to identify a vector $\alpha^*(k-1)$, a vector $\alpha(k)$, a quantities vector $q_\alpha^*(k-1, k)$, and a rate of net product s_α, which give the full employment of labour, whereas NPMP of type k remain partially unemployed.

(b) The second solution will give NPMP of type k fully employed with labour unemployed.

(c) Finally, the third solution will give full utilisation of NPMP and labour.

The procedure for solving this system, in economic terms, is the following: if the α, which are related to $q_\alpha^*(k-1, k)$ and to s_α which satisfy the constraints of full utilisation of the first $k-1$ NPMP, do not give full utilisation of labour, $\alpha^*(k-1)$ must be reduced with a corresponding increase in $\alpha(k)$. In this way, the constraint of the first $k-1$ NPMP is weakened by increasing the weight of the process k and this thereby increases all the quantities produced which incorporate the NPMP as a mean of production. This situation of $\alpha^*(k-1)$ and the corresponding increase in $\alpha(k)$ is arrested as soon as the constraint (27) or (37) becomes operative. The problem of disaggregation consists in splitting the vector $\alpha^*(k-1)$ between the $k-1$ processes in order to pass the matrix (34), $A_\alpha^*(k-1, k)$, to the matrix (20), $A_\alpha(1, ..., k)$, without modifying the solutions obtained.

The mathematical solution is given in appendix 1. This solution determines the splitting coefficients with the distribution of $\alpha_{1j}^*(k-1)$ among the $k-1$ processes with NPMP as follows

$$\alpha_{1j}(\nu) = \alpha_{1j}^*(k-1)\beta(\nu); \quad \nu=1, ..., k-1; j=2, ..., m+1 \tag{38}$$

Matrix (20), $A_\alpha(1, ..., k)$, in the north-east submatrix will therefore have $k-1$ row vectors

$$[\alpha_{12}^*(k-1)\beta(\nu), \alpha_{13}^*(k-1)\beta(\nu), ..., \alpha_{1, m+1}^*(k-1)\beta(\nu)] \tag{39}$$

It should be noted that a distribution of $\alpha_{1j}^*(k-1)$ with non-uniform weights $\beta(\nu)$ in every row is completely useless in that it would imply compensations imposed by (21) and (22). By simplifying for a case with three commodities and two processes with NPMP, it can be shown that if the process with NPMP 1 increases the share of 'corn' supplied to the 'iron' sector, that is, if $\beta_{12}(1)$ is increased above $\beta(1)$, the weight of 'corn' supplied to the 'services' sector must diminish correspondingly, that is, $\beta_{13}(1)$ falls below $\beta(1)$. At the same time, the share of 'corn' supplied to the 'iron' sector by the process with NPMP of type 2 will have to diminish, that is, $\beta_{12}(2)$ will fall below $\beta(2)$, and, correspondingly, the share of 'corn' supplied to the 'services' sector will have to increase, that is, $\beta_{13}(2)$ will rise above $\beta(2)$.

9 Changes in efficiency and activity level

Let us now suppose that the economic system is in a situation of full labour employment, with a number of k NPMP activated, but with the kth not completely utilised. If the labour force increases, it becomes necessary, if an increase in employment is desired, to increase further the utilisation of NPMP of type k. This gives rise to the following results:

(a) a structural change in the global technology whose dimensions, however, do not change, and continue to consist of k processes with NPMP (and of the other m processes);
(b) a continuous change in the efficiency of the global technology in that the k process assumes a greater weight within the technology;
(c) an increase in the quantities produced and in employment.

This is the case of continuous changes in efficiency.

If the increase in the labour force requires also the utilisation of NPMP successive to the kth, which we now suppose exists and that, to simplify, we denote with $k+1$, we will have:

(d) a change in the structure and dimensions of the global technology;
(e) a change, with a discontinuity, in the efficiency of the global technology;
(f) an increase in the quantities produced and in employment.

This is the case of the discontinuous changes in efficiency.

Let us examine the two cases without, however, carrying out a dynamic analysis, that is, without considering the accumulation of the net product. We will restrict our attention for now to comparisons between uniperiodal situations.

10 Changes in efficiency

By taking the uniform rate of net production among the different indicators of the efficiency of the economic system, we can examine its changes as the level of activity increases, by extending, that is, the utilisation of NPMP of type k, employment and production processes.

The mathematical demonstrations for this and the following section can be found in appendix 2. In relation to system (35), and therefore to (34) and to (36), and omitting, for simplicity, the magnitudes $k-1$ and k, we have

$$\frac{\partial \tilde{\lambda}_\alpha}{\partial \alpha_{1j}(k)} = \frac{p_\alpha^* \dfrac{\partial A_\alpha^*}{\partial \alpha_{1j}(k)} q_\alpha^*}{(p_\alpha^*)' q_\alpha^*} \tag{40}$$

where with $(p_\alpha^*)' = [p_1^*(k-1),\ p_1(k),\ p_2,\ \ldots,\ p_{m+1}]$ we denote the left-hand eigenvector of the matrix A_α^*.

This derivation expresses the effect on the net production rate (that is, on the maximum eigenvalue) of A_α^*, of an increase in the splitting coefficients relating to the process with NPMP of type k and therefore the increase in the weight of this process in the economic system.

The mathematical elaboration of (40) gives rise to the following result

$$\frac{\partial \tilde{\lambda}_\alpha}{\partial \alpha_{1j}(k)} = \frac{1}{(p_\alpha^*)' q_\alpha^*} [p_1(k) - p_1^*(k-1)] q_j;\ j = 2,\ \ldots,\ m+1 \tag{41}$$

From (40) and (41) we can derive three alternative cases:
(a) We have the case of increasing efficiency when

$$p_1(k) < p_1^*(k-1) \tag{42}$$

which gives

$$\frac{\partial \tilde{\lambda}_\alpha}{\partial \alpha_{1j}(k)} < 0 \text{ or } \frac{\partial s_\alpha}{\partial \alpha_{1j}(k)} > 0 \tag{43}$$

(b) We have the case of constant efficiency when

$$p_1(k) = p_1^*(k-1) \tag{44}$$

which gives

$$\frac{\partial \tilde{\lambda}_\alpha}{\partial \alpha_{1j}(k)} = 0 \text{ or } \frac{\partial s_\alpha}{\partial \alpha_{1j}(k)} = 0 \tag{45}$$

(c) We have the case of decreasing efficiency when

$$p_1(k) > p_1^*(k-1) \tag{46}$$

which gives

$$\frac{\partial \tilde{\lambda}_\alpha}{\partial \alpha_{1j}(k)} > 0 \text{ or } \frac{\partial s_\alpha}{\partial \alpha_{1j}(k)} < 0 \tag{47}$$

The identification of the three cases depends, therefore, on the relations of magnitude between $p_1^*(k-1)$ and $p_1(k)$ which represent the prices of RMC1 (of 'corn') produced respectively by the aggregated process $k-1$ and by the process k.

If the vector p_α^* is the left-hand eigenvector of the matrix A_α^*, it is the eigenvector of the prices related to an assumed maximum rate of profit for the aggregated global technology. That is

$$(p_\alpha^*)' A_\alpha^* = \tilde{\lambda}_\alpha (p_\alpha^*)' \tag{48}$$

The prices considered here and the assumed profit rate are not, however, those of the price-distribution system related to the global technology A_α. In this case, the price of RMC1 is unique for the whole economy and is given by the least efficient technique (cf. points 5 and 9, section 2 above), that is, the technique which incorporates the least efficient process with NPMP. This technique also determines the rate of profit. The other processes included in the technology, which produce RMC1, and which are more efficient, will have, as a consequence, a rent. In the present case, instead, it is as if the two processes which generate RMC1 produce two commodities which are different and which have two different prices. The assumed profit rate is therefore different from that which corresponds to the usual price-distribution system, with the absence of rent, in this approach, which has a purely instrumental role in the quantities system.

These prices are therefore represented by: $p_1^*(k-1)$ the price based on the cost of production, given by the circulating capital, utilised by the aggregated process $k-1$; $p_1(k)$ the price of the process with NPMP of type k. These can be considered indicators of the produced means of production utilised by the two processes, aggregated and disaggregated, with NPMP.

We therefore have increasing efficiency when $p_1^*(k-1) > p_1(k)$, that is, when we increase the weight of the process which utilises less circulating capital per unit of output. Correspondingly, we have constant efficiency in the case of $p_1^*(k-1) = p_1(k)$, and decreasing efficiency in the case of $p_1^*(k-1) < p_1(k)$.

All three cases are possible, depending, alternatively, on the order of efficiency.

If the order of physical efficiency is followed (6b) – the level of w permitting – we will have decreasing efficiency both when the dimensions of the global technology do not change, and when its dimensions increase. In this case, when another process with NPMP is introduced, the uniform rate of net product falls discontinuously. We could claim this to be an updated version of the Ricardian case. The expansion process of the economy will be arrested when all the viable NPMP have been utilised (see section 2, point 6). This means that if we introduced a further NPMP, the technique A, constructed with this last process (see (8)), would be such that

$$A(k+x)q(k+x) \geq q(k+x),\ x \geq 1 \tag{49}$$

and therefore with a zero or negative rate of net product.

The price–distribution order of efficiency can, however, also give rise to the opposite case so that the techniques $A(h)$ are arranged in such a way that their uniform rates of net product are seen to be increasing.

This situation could be the basis, whenever we are interested in the historical phases of economic development which are not considered here, for analysing a technical progress which saves circulating capital, that is, which only affects the 'new' processes with NPMP not yet activated, and which does not determine – at least within a certain period of time – the disactivation of the 'old' processes. In this case, naturally, also the historical order of price–distribution efficiency should give an increasing efficiency of the processes.

This observation allows us the opportunity to observe that a wider analysis of the problems of the order of efficiency, which does not concern, however, our present purpose, ought to allow the identification of historical orders of efficiency, with or without technological progress, and the logical orders of efficiency, which are those which interest us here. The price–distribution order of efficiency, finally, can give rise to alternating trends in the uniform rates of the net product of the global technology as other processes with NPMP are introduced.

This occurs because a non-univocal order of uniform rates of net product can be related to a univocal order (6a).

11 Growth in activity levels

This is the other aspect to be considered, both in the continuous and discontinuous case.

Let us denote with

$$\tilde{q}' = [\tilde{q}_1(k),\ \tilde{q}_2,\ ...,\ \tilde{q}_{m+1}] \tag{50}$$

the subvector consisting of the last $m+1$ elements of the vector q_α^*, defined by (36) above, and normalised with the first element set equal to 1. It can then be demonstrated that

$$\frac{\partial \tilde{\tilde{q}}_\alpha}{\partial \alpha_{1j}(k)} > 0 \tag{51}$$

whenever

$$\frac{\partial s_\alpha}{\partial \alpha_{1j}(k)} \geq 0; \ \frac{\partial \tilde{\lambda}_\alpha}{\partial \alpha_{1j}(k)} \leq 0; \ p_1^*(k-1) \geq p_1(k)$$

Therefore, when, with greater activation of the process with NPMP of type k, the efficiency of the economic system grows (or remains constant), the quantities produced also increase.

If the efficiency of the economic system diminishes

$$\frac{\partial s_\alpha}{\partial \alpha_{1j}(k)} < 0; \ \frac{\partial \tilde{\lambda}_\alpha}{\partial \alpha_{1j}(k)} > 0; \ p_1^*(k-1) < p_1(k) \tag{52}$$

the mathematical analysis (see appendix 2) shows that the production processes will increase only if $p_1(k)$ does not exceed the amount $p_1^*(k-1)$ beyond certain levels.

The economic interpretation of this condition is not immediately evident on the basis of the mathematical formulation, and probably requires an analysis in terms of vertically integrated sectors. The extreme case should, however, be the following: if the process with NPMP of type k is so inefficient that it generates a negative rate of net product (which is why the subsystem (8b) constructed with this process would have $\tilde{\lambda}_\alpha > 1$), its increased weight in the economic system, with the growth of α, would involve, at a certain point, reducing (or maintaining constant) production processes precisely because the absorption of the means of production exceeds (or equals) the production processes themselves. This situation will never be reached, however, because such a process k, by violating (9), will never be activated.

There is also a second element which supports the conclusion of an increase in production processes also for the case considered by (52). On the basis of (18) of appendix 2, the change in the subvector $\tilde{\tilde{q}}_\alpha$ of the normalised quantities is seen to be linked to the change in the eigenvector $\tilde{\lambda}_\alpha$ by the simple relation

$$\frac{\partial \tilde{\lambda}_\alpha}{\partial \alpha_j} = \frac{\partial \beta_\alpha'}{\partial \alpha_j} \cdot \tilde{\tilde{q}}_\alpha + \beta_\alpha' \cdot \frac{\partial \tilde{\tilde{q}}_\alpha}{\partial \alpha_j} \tag{53}$$

Taking account of (16) in the same section, it is easy to verify that (53) can be expressed as

$$\frac{\partial \tilde{\lambda}_\alpha}{\partial \alpha_j} = [0, \, -e'_{j(m)}].\tilde{\vec{q}}_\alpha + [0, \, (a_1^* - \alpha)'].\frac{\partial \tilde{\vec{q}}_\alpha}{\partial \alpha_j} \tag{54}$$

By inspecting (54), it can be deduced, therefore, that if we assume that (52) holds, we must have

$$[0, \, (a_1^* - \alpha)'].\frac{\partial \tilde{\vec{q}}_\alpha}{\partial \alpha_j} > 0 \tag{55}$$

The increase in a splitting coefficient implies, therefore, that the utilisation of RMC1 as a mean of production, generated by the aggregated process $k-1$, correspondingly increases with the reduction in the net product of that process which produces 'non-augmentable corn'. It is evident that the presupposition, for increasing the utilisation of RMC1 as a means of production, is that the production of at least one of the other m 'industrial' sector processes (as distinct from the two 'agricultural' processes, $k-1$ and k) increases and therefore its requirement of 'corn' will increase. Given that the economic system is indecomposable, it is plausible that the increase in production of the industrial sector and of the agricultural sector k (in which it can be analytically shown that production always increases as α_j grows) induces increases in production in all the other sectors, excluding, obviously, the aggregated 'agricultural' sector $k-1$, which has a fixed output. In all of the sectors, including that of agriculture with variable output, additional means of production, which must be produced, will be required. Finally, compensations with a reduction in those production processes which depend on sector $k-1$ should not occur since this sector's output is fixed.

12 Conclusions

In this chapter we have determined all magnitudes of the quantity system (productions, net products and so on) and their changes by using a 'global technology' which is founded on a scheme of 'joint techniques'.

The main feature of such a technology consists in representing, through a unique matrix, both Leontief-type production processes and production processes based on splitting coefficients regarding the same 'primary commodity' using different NPMP.

On this basis, we have examined two main cases: the case of continuous changes in the efficiency of technology and the case of discontinuous changes in efficiency.

In the first case, the number of processes with activated NPMP does not change; however, the global technology undergoes changes in structure (though not in dimension) and in efficiency as the last activated process with a NPMP takes an increasing weight. These changes take place in the continuum through variations in the 'splitting coefficients', which are determined by splitting input–output coefficients with special analytical tools.

The second case is characterised by discontinuous changes in efficiency because the number of processes with NPMP increases. Then the structural dimensions and efficiency of technology change.

In both cases, our analysis probes into three possibilities: increasing efficiency, constant efficiency and decreasing efficiency. Having chosen the uniform rate of net product of a technology as the index of efficiency, the three above possibilities depend upon the relationship between the price–distribution order of efficiency and the physical order of efficiency among NPMP. The price-distribution order of efficiency is the one among rates of profit (when the unitary wage is given) or among unitary wages (when the rate of profit is given), where each one of these distributive magnitudes is associated with one NPMP. In other words it is the order among the different techniques where each technique includes one NPMP only. The physical order of efficiency is the one among the NPMP (or among the techniques constructed on them) and it is established on the basis of the uniform rate of net product of each technique.

To make clear the consequences of the choice of techniques on the basis of the two different orders, we started from the case in which the two orders coincide. In this case, the efficiency of the economic system declines when the activity level increases. But when the price-distribution order of efficiency gives an ordering of processes which is the reverse of that given by the physical order of efficiency, the economic system displays increasing efficiency with an increase of the activity level. Many other different cases, with constant or with alternating behaviours of efficiency, can be constructed on the basis of different relations between the prices–distribution and the physical order of efficiency.

To conclude: the main result of this analysis, which has been limited to uniperiodic and comparative uniperiodic situations, is to point out the relations existing among technologies, efficiency, and activity level by using the representation of the economic system based upon the scheme of global technologies.

The above approach could be extended to other issues connected to economic dynamics, technical progress and dynamic choice of technologies. But before going into very complex mathematical analysis with the global technology approach it must be taken into account that I have, also with a co-author, already dealt with these problems utilising the 'composite technology' approach with results which are very satisfactory. The global technology approach could therefore more properly be applied to other problems which suggest first of all uniperiodical and comparative uni-periodical consideration and then dynamic analysis.

Notes

* For the original Italian version of this essay see A. Quadrio Curzio, C. F. Manara and M. Faliva, 1987. Changes have been made here to the introduction, conclusions and references. Behind this study there are also some numerical simulations carried out in a research project supported, within the scheme of the National Grants 40%, 1987 by Ministero della Pubblica Istruzione at the Centre of Research in Economic Analysis at the Catholic University of Milan.
1 In the numbering of formulas, the main text and the appendices are considered separately.

Appendix 1 The existence of solutions for aggregated and disaggregated cases

CARLO FELICE MANARA

1.1 In this appendix, we will tackle, at a theoretical mathematical level, the subject matter presented in sections 7 and 8. To this end, we will therefore make constant reference to notations introduced there, departing from these only when it is particularly useful for carrying out demonstrations.

The problems which we will solve in the following pages concern the passage from the system defined 'disaggregated' to the system defined 'aggregated' and vice versa.

Two questions must be answered in mathematical terms:

(a) Is it always possible to obtain an aggregated system, of the kind described earlier in the chapter, by beginning with a disaggregated system, also described above?
(b) Is it always possible to work back from an aggregated system, obtained in this way, to a disaggregated system, which has the 'same' solutions – in the sense which we will clarify – by means of an opportune choice of the splitting coefficients?

As was seen in section 7, the disaggregated economic system, with k techniques, can be described by the square matrix of order $k+m$, denoted by $A_\alpha (1, ..., k)$, subject to the assumptions of section 2. Precisely:

Assumption I

For

$$1 \leq i \leq k-1 \tag{1}$$

we have

$$a_{11} (i) \leq a_{11} (i+1) \tag{2}$$

Assumption II

The matrix $A_\alpha (1, ..., k)$ is non-negative, indecomposable and satisfies conditions such that there exists a real, positive eigenvalue $\tilde{\lambda}_\alpha$, which is the simple root of the characteristic equation of the matrix, and is larger than the modulus of any other eigenvalue, real or complex

$$0<a_{11}(k)<\tilde{\lambda}_\alpha<1 \tag{3}$$

$$0<a_{11}(\nu)<\tilde{\lambda}_\alpha; \; 1\leq\nu\leq k-1 \tag{4}$$

We denote the right-hand eigenvector relating to $\tilde{\lambda}_\alpha$ with

$$q_\alpha(1, ..., k)=[q_1(1), ..., q_1(k-1), q_1(k), q_2, q_3, ..., q_{m+1}] \tag{5}$$

The relations which express the links between the elements of the matrix $A_\alpha(1, ..., k)$, the eigenvalue $\tilde{\lambda}_\alpha$, and the elements of the vector $q_\alpha(1, ..., k)$, are given by the vectorial equation (21) of section 7.

Here we explicitly develop the above-mentioned links

$$a_{11}(j)q_1(j)+\sum_{\nu=2}^{m+1}\alpha_{1\nu}(j)q_\nu=\tilde{\lambda}_\alpha q_1(j); \; (1\leq j\leq k-1) \tag{6}$$

$$a_{11}(k)q_1(k)+\sum_{\nu=2}^{m+1}\alpha_{1\nu}(k)q_\nu=\tilde{\lambda}_\alpha q_1(k) \tag{6a}$$

$$\sum_{\nu=1}^{k}a_{j1}(\nu)q_1(\nu)+\sum_{\nu=2}^{m+1}\alpha_{j\nu}q_\nu=\tilde{\lambda}_\alpha q_j; \; (2\leq j\leq m+1) \tag{7}$$

The well-known theorems on non-negative matrices ensure the existence of maximum $\tilde{\lambda}_\alpha$, as does (3), and the existence of a related, strictly positive eigenvector $q_\alpha(1, ..., k)$.

1.2 We will now set out that procedure called 'aggregation' in section 8. By means of this procedure, beginning with the system described by the equations (6), (6a) and (7), we can construct an 'aggregated' system. To this end we have

$$\bar{q}_1^*(k-1)=\sum_{\nu=1}^{k-1}\bar{q}_1^*(\nu) \tag{8}$$

$$\beta(\nu)=\bar{q}_1(\nu)/\bar{q}_1^*(k-1) \tag{9}$$

For the numbers – called 'weights' – (obviously real and positive) $\beta(\nu)$, the following relation holds

$$\sum_{\nu=1}^{k-1}\beta(\nu)=1 \tag{10}$$

Moreover, we have

$$\alpha_{1j}^*(k-1)=\sum_{\nu=1}^{k-1}\alpha_{1j}(\nu); \; (2\leq j\leq m+1) \tag{11}$$

$$\alpha_{i1}^*(k-1)=\sum_{\nu=1}^{k-1}\alpha_{i1}(\nu)\beta(\nu);\ (2\leq i\leq m+1) \tag{12}$$

$$\alpha_{11}^*(k-1)=\sum_{\nu=1}^{k-1}\alpha_{11}(\nu)\beta(\nu) \tag{12a}$$

In words, it could be said that the numbers $\alpha_{1j}^*\ (k-1)$ are obtained by summing, 'by column', the elements of the matrix $A_\alpha(1,\ ...,\ k)$ which belong to the columns identified by the indices (of the column) that go from 2 to $m+1$, and belong to the first $k-1$ rows; analogously, it could be said that, for $2\leq i\leq m+1$, the elements $a_{i1}^*\ (k-1)$ were obtained by summing 'by row' the elements of the first $k-1$ columns of the matrix $A_\alpha(1,\ ...,\ k)$, multiplied by the corresponding 'weights' given by the co-efficients in (9).

Analogously, the element $a_{11}^*(k-1)$ is obtained by summing all the elements $a_{11}(\nu)$, multiplied by the corresponding weights $\beta(\nu)$.

By these summations an 'aggregated' matrix is obtained which we will denote with the symbol, $A_\alpha^*(k-1,\ k)$; this is represented in matrix (34a) of section 8.

The following system of equations corresponds to this matrix

$$a_{11}^*(k-1)\bar{q}_1^*(k-1)+\sum_{j=2}^{m+1}\alpha_{1j}^*(k-1)q_j=\tilde{\lambda}_\alpha\bar{q}_1^*(k-1) \tag{13}$$

$$a_{11}(k)q_1(k)+\sum_{j=2}^{m+1}\alpha_{1j}(k)q_j=\tilde{\lambda}_\alpha q_1(k) \tag{14}$$

$$a_{j1}^*(k-1)\bar{q}_1^*(k-1)+\alpha_{j1}(k)q_1(k)+\sum_{\nu=2}^{m+1}a_{j\nu}q_\nu=\tilde{\lambda}_\alpha q_j \tag{15}$$

for $2\leq j\leq m+1$.

It should be observed that equations (13) and (14) are obtained respectively from the first and second row of the aggregated matrix. Equation (13) is obtained by summing member by member the first $k-1$ equation of system (6), and therefore derives from these; (14) coincides with (6a); and, finally, bearing in mind (8), (9), (11) and (12), we have that (15) derives from (7).

We now define the vector

$$(q_\alpha^*(k-1,\ k))'=[\bar{q}_1^*(k-1),\ q_1(k),\ q_2,\ ...,\ q_{m+1}] \tag{16}$$

We can summarise the observations made so far as follows:

Theorem 1

If equations (6), (6a) and (7), which describe the system of equations for matrix $A_\alpha(1, 2, ..., k)$, have as solutions the elements of the vector $q_\alpha(1, ..., k)$, given by (5), then equations (13), (14) and (15), which describe the aggregated system for the matrix $A_\alpha^*(k-1, k)$ have for solutions the elements of the vector $q_\alpha^*(k-1, k)$ given by (16), with the same eigenvalue $\tilde{\lambda}_\alpha$ appearing in both systems of equations.

1.3 It can now be asked, given that there is a system represented by equations such as (13), (14) and (15), whether it is still possible to consider this system to be obtainable with an operation of aggregation from a system of the kind described by the equations (6), (6a) and (7).

To this end, we assume the following data are known

1   the elements of the matrix $A_\alpha^*(k-1, k)$;
2   the coefficients $a_{11}(v)$ (for $1 \leq v \leq k-1$) of the matrix $A_\alpha(1, 2, ..., k)$, satisfying conditions (1) and (2);
3   the vector $q_\alpha^*(k-1, k)$ given by (16);
4   the weights $\beta(v)$ given by (9), and therefore also the elements $q_1(v)$ (for $1 \leq v \leq k-1$) of the vector $q_\alpha(1, 2, ..., k)$.

The problem set out above can be formulated more precisely by requiring that, under these conditions, the elements $\alpha_{1j}(v)$ for $2 \leq j \leq m+1$ and for $1 \leq v \leq k-1$ of a matrix $A_\alpha(1, 2, ..., k)$ be determined in such a way that equations (6) and (11) are satisfied.

To this end, we observe that the relations (6), (6a) and (11) cited above, form a system of $m+k-1$ linear equations in $m(k-1)$ unknown values given by the unknown elements $\alpha_{1j}(v)$ of the matrix $A_\alpha(1, 2, ..., k)$ which we are searching for. Now it can be observed how we obviously have

$$m(k-1) \geq m+k-1 \tag{17}$$

as soon as

$$m \geq 2 \text{ and } k \geq 3 \tag{18}$$

Conditions (18) are always satisfied; on the other hand, the problem of aggregation and disaggregation is not even posed. However, these conditions only ensure that the number of unknown values $\alpha_{1j}(v)$ in the system of relations (6) and (11) exceeds the number of equations.

However this is not sufficient to guarantee the system consistency.

To this end, we could examine the coefficient matrix of the linear system – in the unknown quantities $\alpha_{ij}(v)$ – given by (6) and (11), but such an approach is not advisable due to the computational burdens implied in it.

It is therefore preferable to verify directly whether the above-mentioned equations have solutions, at least for properly chosen values of the $a_{11}(\nu)$ coefficients.

Even if some loss of generality cannot be avoided, this approach to the problem has the advantage of leading to the desired results in a straightforward manner.

In this connection, we will now prove the following lemma.

Lemma
The following relations hold

$$a_{11}(1) \leq a_{11}^*(k-1) \leq a_{11}(k-1) \tag{19}$$

Proof: For the proof observe that we have (see (12a))

$$a_{11}^*(k-1) = \sum_{\nu=1}^{k-1} a_{11}(\nu)\beta(\nu) \tag{20}$$

From (10) and (2) we can easily find that

$$a_{11}(1)\sum_{\nu=1}^{k-1}\beta(\nu) \leq \sum_{\nu=1}^{k-1} a_{11}(\nu)\beta(\nu) = a_{11}^*(k-1) \tag{21}$$

and similarly that

$$a_{11}(k-1)\sum_{\nu=1}^{k-1}\beta(\nu) \geq \sum_{\nu=1}^{k-1} a_{11}(\nu)\beta(\nu) = a_{11}^*(k-1) \tag{22}$$

Now pick up a number a, between $a_{11}(1)$ and $a_{11}(k-1)$, and assume, referring to the equation system (6) and (11), that

$$a_{11}(\nu) = a, \text{ per } 1 \leq \nu \leq k-1 \tag{23}$$

Accordingly, equations (6) specialise into

$$aq_1(j) + \sum_{\nu=2}^{m+1} \alpha_{1\nu}(j)q_\nu = \tilde{\lambda}_a q_1(j); \; 1 \leq j \leq k-1 \tag{24}$$

By setting

$$\alpha_{1j}(\nu) = \beta(\nu)\alpha_{1j}^*(k-1), \text{ being } 1 \leq \nu \leq k-1, \; 2 \leq j \leq m+1 \tag{25}$$

it can be easily shown that the equations (24) and (11) are satisified.

It follows that the equation system (6) and (11) is consistent, at least when the subset of coefficients $\alpha_{1j}(\nu)$ satisfies (23).

In fact, the coefficient matrix and the right-hand side vector of the linear system satisfy, in this case, the Rouché–Capelli conditions for consistency. Now, the hypotheses of the above-mentioned theorem can be stated in terms of non-nullity of the determinants of a set of square matrices derived from the coefficient matrix and the right-hand side vector. Such determinants are obviously rational – and consequently continuous – functions of the elements of the argument matrix.

We can therefore extend our proposition about the consistency of the system in accordance with assumption (23) to a more general case. In fact it can be stated that the equation system (6) and (11) are solutions for the set of positive real numbers ϵ which satisfy the following condition

$$a-\epsilon \leq a_{11}(1) \leq \ldots \leq a_{11}(k-1)=a+\epsilon \tag{26}$$

We can, consequently, enunciate the following theorem.

Theorem 2

Given a coefficient matrix $A_\alpha^*(k-1, k)$ and a set of weights $\beta(\nu)$, satisfying condition (10), a set of coefficients $\alpha_{1j}(\nu)$ can be found so that at least one disaggregated matrix $A_\alpha(1, 2, \ldots, k)$, deriving from a given aggregated matrix $A_\alpha^*(k-1, k)$, can be obtained.

Both matrices will have the same maximal eigenvalue $\bar{\lambda}_\alpha$ and the same associated right-hand eigenvector as far as the unaggregated components are concerned.

Proof: The proof can be obtained straight away from the previous considerations. Besides, it can be noticed that the solutions $\alpha_{1j}(\nu)$ of the equation system (6) and (11) can always be assumed positive, provided that the parameter ϵ in (26) is properly chosen, as it can be easily understood on the basis of continuity arguments.

Appendix 2 The differentiation of the maximal eigenvalue and of the associated right-hand eigenvector

MARIO FALIVA

2.1 Let us consider the partitioned matrix (see section 8) omitting, in order to simplify the notation, the argument $(k-1, k)$

$$A_\alpha^* = \begin{bmatrix} a_{11}^*(k-1) & 0 & (a_1^*-\alpha)' \\ 0 & a_{11}(k) & \alpha' \\ a_1^*(k-1) & a_1(k) & A(m) \end{bmatrix} \tag{1}$$

Since A_α^* is non-negative, irreducible and viable, its maximal eigenvalue $\tilde{\lambda}_\alpha$ is a real, positive, less than one, simple root of the characteristic equation.

We need, for the analytical development of section 10, to find out a formal expression of the sensitivity of $\tilde{\lambda}_\alpha$ to variations of elements $\alpha_j (j=1, 2, ..., m)$ of the parametric vector α, which leads to the computation of the partial derivatives $\dfrac{\partial \tilde{\lambda}_\alpha}{\partial \alpha_j}$ (where $j=1, 2, ..., m$).

The characteristic equation

$$\det(A_\alpha^* - \tilde{\lambda}_\alpha I) = 0 \tag{2}$$

is the customary starting point for this computation.

Observe, first of all, that (2) implies

$$\frac{\partial \det(A_\alpha^* - \tilde{\lambda}_\alpha I)}{\partial \alpha_j} = 0 \text{ (where } j=1, 2, ..., m) \tag{3}$$

The derivative in the left-hand side of (3) may be easily computed by means of formal rules of differentiation in matrix notation, as can be found in Faliva (1975b). Rule 8 of Faliva, for composite functions differentiation, leads to the following result[1]

$$\frac{\partial \det(A_\alpha^* - \tilde{\lambda}_\alpha I)}{\partial \alpha_j} = \left\{ \text{vec} \frac{\partial \det(A_\alpha^* - \tilde{\lambda}_\alpha I)}{\partial (A_\alpha^* - \tilde{\lambda}_\alpha I)} \right\}' \cdot \left\{ I \otimes \frac{\partial (A_\alpha^* - \tilde{\lambda}_\alpha I)}{\partial \alpha_j} \right\} \cdot \text{vec } I \tag{4}$$

133

By making use of the formulae (6) and (15) of Faliva, it is easy to establish that the derivative (4) can be expressed as follows:

$$\frac{\partial \det(A_\alpha^* - \tilde{\lambda}_\alpha I)}{\partial \alpha_j} = \left\{ \text{vec}\,[(A_\alpha^* - \tilde{\lambda}_\alpha I)^+]' \right\}' \cdot$$

$$\cdot \left(I \otimes \frac{\partial A_\alpha^*}{\partial \alpha_j} \right) \cdot \text{vec}\,I - \left\{ \text{vec}\,[(A_\alpha^* - \tilde{\lambda}_\alpha I)^+]' \right\}' \cdot$$

$$\cdot \left[I \otimes \left(\frac{\partial \tilde{\lambda}_\alpha}{\partial \alpha_j} I \right) \right] \cdot \text{vec}\,I = \text{tr} \left[(A_\alpha^* - \tilde{\lambda}_\alpha I)^+ \frac{\partial A_\alpha^*}{\partial \alpha_j} \right] -$$

$$\frac{\partial \tilde{\lambda}_\alpha}{\partial \alpha_j} \cdot \text{tr}(A_\alpha^* - \tilde{\lambda}_\alpha I)^+ \tag{5}$$

where $(A_\alpha^* - \tilde{\lambda}_\alpha)^+$ denotes the adjoint matrix of $A_\alpha^* - \tilde{\lambda}_\alpha I$.

By substituting the final expression of (5) into the left-hand side of (3), it may be easily verified that the derivative of $\tilde{\lambda}_\alpha$ with respect to α_j is expressible as

$$\frac{\partial \tilde{\lambda}_\alpha}{\partial \alpha_j} = \frac{\text{tr} \left[(A_\alpha^* - \tilde{\lambda}_\alpha I)^+ \cdot \frac{\partial A_\alpha^*}{\partial \alpha_j} \right]}{\text{tr}(A_\alpha^* - \tilde{\lambda}_\alpha I)^+} \tag{6}$$

Since, as we have already observed, $\tilde{\lambda}_\alpha$ is a non-repeated root of the characteristic equation $\det(A_\alpha^* - \lambda I) = 0$, the adjoint matrix $(A_\alpha^* - \tilde{\lambda}_\alpha I)^+$ has unit rank.

From the orthogonality of $A_\alpha^* - \tilde{\lambda}_\alpha I$ and its adjoint and from the equation systems defining the right-hand and left-hand eigenvectors – denoted by q_α^* and p_α^* respectively[2] – we can argue that the adjoint matrix can be represented, in terms of the above mentioned vectors, as follows

$$(A_\alpha^* - \tilde{\lambda}_\alpha I)^+ = \mu q_\alpha^* (p_\alpha^*)' \tag{7}$$

where μ denotes an *ad hoc* scalar factor. By making use of (7) and of elementary properties of the trace operator, the derivative (6) can be written in the following form (see also Reddy (1967))

$$\frac{\partial \tilde{\lambda}_\alpha}{\partial \alpha_j} = \frac{(p_\alpha^*)' \cdot \frac{\partial A_\alpha^*}{\partial \alpha_j} \cdot q_\alpha^*}{(p_\alpha^*)' \cdot q_\alpha^*} \tag{8}$$

The result (8) can be written in a way as to provide a more straightforward economic interpretation (see section 10). For this purpose notice how

$$
\frac{\partial A^*_\alpha}{\partial \alpha_j} =
\begin{bmatrix}
\dfrac{\partial a^*_{11}(k-1)}{\partial \alpha_j} & 0 & \dfrac{\partial(a^*_1-\alpha)'}{\partial \alpha_j} \\[2ex]
0 & \dfrac{\partial a_{11}(k)}{\partial \alpha_j} & \dfrac{\partial \alpha'}{\partial \alpha_j} \\[2ex]
\dfrac{\partial a^*_1(k-1)}{\partial \alpha_j} & \dfrac{\partial a_1(k)}{\partial \alpha_j} & \dfrac{\partial A(m)}{\partial \alpha_j}
\end{bmatrix}
=
\begin{bmatrix}
0 & 0 & -e'_{j(m)} \\
0 & 0 & e'_{j(m)} \\
o & o & O
\end{bmatrix}
\tag{9}
$$

where $e_{j(m)}$ denotes the jth elementary vector (with m components).

By making use of the symbolic notation adopted for the elements of the eigenvectors p^*_α and q^*_α earlier

$$
p^*_\alpha =
\begin{bmatrix}
p^*_1(k-1) \\
p_1(k) \\
p_2 \\
\vdots \\
p_{m+1}
\end{bmatrix}
\tag{10}
$$

$$
q^*_\alpha =
\begin{bmatrix}
\bar{q}^*_1(k-1) \\
q_1(k) \\
q_2 \\
\vdots \\
q_{m+1}
\end{bmatrix}
\tag{10bis}
$$

and by substituting (9) into (8) we obtain, with simple computations, the following expression for the derivative of $\tilde{\lambda}_\alpha$ with respect to $\alpha_j (j=1, 2, \ldots m)$

$$
\frac{\partial \tilde{\lambda}_\alpha}{\partial \alpha_j} = \frac{1}{(p^*_\alpha)' \cdot q^*_\alpha} \cdot (p_1(k) - p^*_1(k-1)) \cdot q_{j+1}
\tag{11}
$$

Correspondence between (11) (see above) and (41) in section 10 is easily established by considering that, according to the previously introduced notations (see relations (33), section 8), we have

$$
\alpha_j \equiv \alpha_{1,j+1}(k), \quad (j=1, 2, \ldots, m)
\tag{12}
$$

2.2 The right-hand eigenvector q^*_α corresponding to the maximal eigenvalue $\tilde{\lambda}_\alpha$ is, by definition, the non-trivial solution of the homogeneous linear system

$$(A_\alpha^* - \tilde\lambda I) \cdot q_\alpha^* = O \tag{13}$$

Since q_α^* is determined up to a scalar multiple,[3] the value of one component – which we identify with the first element of the vector, in order to conform to section 11 – can be fixed equal to one, without loss of generality.

As a result, we obtain a normalised eigenvector which can be written in this way (compare with (50), section 11)

$$q_{(n)}^* = \begin{bmatrix} 1 \\ \tilde{\tilde{q}}_1(k) \\ \tilde{\tilde{q}}_2 \\ \vdots \\ \tilde{\tilde{q}}_{m+1} \end{bmatrix} = \begin{bmatrix} 1 \\ \tilde{\tilde{q}}_\alpha \end{bmatrix} \tag{14}$$

We intend now to find out the analytical expression for the sensitivity of the components of $\tilde{\tilde{q}}_\alpha$, defined above, to variations of the elements of the parametric vector α.

Formally the problem is that of computing the vectors of partial derivatives $\dfrac{\partial \tilde{\tilde{q}}_\alpha}{\partial \alpha_j}$, with $j = 1, 2, \ldots, m$.

For this purpose, it is convenient to refer to the relation (13), along with minor modifications made in order to tally with the normalisation rule applied to q_α^* (see formula (14)).

In this connection the coefficient matrix A_α^* can be rewritten in a partitioned form such as

$$A_\alpha^* = \begin{bmatrix} a_{11}^*(k-1) & \beta_\alpha' \\ b & B_\alpha \end{bmatrix} \tag{15}$$

where the blocks β_α, b and B_α are connected with the blocks in the right-hand side of (1) by the following relations

$$\beta_\alpha = \begin{bmatrix} 0 \\ a_1^* - \alpha \end{bmatrix} \tag{16}$$

$$b = \begin{bmatrix} 0 \\ a_1^*\ (k-1) \end{bmatrix} \tag{16bis}$$

$$B_\alpha = \begin{bmatrix} a_{11}(k) & \alpha' \\ a_1(k) & A(m) \end{bmatrix} \tag{16ter}$$

By reformulating the linear system (13) in terms of the normalised vector $q_{(n)}^*$ (see (14)) and of the right-hand side of (15), we obtain

$$\begin{bmatrix} a_{11}^*(k-1) & \beta_\alpha' \\ b & B_\alpha \end{bmatrix} \cdot \begin{bmatrix} 1 \\ \tilde{\tilde{q}}_\alpha \end{bmatrix} = \tilde{\lambda}_\alpha \cdot \begin{bmatrix} 1 \\ \tilde{\tilde{q}}_\alpha \end{bmatrix} \tag{17}$$

Simple computations enable us to realise that equation (17) can be equivalently stated in the form of the following pair of relations

$$\begin{cases} \tilde{\lambda}_\alpha = a_{11}^*(k-1) + \beta_\alpha' \tilde{\tilde{q}}_\alpha \\ (\tilde{\lambda}_\alpha I - B_\alpha) \cdot \tilde{\tilde{q}}_\alpha = b \end{cases} \tag{18}$$
$$\tag{18bis}$$

By solving (18bis) for $\tilde{\tilde{q}}_\alpha$ we get[4]

$$\tilde{\tilde{q}}_\alpha = (\tilde{\lambda}_\alpha I - B_\alpha)^{-1} \cdot b \tag{19}$$

The analytical expression of $\dfrac{\partial \tilde{\tilde{q}}_\alpha}{\partial \alpha_j}$ can, at this point, be worked out by making use of convenient formal rules of differentiation in compact form, as can be found in Faliva (1975b). Thanks to Rules 2 and 4 (formulae (16) and (18) of Faliva) the following result is obtained

$$\frac{\partial \tilde{\tilde{q}}_\alpha}{\partial \alpha_j} = -(\tilde{\lambda}_\alpha I - B_\alpha)^{-1} \cdot \frac{\partial (\tilde{\lambda}_\alpha I - B_\alpha)}{\partial \alpha_j} \cdot (\tilde{\lambda}_\alpha I - B_\alpha)^{-1} \cdot b \tag{20}$$

In addition to this it can be easily shown that

$$\frac{\partial (\tilde{\lambda}_\alpha I - B_\alpha)}{\partial \alpha_j} = \frac{\partial \tilde{\lambda}_\alpha}{\partial \alpha_j} I - \begin{bmatrix} 0 & e_{j(m)}' \\ 0 & 0 \end{bmatrix} \tag{21}$$

By combining (20) with (19) and (21), the vector of partial derivatives $\dfrac{\partial \tilde{\tilde{q}}_\alpha}{\partial \alpha_j}$ can be rewritten as follows

$$\frac{\partial \tilde{\tilde{q}}_\alpha}{\partial \alpha_j} = -(\tilde{\lambda}_\alpha I - B_\alpha)^{-1} \cdot \left\{ \frac{\partial \tilde{\lambda}_\alpha}{\partial \alpha_j} I - \begin{bmatrix} 0 & e_{j(m)}' \\ o & O \end{bmatrix} \right\} \cdot \tilde{\tilde{q}}_\alpha$$

$$= (\tilde{\lambda}_\alpha I - B_\alpha)^{-1} \cdot \left\{ \begin{bmatrix} e_{j+1(m+1)}' \\ O \end{bmatrix} - I \frac{\partial \tilde{\lambda}_\alpha}{\partial \alpha_j} \right\} \cdot \tilde{\tilde{q}}_\alpha$$

$$= (\tilde{\lambda}_\alpha I - B_\alpha)^{-1} \left(e_{1(m+1)} \tilde{\tilde{q}}_{j+1} - \tilde{\tilde{q}}_\alpha \frac{\partial \tilde{\lambda}_\alpha}{\partial \alpha_j} \right) \tag{22}$$

Hence by substituting (11) into the final expression of (22), the following result for $\dfrac{\partial \tilde{\tilde{q}}_\alpha}{\partial \alpha_j}$ is obtained, by means of simple computations

$$\frac{\partial \tilde{\tilde{q}}_\alpha}{\partial \alpha_j} = (\tilde{\lambda}_\alpha I - B_\alpha)^{-1} \left\{ e_{1(m+1)} + \tilde{\tilde{q}}_\alpha \cdot \frac{p_1^*(k-1) - p_1(k)}{(p_\alpha^*)' \cdot q_\alpha^*} \right\} \cdot \tilde{\tilde{q}}_{j+1} \tag{23}$$

Expression (23) is the fundamental result on which the discussion of section 11 is based.

Notes

1 For what concerns definitions of Kronecker product and vec and trace operators, used, in the following formulae, one can refer to Faliva (1975a).
2 Formally, the homogeneous linear systems defining the eigenvector pair q_α^* and p_α^* are given by

$$(A_\alpha^* - \tilde{\lambda}_\alpha I) q_\alpha^* = o$$
$$(p_\alpha^*)' (A_\alpha^* - \tilde{\lambda}_\alpha I) = o'$$

3 Remember that, according to our assumptions, the eigenvalue $\tilde{\lambda}_\alpha$ is a non-repeated root of the characteristic equation $\det(A_\alpha^* - \tilde{\lambda}_\alpha I) = 0$.
4 Since A_α^* is, by hypothesis, a non-negative indecomposable matrix, every eigenvalue of its principal submatrix B_α is (in modulus) smaller than $\tilde{\lambda}_\alpha$. It follows that the matrix $\tilde{\lambda}_\alpha I - B_\alpha$ is non-singular (and moreover its inverse is a strictly positive matrix).

References

Faliva, M. (1975a) 'Aspetti particolari di calcolo matriciale: operatore "vec", prodotto di Kronecker, traccia, differenziazione di semplici funzioni', *Rivista Internazionale di Scienze Sociali*, 83: 383–92.
—— (1975b) 'Alcune regole di derivazione in termini matriciali', *Statistica*, 35: 329–40.
Leontief, W. W. (1941) *The Structure of the American Economy 1919–1929*, Cambridge, Mass., Harvard University Press.
—— (1951) *The Structure of the American Economy 1919–1939*, New York, Oxford University Press, 2nd edition.
Lowe, A. (1952) 'A Structural Model of Production', *Social Research*, 19: 135–76.
—— (1995) 'Structural Analysis of Real Capital Formation', in M. Abramovitz (ed.), *Capital Formation and Economic Growth*, Princeton, NJ, Princeton University Press, pp. 581–634.
Neumann J. von (1945/6) 'A Model of General Equilibrium', *Review of Economic Studies*, 13: 1–9 (English translation from the 1937 German original).
Pasinetti L. L. (1981) *Structural Change and Economic Growth. A Theoretical Essay on the Dynamics of the Wealth of Nations*, Cambridge, Cambridge University Press.

Quadrio Curzio, A. (1967) *Rendita e distribuzione in un modello economico plurisettoriale*, Milano, Giuffré.

(1975) *Accumulazione del capitale e rendita*, Bologna, il Mulino.

(1977) 'Rendita e distribuzione del reddito, ordine di efficienza e di redditività', in L. L. Pasinetti (ed.), *Contributi alla teoria della produzione congiunta*, Bologna, il Mulino, pp. 301–27.

(1980) 'Rent, Income Distribution, Order of Efficiency and Rentability', in L. L. Pasinetti (ed.), *Essays on the Theory of Joint Production*, London, Macmillan, pp. 218–40 (English translation of the 1977 original).

(1986) 'Technological Scarcity: an Essay on Production and Structural Change', in M. Baranzini and R. Scazzieri (eds.), *Foundations of Economics. Structures of Inquiry and Economic Theory*, Oxford, Basil Blackwell, pp. 311–38.

(1987) 'Land Rent', in *The New Palgrave Dictionary: A Dictionary of Economics*, vol. III, ed. by J. Eatwell, M. Milgate and P. Newman, London, Macmillan, pp. 118–21.

Quadrio Curzio, A., Manara, C. F. and Faliva, M. (1987) 'Produzione ed efficienza con tecnologie globali', in *Economia Politica. Rivista di teoria e analisi*, 4 (1, April): 11–47.

Quadrio Curzio, A. and Pellizzari, F. (1991) 'Structural Rigidities and Dynamic Choice of Technologies', *Rivista Internazionale di Scienze Economiche e Commerciali* (6–7, June–July): 481–517.

(1996) *Risorse, Tecnologie, Rendita*, Bologna, il Mulino.

Reddy, D. C. (1967) 'Evaluation of the Sensitivity Coefficient of an Eigenvalue', IEEE Transactions on Automatic Control, p. 79.

Ricardo, D. (1817–21) *On the Principles of Political Economy and Taxation*, London, Murray. (Also published as vol. I of *The Works and Correspondence of David Ricardo*, ed. P. Sraffa with the collaboration of M. H. Dobb, Cambridge, Cambridge University Press.)

Sraffa, P. (1960) *Production of Commodities by Means of Commodities*, Cambridge, Cambridge University Press.

4 Efficient traverses and bottlenecks: a structural approach*

CHRISTIAN GEHRKE AND HARALD HAGEMANN

1 Introduction

Within the analysis of multisectoral growth models emphasis has in the last two decades shifted to problems of structural change and technological unemployment. The analysis of an economy which originally has been in a steady-state equilibrium but which was disturbed by a change in one of the exogenous determinants of growth, such as technical progress, the supply of labour or natural resources, is one of the most challenging problems in economics. The investigation of the macroeconomic consequences of such disturbances and of the conditions that have to be fulfilled in order to bring the economy back to an equilibrium growth path, is at the centre of *traverse analysis*, which 'is the easiest part of skiing, but the hardest part of economics'.[1] Although traverse analysis is linked with equilibrium growth which it takes as a starting point, in contrast to long-run balanced growth analysis it is a short- or medium-run analysis which marks an important step forward in coping with the dynamic nature of the problems and thus rejuvenating growth theory by liberating it from the overall preoccupation with steady-state growth paths. Pioneers in the field of traverse analysis are Adolph Lowe (1976) and John Hicks (1965, 1973) who in chapter 16 of his *Capital and Growth* was the first to formally define a traverse.

Suppose that we have an economy which has in the past been in equilibrium in one set of conditions; and that then, at time 0, a new set of conditions is imposed; is it possible (or how is it possible) for the economy to get into the new equilibrium, which is appropriate to the new conditions? We do not greatly diminish the generality of our study of disequilibrium if we regard it in this way, as a *Traverse* from one path to another.[2]

The decisive problem that the economy faces after a new set of conditions is imposed is the inappropriateness of its capital stock. The necessary adjustment path requires both time and costs, i.e., in traverse analysis historical and no longer logical time matters. Hicks later became dissatisfied with the deficient modelling of time in his 'embryonic theory of traverse'[3] of the 1965 vintage and therefore in *Capital and Time* (1973) switched from a two-sectoral fixed-coefficient model to a neo-Austrian model of production in which a stream of labour inputs is transformed into a stream of consumption goods.

Lowe, on the other hand, not only explicitly adopted Hicks's 'traverse' term[4] but also adhered to a model with a circular flow, i.e., an inter-industry model instead of a vertically integrated model. However, the abandonment of the single capital good assumption in Lowe's tripartite model constitutes an important difference to the two-sectoral Hicksian model, since it enables us to take into account the structural dynamics within the group of investment sectors itself.[5] This subdivision of the equipment-goods group becomes relevant for the investigation of the structural conditions for steady growth and especially for the analysis of traverse processes when a restructuring of the economy has to take place. When the problem of structural change arises, the importance of the industrial structure and physical *bottlenecks* in production immediately comes into focus. The existence of an inherited stock of fixed capital goods implies a structural barrier to short-term responses when changes in the growth rate occur. The dynamic traverse from one steady growth path to another necessarily involves a change in the whole quantity structure of the economy, especially the rebuilding of the capital stock. Traverse analysis thus illuminates

the key position that 'real capital' holds in the growth of an industrial economy. It is this factor that, at all levels of industrialization, is responsible for the major bottlenecks when the rate of growth rises, and for waste of available inputs when it falls. For this reason our investigation will center on the *formation, application, and liquidation of real capital.*[6]

Lowe's structural analysis of traverse processes is concerned with the structural conditions required to achieve the macrogoal of balanced growth in the most efficient way. Far more emphasis is put on the 'ultimate' steady state to which the economic system is to move than in neo-Austrian traverse analysis, in which Hicks concentrates on the short- and medium-run effects of an innovation – the 'early phase' – and plays down the problem of convergence which comes up in the late phase. This points to an important methodological difference. Lowe makes it clear from the outset that his structural theory of economic growth is not designed to describe the actual dynamics of economic systems: 'I strongly believe that the Mecca of the modern growth theorist does not lie where prevailing opinion looks for it; namely, in "positive" analysis. . . . we shall base our trust in *prescriptive* rather than *descriptive* analysis.' But Lowe's specific methodological approach, which he termed '*instrumental analysis*',[8] differs considerably not only from positive economics but also from what is conventionally taken to be implied by prescriptive analysis, namely a normative approach to economic theory. Whereas the conventional procedure of the hypothetico-deductive method predicts an unknown terminal state from the knowledge of an initial state and a behavioural law which is supposed to describe the reactions of the microunits involved, contrariwise the heuristic procedure of Lowe's instrumental analysis treats not only the initial state of the economy but also the terminal state as known – as a stipulated goal like balanced growth and full resource utilisation. According to Lowe, economists must face the fact that the macroeconomic goals are set in the democratic process, i.e., accept the stipulated goals as data. What is unknown and thus the object of economic analysis are the motions of the structural elements which will transform the initial state into the stipulated terminal state. This includes the derivation of a feasible adjustment path based on structural requirements as the important first step; this, however, has to be supplemented by what Lowe termed *force analysis*, i.e., by establishing patterns of microbehaviour, motivations and a state of the environment (including, though not necessarily, measures of economic policy) which induce suitable reactions on the side of the microunits which will set the economy on a goal-adequate traverse. The regressive inference of Lowe's instrumental analysis is, then, 'a generalization of Keynes's concern with the requirements for the attainment of full employment; it . . . is . . . a procedure by which suitable means are derived from given ends'.[9] It is this *inversion of the problem* which gives the macrogoal the strategic role in Lowe's instrumental analysis, thus essentially distinguishing it from positive analysis of traditional economics.

The purpose of the present chapter is to evaluate Lowe's contribution to the analysis of traverse processes. This will be done by scrutinising some objections that have been raised against Lowe's analysis and by contrasting Lowe's instrumental approach with the alternative, positive approach to traverse analysis proposed by J. Hicks. We shall argue that both Lowe's representation of the production system and his method of analysis are highly relevant to the further elaboration of a theory of traverse processes.

The structure of the chapter is as follows. In section 2 we shall delineate the characteristic features of Lowe's structural model of production and briefly examine the steady-state properties of his model. Section 3 contains a summary of Lowe's instrumental analysis of traverse processes initiated by changes in the rate of growth of labour supply and by non-neutral process innovations. In the final section we shall first discuss some methodological problems associated with a descriptive theory of traverse processes and then examine some objections that have been raised against Lowe's analysis.

2 Lowe's structural model of production

For an analysis of the implications of a change in the rates of expansion or contraction in the overall level of activity or of a change in the rate of change of a given 'impulse', such as technical progress, the underlying structure of the productive system is a decisive factor. The first relevant question concerns the degree of aggregation. By focusing exclusively on Keynesian aggregates, one would fail to take into account the phys-ical–technical relations among the main sectors of an industrial system. On the other hand, it would be extremely difficult to trace the traverse for a highly disaggregated input–output model of the Leontief type. 'Thus the task consists in choosing a level of aggregation between those chosen by Keynes and Leontief – high enough to permit analytical manipulation of complex dynamic processes, low enough to reflect those physical proper-ties of an industrial market which affect its general stability.'[10]

Lowe developed the structural model of production which he later used for his traverse analysis in the two papers 'A Structural Model of Production' (1952) and 'Structural Analysis of Real Capital Formation' (1955).[11] However, the central idea of his model dates far back to the research achievements of the Kiel school which in the second half of the Weimar Republic attempted to develop a theory of accumulation, techni-cal progress and structural change.[12] The major research interest of the Kiel group consisted in the construction of a theoretical model of cyclical growth in which the 'short-run' and the 'long run' were not artificially separated. In contrast to monetary explanations of the business cycle, technical progress was recognised as the central determinant of the cycle as well as of the long-run growth trend.[13] In order to develop a frame of refer-ence for these studies, attention of the Kiel group was directed towards the two most important alternative ways of conceiving the productive system, the schemes of the circular flow in Böhm-Bawerk and Marx. It was Lowe's closest collaborator, Fritz Burchardt, who in 1931/2 set out to compare, contrast and combine these schemes and thus undertook the first synthesis of the sector model and the stage model.[14] The central ideas of Burchardt's two essays reappear in the 'schematic representation of industrial produc-tion' (see figure 4.1) which underlies Lowe's investigation of traverse pro-cesses. Starting from Marx's reproduction schema, both Lowe and Burchardt emphasised the necessity of one important modification, namely the splitting up of the capital-goods sector into two parts. Thus, in Lowe's model one capital-goods sector produces the equipment for the

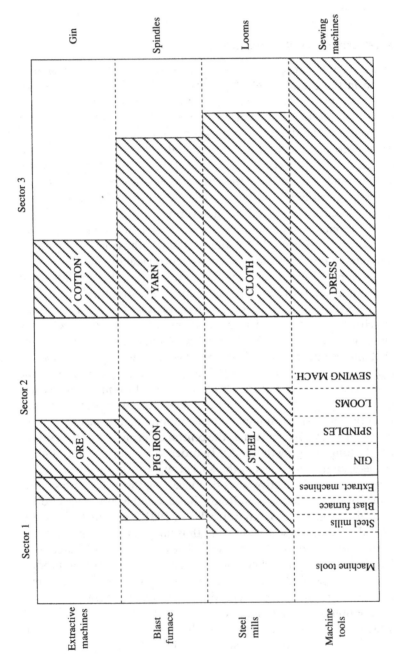

Figure 4.1

replacement and expansion of both equipment-goods sectors and the other produces the equipment for the consumer-goods sector.

Lowe's schema of industrial production, however, comprises not only three sectors but also four successive stages within each sector that lead up to the finished goods. Thus Lowe's category of equipment-goods industries includes not only the production of the final fixed capital goods but also the preceding stages of mining and the production of pig iron and steel. Similarly, the consumer-goods industries include not only the making of the finished dress ready for sale to the individual consumer but also the preceding stages of cultivating cotton, spinning yarn and weaving clothes. The fact that all sectors are divided into stages representing the successive maturing of natural resources into final goods with the help of labour and fixed capital goods brings into light the often neglected role of *working capital* goods as goods in process. However, one important point should not be overlooked. Whereas the output of working capital or intermediate goods of the preceding stage serves as an input in the subsequent stage from the second stage onwards, it is already the very first stage in which fixed capital goods are to be applied in the production process. The lack of attention paid to the circular flows, especially the tracing back of all finished goods to nothing but labour and natural resources, i.e., the treatment of fixed capital goods as the output of some intermediate stages in the vertical model, was an essential critique raised by Burchardt against Böhm-Bawerk's Austrian concept of the structure of production. It should also be noted that the equipment-goods *industries* always belong to both sectors 1 and 2. The division into *sectors* is a purely analytical device; the 'fictitious' sectors are not to be identified with concrete industries like coal mining or chemical production. In contrast to Marx's analysis, which was essentially related to *flows*, Lowe explicitly added the appropriate *stocks* – like blast furnaces and spindles at stage 2 – which play a significant role when accumulation and structural change are to be analysed.

A central idea this schema is meant to depict is the perception that there exists a group of fixed capital goods classified as 'machine tools' which have the capacity for physical self-reproduction and therefore hold the strategic position in any industrial system similar to seed corn in agricultural production. This idea carries over to the three-sectoral model, which can be constructed from the complete schema by consolidating the various stage inputs and outputs of the three sectors in terms of certain aggregates of finished goods. *Machine tools*, the output of sector 1, can be maintained and increased only with the help of a circular process in which these machine tools also act as inputs. Machine tools are directly used in sectors 1 and 2 and indirectly in sector 3 because the secondary equipment goods – the output of sector 2 – are used as inputs only in sector 3, thus implying that the capital stock in the consumer-goods sector is specific and not transferable to other sectors. According to Sraffian terminology, sector 1 therefore represents the 'basic sector'. The production of machine tools is the bottleneck which any process of accelerated accumulation must overcome. This can be seen when we look at the methods of production as represented in the A matrix of machine-input coefficients a_{ji} and the l vector of direct labour coefficients l_i.[15]

$$A = \begin{bmatrix} a_{11} & 0 & 0 \\ a_{12} & 0 & 0 \\ 0 & a_{23} & 0 \end{bmatrix} \quad l = \begin{bmatrix} l_1 \\ l_2 \\ l_3 \end{bmatrix}$$

It is a characteristic feature of the Lowe model that there exists a definite hierarchy of sectors, from 1 via 2 to 3, which implies a unique intertemporal complementarity when processes of structural change are taking place. Even if we disregard the stages aspect and only look at the three vertically integrated sectors, there still remains a touch of Austrian flavour which makes possible the analysis of adjustment processes in historical time.

Lowe's main concern is with the different kinds of disequilibria that arise under the impact of changes in major growth stimuli and with the traverses an economy must follow in order to leave behind these disequilibria. Since he generally stipulates '*dynamic equilibrium* or *steady growth* as both the initial and the terminal state of the system',[16] we start with the discussion of different growth equilibria, i.e., compare economies which are in long-run equilibrium but differ in the growth or distribution patterns, as a necessary prelude for the analysis of traverse, i.e., the path that connects two dynamic equilibria associated with different rates of growth. The comparison shows the terminal position from a structural point of view. In competitive equilibrium with continuous, full and efficient utilisation of the available inputs, we get the following system of *quantity equations*

$$a_{11}(g+d)f_1 + a_{12}(g+d)f_2 = f_1$$

$$a_{23}c = f_2$$

$$l_1(g+d)f_1 + l_2(g+d)f_2 + l_3c = 1 \tag{1}$$

Making the usual assumption that the technical parameters – including the uniform rate of depreciation d – are given, the quantity system provides us with three equations in the four variables c, g, f_1 and f_2, where c denotes consumption per unit of total employment, g the rate of growth and f_j the input of fixed capital of type j per unit of total employment.

Thus we can express all the other quantity variables as functions of g, e.g., for economies which use the same technique but operate under a different growth rate we get the monotonically inverse *consumption-growth curve*

$$c=\frac{1-a_{11}(g+d)}{l_3+(a_{23}l_2-a_{11}l_3)(g+d)+a_{23}(a_{12}l_1-a_{11}l_2)(g+d)^2}$$

In a similar way, we can calculate a whole set of quantity relations.[17] Any path of balanced growth requires certain proportions in the allocation of resources and composition of production between the three sectors. The higher the growth rate of an economy, the higher the share of its labour force employed in the production of machine tools, the higher the percentage of its machines used in sector 1 rather than in sector 2, etc.

Competitive equilibrium in a capitalist economy also implies that the price of a unit of output must cover its cost of production including 'normal' profits at a uniform rate. Thus we have

$$(r+d)Ap+wl=p$$

or, by choosing the consumer good as the *numéraire*, the following system of *price equations*

$$a_{11}(r+d)p_1+l_1w=p_1$$
$$a_{12}(r+d)p_1+l_2w=p_2$$
$$a_{23}(r+d)p_2+l_3w=1 \tag{2}$$

Note that the price system provides us with three equations in four variables: w, r, p_1 and p_2, where the price of machines and the price of secondary equipment goods, p_1 and p_2, are relative prices. Like the wage rate w (which is assumed to be paid *ex post*) these prices are expressed in units of the consumer good. The degree of freedom can be removed by fixing one variable. Expressing all the other price variables as functions of r, we get a set of equations for economies which use the same technique but operate under a different rate of profit (wage rate). With only one type of consumer good in the Lowe model, the *wage–profit curve* turns out to be the dual of the consumption-growth curve.

As is well known, some assumption about *saving* provides a direct link between capital accumulation and income distribution, i.e., between the quantity system and the price system. The postulation of a saving function in connection with the Keynesian equilibrium condition of saving–investment equality constitutes a relationship between the rate of profit and the growth rate. Whereas with a general Kaldorian saving function this r–g relationship can be very complex and depend on the distribution of income as well as on technology, for purposes of traverse analysis Lowe makes the simplifying assumption that 'dynamic equilibrum' is bound up with the 'golden rule of accumulation',[18] i.e., the rate of profit and the growth rate coincide. The remaining degree of freedom is removed in the Lowe model through the exogenously given natural rate of growth.

3 Instrumental analysis of traverse processes

The constitutive element of Lowe's instrumental analysis is the stipulated terminal state of the economic system. Lowe generally takes the *'continuous, full, and efficient utilization* of the available inputs' (Lowe, 1976, p. 21) as being the stipulated macrogoal to be accomplished and therefore considers states of stationary or dynamic equilibrium – steady-state growth paths, on which the economic system expands in accordance with the exogenously given natural rate of growth – as being the aspired terminal states of the system.[19] In general, the natural rate of growth consists of two components, the rate of growth of labour supply and the rate of growth of productivity. Accordingly, we shall be concerned, first, with the traverse that leads from an initial dynamic equilibrium to a terminal dynamic equilibrium under the impact of a once-and-for-all rise in the exogenously given rate of growth of labour supply and, second, with the traverses caused by non-neutral process innovations.

3.1 Adjustment to changes in the rate of growth: structural analysis

When the economic system starts off from a state of full-capacity utilisation, it is clear that the employment of an additional influx of labour, given the assumption of short-run rigidity in the technical coefficients, presupposes the formation of additional real capital. This is a time-consuming and, as we shall see, rather complex process, so that in Lowe's model a full-employment traverse path is generally impossible.

Since Lowe has taken the terminal goal to be accomplished to be the 'continuous, full utilisation of all productive resources', it is close at hand to assume that the additional labour force should be equipped with plant and equipment as soon as possible. Accordingly, Lowe chooses the *'maximum speed of adjustment constrained by the condition that malinvestment must be avoided'* (Lowe, 1976, p. 124) as a suitable 'path criterion' for the determination of efficient structural adjustment paths.[20] However, although Lowe's traverse analysis has some similarities with the solution of a constrained maximisation problem, it should not be interpreted as being analogous. We shall come back to this below. In the

Lowe model an efficient structural adjustment path to a higher rate of growth of labour supply can be envisaged as a sequence of four successive phases:

Phase of partial capacity liberation in sector 2

Although a continuous additional supply of labour calls for a rise in the system's overall growth rate, the three sectors cannot be expanded simultaneously at a uniform rate. The expansion of consumption-goods output in sector 3 unequivocally requires additional equipment which cannot be supplied unless sector 2 has increased its own stock of machines. Such an increase must be obtained from the machine-producing sector, i.e., the key to a higher overall growth rate lies in increasing the shares of the basic sector 1. The same logic which requires that the system as a whole first has to change inputs before it can change outputs makes such an increase dependent on the prior expansion of the capital stock in sector 1. The decisive question therefore is: by what procedure can the capital stock of the industries in sector 1 be expanded above the net investment and replacement demand in the old growth equilibrium? The fixed capital of the industries in sector 1 is provided by the 'machine tools' industry, and since the fixed capital of the industries which supply the 'machine tools' industry with working capital goods is fully utilised in the old growth equilibrium and can be augmented only with the help of additional 'machine tools', a vicious circle seems to emerge. Here a characteristic property of the Lowe model comes into play: the twofold serviceability of 'machine tools', which can either be used, in sector 1, in the production of equipment goods for the industries of the equipment-goods sectors 1 and 2 or, in sector 2, in the production of equipment goods for the industries of the consumer-goods sector 3. The necessary horizontal 'transfer' of machine tools from sector 2 to sector 1 means that simultaneously part of the stocks of fixed and circulating capital that are employed in the industries of the stages preceding the machine tools industry is 'transferred' from sector 2 to 1. Since this 'transfer' of machine tools must lead to a reduction in the production of equipment goods for the consumer-goods industries compared with its previous level, we arrive at the somewhat paradoxical result that, in order ultimately to increase the growth rate of consumption output, at first a temporary fall in this growth rate is necessary.

The analysis bears a close resemblance to Fel'dman's notion that investment priority for the capital-goods sector is a precondition for attaining a higher growth rate of national income, developed during the Soviet industrialisation debate in the late twenties.[21] The main lesson to be learnt is that the capacity of the machine tools sector is the crucial bottleneck which limits the rate of growth in a closed economy, in which the insufficient domestic output of machine tools cannot be supplemented with imports.

Structural incapacity to supply enough capital goods will prevent a rise in the saving ratio from being fully transformed into the desired level of investment. But it has to be taken into account that a one-sided preoccupation with this 'Fel'dman constraint' on the investment capacity size may bring the 'Preobrazhenski constraint' on the consumption side into action. If the initial capacity of the capital goods industry is just sufficient to replace the worn-out machines, growth can only take place as a result of a temporary reduction in the output of consumer goods which may be impossible for subsistence reasons. In this case a *circulus vitiosus* will emerge.[22]

This points towards the fact that there can exist harder or softer variants of a temporary reduction in consumption, e.g., a fall in the *absolute* level or a *relative* reduction, i.e., a fall in the rate of growth of consumer-goods output. If Lowe's traverse analysis were interpreted as a constrained maximisation problem, a predetermined downwards barrier on consumption (per unit of total employment) would have to be introduced into the analysis from the outset. Yet in Lowe's instrumental approach this downwards barrier must emerge as the result of a collective decision made in the course of the adjustment process; i.e., it cannot be specified *ad hoc*. As has been said before, Lowe's instrumental analysis is a heuristic procedure in which ends and means have continuously to be adapted. For expositional purposes Lowe regards a zero rate of growth as the downwards barrier in his calculations.[23]

Phase of self-augmentation of machine tools

Lowe's path criterion of maximum speed of adjustment requires that the phase of partial capacity liberation, in which sector 1 is expanded at the expense of sector 2, is followed by a second phase, in which all savings are invested in sector 1, up to the 'point of maximum expansion from within', where the terminally required additions to the capital stock in sector 1 have been accomplished. Taking explicitly into consideration the stage aspect of Lowe's industrial scheme of production, it is clear that this self-augmentation must follow a predetermined sequence and start in the earliest stage. It should be stressed that only after the shift of the liberated fixed and working capital goods of all stages of sector 2 to sector 1 has taken place, and the necessary addition to the stock of fixed capital in the earliest stage has been built up, can the process of genuine self-augmentation in a steady interplay with the expansion of the corresponding working capital goods occur.[24]

Phase of adjustment of the capital stock in sectors 2 and 3

The third phase of the traverse is characterised by the adjustment of the capital stock of the industries in sector 2 to the higher rate of growth, i.e., after having reached its new required level the machine-tools industry will devote its net output to the building up of the capital stock of the intermediate sector's industries. Of course, the adjustment requirements include an analogous expansion of the stock of working capital in this sector.

Adjustment of consumer-goods output

Adjustment will come to an end and the traverse will be completed, when the enlarged output of sector 2 is finally applied in sector 3 for the expansion of consumer-goods output. When the terminal equilibrium path has been reached, all sectors will again expand at the same rate – the new and higher rate of growth of the labour force.

One might be tempted to suspect that it is Lowe's assumption of rigidly fixed technical coefficients that leads to this rather complex adjustment pattern and that acknowledging the possibility of some degree of variability in input proportions will make a smooth adjustment possible. Yet although Lowe does not deny the (empirical) possibility of a short-period variability in the capital–labour ratio, he immediately dismisses what is the centrepiece of Wicksell's[25] 'solution' to Ricardo's machinery problem, namely a change of factor input proportions in response to a change in relative factor prices, by arguing that 'such variations of the capital–labour ratio are of a long-period nature insofar as they require the previous formation or transformation of real capital' (Lowe, 1976, p. 115).[26] What is at stake is variability with regard to the existing capital stock in its given form and here Lowe sees 'at least three instances in which considerable variability seems to prevail: underutilization of the available capital stock; a margin between the optimum and the maximum utilization of the initially given equipment; and the working of this equipment over more than one shift'.[27] However, Lowe's structural analysis of traverse paths to a higher rate of growth, on which one of the latter two options for temporary overutilisation of equipment is adopted (see Lowe, 1976, chapter 13), leads him to the conclusion that, although initially temporary additions to the aggregate employment opportunities of the system will be provided, there must ultimately be a phase of new capital formation followed by a phase of reductions in per-capita consumption.[28] Such traverses can therefore be considered as an alternative to the previous scenario on which the succession of phases is reversed, but on which nevertheless each of the four phases described before must inevitably occur.

3.2 Adjustment to different types of technological change: structural analysis

Let us now turn to Lowe's analysis of traverse processes caused by the introduction of non-neutral process innovations. Lowe regards technological change as the 'true stimulus of economic growth' and identifies technological change with process innovations, because of the 'practical reason' that 'product-innovation has so far proved refractory to economic analysis' (Lowe, 1976, p. 236). Like Hicks, Lowe distinguishes between the short-run and the long-run effects of an innovation and shows that the employment effects depend heavily on investment behaviour during the transitional disequilibria. Both authors take as their starting point Ricardo's famous investigation 'On Machinery', which according to Sraffa (1951, p. lvii) marks 'the most revolutionary change' in the third edition of Ricardo's *Principles*.[29] But whereas Hicks mainly investigates the circumstances under which *displacement* of labour as a consequence of the introduction of (new) machinery will manifest itself,[30] Lowe centres his analysis on the determination of the (structural and motorial) requirements for the *compensation* of technological unemployment. According to him, the

question is neither whether, as a rule, nonneutral innovations initially create unemployment (they do) nor whether, given sufficient time, compensation is possible (it certainly is). The question is whether a free market is endowed with a *systematic mechanism that assures compensation within the Marshallian short period*, thus precluding any secondary distortions that could upset dynamic equilibrium.[31]

It should be noticed from the outset that Lowe does not explicitly consider the time phase, in which the transformation of the productive capacity, i.e., the building and embodiment of new capital goods, takes place. The traverse analysis is thus confined to the study of labour- and/or capital-displacing process innovations and the structural adjustments required for compensation, i.e., for achieving the macrogoal of full-employment growth. Thus the starting point of his traverse analysis of a *pure labour-displacing innovation* is a state of the system in which 'a capital stock equal to the original one in terms of wage units can now produce the original output with less labour input, because either the *given* physical stock is more efficiently organized or a new more efficient stock *was built* after the original stock was fully depreciated' (Lowe, 1976, p. 256, emphases added).[32]

Lowe stresses the industry-specific nature of most technical progress and starts with the discussion of a *pure labour-displacing innovation* introduced in some industry in the consumer-goods sector 3. This is the clearest case to study both the initial impact and the structural adjustment processes required for compensation, because it is the only case without additional complications arising from the secondary effects of innovations occurring in other sectors. The traverse analysis starts with the hypothesis that some pioneering firms in sector 3 have introduced an innovation that allows the production of the same output quantity as before with less labour input. This pure reduction of the coefficient l_3, which is equivalent to an increase in labour productivity, implies a displacement of workers as long as output does not increase with productivity. Thus the starting point of Lowe's traverse analysis is a state of the system in which, 'after the displacement of labour has occurred, the system as a whole, excluding the displaced, is again in equilibrium' (Lowe, 1976, p. 257 n.5). The necessary precondition for a successful compensation of the initial temporary unemployment is a process of additional capital formation. Structural analysis reveals the close analogy between a successful and rapid compensation process of technological unemployment in the case of a pure labour-displacing innovation in sector 3 and an efficient traverse to a higher growth rate of labour supply. The reabsorption of the workers displaced in sector 3 can proceed only to the extent to which net investment takes place, which implies that some workers are transferred to sectors 1 and 2, first for the construction of additional capital goods and later on for their replacement. On the assumption that during the first phase of the traverse the price of the consumption goods remains constant, the gains of the productivity increase are distributed to the innovating firms as 'extra profits', the immediate reinvestment of which is the necessary precondition for successful compensation.[33]

What difference does it make if a pure labour-displacing innovation is introduced in some industry producing secondary equipment instead of an industry producing a final consumption good, i.e., in an industry of sector 2 instead of one of sector 3? The major modification consists in the secondary effect of the innovation on the prices and output of the consumption-goods sector, which uses the output of sector 2 as an input. Therefore in the final equilibrium not only the price of the secondary equipment good but also that of the consumption good will be lower than in the initial steady state. If a pure labour-displacing innovation occurs in sector 1, the secondary effect affects the entire system, because such an improvement in the production of primary machines reduces prices of equipment inputs in both equipment-goods sectors. But in both cases of a pure labour-displacing innovation introduced in one of the two equipment-goods sectors, compensation for displaced labour is, just as in the case of an introduction in the consumer-goods sector, conditional on the formation of additional real capital. But since the elasticities of demand for secondary equipment and, more indirectly, also for primary equipment in the long run depend on the elasticity of final demand for consumption goods, compensation also depends on the latter, after the competitive generalisation of technical progress, a process in which the technological profits and thus the funds for the financing of net investment gradually disappear, i.e., the gains of productivity increases are transferred to the buyers of cheapened output.

Contrary to the case of a pure labour-displacing innovation, the introduction of a *pure capital-displacing innovation* in the consumption-goods sector has secondary effects for the two other sectors. Since real capital, in contrast with labour, is not only an input but also an output, a decrease of the coefficient a_{23} is bound to reduce output as well as capital input in both equipment-goods sectors. In a fixed-coefficient model of the Lowe type, a capital-displacing innovation in the production of consumption goods thus creates a compensation problem for *indirectly displaced labour* in sectors 1 and 2. In the case of a capital-displacing innovation introduced in sector 2, this secondary labour-displacement effect would be limited to sector 1, and it would be completely absent in the case of a capital-displacing innovation occurring in sector 1. But also in the latter case some displacement of labour is inevitable, since a decrease in the capital-input requirement in the production of primary equipment (a decrease in a_{11}) will (initially) reduce the output of primary equipment.

The study of pure labour-displacing and pure capital-displacing innovations supplies us with the basic structural adjustment patterns, from which the more complex and (empirically) more important cases of *combined changes in labour- and capital-input requirements* per unit of output can be derived. The (historically) most important of these cases is represented by a *capital-attracting and labour-displacing innovation*.[34] As far as the structural adjustment requirements are concerned, this case presents the same problems as have been discussed for pure labour-displacing innovations, the fundamental difference being that its capital-attracting nature requires an initial process of additional net capital formation combined with the gradual transformation of the original capital stock, before the innovational impact can even get under way.[35]

3.3 Force analysis as a necessary complement to structural analysis

Our brief sketch of Lowe's structural analysis of traverse processes shows that he is not concerned with the descriptive analysis of the changes and movements in the structural relations, as they occur in actual economic systems in historical time, but with establishing the structural conditions required to achieve a stipulated macrogoal in the most efficient way. Yet the determination of feasible adjustment paths based on structural requirements is only the necessary first step in Lowe's instrumental approach to political economics. It has to be supplemented by establishing behavioural and motivational patterns, which induce decisions on (sectoral and aggregate) savings and investments that will set the economy on these goal-adequate traverses. This is the task of force analysis, in which the social relations in the economic system under investigation have to be taken into account, since these decision processes are clearly organised in different ways in free-market and in collectivist systems.

Force analysis is especially relevant for the analysis of adjustment processes in free-market systems and reveals the *crucial role of expectations* and the significance of a functioning price mechanism. During the traverse disequilibrium manifests itself also in price changes and a divergence of sectoral profit rates, which acts as a strong incentive for the whole adjustment process taking place. Nevertheless a functioning price mechanism alone is not sufficient and must be supplemented by other guides for long-term decisions.[36] This can be illustrated by looking back at the first two phases of the traverse to a higher growth rate of labour supply. Partial capacity liberation in sector 2 requires a fall in aggregate demand for consumption goods. According to Lowe, the mechanism by which this is achieved in a free-market economy is 'involuntary savings', i.e., because an increase in labour supply leads to a reduction of the wage rate, it is workers' consumption that is reduced.[37] An efficient structural adjustment path requires that simultaneously with the contraction of output in the consumer-goods sector positive investment decisions in sector 1 have to be realised. What are the motorial conditions for these decisions to be formed, in view of the fact that primary equipment serves indirectly as an input into the production of consumption goods? Obviously the investment of all profit incomes in sector 1 presupposes investors' anticipation of a long-run increase in demand for consumer goods (and thereby via secondary equipment also for primary equipment) despite the current demand reduction and price decline, i.e., *negative elasticities* of both quantity and price expectations. Since it is probable that the expectations which are *required* to assure positive investment decisions differ from those which are *likely* to be formed in the prevailing situation, it will be the function of public controls to transform actual behaviour into required, goal-adequate behaviour.

As far as the structural processes are concerned, the compensation process for technological unemployment arising from pure labour-displacing innovations introduced in the consumption-goods sector resembles the adjustment pattern of the traverse to a higher rate of growth of labour supply. Thus from a structural point of view it is irrelevant whether the labour increment originates outside or inside the system. Things look quite different concerning force analysis, since in the former case the technologically induced profits of the innovating firms provide an alternative source of investment funds besides the decreasing wages emerging from excess supply in the labour market. Because Lowe regards the source of these funds, the extra profits of the innovators, as being made at the expense of the former wages of the displaced workers, he again speaks of 'involuntary savings'. It is the vanishing of the displaced workers' demand for consumer goods that liberates part of the stock of equipment goods for self-augmentation of the system's capital stock. Considering the at least temporary competitive superiority of the pioneering firms, investors' risks are much lower than in the case of an additional influx of labour, especially since their lower costs of production enable them to increase their market share by lowering prices, thereby transferring the compensation problem to the non-pioneering firms.

4 Lowe's contribution to the analysis of traverse processes: an evaluation

To focus more clearly on the significance of Lowe's *methodological approach* it might be useful to give a brief account of the most common alternative approach that has been applied in the analysis of traverse processes. This method was first set out by J. Hicks in his *Capital and Time* (1973) and has subsequently been used by various authors.[38] The Hicksian traverse analysis is based on a neo-Austrian, vertically integrated representation of the productive system,[39] a significant property of which is that the intertemporal complementarities in the productive process are put into sharp focus. This property of the neo-Austrian approach makes possible, according to Hicks and his followers, the *descriptive* analysis of the evolution of an economic system outside of steady-state equilibrium. Starting from a long-run equilibrium path which is disturbed by the introduction of some specified process innovation, two different traverse paths, considered as sequences of temporary equilibria, are investigated. Given some behavioural assumptions, the 'rate of start of new processes' can be determined endogenously, when either the real wage rate ('fixwage-path') or the employment ('full-employment path') is treated as exogenously given *and* when the system is assumed to function at 'full performance'.

It is the latter assumption which causes difficulties for the Hicksian methodology. Except for the case of very restrictive assumptions on technology (the so-called 'standard case'), the 'full-performance condition' can give rise to negative solutions for the rate of starts of new processes during the 'early phase' of the traverse, signalling the emergence of an incompatibility between the supply with output goods and the input requirements of the elementary processes that have been started earlier and are still operative. It cannot be denied that such phenomena, which have properly been termed 'Hayek-effects', can actually occur and may even be of considerable importance in the explanation of slack capacity. However, from a methodological point of view the emergence of these phenomena gives rise to a true disequilibrium situation, implying that the Hicksian methodology of treating the traverse as a sequence of temporary equilibria becomes an insufficient tool for a descriptive theory of non-steady-state growth paths.[40]

Another objection against the Hicksian methodology arises from the fact that the convergence of the traverse paths to the steady-state equilibrium compatible with the new technique can be assured only under very special conditions.[41] According to Hicks[42] the convergence problem can be considered to be of minor importance only, as various kinds of new phenomena would have occurred (a second change in technique for example) before the economy could, at best, asymptotically reach the steady-state equilibrium compatible with the first change in technique. While this argument is plausible with regard to 'real' growth processes taking place in 'real' economic systems, it is problematical from a methodological point of view. In his investigation of traverse processes Hicks uses a steady-state growth path as a starting point (and as a reference path). This, however, logically requires that steady-state paths can be shown to exhibit sufficient stability, i.e., that convergence of traverse paths to a steady-state equilibrium can be assured.

The outstanding feature of Lowe's *instrumental approach* to the analysis of traverse processes is that it enables him to point out possible factors that might lead to malfunctioning in free-market economies facing structural adjustment processes. The fundamental source of these adjustment problems is identified by Lowe in the existence of *physico-technical bottlenecks* that emerge during processes of restructuring the economic system, that is, during processes of formation or liquidation of real capital. Since real capital is itself an element of a circular production process, its augmentation is constrained by the volume and structure of the preexisting real capital stock and therefore can only be accomplished by conversions in the economy's productive structure, making necessary a temporary contraction of output in the consumption-goods industries. Since these physico-technical bottlenecks preclude a transition path on which the resources of the economic system can be continuously fully utilised, the speed of the adjustment process becomes a meaningful criterion for the selection of *efficient traverse paths*. Full employment throughout the traverse path is nearly always precluded in Lowe's model, however flexible the real wage may be. Contrary to the Hicksian traverse model, in which the 'bottleneck'

for the full employment of the available work force in any period is constituted by the 'wage-fund', so that it can be overcome by simply reducing the
real wage, in Lowe's model temporary unemployment is unavoidable,
because any attempt to rapid expansion is constrained by the existing
stock of real capital. Lowe's structural analysis then shows the successive
stages through which the economic system must pass in order to reach the
aspired macrogoal of steady growth in the most efficient way.[43]

The identification of these physico-technical bottlenecks and of their
significance during processes of restructuring the economic system is due
to Lowe's production schema, which combines elements of flexibility and
of rigidity in the productive structure. That both these elements should be
given proper consideration in an analysis of the dynamics of production
systems was already pointed out by Burchardt (1931–2). He recognised
that in any modern industrial system, a characteristic feature of which is
that in none of its industries commodities are produced by means of 'unas-
sisted labour' alone, there must exist certain types of capital goods that can
serve different purposes, i.e., that can be utilised to produce different types
of output, for otherwise a restructuring (expansion or contraction) of the
economic system would be impossible. If all capital goods (fixed and circulating) were considered to be totally specific, the only possible representation of the productive structure would be one of the Austrian type, i.e.,
there could be no circularity. Burchardt at the same time clearly recognised
that a two-sectoral schema like the Marxian one must lead to a representation in which the non-specificity of capital goods is much overstated. It is a
specific characteristic of Lowe's 'tripartite schema of industrial production' that it combines these elements of flexibility and rigidity (or of specificity and non-specificity), that must simultaneously be present in every
modern industrial system, in a simple and comprehensive schema. That
the three-sectoral model, which emerges from Lowe's complete schema by
vertical integration, can be fruitfully exploited in the analysis of growth
and developmental problems has been proved by various authors.[44] But it
is only in Lowe's complete schema, in which different stages of production
in each of these sectors are made explicitly visible, that a unique synthesis
of the circular interdependence and of the vertical integration approach
has been provided.

The full significance of Lowe's analytical schema can be illustrated by
examining the statement that in models with a sectoral representation the
adjustment to a new constellation of data is effectuated through simple
horizontal transfers between sectors and that such a representation loses
its relevance 'as capital goods become more and more specialized and
hence less and less transferable' (Amendola and Gaffard, 1988, p. 29). A
close examination of Lowe's 'analytical schema of production' (see

section 2) reveals that it is not 'a simple transfer of capital between sectors', if with that expression one associates the idea of 'malleable' or 'totally unspecific' capital that can easily be moved from one industry to another. If, for example, in Lowe's model, capacity is liberated in sector 2 and 'transferred' to sector 1, this means that *part of the output* of those industries classified as belonging to both equipment-goods sectors 1 and 2 (the 'extractive industries', the 'iron industry', the 'steel industry'), which formerly served as an input to the production of equipment for the consumer-goods industries, is now used as an input to the production of equipment for the equipment-goods industries themselves. Thus from an analytical point of view *part of the capacity* of these industries is 'transferred' from sector 2 to 1, although the equipment in these industries (i.e., 'extractive machinery', 'steel mills', etc.) is and remains totally specific. The only capital goods considered to be 'non-specific' are machine tools, which can be used to produce different types of equipment. To sum up: There is no idea of 'malleable' capital goods in Lowe's model – it is on the contrary clearly recognised by him that most capital, once installed in particular industries, is highly specific. But since every circular system of production must contain at least one non-specific capital good, a change of the proportions, in which this good is used in its different applications, simultaneously changes the proportions in which the capacity of other industries is analytically divided between the purely fictitious sectors 1 and 2.

A more serious objection against Lowe's traverse analysis concerns his investigation of traverse processes initiated by technological changes. Amendola and Gaffard (1988, p. 29) are certainly right in claiming 'that the phase of the embodiment of the new technology must be taken explicitly into consideration'. It is no doubt a shortcoming of Lowe's analysis of the traverse processes caused by the introduction of process innovations that the initial phase, in which the building and instalment of the new technology takes place, is largely left in the dark. But Amendola and Gaffard's further claim, that it is only vertically integrated production models which neglect circular structures in production that would permit a proper analysis of this phase, has been proved erroneous by the results reached both in non-integrated neo-Austrian models (Belloc, 1980; Violi, 1982) and in interindustry production models (Baldone, 1984). Baldone has also shown conclusively that the Hicksian methodology, when applied to more general models of production (which can either be of the non-integrated neo-Austrian variety or of the industry approach type), leads to an *indeterminateness* of the traverse paths. This is due to the fact that Hicks's 'full performance' hypothesis will necessarily have to be modified in the context of more general productive structures (see Baldone, 1984, section 3). Thus

Amendola's and Gaffard's statement seems to miss the point. It is not a more general model of production including circular structures that obstructs 'a proper analysis of this phase', but it is the Hicksian method of analysis, which becomes insufficient for the derivation of determinate traverse paths in the context of more general models.

We therefore conclude that Lowe's instrumental approach to the analysis of traverse processes can be considered, in view of the methodological problems associated with a descriptive approach to traverse theory, a most relevant method of analysis in this field of investigation. Furthermore, Lowe's representation of the productive system proves to be a highly original contribution to the analysis of the dynamics in production systems: it provides a unique synthesis of Austrian sequentiality and classical (or Sraffian) circularity.

Notes

* The essay was written in winter 1989–90 when the second author stayed as a Visiting Fellow at Clare Hall and the Department of Economics of Cambridge University. We thank Heinz Kurz for his helpful comments and Michael Landesmann for the possibility of presenting and discussing the paper in his seminar on 'Structural Change and Economic Dynamics'.

1 Solow (1984, p. 21).

2 Hicks (1965, p. 184, our italics).

3 Hicks (1977, p. 190).

4 See Lowe (1976, p. 10).

5 The importance of this modification was recognised by Hicks himself who emphasised in his *Methods of Dynamic Economics*: 'I do not believe . . . that the fixity of technique . . . is the vital point. The big change occurs . . . at the point where we abandon the single capital good' (Hicks, 1985, p. 137).

6 Lowe (1976, p. 10).

7 Lowe (1976, pp. 7–8).

8 For a detailed elaboration of his instrumental analysis see Lowe (1965), for a critical evaluation by a variety of authors the essays in Heilbroner (1969).

9 Lowe (1987, pp. 171–2).

10 Lowe (1987, p. 31).

11 The articles are reprinted as the first two essays in Lowe (1987).

12 For a more detailed exposition of the research achievements of the Kiel School and the development of Lowe's thinking on structural analysis of real capital formation over six decades, see Hagemann (1990, esp. section II).

13 See Lowe's recent retrospective view on the debates on business cycle theory in Germany during the Weimar period in Lowe (1989, esp. pp. 84–6). Lowe's leading role in these debates can also be seen in his main opponent's work, Hayek's *Monetary Theory and the Trade Cycle*, in which the dispute with Lowe, and the other members of the Kiel group like Burchardt and Neisser, is an important issue.

14 Alfred Kähler (1933) first applied Burchardt's synthetical model to genuine dynamic analysis in his study of the displacement effects of workers by machinery.

15 The a_{ji}'s and the l_i's denote, respectively, the inputs of fixed capital of type $j=1,2$ (primary and secondary equipment) and of total labour per unit of sectoral output in sector $i=1,2,3$.

16 Lowe (1976, p. 16).

17 See Hagemann (1990, section III) and for a detailed elaboration of all the quantity and price equations the analysis in Hagemann and Jeck (1981).

18 Lowe (1976, p. 87).

19 It should be noted that in Pasinetti's (1981) model of an expanding economy, in which the structure of demand changes over time and in which productivity growth rates differ between different (vertically integrated) sectors, the growth path followed is also characterised by continuous full-employment and full-capacity utilisation. Therefore steady or stationary states do not seem to be the only possible equilibrium growth paths fulfilling Lowe's conditions.

20 This entails that the criticism of Lowe's path criterion in Metcalfe (1977) and Steedman (1977), both of which suggest Lowe's choice to be an arbitrary one, is unfounded.

21 The production-theoretic structure of Fel'dman's model in the version of Robinson and Eatwell (1973, pp. 288–92) is identical with the three-sectoral Lowe model.

22 Hagemann (1987, p. 346).

23 See, e.g., Lowe (1976, p. 125).

24 This is also made clear in Lowe's comment on Johansson: 'Johansson too insists that expansion proceeds in linear fashion from the earliest to the latest stage, because "as no stocks exist that can be used in the later stages of production, an increase of production must necessarily start in the first stage" (Johansson, as quoted by Lundberg, 1937, p. 70). However, in this quotation, he is apparently concerned only with the *outputs* in successive stages, not with the *capital stocks* that are to produce these outputs. Nonetheless, if there were no free capacity available in the first stage, . . . how could production be increased anywhere – unless workers extracted the ore, in good Austrian fashion, with their bare hands? For this reason, what needs stressing is the strategic function of a reduction in the output of consumer goods for the *technical* feasibility of expansion in an equilibrating system' (Lowe, 1976, pp. 177–8).

25 See Wicksell (1934, pp. 133–44) and Jonung (1981).

26 For a critical evaluation of Wicksell's basic objection to Ricardo's analysis of the problem of technological unemployment see also Neisser (1990).

27 Lowe (1976, pp. 115–6).

28 Since Lowe argues that temporary overutilisation of equipment must raise the effective rate of wear and tear, the need for an additional formation of new real capital will only be postponed to later periods by taking such measures. Interestingly, Hicks's view on the effects of overutilising the productive capacities in existence comes close to Lowe's (see Hicks, 1965, pp. 193–7).

29 In Ricardo's numerical example, the economy takes off from a stationary-state equilibrium and the evolution of the gross and net produce is calculated for three successive periods, depicting the effects of the construction and utilisation of machinery on aggregate output. There is, however, no indication that the economy will arrive at another uniquely determined equilibrium, i.e., the development of profits, investment, employment and output are largely left indeterminate. Accordingly, his example can be regarded as an 'early and rude type of traverse analysis' (see Kurz, 1984) which contains a capital shortage theory of temporary technological unemployment. In two recently published articles Samuelson (1988, 1989) set out to vindicate Ricardo's propositions. His exposition contains numerical examples that lead to permanent technological unemployment, i.e., to a new long-run equilibrium position with unemployed labour. It is to be noted that there is nowhere in Ricardo's chapter any evidence to be found in support of this scenario. According to Ricardo's view capital accumulation and output expansion will in the long run act as a compensating factor to the initial displacement effect of machinery.

30 Hicks's fixwage model (1973, chapter VIII), which provides almost an exact replica of Ricardo's assumptions, shows that the introduction of machinery has an adverse effect on employment in the short run only in the case of 'strongly forward biased' innovations, a case which may be termed, following Zamagni (1984), a 'mechanisation' of production. However, Violi (1984a, 1984b) shows that all cases of innovations can lead to temporary unemployment, when neo-Austrian production processes with more general profiles are considered (although the case of a 'mechanisation' combined with a lengthening of the construction period is the one that leads to it with highest probability), and that the crucial condition for technological unemployment to occur is not the specific form of the innovation, but the effect on the development of the 'gross produce', a point that was already grasped by Ricardo.

31 Lowe (1976, p. 250).

32 Lowe's procedure has been criticised by Amendola and Gaffard (1988, p. 28): 'The fact that the "traverse" is accomplished through a reallocation of capital goods between the different sectors entails . . . that technical progress, in effect, does not require a qualitative transformation of the productive capacity, but a simple reshuffling, which analytically is an instantaneous "operation".' In our view, Amendola and Gaffard misunderstand the scope of his investigation. Lowe's analysis is only concerned with those phases of the traverse path that *follow* the phase of the embodiment of the new technology.

33 Alternative ways of distributing the gains of productivity increases would consist of prices decreasing *uno actu* with the costs of production as is assumed in traditional compensation theory, or wages increasing with labour productivity in the economy as a whole. As should be clear since J. S. Mill's famous dictum that 'demand for commodities is not demand for labour', these alternatives do not provide a mechanism for automatic short-term compensation, since the additional expenditures on the part of the beneficiaries of the cheapened output can only compensate for the lack of demand on the part of the displaced. Only to the extent that the additions to consumers' purchasing power

will be saved and invested, can their reemployment be achieved. To assume the emergence of technological extra profits in connection with Lowe's (super-classical) saving (=investment) assumption is most favourable for compensation.

34 This case is also at the centre of Marx's analysis of technical innovations. Its dominant role in the evolution of capitalist economies is also stressed in Hicks (1969).

35 Lowe's fragmentary treatment of the traverse problems originating from this form of innovation (see Lowe, 1976, chapter 26) shows the necessity of taking the phase of the embodiment of a new technology explicitly into consideration (see also section 4).

36 Interestingly, Malinvaud arrives at a similar conclusion in his evaluation of Hicks's traverse studies. See Malinvaud (1986, p. 379).

37 It should be noted that in Hicks's analysis of the full-employment traverse path a similar mechanism is at work, i.e., the start of a sufficient number of processes to keep the labour force fully employed is achieved by a reduction in workers' per capita consumption.

38 Magnan de Bornier (1980), Gozzi and Zamagni (1982), Zamagni (1984), Violi (1984a, 1984b), Amendola (1984) and Amendola and Gaffard (1988) applied Hicks's methodological approach in the context of vertically integrated production models; Belloc (1980) and Violi (1982) extended its application to the case of non-integrated neo-Austrian models.

39 For a detailed exposition of the characteristic features of Hicks's neo-Austrian production model see Hicks (1970, 1973) and Magnan de Bornier (1990). A critical examination of this model is provided in Burmeister (1974), Hagemann and Kurz (1976) and Baldone (1984). The advantages and drawbacks of neo-Austrian production models in the analysis of traverse processes have been investigated in Hagemann (1990, pp. 164–7). In the following we will concentrate on the methodological problems associated with the Hicksian approach to traverse analysis.

40 This deficiency has been clearly recognised by Magnan de Bornier (1980), who implicitly adopts Lowe's instrumental methodology when analysing a 'planned' traverse path in a neo-Austrian model.

41 See Gozzi and Zamagni (1982), Violi (1982, 1984b) and Malinvaud (1986).

42 See Hicks (1977, pp. 194–5) and, for a similar statement, Zamagni (1984, p. 148).

43 Lowe openly admits that his procedure 'resembles comparative statics rather than genuine dynamics' (Lowe 1976, p. 114).

44 See, e.g., Dobb (1960, 1967), Chng (1980), Chakravarty (1987).

References

Amendola, M. (1984) 'Towards a Dynamic Analysis of the "Traverse"', *Eastern Economic Journal*, 10: 203–10.

Amendola, M. and Gaffard, J.-L. (1988) *The Innovation Choice. An Economic Analysis of the Dynamics of Technology*, Oxford, Basil Blackwell.

Baldone, S. (1984) 'Integrazione verticale, struttura temporale dei processi produttivi e transizione fra le tecniche', *Economia Politica*, 1: 79–105.

Belloc, B. (1980) *Croissance économique et adaptation du capital productif*, Paris, Economica.

Burchardt, F. A. (1931–2) 'Die Schemata des stationären Kreislaufs bei Böhm-Bawerk und Marx', *Weltwirtschaftliches Archiv*, 34: 525–64; 35: 116–76.

Burmeister, E. (1974) 'Synthesizing the Neo-Austrian and Alternative Approaches to Capital Theory: A Survey', *Journal of Economic Literature*, 12: 413–56.

Chakravarty, S. (1987) *Development Planning. The Indian Experience*, Oxford, Clarendon Press.

Chng, M. K. (1980) 'Dobb and the Marx-Fel'dman Model', *Cambridge Journal of Economics*, 4: 393–400.

Dobb, M. (1960) *An Essay on Economic Growth and Planning*, London, Routledge and Kegan Paul.

—— (1967) 'The Question of "Investment Priority for Heavy Industry"', in *Papers on Capitalism, Development and Planning*, London, Routledge and Kegan Paul, pp. 107–23.

Fel'dman, G. A. (1928–9) 'On the Theory of Growth Rates of National Income, I and II', in N. Spulber (ed.), *Foundation of Soviet Strategy for Economic Growth, Selected Essays 1924–1930*, Bloomington, Indiana University Press, pp. 174–99 and 304–31.

Gozzi, G. and Zamagni, S. (1982) 'Crescita non uniforme e struttura produttiva: un modello di traversa a salario fisso', *Giornale degli Economisti e Annali di Economia*, 41: 305–45.

Hagemann, H. (1987) 'Capital Goods', in J. Eatwell, M. Milgate and P. Newman (eds), *The New Palgrave. A Dictionary of Economics*, London, Macmillan, vol. I.

—— (1990) 'The Structural Theory of Growth', in M. Baranzini and R. Scazzieri (eds), *The Economic Theory of Structure and Change*, Cambridge, Cambridge University Press, pp. 144–71.

Hagemann, H. and Jeck, A. (1981) 'Wachstum und Einkommensverteilung. Strukturanalyse auf der Basis eines dreisektoralen Modells vom Lowe-Fel'dman-Dobb-Typ', in W. J. Mueckl and A. E. Ott. (eds), *Wirtschaftstheorie und Wirtschaftspolitik. Gedenkschrift für Erich Preiser*, Passau, Passavia Universitätsverlag, pp. 99–124.

Hagemann, H. and Kurz, H. D. (1976) 'The Return of the same Truncation Period and Reswitching of Techniques in Neo-Austrian and More General Models', *Kyklos*, 29: 678–708.

Hayek, F. A. (1929) *Geldtheorie und Konjunkturtheorie*, Vienna and Leipzig: Hölder-Pichler-Tempsky. Transl. *Monetary Theory and the Trade Cycle*, London 1933, Routledge and Kegan Paul.

Heilbroner, R. (ed.) (1969) *Economic Means and Social Ends. Essays in Political Economics*, Englewood Cliffs, NJ, Prentice-Hall.

Hicks, J. (1965) *Capital and Growth*, Oxford, Clarendon Press.

—— (1969) *A Theory of Economic History*, Oxford, Clarendon Press.

(1970) 'A Neo-Austrian Growth Theory', *Economic Journal*, 80: 257–81.

(1973) *Capital and Time*, Oxford, Clarendon Press.

(1977) *Economic Perspectives. Further Essays on Money and Growth*, Oxford, Clarendon Press.

(1985) *Methods of Dynamic Economics*, Oxford, Clarendon Press.

Jonung, L. (1981) 'Ricardo on Machinery and the Present Unemployment: An Unpublished Manuscript by Knut Wicksell', *Economic Journal*, 91: 200–5.

Kähler, A. (1933) *Die Theorie der Arbeiterfreisetzung durch die Maschine*, Greifswald, Julius Abel.

Kurz, H. D. (1984) 'Ricardo and Lowe on Machinery', *Eastern Economic Journal*, 10: 211–29.

Lowe, A. (1965) *On Economic Knowledge: Toward a Science of Political Economics*, New York, Harper and Row.

(1976) *The Path of Economic Growth*, Cambridge, Cambridge University Press.

(1987) *Essays in Political Economics: Public Control in a Democratic Society*, ed. A. Oakley, Brighton, Wheatsheaf Books.

(1989) 'Konjunkturtheorie in Deutschland in den zwanziger Jahren', in B. Schefold, (ed.), *Studien zur Entwicklung der ökonomischen Theorie VIII*, Berlin, Duncker & Humblot, pp. 75–86.

Lundberg, E. (1937) *Studies in the Theory of Economic Expansion*, London, P. S. King.

Magnan de Bornier, J. (1980) *Capital et déséquilibres de la croissance*, Paris, Economica.

(1990) 'Vertical Integration, Growth and Sequential Change', in M. Baranzini and R. Scazzieri (eds), *The Economic Theory of Structure and Change*, Cambridge, Cambridge University Press, pp. 122–43.

Malinvaud, E. (1986) 'Reflecting on the Theory of Capital and Growth', *Oxford Economic Papers*, 38: 367–85.

Metcalfe, J. S. (1977) 'Review of "The Path of Economic Growth" by A. Lowe', *The Manchester School*, 55: 193–5.

Neisser, H. (1990) 'The Wage Rate and Employment in Market Equilibrium', *Structural Change and Economic Dynamics*, 1: 141–63.

Pasinetti, L. L. (1981) *Structural Change and Economic Growth. A Theoretical Essay on the Dynamics of the Wealth of Nations*, Cambridge, Cambridge University Press.

Ricardo, D. (1951) *On the Principles of Political Economy and Taxation* (1st edn. 1817; 3rd edn. 1821), vol. I of: *The Works and Correspondence of David Ricardo*, ed. P. Sraffa with the collaboration of M. H. Dobb, Cambridge, Cambridge University Press.

Robinson, J. and Eatwell, J. (1973) *An Introduction to Modern Economics*, London, McGraw-Hill.

Samuelson, P. A. (1988) 'Mathematical Vindication of Ricardo on Machinery', *Journal of Political Economy*, 96: 274–82.

(1989) 'Ricardo Was Right!', *Scandinavian Journal of Economics*, 91: 47–62.

Solow, R. M. (1984) 'Mr. Hicks and the Classics', in D. A. Collard *et al.* (eds),

Economic Theory and Hicksian Themes, Oxford, Clarendon Press, pp. 13–25.

Sraffa, P. (1951) 'Introduction' to *The Works and Correspondence of David Ricardo*, ed. P. Sraffa with the collaboration of M. H. Dobb, Cambridge, Cambridge University Press, vol. I, pp. xiii–lxii.

Steedman, I. (1977) 'Review of "The Path of Economic Growth" by A. Lowe', *Economic Journal*, 87: 584–5.

Violi, R. (1982) *L'economia della traversa. Struttura del capitale e crescita non uniforme*, Tesi di laurea, Università di Parma.

—— (1984a) 'I processi dinamici di transizione indotti dall'innovazione tecnologica', *Annali della Fondazione Luigi Einaudi*, 18: 53–96.

—— (1984b) 'Sentiero di traversa e convergenza', *Giornale degli Economisti e Annali di Economia*, 43: 153–96.

Wicksell, K. (1934) *Lectures on Political Economy*, vol. I, London, Routledge and Kegan Paul.

Zamagni, S. (1984) 'Ricardo and Hayek Effects in a Fixwage Model of Traverse', in D. A. Collard *et al.* (eds), *Economic Theory and Hicksian Themes*, Oxford, Clarendon Press, pp. 135–51.

5 Structural change and macroeconomic stability in disaggregated models

RICHARD GOODWIN AND MICHAEL LANDESMANN

1 Introduction

This paper considers a number of contributions which have attempted to formulate business cycle models in a disaggregated framework. In the history of economic thought the fact that 'structural change' in the sense of changes in the relationships of components (industries, firms, activities) of an economic system to each other plays an important role in the dynamics of aggregate economic fluctuations has long been recognised. Most prominently, we find a strong emphasis on this relationship in the writings of Marx and Schumpeter. But a host of other writers have picked up this theme, from the late nineteenth- and early twentieth-century contributions of Michail Ivanovic Tugan-Baranowski, Mentor Bouniation, Albert Aftalion, Arthur Spiethoff to the interwar contributions of such diverse figures as Rudolf Hilferding, Otto Bauer, Friedrich August von Hayek and Dennis Robertson. They all emphasised the importance of industrial structural change in the form of repercussions of the phases of the industrial cycle upon technical change, the uneven growth of industries, the degree of market concentration, etc. With Keynes and the advent of short-run aggregate macroeconomic analysis these issues were pushed into the background, only to reemerge after 1973 when the experience of two oil crises and the strong competitive challenge from newly industrialising countries put the issue of industrial structural change again near the top of the agenda.

2 Early disaggregated formulations of economic dynamics: dynamic coupling, lag structures and degree of connectedness

The first crop of disaggregated models which were explored for their inherent dynamic features were linear models which tried to analyse either the stability of interactive behaviour on markets (Hicks, 1939; Samuelson, 1944; Metzler, 1945, 1950; Goodwin, 1947) or the dynamic properties of Leontief-type systems which depicted production

167

interdependencies (Hawkins, 1948; Goodwin, 1949, 1950; Chipman, 1950; Solow, 1952).

In all these models it was shown that – given overall stability of the system – oscillatory behaviour in the course of an adjustment process was possible and, indeed, likely and that such oscillations would be dampened if no further shocks (in the form of impulses which push the economy away from an equilibrium configuration) were received.

In a series of models (1947, 1949, 1950, 1953), Goodwin discussed the possibility of oscillatory behaviour in multisectoral models. For example, in Goodwin (1950) he discusses a simple model of the type

$$y(t+1)=Ay(t)+b+\Delta b \tag{1}$$

where y is the vector of output or sales, A the matrix of input–output coefficients; b refers to a vector of constant injections which change at time $t=0$ by Δb (the elements of Δb need not be of the same sign).

Goodwin first considers the associated system of homogeneous equations

$$y(t+1)=Ay(t) \tag{2}$$

and introduces the linear transformation of that system to *normal* or *principal coordinates*.[1]

$$y=H^{-1}\eta \tag{3}$$

such that substituting back into (2) we get

$$\eta(t+1)=\underbrace{HAH^{-1}}\eta(t)$$
$$\equiv[\lambda] \tag{4}$$

where $[\lambda]$ is a diagonal matrix with the n distant roots λ_i of A along the diagonal.

As pointed out by Goodwin (1983 [1949], pp. 13–14):

In the new coordinates, η_i, the variables are independent of one another ('uncoupled') and we have n simple, separate first-order difference equations

$$\eta_i(t+1)=\lambda_i\eta_i(t)\ i=1, 2, ..., n \tag{5}$$

which are obviously satisfied by the n solutions

$$\eta_i=N_i\lambda_i^t \tag{6}$$

with the n arbitrary constants N_i.

The n coordinates are called *normal coordinates*, and their usefulness in examining the disaggregated dynamics of an interdependent production system is emphasised:

by their use we see that there are in our system n modes of behaviour, all independent of one another, anyone or all of which may be excited at any one time. This fact is a direct, though scarcely obvious, consequence of the linearity of the system, and it is known as Daniel Bernoulli's Principle of the Superpositions of Motions. (Goodwin, 1983 [1949]).

The structure of the A matrix may explain the non-oscillatory or oscillatory dynamics of the system, as well as the frequency of oscillations:

Since matrix A is not symmetric, the roots of that matrix can be real or complex. If all the roots are real and positive, the system is non-oscillatory. If any of the roots are real and negative there may be oscillations of period two. If any of the roots are complex there will be longer-period oscillations; indeed oscillations of any length are possible on the basis of the multiplier mechanism alone. (Goodwin, 1983 [1949], p. 19)

Returning to the original (untransformed) system (3) we have

$$y(t) = H^{-1}\eta(t) = H^{-1}[\lambda]^t N \tag{7}$$

The dynamical motion of the $y_i(t)$ are determined as linear combinations of the independent motions of the diagonalised system (4)

$$y_i(t) = K_{i1}N_1\lambda_1^t + K_{i2}N_2\lambda_2^t + \ldots + K_{in}N_n\lambda_n^t \tag{8}$$

where K_{ij}'s are the elements of H^{-1}.

All sectors of the system have the same 'latent set' of constituent motions but the proportions in which the motions are combined may be different from one sector to another (see Goodwin, 1983, p. 25.)

Going back to system (1) with variable injections Δb, Goodwin concludes that such a system is liable to oscillations:

The reason, presumably . . . is the Slutsky effect, i.e., the cumulation of random disturbances will produce cycles. Beyond this property common to [both the simple and the matrix multiplier system], the matrix multiplier has another, which consists of the fact that the transition from one level of activity to another is likely to set up internal or *structural vibrations* within the aggregate system. (Goodwin, 1983, p. 28)[2]

A second interesting insight into the characteristics of economic fluctuations in disaggregated models was obtained by Goodwin when he analysed the interaction of sectors (or markets) with *differences in lag structures* (see Goodwin, 1947).

Take the case of the coupling of two sectors where one has twice the production lag of the other and their system of price determination is coupled in the following way

$$p_1(t) + a_1 p_1(t-1) + b_1 p_2(t) = 0$$
$$p_2(t) + a_2 p_2(t-2) + b_2 p_1(t) = 0 \tag{9}$$

In matrix notation

$$\begin{bmatrix} 1+a_1E & b_1 \\ b_2 & 1+a_2E^2 \end{bmatrix} \begin{Bmatrix} p_1 \\ p_2 \end{Bmatrix} = \begin{Bmatrix} 0 \\ 0 \end{Bmatrix} \tag{10}$$

The characteristic equation of such a system is

$$(1-b_1b_2)\lambda^3+a_1\lambda^2+a_2\lambda+a_1a_2=0 \tag{11}$$

With a_1, a_2 and b_1, b_2 positive and real, all the roots cannot be real. The roots must be of the form

$$\begin{aligned} \lambda_1 &= r\,e^{i(2n+1)\pi} \\ \lambda_2 &= r\,e^{i(2n\pi+\varepsilon)} \qquad n=0\pm1\pm2,\ldots \\ \lambda_3 &= r'\,e^{i(2n\pi-\varepsilon)} \end{aligned} \tag{12}$$

where r, r' and ε are determined by the parameters a_1, a_2, b_1 and b_2 in (11).

The situation above leads to a complicated combination of oscillatory movements, such that, as a rule, simple periodicity can be excluded even in the absence of external disturbing factors:

[A]ll the periods will be 2 or less, except one, which must be larger and has no limit on its length. The coupled periods . . . depend in a complicated way on both the uncoupled periods and on the structural parameters. Neither market, barring an exceptional case, will have the same maximum period as before. The two independent periods get scrambled into a complicated set of periods, the same set being exhibited by both markets. The longest of these may be longer than the longest of the two independent cycles . . . [and] there is a strong likelihood of lengthening of the duration of the cycle as a result of the coupling.

Even more remarkable is the fact that it is no longer simply periodic, it does not repeat itself, even with no outside disturbance or natural dampening. Except by accident the various periods will not dovetail, because they are not integral multiples of one another, and hence in each cycle they will join in a new way, resulting in an ever changing wave shape. (Goodwin, 1983, p. 61; originally published as Goodwin, 1947))[3]

Another important instance of 'dynamic coupling' was given by Goodwin in another paper (see Goodwin, 1988). It refers to the *interaction between two types of cycles*, the shorter but more violent inventory cycle and the longer fixed equipment accelerator cycle.

That inventory adjustment behaviour can give rise to considerable instability in market economies has long been recognised in economic analysis.[4]

Goodwin uses a simple partial inventory adjustment model which can give rise to unstable oscillatory behaviour[5]

$$q = -\beta(s - s^*)$$
$$= \beta(s - \alpha q) \tag{13}$$

where q is output or sales, s and s^* the current and desired level of stocks respectively; $\alpha > 0$.

$$q^d = \bar{a}q + A(t) \tag{14}$$

where q^d is total demand with $\bar{a}q$ intermediate demand and $A(t)$ other (exogenous) components of demand.

In deviations from equilibrium, $A(t)$ is set to zero so that

$$\dot{s} = q - \bar{a}q$$

The simple structure of the inventory cycle model can then be written as

$$\begin{Bmatrix} \dot{q} \\ \dot{s} \end{Bmatrix} = \begin{bmatrix} \alpha\beta & -\beta \\ (1-a) & 0 \end{bmatrix} \begin{Bmatrix} q \\ s \end{Bmatrix} \tag{15}$$

Such a system can give rise to unstable oscillations. It will, however, reach a 'floor' at $s = 0$ which will constrain any downward spiral of the system.

The longer fixed equipment accelerator model endogenises another component of demand, the demand for fixed capital

$$I = \kappa \dot{k} \tag{16}$$

where capital goods are measured in terms of output capacity and investments I is a function of desired increase in capacity $\dot{k}$, with $\kappa > 1$

$$\dot{k} = -\gamma(k - q) \tag{17}$$

a flexible accelerator with $0 < \gamma < 1$.

q now becomes

$$\dot{q} = -\mu(q - (aq) + I)$$
$$= -\mu((1-a)q - \kappa\gamma(k - q))$$
$$= \mu(\kappa q - (1-a)q - \kappa\gamma k) \tag{18}$$

The system can be written as

$$\begin{Bmatrix} \dot{q} \\ \dot{k} \end{Bmatrix} = \begin{bmatrix} \mu(\kappa\gamma - (1-a)) & -\mu\kappa\gamma \\ \gamma & -\gamma \end{bmatrix} \begin{Bmatrix} q \\ k \end{Bmatrix} \tag{19}$$

This system is constrained by an upper bound on q when full employment is reached.

Goodwin remarks that the two systems are complementary in the sense that the inventory cycle provides a reason for a lower turning point (when zero stocks are reached and the accelerator can turn around), while full employment can serve as an upper bound to a (potentially) explosive oscillatory system. Both models represent self-generating oscillators but, of course, they will be related through their effect on aggregate demand, q^d. They have to be seen as two parts of a *coupled* dynamical system.

Goodwin (1988, pp. 165–7) discusses linear and non-linear versions of the coupling of the two oscillators and showed how the frequencies of the two types of cycles are affected through their interdependence.

Hawkins (1948) in an influential paper discussed the relationship between the degree of connectedness (he used the word 'coupling') between different sectors of the economy and dynamic instability.

Take a linear system of the type

$$x_i = \sum_{j=1}^{n} a_{ij} x_j + \dot{C}_{ij} \qquad (20)$$

where C_{ij} is capital from sector i stocked in process j.

If $c_{ij} = C_{ij}/x_j$ is assumed constant, we may write

$$x_i = \sum_{j=1}^{n} (a_{ij} x_j + c_{ij} \dot{x}_j) \qquad (21)$$

where c_{ij} is the *rate* at which output from i goes to form new productive capital in j, where

$a_{ij} > 0$ for all i, j
$1 - a_{ii} > 0$ for all j
$c_{ij} > 0$ for all i, j

c_{ij}/a_{ij} is the time required for capital from i to turn over in the productive process j.

The general solution of (21) can be written as

$$x_i = \sum_{j=1}^{n} A_j B_{ij} e^{\alpha_j t} \qquad (22)$$

where

$b_{ij} = a_{ij}$ for $i \neq j$
$b_{ii} = a_{ii} - 1$ for all i

The α_j are the roots derived from the characteristic equation of system (21), the A_j are constants and the B_{ij} are determined by (21).[6]

The well-known Hawkins–Simon theorem (Hawkins and Simon, 1949) stated that there was one root, call it α_1, which led to a steady-state solution of system (21); the other roots were *transients* which would be superimposed upon the steady state. In order for the transient terms in the solution of (21) to become negligible in comparison with the steady-state terms, the real parts of roots $\alpha_2, ..., \alpha_n$ should be smaller than α_1 (which is real and positive).

In the particular case of a two-sector model, Hawkins found that this would be assured if the two sectors were sufficiently *coupled* in the sense that each sector 'must contribute a proportion of the capital in the other [sector] greater than the proportion in which it contributes to its own capital' (Hawkins, 1948, p. 317). If the sectors are *closely coupled* (in the above sense), the system is stable; if it is *loosely coupled*, the system is unstable;[7] and, if the sectors are *completely uncoupled*, they could just be considered as independent systems.

Hawkins generalises his argument to the case of three sectors and arrives at similar conclusions concerning the importance of close (especially indirect) coupling of sectors. If the roots of the characteristic equation of such a system are conjugate complex quantities, the solution is *oscillatory*.

The oscillatory term will be of the form

$$k_i e^{\beta t} \sin (\gamma t + T_i)$$

in which the complex roots are $\alpha_2, \alpha_3 = \beta \pm i\gamma$ where k_i are the amplitude and the T_i the phase constants of the oscillations in each sector.

Hawkins does not derive the precise conditions of *oscillatory* solutions but suggests their dependence upon indirect coupling. Furthermore, oscillations in the different sectors will tend to compensate each other.

In the concluding section of his paper, Hawkins discusses the possibility for instabilities which emerged in his model in relation to the assumptions of fixed coefficients and of full employment (of all resources). He emphasises that these assumptions could be weakened but nonetheless the potential for instabilities will remain (and possibly be reinforced through unstable behavioural response mechanisms) since the technological constraints will still be binding at certain boundaries.

According to Hawkins:

A . . . radical sort of generalisation is that which gets away from the assumption of constant technical coefficients and time constants. If the ingredients of production may be mixed in varying proportions with varying capitals and outputs corresponding, then even under full employment the number of unknowns will exceed the number of technological relations. The way is then prepared for the introduction of marginal or other teleological assumptions, as a means of getting additional equations among the variables of the system. It is important to recognise, however, that certain features of such a system are invariant with respect to the particular teleological assumptions made. Any reasonable production function is such that the corresponding technical coefficients (ratios of inputs to output) and turnover times are variable only within limits. Especially they have lower bounds which, in a given state of society and technology, are entirely fixed. This means that in the n-space of outputs there is a cone-shaped region within which the system will have to move if it is to be unaffected by transients of technological origin. Each point outside this steady-state region is the vertex of a horn-shaped region, within which the system must remain (under full employment) if it starts at that point. If compartments [or sectors] of the system are sufficiently loosely coupled, this region will not re-enter the steady-state region, but will curve away from it; full employment will then bring about a crisis of disproportion. The present paper deals with a limiting case, for which the regions in question are shrunk to single lines of development. Whereas the more general model has its solutions *bounded* technologically, in the limiting case they are *determined* technologically. (Hawkins, 1948, p. 322)

3 The dynamics of decomposable systems

We come now to an interesting early contribution to dynamic analysis in disaggregated systems by Simon and Ando (1961) in their paper on 'Aggregation of Variables in Dynamic Systems'.[8] One can think of their analysis as an application of a Marshallian *period analysis* to the dynamics of a disaggregated model in which the hierarchy of stages (short-short-run, short-run, medium-run, long-run, etc.) becomes a function of the *degree of interdependence* within and between the subsystems of an economic system.

Let us – following Ando and Simon – start with a completely decomposable system

$$P^* = \begin{bmatrix} P_1^* & & & \\ & \ddots & & \\ & & P_I^* & \\ & & & \ddots \\ & & & & P_N^* \end{bmatrix} \tag{23}$$

where the P_I^* are square submatrices and the remaining elements are zero.

Next consider a slightly altered matrix P defined as

$$P = P^* + \varepsilon C \tag{24}$$

where ε is a very small number and C is an arbitrary matrix of the same dimension as P^*. P is a *nearly decomposable matrix*.

A simple linear dynamical system can now be postulated which describes the paths of the output vector x through time

$$x(t+1) = x(t)P \tag{25}$$

Let the roots of submatrix P_I^* be $\lambda_{1_I}^*, \lambda_{2_I}^*, ..., \lambda_{n_I}^*$. These roots are assumed to be distinct, and the subscripts so arranged that $\lambda_{1_I}^* > \lambda_{2_I}^* >, ..., > \lambda_{n_I}^*$. Since the roots of a matrix are continuous functions of its elements, we can define, for any positive real number δ, however small, a small enough ε so that, for every root of P^*, λ_i^*, there exists a root of P, λ_i, such that

$$| \lambda_i - \lambda_i^* | < \delta \tag{26}$$

Because of the correspondence of the characteristic roots of P and P^* described above, we expect $x(t)$, when its time path is defined by (25), to show the *dynamic behaviour* described below.

(i) In the short run, the behaviour of $x_{i_I}(t)$ is dominated by roots belonging to the Ith subset, so that the path of $x_{i_I}(t)$ will be very close to the path of $x_{i_I}^*(t)$, and almost independent of $x_{i_J}(t)$, $J \neq I$, and $P_J \neq I$. Here, P_J is defined as the submatrix of P which corresponds to submatrix P_J^* of P^*. In order to analyse the behaviour of the system at this stage, we can treat the system as though it were completely decomposable.

(ii) Unlike P^*, P is not completely decomposable, so that the weak links among subsystems will eventually exert an influence. However, the time required for these influences to show themselves is long enough, so that when they become manifest, within each subsystem the largest root, λ_{1_I}, will have dominated all other roots $\lambda_{2_I}, \ldots, \lambda_{n_I}$. Thus, at this stage, the variables within each subset, denoted by $x_{i_I}(t)$, will move proportionately, and the behaviour of the whole system will be dominated by the N roots $\lambda_{1_I}, \ldots, \lambda_{1_N}$.

(iii) In the very long run, however, the behaviour of $x(t)$ will be dominated by the largest root of P, which is a feature shared by any linear dynamic system.

We can think of the system as moving through a succession of four stages.

In the first stage, the subsystems have not yet settled down to a steady-state equilibrium path (see the discussion above of Hawkins' contribution); the dynamic pattern within each subsystem is not yet exclusively dominated by the dominant roots λ_{1_I}, but the transient roots still make themselves felt; this is the stage of *short-run dynamics*.

In the second stage, each subsystem has settled down to a steady-state path. Within each subsystem the largest root λ_{1_I} will dominate all other roots. However, since the links between the different subsystems are weak they can follow different steady-state paths. Once variables within each subsystem have settled down to an equilibrium configuration, relations within each subsystem can be ignored since variables move proportionately; this phase is the phase of *short-run equilibrium*.

In the third place, relationships between the subsystems will make themselves felt, but the behaviour of the overall system is not yet dominated by the largest root of the overall system P, but all roots $\lambda_{1_I}, \ldots, \lambda_{1_N}$ will be relevant in determining the system's dynamics. There will still be non-steady dynamics in the system as a whole; this is the stage of *long-run dynamics*.

The last, fourth, stage is finally one where the largest root of P dominates the overall dynamics of the system and the system settles down to long-run steady-state growth; it is the stage of *long-run equilibrium*.

The system dynamics just described can be generalised to take account of more than two levels in a hierarchy determined by degrees of interdependence within and between different subsystems of the economy.

$$P^* = \begin{bmatrix} P_1 & 0 & 0 & 0 \\ 0 & P_2 & 0 & 0 \\ 0 & 0 & P_3 & 0 \\ 0 & 0 & 0 & P_4 \end{bmatrix} \quad P^\epsilon = \begin{bmatrix} P_1 & Q_1 & \vdots & 0 & 0 \\ Q_2 & P_2 & \vdots & 0 & 0 \\ \cdots & \cdots & \cdots & \cdots & \cdots \\ 0 & \vdots & \vdots & P_3 & Q_3 \\ 0 & \vdots & \vdots & Q_4 & P_4 \end{bmatrix} = \begin{bmatrix} P_1 & 0 \\ 0 & P_{II} \end{bmatrix}$$

$$P = \begin{bmatrix} P_1 & Q_1 & \vdots & R_1 & R_2 \\ Q_2 & P_2 & \vdots & R_3 & R_4 \\ \cdots & \cdots & \cdots & \cdots & \cdots \\ S_1 & S_2 & \vdots & P_3 & Q_3 \\ S_3 & S_4 & \vdots & Q_4 & P_4 \end{bmatrix} = \begin{bmatrix} P_1\epsilon & \vdots & R \\ \cdots & \cdots & \cdots \\ S & \vdots & P_{II}\epsilon \end{bmatrix}$$

where $P^\epsilon = P^* + \epsilon C$ and $P = P^\epsilon + \delta D$. We assume $\epsilon C \ll \delta D$.

The progression here is from a completely decomposable system P^* where all the interdependencies between subsystems P_1^*, P_2, ..., P_4 can be ignored, to P^ϵ where higher level subsystems P_I, P_{II} are formed and interdependencies within these subsystems have to be observed but no interdependencies between the higher-level subsystems P_I and P_{II} are yet of any relevance, to the full system P where also the weak interdependencies between P_I and P_{II} make themselves felt. In such a system, five phases in the overall system dynamics may be distinguished:

(i) the dynamics of a completely decomposable system;
(ii) the short-run dynamics of *intra* subsystems interdependencies;
(iii) equilibrium configurations within the higher-level subsystems P_I and P_{II} get established;
(iv) *inter* subsystem disequilibrium dynamics take place;
(v) long-run equilibrium configuration within the system as a whole gets established.

In the example given above, a further generalisation could be introduced, if the elements of submatrix R are much smaller than the elements of submatrix S; i.e., $r_{ij} \ll s_{ij}$. In this case, an asymmetric type of dependence between the higher-level submatrices gets established in a first phase (phase v'), i.e., the intra-subsystem dynamics in P_I affects P_{II} but not the other way round, and only in the next stage (phase v") does P_{II} affect P_I and the overall system dynamics is affected by all types of interdependencies, however small.

4 Decomposing dynamic behaviour in interdependent systems

In order to discuss more recent contributions by Goodwin and others on the disaggregated dynamics of economic systems we start by giving a more detailed discussion of the *spectral* properties of linear disaggregated systems, in other words we shall discuss *distinct modes* of dynamic behaviour in disaggregated systems. (For details see Punzo, 1990; and Punzo, in Goodwin and Punzo, 1987).

Take the case of a real square matrix Z of dimension n which has at most n distinct eigenvalues λ_i associated with it.

The *spectrum* of matrix Z is then defined as the set of eigenvalues of Z

$$sp(Z) = \{\lambda_i(Z)\}[9]$$

Take a system common in linear economic models, such as

$$[sI - A]q = 0 \tag{27}$$

for the homogeneous case or

$$[sI - A]q = b \tag{28}$$

for the non-homogeneous case, where A is a real square matrix of input–output coefficients of dimension n, I is the identity matrix, s is a scalar and q is a vector.

A solution of a system such as (27) is an $(n+1 \times 1)$ vector $(\lambda^i, q^{(i)})$ where λ^i is the spectrum of A and $q^{(i)}$ is one of its associated eigenvectors.[10]

Let X be the matrix formed by the eigenvectors of A.[11] Since eigenvectors associated with distinct eigenvalues are linearly independent we can say that they span k *disjoint* linear subspaces if k is the number of distinct eigenvalues of A.

We can then think of matrix X as a coordinate system where each sector of X provides a principal axis along which a sector undergoes expansion at the associated factor λ_j. Such a coordinate system is 'efficient' if it provides enough coordinates to identify a point in C^n. This is efficient if X contains exactly n linearly independent vectors. (This is usually not satisfied for joint production systems; see Punzo and Velupillai (1984) for a discussion of such systems.) Efficiency thus amounts to the requirement that the associated matrix X (i.e., associated with A) is able to provide an alternative set of coordinate axes (or an alternative *basis*) in a space of dimension n.

Let us now come to the crucial procedure of *diagonalisation* of a coefficient matrix. In the diagonal representation of a system, an empirically given network of relations is split into a fictitious simpler system.

If X is the matrix of eigenvectors associated with the coefficient matrix A, a diagonal representation of $[I-A]$ is obtained via a description

$$X^{-1}[I-A]X = X^{-1}X - X^{-1}AX = [I-\Lambda] \tag{29}$$

where Λ is a diagonal matrix containing the set of eigenvalues $\lambda^1, ..., \lambda^n$ on its diagonal. Λ is called the canonical form of matrix A.[12]

Thus, matrix $[I-\Lambda]$ is the presentation of the structural matrix $[I-A]$ along the coordinate axes in R^n supplied by the eigenvectors of A. The axes provided by X are called *principal coordinates*. While with $[I-A]$, n^2 parameters are needed to identify the system's structure, in principal coordinates only n eigenvalues suffice. Diagonalising the structural matrix is therefore a technique to synthesise the *dynamical* properties of the system into a lower-dimensional space of parameters. It is also a method to find the *distinct modes of dynamic behaviour* in a linear system of interdependence.

Let us explain that last statement a bit further: any eigenvector $x^{(i)}$ can be interpreted as a *direction of expansion* of a vector. The coordinate transformation is affected by a linear map which associates with an x in C^n a vector y in C^n such that

$$y = \lambda_i x \tag{29'}$$

where x is a $q^{(i)} \in [x^{(i)}]$ of matrix X; $[x^{(i)}]$ being the eigenspace associated with eigenvalue λ_i.[13]

As any $q^{(i)}$ is transformed (through this linear operation) into a multiple of itself, it is natural to interpret λ_i as its *expansion factor*.

A system such as (29), which has been transformed into its canonical form, synthesises the coefficients of each eigensector by a scalar $(1-\lambda_i)$. Such a diagonal description

solves the problem of synthesising the structure of an economic system not by aggregating into one commodity, but by rearranging industries into pseudo-producing sectors . . . Each eigensector . . . transforms a basket of commodities as input into its scalar multiple as output.

Commodities are the same throughout the eigensectors. However, both their relative proportions and the multiplication scalar [the expansion factor] differ, and it is these two data that identify different eigensectors.

At unit level of operation, an eigensector produces one unit and uses as replacement λ_j units of the same [composite] commodity.

Thus, the output vector of the jth eigensector is linked to the output vector of the system as a whole by the equation

$$[X^{-1}]_j x = y_j$$

where $[X^{-1}]_j$ is the jth row of matrix X^{-1}. (Goodwin and Punzo, 1987, p. 202)

Diagonalisation may thus be considered as an important *technique of decomposition* of the different dynamic modes of behaviour inherent in a disaggregated linear system. The dynamics of the original sectors or industries (defined in the orthogonal and not the principal coordinate system) are then linear combinations of these distinct modes of dynamic behaviour.

Let us now come to the use which has been made of the transformation of a disaggregated system into its canonical (or diagonalised) form by Richard Goodwin and some of his followers.

First, the system transformed into its generalised coordinates may easily be seen as a generalisation of Sraffa's solution to the Ricardian value-theoretical problem, where inputs, outputs and shares in the value added of an economy can all be measured in terms of a 'standard commodity'. In Goodwin's system, using the decomposition technique discussed above, there are n such standard commodities corresponding to n eigensectors.

For the ith sector we have

$$P_i = \underset{\substack{\text{intermediate} \\ \text{input costs}}}{p_i \lambda_i} + \underset{\substack{\text{labour costs} \\ \text{profit on invested capital}}}{\pi(p_i \lambda_i + w b_{li})} \tag{30}$$

Both the real wage and distributive shares can be unambiguously measured in terms of 'eigengoods'. Dividing (30) by p_i gives distributive shares in gross outputs

$$0 \;\vert\; \underset{\lambda_i}{\quad} \quad \underset{(w/p)b_{li}}{\quad} \quad \underset{\pi\{\lambda_i + (w/p_i)b_{li}\}}{\quad} \;\vert\; 1$$

If we denote by θ_i and σ_i the share of wages and the share of profits in the gross output of sector i we may write

$$1 = (1+\pi)(\lambda_i + \theta_i) = \lambda_i + \theta_i + \sigma_i \tag{31}$$

The decomposition of the system through its analysis in generalised coordinates allows a discussion of distributional problems irrespective of any valuation problems.

If, for example, we want to analyse the effect of a change in the two macrodistributional variables, w and π, taken to be the same in all sectors of the economy, then any increase in π will lead to, with λ_i constant, a decline in θ_i, the share of wages. With b_{ij} constant, the sectoral real wage w/p_i will also decline. The effect, however, will be different in each sector.

Consider now sectoral labour and product markets in principal coordinates and see how Goodwin's Lotka–Volterra system of distributional conflict (Goodwin, 1967) generalises into an n (eigen) sector model of fluctuating growth.

Assume that profits are equal to investment and to output growth

$$\pi_i = \dot{q}_i/q_i = 1 - \lambda_1 - a_{I_i} w_i = 1 - \lambda_i - u_i \qquad (32)$$

where $u_i = a_{I_i} w$ is the real unit wage cost (also share of labour).

$$\dot{u}_i/u_i = \dot{w}_i/w_i - g_{ai} \qquad (33)$$

where g_{ai} is (labour) productivity growth in sector i.

Assume that wage rates are changing as a linear function of the (sectoral) employment level

$$\dot{w}_i/w_i = r_i v_i - \gamma_i \qquad (34)$$

where $v_i = I_i/N_i$ is the ratio of employment (I_i) to the available labour force in the ith sector (N_i); N_i grows at a given rate g_{Ni}.

With given labour-input coefficients, the sectoral employment rate v_i will be proportionately related to output growth and negatively to productivity growth and the growth of the (sectorally) available labour force

$$\dot{v}_i/v_i = \dot{q}_i/q_i - (g_{ai} + g_{Ni}) \qquad (35)$$

The system is then composed of $2n$ equations

$$\dot{u}_i/u_i = r_i v_i - (\gamma_i + g_{ai}) \qquad (36)$$

$$\dot{v}_i/v_i = -u_i + (1 - \gamma_i) - (g_{ai} + g_{Ni}) \qquad (37)$$

Or in matrix form

$$\begin{Bmatrix} \dot{u}/u \\ \dot{v}/v \end{Bmatrix} = \begin{bmatrix} [0] & [\mu] \\ -[I] & [0] \end{bmatrix} \begin{Bmatrix} u \\ v \end{Bmatrix} + \begin{bmatrix} -(\gamma + g_a) \\ (1 - \lambda) - (g_a + g_N) \end{bmatrix} \qquad (38)$$

The above system will exhibit the following dynamic: as output and employment expands at a faster rate than the labour force, real wages will rise sufficiently to reduce the profit share which in turn forces a deceleration of output growth; the movements are symmetric in the downturn.

Goodwin adds

It is important that the structure [of the system] is linear, and only the growth rates are not. This has the valuable consequence that qualitatively, or generically, the solutions behave similarly to those of the more familiar linear systems. Still more remarkable, this remains true even if we introduce non-linear functional relations to limit u and v to the unit positive square. (Goodwin and Punzo, 1987, p. 108)

As a system of n oscillators, it has the following features

All pairs, u_i, v_i will oscillate but with different periods and phases, any two pairs constituting a two-dimensional torus, the system an n-dimensional one. Weighted sums of these eigenoscillations determine the behaviour of each actual [original] sector. The n constituent, empirical periodicities produce resulting wave forms that are highly irregular and repeat only at long intervals; in fact, if one or more periods form an irrational ratio, the wave form will *never* repeat: hence it is generic that in almost every case there will be no observable periodicity. Thus, disaggregation can play an important part in explaining the irregularity of economic statistics. (Goodwin and Punzo, 1987, pp. 110–12)

Goodwin's model as represented in (38) is a disaggregated formulation of his previously aggregate model of distribution conflict and fluctuating growth.

There are, however, a number of drawbacks of this formulation: one is the use of the decomposition technique (in terms of principal coordinates) which leads to a specification of labour-market dynamics in each separate (eigen) sector without considering any interdependence between them. Thus, wage–profit and employment dynamics are specified for each (eigen) sector separately, without any explicit formulation of spillovers or inter-dependencies across sectors.

Secondly, while the model can exhibit cyclical movements, it is also structurally unstable just as has been stated by Kolmogoroff with respect to the original predator–prey model put forward by Volterra (see Kolmogoroff, 1936).

More recently, an attempt to overcome this difficulty has been to employ a linear formulation of a locally unstable multisectoral model which is then constrained by macroeconomic non-linearities such as the full-employment constraint. These non-linearities impose a constraint upon an otherwise explosive linear model and push the system always back into a region from which it can grow again. Underlying long-term patterns of productivity growth and demographic changes assume, furthermore, that the (irregular) cyclical movements are not around a stationary position but around a growth or long-wave trajectory (see Goodwin, 1989, essays 2, 3 and 5).

However, a drawback of such a formulation of an unstable linear multi-sectoral system constrained by macroeconomic non-linearities is that it cannot precisely describe the interaction between these two components of its overall model.

In this respect, some recent contributions by Alfredo Medio (1985, 1987), which use the tools of synergetic analysis,[14] have made some progress in understanding what happens when the linear structure of a multisectoral model breaks down.

Medio starts with an equilibrium version of a closed dynamic input–output model of the type:

$$x = Ax + B\dot{x} \tag{39}$$

where total demand for commodity i is composed of

$$x_i^D = x_i^C + x_i^I$$

with $x_i^C = \sum_{j=1}^{n} a_{ij} x_j$ intermediate consumption demand and $x_i^I = \sum_{j=1}^{n} b_{ij} \dot{x}_j$ investment demand determined by a simple multisectoral acceleration mechanism.

In this type of model, Medio introduces non-linearities by making the accelerator coefficients b_{ij} a function of the levels of output of the different sectors, and by introducing lag structures both in the adjustment of actual investment to desired investment, and in the adjustment of the supply of a commodity to its demand.

x_i^I now becomes

$$x_i^I (L_i^I D + 1) = \sum_{j=1} b_{ij}(x_1, x_2, \ldots, x_n) \dot{x}_j$$

where L^i is the length of the lag of actual to desired investment and $D = d/dt$.

Also $x_i(L_i^q D + 1) = x_i^D$ where $x_i^D = x_i^C + x^I$
with L_i^q the length of the supply–demand lag for a commodity.

Setting $\dot{x}_j = dx_j/dt$ and $\ddot{x}_j = d^2 x_j/dt^2$, I being the identity matrix, and the symbol (^) indicating diagonal matrices, the system becomes

$$[\hat{L}^q \hat{L}^i]\ddot{x} - [\hat{L}^q + \hat{L}^i(I - A) - B(x)]\dot{x} + [I - A]x = 0 \tag{40}$$

Introducing two vectors $z_1 = \dot{x}$ and $z_2 = x$
and setting

$$G_1 = [\hat{L}^q \hat{L}^i]^{-1}[I - A]$$
$$G_2 = -[\hat{L}^i]^{-1} - [\hat{L}^q]^{-1}[I - A] + [\hat{L}^q \hat{L}^i]^{-1}B$$

the system may be written as

$$\dot{z} = Gz \text{ or } \begin{Bmatrix} \dot{z}_1 \\ \dot{z}_2 \end{Bmatrix} = \begin{bmatrix} G_2 & G_1 \\ I & 0 \end{bmatrix} \begin{Bmatrix} z_1 \\ z_2 \end{Bmatrix} \tag{41}$$

$\hat{L}^q$ and $\hat{L}^i$ are diagonal matrices with positive elements on the diagonal and so are their inverses; hence $\det[\hat{L}^q \hat{L}^i]^{-1} > 1$. This implies that, with the flow input–output matrix A being viable and hence $\det(I - A) > 0$, the characteristic roots of system (41) with real (positive or negative) parts must be in *even numbers*. Hence, *when the system moves from stability to instability* there must be two complex conjugate roots whose real parts simultaneously cross the imaginary axis. This property allows Medio to use the *Hopf bifurcation theorem*[15] to show how a system which loses its stability might exhibit limit cycle movements in the neighbourhood of the bifurcation.

The control parameter which Medio uses to push the system to instability is the size of the accelerator coefficients B. Take the simple case in which the accelerator coefficients in matrix B change in scale but not in relation to each other

$$B = \alpha B_0$$

where α is a scalar and B_0 is a non-negative constant matrix.

For sufficiently small values of x – i.e., when the accelerator coefficients are small relative to the savings coefficients $[I - \alpha_{ij}]$ and the lengths of the lags – Medio shows that the system (41) will be stable. When x becomes sufficiently large, the system will lose its stability and at a critical value $\alpha = \alpha_c$ the 'true system', which is the non-linear system of which the system (41) is a linearisation around the equilibrium point, undergoes a *Hopf bifurcation*, that is, besides the stationary solution $z_1 = 0$, for values α near α_c there will be a family of periodic solutions. This entails loss of stability for this particular multisectoral multiplier–accelerator model, and generates an oscillatory behaviour (see Medio, 1987, pp. 308 and 311). A major contribution of aggregate trade cycle theory of the Keynesian type is thus generalised to the n-dimensional case.

Notes

1 The early reference given by Goodwin to this transformation is Whittaker (1937), pp. 177–87. Whittaker in turn invokes Weierstrass (1894 [1858]): 'The universal possibility of the reduction to normal coordinates for dynamical systems was established by Weierstrass in 1858' (Whittaker, 1937, p. 183). (Here the reference is to vol. I, p. 233 of Weierstrass' collected works, see Weierstrass, 1894–1927.) For a recent discussion see Punzo (1990).

2 See also Whittaker (1937 chapter III) on the 'Theory of Vibrations'.

3 For a more recent example of analysis of dynamical coupling of a number of sectors, see Lorenz (1987).

4 See the early papers by Metzler (1941, 1962; reprinted in 1973).

5 See also the discussion in Lovell (1961) and Metzler (1962, 1973).

6 If α_k is one of the roots derived from the characteristic equation of system (21) and we substitute the particular solution $B_{ik} e^a k^t$ in (21) we obtain

$$B_{ik} = \sum_{j=1}^{n} (a_{ij} + c_{ij}\alpha_k)$$

7 Hawkins describes the economic meaning of instability in the following way:

> If α_2 is larger than α_1 (the steady state root) and if $A_2 \neq 0$ from the initial conditions, then the two rates of production x_1 and x_2 will deviate more and more from the steady state solution given by the first term. After sufficient time the derivative of one of the rates of production will become negative. When in particular it becomes small enough so that its demand upon the other compartment falls to zero, i.e., $a_{ij}x_j + c_{ij}\dot{x}_j = 0$, then this compartment has reached its own natural decay rate, and beyond this point we will have negative demand, which has no meaning in terms of the model. The assumption of full employment breaks down, which may be interpreted as a crisis for this kind of system – a crisis of disproportionate development. (Hawkins, 1948, pp. 317–18).

8 See also the follow-up papers by Ando and Fisher (1963), Fisher and Ando (1962), Fisher (1963); all contained in the collection of essays edited by Ando, Fisher and Simon (1963).

9 Punzo (in Goodwin and Punzo, 1987, mathematical appendix) summarises the general properties which are known about the spectra of real matrices:

> Property 1: The spectrum of a matrix Z is a non-empty set, made up of *at most* as many distinct scalars λ_i as is the order of the matrix.
> Property 2: The spectrum of a *real* matrix Z lies in the complex plane. All eigenvalues with non-zero imaginary parts come in complex conjugate pairs.

10 We know the following properties about the set of eigenvectors associated with a matrix A (see Punzo, mathematical appendix, in Goodwin and Punzo, 1987).

> Property 3: Eigenvectors associated with distinct eigenvalues are linearly independent.
> Property 4: The *minimal* number of independent eigenvectors (in other words, the minimal rank of the matrix X where X is the matrix formed by the eigenvalues of A) is equal to the number of distinct eigenvalues in its spectrum.

11 Vectors $q^{(i)}$ which are solutions of equation (27) are called *right* eigenvectors of matrix A. Left eigenvectors, which are associated with the same spectrum $\mathrm{sp}(A)$, are eigenvectors of the transpose of A. We concentrate in the following on the set of right eigenvectors, calling them simple eigenvectors.

12 See also Hirsch and Smale (1974, chapter 4). For a detailed discussion of when matrices are diagonalisable, see Goodwin and Punzo (1987, pp. 204–5 and 339–42).

13 In general, the eigenspace associated with a given eigenvalue is spanned by a *set* of linearly independent eigenvectors of the submatrix of X:

$$[x^{(i)}] = [q^{(i, 1)}, q^{(i, 2)}, \ldots, q^{(i, k)}].$$

Only if an eigenvalue is *simple* will there be only one vector in submatrix $[x^{(i)}]$ corresponding to it. Geometrically, the eigenspace is then a line through the origin of the space of n-dimensional complex vectors, C^n. However, in general, we can expect to find eigenspaces of dimensions greater than one.

14 See, e.g., Haken (1983a, 1983b).
15 See Guckenheimer and Holmes (1983, p. 151) or Lorenz (1989, pp. 75–87).

References

Ando, A. and Fisher, F. M. (1963) 'Near-Decomposability, Partition and Aggregation, and the Relevance of Stability Discussions', *International Economic Review*, 4 (1): 53–67.

Ando, A., Fisher, F. M. and Simon, M. A. (1963) *Essays on the Structure of Social Science Models*. Cambridge, Mass., The MIT Press.

Benhabib, J. and Nishimura, K. (1979) 'The Hopf Bifurcation and the Existence of Closed Orbits in Multi-sector Models of Optimal Economic Growth', *Journal of Economic Theory*, 21: 421–44.

Boldrin, M. and Montrucchio, L. (1986) 'On the Indeterminacy of Capital Accumulation Paths', *Journal of Economic Theory*, 40: 26–38.

Chipman, J. S. (1950) 'The Multisector Multiplier', *Econometrica* (October): 355–79.

Fisher, F. M. (1963) 'Decomposability, Near Decomposability, and Balanced Price Change under Constant Returns to Scale', *Econometrica*, 31 (1–2, January–April): 67–89.

Fisher, F. M. and Ando, A. (1962) 'Two Theorems on Ceteris Paribus in the Analysis of Dynamic Systems', *The American Political Science Review*, 56 (1): 108–13.

Goodwin, R. M. (1947) 'Dynamical Coupling with Especial Reference to Markets Having Production Lags', *Econometrica*, 15 (3, July): 181–204.

(1949) 'The Multiplier as a Matrix', *Economic Journal*, 59 (December): 537–55, reprinted in Goodwin (1983).

(1950) 'Does the Matrix Multiplier Oscillate?', *Economic Journal*, 60 (December): 764–70.

(1953) 'Static and Dynamic Linear General Equilibrium Models, Discussion', in *Proceedings of the Conference on Inter-Industrial Relations held at Driebergen, Holland, Netherlands Economic Institute*, Leiden, H. Stenfert Kroese, pp. 54–98.

(1967) 'A Growth Cycle', in C. H. Feinstein (ed.), *Socialism, Capitalism and Economic Growth*, Cambridge, Cambridge University Press.

(1974) 'The Use of Normalized General Co-ordinates in Economic Analysis', in A. Mitra (ed.), *Economic Theory and Planning. Essays in Honour of A. K. Dasgupta*, Calcutta, Oxford University Press, pp. 26–38.

(1983) *Essays on Linear Economic Structures*, London, Macmillan.

(1988) 'The Multiplier/Accelerator Discretely Revisited', in G. Ricci and K. Velupillai (eds.), *Growth Cycles and Multisectoral Economics: The Goodwin Tradition*, Berlin–Heidelberg, Springer Verlag.

(1989) *Essays on Nonlinear Economic Dynamics*, Frankfurt, P. Lange.

Goodwin, R. M. and Punzo, L. F. (1987) *The Dynamics of a Capitalist Economy*, Oxford, Polity Press.

Guckenheimer, J. and Holmes, P. (1983) *Nonlinear Oscillations, Dynamical Systems, and Bifurcations in Vector Fields*, Berlin, Springer Verlag.

Haken, H. (1983a) *Synergetics. An Introduction*, Berlin, Springer Verlag.

(1983b) *Advanced Synergetics*, Berlin, Springer Verlag.

Hawkins, D. (1948) 'Some Conditions of Macroeconomic Stability', *Econometrica*, 16 (October): 309–22.

Hawkins, D. and Simon, H. A. (1949) 'Note: Some Conditions of Macroeconomic Stability', *Econometrica*, 17 (July–October): 245–8.

Hicks, J. R. (1939) *Value and Capital*, Oxford, Clarendon Press.

Hirsch, M. W. and Smale, S. (1974) *Differential Equations, Dynamical Systems and Linear Algebra*, Orlando, Academic Press.

Kolmogoroff, A. (1936) 'Sulla teoria di Volterra della lotta per l'esistenza', *Giornale dell'Istituto Italiano degli Attuari*, vol. II (January): 74–80.

Lorenz, H. W. (1987) 'Strange Attractors in a Multisector Business Cycle Model', *Journal of Economic Behaviour and Organisation*, 8: 397–411.

(1989) *Nonlinear Dynamical Economics and Chaotic Motion*, Berlin, Springer Verlag.

Lovell, M. (1961) 'Manufacturers's Inventories, Sale Expectations, and the Acceleration Principle', *Econometrica*, 29 (July): 293–314.

Medio, A. (1985) 'Synergetics and Dynamic Economic Models', in R. M. Goodwin, M. Krüger and A. Vercelli (eds.), *Nonlinear Models of Fluctuating Growth*, Berlin, Springer Verlag.

(1987) 'A Multisector Model of the Trade Cycle', in D. Batten, J. Casti and B. Johansson (eds.), *Economic Evolution and Structural Adjustment*, Berlin, Springer Verlag.

Metzler, L. A. (1941) 'The Nature and Stability of Inventory Cycles', *Review of Economics and Statistics*, 23 (3, August): 113–29.

(1945) 'Stability of Multiple Markets: The Hicks Conditions', *Econometrica*, 13 (October): 277–354.

(1950) 'A Multiple Region Theory of Income and Trade', *Econometrica*, 18 (October): 329–54.

(1962) 'Partial Adjustment and the Stability of Inventory Cycles' (ms), Prepared for the International Statistical Institute, Dublin, September, 1962, now published in Metzler (1973), pp. 429–39.

(1973) *Collected Papers, Harvard Economic Studies*, vol. 140, Cambridge, Mass., Harvard University Press.

Punzo, L. F. (1990) 'Generalised Diagonal Coordinates in Dynamical Analysis and Capital and Distribution Theory', in K. Vellupillai (ed.), *Non-Linear and Multisectoral Macrodynamics, Essays in Honour of Richard Goodwin*, London, Macmillan.

Punzo, L. F. and Velupillai, K. (1984) 'Multisectoral Models and Joint Production', in F. van der Ploeg (ed.), *Mathematical Models in Economics*, Chichester, John Wiley.

Samuelson, P. A. (1944) 'The Relation between Hicksian Stability and the Dynamic Stability', *Econometrica*, 12 (July–October): 256–7.

Silverberg, G. (1984) 'Embodied Technical Progress in a Dynamic Model: The Self-Organisation-Paradigm', in R. M. Goodwin, M. Krüger and A. Vercelli (eds.), *Non-Linear Models of Fluctuating Growth*, Berlin, Springer Verlag.

Simon, H. A. and Ando, A. (1961) 'Aggregation of Variables in Dynamic Systems', *Econometrica*, 29 (2): 111–37.

Solow, R. M. (1952) 'On the Structure of Linear Models', *Econometrica* (January): 29–46.

Weierstrass, K. (1894–1927) *Mathematische Werke*, volumes 1–7, Berlin, Mayer and Müller; Leipzig, Akademische Verlagsgesellschaft.

Whittaker, E. T. (1937) *A Treatise on the Analytical Dynamics of Particles and Rigid Bodies*, Cambridge, Cambridge University Press.

II Production organisation and economic dynamics

6 The production process: description and analysis

MICHAEL LANDESMANN AND ROBERTO SCAZZIERI

1 Introduction

In this and the following chapters we are going to examine how a novel analytical treatment of production processes may contribute to the analysis of structural dynamics of economic systems.

The distinguishing characteristic of the approach we adopt is one that isolates three levels of analysis of a production process:

(i) task identification and task arrangement;
(ii) fund factor analysis (the bundling and utilisation of capabilities);
(iii) material transformation and the organisation of materials-in-process flows.

2 The production process: appearance and conceptualisation

Let us start with a descriptive account of a particular production process in operation:[1] in such a process – think in the first instance of a manufacturing process – 'materials' are being shaped and are changing their characteristics from one stage of the process to another. We may see, at any one time, different materials moving through different stages of transformation alongside each other; they may be merged or separated. There are also what one could call 'agents' of the production process, that is 'objects' or 'people' who are involved in the process of shaping and 'changing' materials. Such objects or people are involved in certain types of productive operations, for example they are handling materials in a particular way at a particular stage and may in fact perform a number of such operations either at the same time or in a sequence over time.

Even from a heuristic description of the production process it appears that the various operations which the different agents are involved in are dependent on each other. For example, certain operations performed by a particular agent at a particular time require that another type of operation be performed by another agent (of a similar or a different type) either at the same time or consecutively. It thus seems that the various agents 'cooperate' with each other and that their actions are coordinated both in type as well as in sequence. Similarly, the steps in the transformation processes of different materials might appear to be clearly dependent upon each other in sequence. For example, particular materials might have to undergo a sequence of transformation stages before they can be merged with other materials, or, separation of different components of the same material will occur as a result of a particular stage in its transformation process. It is also likely that one will observe time intervals when it seems that certain agents are not performing any operation at all or only a limited use is being made of their 'potential'. Similarly, there are periods when the materials do not seem to undergo any transformation at all, or, in which they undergo change without any agent visibly acting upon them. Separate storage facilities might or might not be used in such periods.

It is worth noting that, whatever the scope of the observational exercise, there will always be instances of certain materials or agents (being objects or people) 'moving in' or 'moving out' of the descriptive horizon constructed for that particular exercise. Such elements of the production process are 'crossing the boundaries' into and out of the productive system under observation. A particular production process might therefore be identified by particular sequences of material transformations, agents (objects, people) having the 'potential' to participate in such sequences and doing so through particular actions. Since there are always materials and agents crossing the descriptive (and analytical) boundary in and out of such a process, there is always scope to include further stages of transformation, actions by agents, etc. and thus widen the definition of a particular production process.

3 The notion of a production process

The heuristic picture of a productive system that has been presented in the previous subsection suggests that the starting point of production analysis should be identified in the inherently dynamic character of that system. This is, in our view, the reason for the importance of the concept of a *'process'* in production analysis. We may identify three essentially dynamic features of the concept of a process that are important for production analysis.

(i) The first is that a process has an inherent dimension of *sequentiality*. This means that, at whatever points we cut through a process, the relationship between two points (or 'stages') of that process is unidirectional. A switching in time of these stages, that is, a change in the 'sequential ordering' of these stages will not be possible unless the identity of a process is changed.

(ii) The second dynamic feature of an individual process is its *non-stationarity*. By this we mean that, whatever analytical process description (defining the 'scope' of the process) we choose and whatever process stage we identify, it will always be possible to find an interval long enough within that process so that the precise sequence of stages will not be repeated.

(iii) A third dynamic feature of a process is the fact that it is '*bounded*' along the time dimension so that the analytical description of such a process must always include the specification of an initial and a final stage.

One should note, of course, that the end of one process could be adjacent to the starting point of another process of the same (or different) kind; the two features of non-stationarity and time boundedness are important for the identification of individual processes rather than ruling out the continued operation of processes in the course of time. It will be seen that production activity can be characterised by the above three general features of a process and this will provide the starting point for the *process-based analysis* of productive systems that we will adopt in the following.

Processes subsequent to each other can be either dependent on or independent of each other's performance; if one process is essential to the starting of another process the feature of sequentiality is extended to the relationship between different processes. Hence a productive system (depending again upon the scope of its analytical description) will not only be characterised by a set of individually specified 'elementary production processes' (using the criteria set out above) but also by the various dependency relationships amongst such processes. These dependency relationships will be further identified after setting out in more detail the 'content' of a process.

4 The content of a process

Three elements determine the content of a production process:

(i) The set of *tasks* to be performed. These may in turn be defined as combinations of elementary operations; however, tasks may in turn be seen as primitive components as far as the analysis of the internal structure of a particular process is concerned. Such tasks specify what has to be performed in a process.[2]

(ii) The set of *agents* participating in that process which could be either physical objects (tools, machines) or human beings (workers, supervisors, managers).[3]

(iii) *Materials* that enter the process and undergo a process of transformation thereby changing their characteristics in the course of productive activity.[4]

Production theory has generally avoided a complete description and analysis of the production process in terms of all the three above components which interact in a way that brings about a clearly identifiable pattern of productive activity. Instead, the attention of economists has generally concentrated upon one or another category of productive elements to the exclusion of others. Thus, for example, the category of 'production factors' is often introduced. This pools together 'agents' and 'materials' thus losing sight of an important feature of production processes. Also, the clear dependence of hiring particular sets of agents given the task specification of a process, or reversely, the dependence of task definition and task allocation upon the availability of a particular collection of agents (fund elements)[5] has been insufficiently explored in the recent literature. Thirdly, availability of particular materials and knowledge about these materials constrains the set of transformation processes which need to be followed and the tasks which need to be executed, as has only been emphasised by a rather specialised group of analysts (see, e.g., Cohendet *et al.*, 1988).

5 The internal structure of a production process

Once a particular production process has been identified by means of a precise identification of its 'vertical' boundaries with respect to the processes that precede or follow it along the time dimension, and also of its 'horizontal' boundaries with respect to the processes that are taking place alongside it at a given point of time, it is possible to consider the internal arrangements within a process. Given the three sets of elements which make up the content of a process there are also three distinct but complementary ways of characterising the internal 'structural' characteristics of a production process.

First, a particular production process may analytically be represented as a particular *network of interrelated tasks*. Second, it may be described as a *specific pattern of coordination* amongst 'active operators' (we will distinguish these from materials which are being transformed) executing particular sets (and sequences) of tasks. Third, the production process may be described by the *sequence of transformations* which the 'material in process' undergoes; such sequences of transformations require, of course, coordination in time and quantity.[6]

The complete structure of a production process cannot be identified unless the relationship among the three above patterns or analytical representations is fully explored. The three following subsections will consider in some detail the structural features of productive activity that are specially related to tasks, agents and materials in process respectively.

5.1 The structuring of tasks in a process

A production process may be described as an arrangement of tasks. The arrangement (in particular the clustering and sequencing of tasks) is such that the process as a whole may be considered as a purposeful activity, that is as an activity deliberately aimed at a certain result and designed for that purpose (see also Scazzieri, 1993). Tasks themselves gain purpose only because they have a particular position in the internal organisation of a process.

Tasks are made up of 'primitive operations' that describe elementary acts such as particular types of movements, holding operations, and so on. Primitive operations in themselves are not purposeful. They become purposeful only after a certain number of primitive operations are put together into tasks and a structuring of these tasks occurs within a process. In this case, primitive operations become elementary components of a purposeful overall activity.

We shall find that there are various ways of combining primitive operations into tasks. These ways depend upon the physical characteristics of the materials needed for the execution of tasks and the capabilities and capacities of 'actors' (fund factors) with which such tasks are performed. Tasks thus have to be defined both in relation to the stages in the processes of transformation of specific materials as well as in relation to the activities of fund-input elements. The specific skills and capacities of different fund elements constrain the specification of tasks and the type of task arrangement that can be implemented in a productive process.[7]

Some agents may be capable of performing a large set of primitive operations, while other agents may only be able to perform a much narrower set of such operations. On the other hand, primitive operations may (and in many cases will) be complementary to each other (such as 'holding' and 'cutting'). This has an important implication: if a primitive operation complementary to another is not included in the same task, it has to be included in another task and this requires strict coordination in the activities of those who perform these two tasks. It may be that two primitive operations are complementary in the sense that they have to be performed in a sequence. If such operations are not included in the same task, the two tasks in which they are included will have to be sequentially arranged. However, not all precedence patterns of tasks derive from this type of complementarity. As we will see, it might be the nature of the available fund inputs and the issue of capacity (or capability) utilisation which requires a particular sequencing of tasks. Or it could lie in the nature of the material in process (for which N. Georgescu-Roegen uses the notion *process fund*)[8] that tasks have to be performed in a particular sequence. In this respect, sequentiality could imply *strict continuity* (for example, when different operations have to be performed on hot iron) or it might allow *interruptions* so that stages of transformation of a given material in process do not have to immediately follow one another.

In general, then, any given production process will require the execution of a number of tasks according to a definite precedence pattern. In many cases, however, there will be options as to the precise sequencing of fabrication stages and in the sequencing of tasks linked to such stages. The choice of task specification and task arrangement deals with the organisational issues related to this analytical dimension of a productive process. As we saw, the choice of such arrangements is dependent upon the two other dimensions of the productive activity.

5.2 The coordination of productive agents

As mentioned above, it is generally possible to identify, within a production process, a set of elements that are responsible for the actual transformation of the material in process, without being in any relevant physical sense embodied in the commodity (commodities) that is (are) being produced. We may call productive elements which are required for the transformation process to take place without themselves getting materially absorbed by it, the *active operators* of the process under consideration.

As a first approximation, the active operators may be identified if we describe that process in terms of the distinction between 'who (or what) is acting' and 'what is acted upon'. When considering the pattern of coordination among active operators that makes any specific productive transformation possible, it may be useful to distinguish between two types of active operators: *flow agents and fund agents*. This distinction refers to the degree of permanence of such agents in the course of the productive transformation associated with a given process.

Flow agents are active elements (examples could be fuel or chemical catalysts) that are supplied either from other processes or from external sources and which participate when they are required for certain stages of the process. Flow agents ought to be distinguished from work-in-process materials, for the latter cannot be considered as active elements of the production process, due to the fact that such materials are the building blocks from which the finished commodities are made. However, the distinction between materials in process and flow agents might be rather fluid in a number of cases.

A distinctive feature of *fund elements* is that their definitional characteristics remain substantially unaltered from the beginning to the end of the production process. It is worth noting that by 'substantially unaltered' we do not mean a complete preservation of the entire set and structure of characteristics. Some degree of change in the bundle of characteristics is allowed as long as the fund element under consideration is structurally preserved.[9] There are tolerance thresholds beyond which a given fund element changes its characteristics fundamentally at least as far as its usability in particular production processes is concerned (a bridge or machine breaks down, etc.). Within certain limits, the performance characteristics of a given fund element might change without any qualitative difference in its capabilities to perform a particular set of tasks. Fund agents, of which machines and hired workers are examples, are often associated with a particular production process even at times when they do not perform any particular task(s) within that process.

A critical feature in the arrangement of fund inputs within a production process is the way in which fund inputs are allocated to the execution of particular tasks. In this connection, it is generally important to determine the adequate degree of 'task specialisation' of the different fund inputs. To this purpose, we may regard fund inputs as bundles of *capabilities* (see also Landesmann, 1986). Each fund-input element f^k may be defined in an n-dimensional capability space C as a vector of measurable capabilities

$$f^k = \{\bar{c}_i^k\}$$

where $\bar{c}_i^k$ are in R^n.

The reason why such a representation is possible is that capabilities have in most cases a clear quantitative expression.[10] For example, capabilities such as speed can be expressed in terms of a certain number of particular types of movements which can be performed over a certain time interval; memory can be expressed as a capacity to store a particular number of pieces of information at a moment in time. Other capabilities, such as accuracy, can be measured by certain quantitative boundaries, such as the ability to distinguish (and work upon) size differences of particular materials down to, say 0.001mm. In most circumstances, therefore, we are safe to assume that the capabilities of different fund-input elements with respect to particular tasks can be compared in cardinal space.

The *performance* of fund-input elements *vis-à-vis* particular tasks is a multidimensional concept in the same way that capabilities are defined in multidimensional space. In order to arrive at an overall performance indicator, different performance criteria, such as accuracy, speed, etc. have to

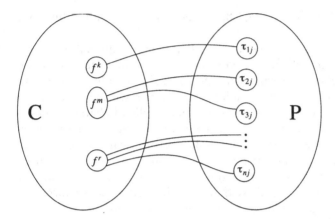

Figure 6.1   Capabilities, tasks and the job specification programme
Note: C refers to the space of capabilities, P to the space of 'primitive' or 'elementary operations', f^k, f^m, f^r refer to different fund-input elements and τ_{ij} refers to tasks ($i=1, ..., n$) to be executed in a process j.

be weighted. Any ranking of different fund inputs' abilities to perform particular tasks will be a function of the weighting scheme adopted. Given a particular weighting scheme, an ordering of fund inputs in terms of *relative task adequacy* with respect to particular tasks can be obtained.

Take the case of three types of fund elements f^k, f^m and f^r which are being ordered in terms of their task adequacy with respect to two tasks τ_i and τ_j. Denoting by $f^k \rightarrow \tau_j$ the allocation of fund element of type k to undertake task j, we may have the following orderings

$$f^k \rightarrow \tau_i > f^m \rightarrow \tau_i > f^r \rightarrow \tau_i$$

$$f^r \rightarrow \tau_j > f^m \rightarrow \tau_j > f^k \rightarrow \tau_j$$

where the symbols $>$ and $<$ denote, respectively, the relations 'more adequate (task performance) than' and 'less adequate (task performance) than'.

Such an ordering of 'task performances' will be taken into account when allocating fund inputs to particular tasks such that all the tasks belonging to a particular process would actually be performed; as we will see, however, this will not be the only criterion which will be taken into account when deciding upon a particular '*job specification programme*'. The latter can be defined as a mapping from the set of capabilities (or skills) embodied in the different fund-input elements to the set of tasks to be performed in a particular production process (remember that tasks themselves were defined as sets of 'primitive operations') (see figure 6.1).

We may say that a job specification programme is *complete* if all the tasks to be performed in a given process are allocated to particular types of funds. Furthermore, if only the *criterion of 'relative task adequacy'* were to be applied in deciding upon a particular job specification programme, then this would lead to a particular ranking of such programmes of the type: $J(\alpha)>J(\beta)>J(\gamma)>...$ where each $J(\omega)$ ($\omega=\alpha$, β, γ, $...\subset\Omega$) refers to a particular job specification programme. We can see that the job specification programme determines the pattern of coordination between fund-input elements. The sequencing of tasks and the contents of these tasks in terms of bundles of primitive operations implies a pattern of coordinated activity of fund-input elements; on the other hand, the existing capability structure of fund inputs will affect the appropriate specification and sequencing of tasks to make the best use of available capabilities.

We now come to the crucial issue of *fund-input utilisation*. As pointed out above, fund elements are generally available in productive units whether or not they are currently used to execute tasks. This introduces the second relevant criterion in deciding upon a particular fund-task allocation (or job specification) scheme, namely to take account of the problem of utilisation of available fund-input elements. As was discussed earlier on, the definition of fund-input elements in a multi-dimensional capability space implies that the problem of 'capacity utilisation' must also be seen as a problem with as many dimensions (i.e., whether and to which degree a particular fund-input element is utilised in all of its dimensions, speed, accuracy, etc. when executing a particular task or set of tasks). Traditionally, the notion of capacity utilisation in production analysis has often been limited to a single dimension and at times we will also proceed in this way. However, at other times, organisational production analysis will have to consider the multidimensionality of the utilisation problem as we will see in chapter 8.

The issue of fund-input utilisation leads us to the arrangement of task executions over time and also to the arrangement of different processes of the same or different types over time. Figure 6.2 shows three such arrangements.

In (i) we have the same type of fund-input element involved sequentially in the three tasks which constitute a process P_1. If we look at the utilisation profile (right-hand side) we can see that the degree of utilisation (here demonstrated in only one dimension) will change over time as the different tasks require different 'capacities' in one or more capability dimensions; the fund-input element does not change its own capacities according to these varying needs.

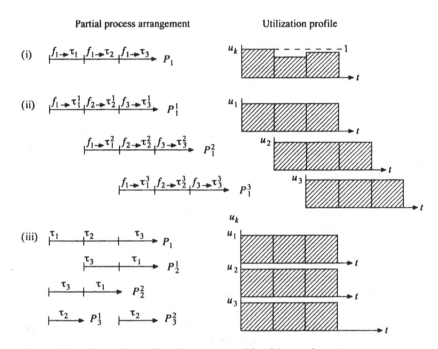

Figure 6.2   Alternative utilisation patterns of fund-input elements

In (ii) we have three types of fund-input elements executing the three different types of tasks associated with process P_1. We show an arrangement *in series* in which it is possible to organise a number of processes of the same type in such a way that the different fund-input elements can always be involved in the same type of task (they are *specialised*) but shift over time from executing this task first in process P_1^1, then in process P_1^2 and then in process P_1^3. The utilisation profile shows that the different fund-input elements will – through this arrangement – be continuously utilised to the same degree.[11]

In (iii) we have the case where three different fund-input elements are involved in executing tasks in three different types of processes which are distinguished by the sequence and set of tasks to be performed. Here we can see that the utilisation problem could be solved through the scheduling (both in time and in scale) of different types of processes which are complementary in their utilisation profiles of different funds' available capabilities.

The utilisation pattern of fund elements is an important explanatory feature of different forms of production organisation and of 'networks' in industrial organisation and will be discussed in greater detail in the following two chapters.

5.3 Material transformation processes

A critical feature of production processes is that certain materials go through distinct and interrelated stages of fabrication. The *sequentiality* of such stages, as well as the *continuity* of the whole transformation process as materials move from one stage to another, is an important characterising feature of a number of different forms of production organisation. An example may be found in Marx's discussion of the factory system, in which material in process in all its stages of fabrication moves continuously through the different lines of production.[12] In other forms of production organisation, on the other hand, the continuity aspect is not much stressed, for stoppages of the material in process occur quite often, although there may be a strong emphasis upon a high degree of utilisation of certain types of fund inputs.

The sequentiality of fabrication stages may or may not require continuity of the transformation process as well; this depends upon the physical characteristics of the material in process and the transformation process itself. This may explain different forms of production organisation in certain types of production activity. For example, the need of ensuring the continuity of the transformation process is particularly relevant if certain stages of fabrication produce continuous flow outputs such as red-hot iron, rather than units of indivisible output elements, such as a table, a pair of shoes, an automobile, and so on. This could explain the pressure to move away from the 'job-shop' pattern of fabrication in medieval craft production. This was originally based on stop and go phases of the material transformation process, and hence the pressure was particularly strong in those processes in which the continuous flow of half-finished materials was an essential prerequisite of certain intermediate stages; this was the case, for example, in the dying process in textile production. Production units in which output emerged in indivisible quantities, such as the carpenter's or blacksmith's workshop, were less exposed to such pressure.

Linked to the difference between *continuous flow* and *indivisible output processes* are differences in the characteristics of *inventory management*. In the former case (continuous flow) the storage capacities that are required will be (in the general case) of continuously varying size and storage movements will be continuous, whereas in the latter case (indivisible output processes) storage space will be of particular unit sizes (for instance shelves of given lengths) and storage movements will take place at particular points in time. The storage patterns in the continuous flow and indivisible output cases are represented in a stylised way in figure 6.3. In chapter 8 we will show that the characteristics of stock movements and the organisation of storage capacities was of significant importance in a number of changeovers between different forms of production organisation.

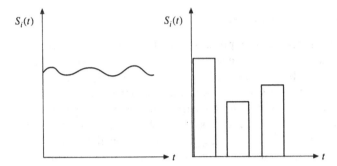

Figure 6.3   Storage dynamics in (a) continuous flow production (b) indivisible output production

Just as the overall production process can be decomposed into a set of tasks (the arrangement of which defines the job programme to be executed by the different available fund-input elements) so does the view of the production process as a *process of material transformation* allow a *decomposition into transformation stages*. The scope for such a decomposition and the organisational arrangement of such stages is dependent upon two factors: the knowledge of the properties of the material which is being transformed, and the possibilities which the capabilities/skills of fund factors provide to organise the transformation process in a particular way. The material transformation process can be visualised as a (sometimes complex) *system of pipelines* which represents the timing and sequential and also parallel arrangement of stages in the material transformation process. It is clear that further decomposition of material in process into its constituent components and further differentiation or the integration of stages of material transformation do affect such an organisational scheme. Let us illustrate some of the scope for organisational arrangements of material in process flows.

Consider the example of a production process P which consists of fabrication stages a, b, c and d and assume that stages b and c can (due, for example, to new insights into the transformation processes involved in these stages) be further decomposed into two chains of fabrication stages (u, v, w) and (x, y, z). While stages b and c were 'sequentially dependent' upon each other (we use the notation $b \rightarrow c$ to denote such sequential dependence), because c could not start without some input from b, the two chains $(u \rightarrow v \rightarrow w$ and $x \rightarrow y \rightarrow z)$ might be sequentially independent of each other. The reason for such a decomposition of an original combined transformation sequence into independent subsequences could for example be the decomposition of a given material into its metallic and non-metallic components; upon these components transformation could, over a certain sequence of stages, proceed independently from each other until some end products would be recombined in the final stages of the overall production process. Such a decomposition of materials-in-process flows allows a parallel organisation of strings of fabrication stages which were formerly sequentially arranged; this might lead to a substantial shortening of the overall process length (T). We illustrate this in the following schema.

Production process P was initially characterised by the transformation sequence ($a{\to}b{\to}c{\to}d$) with overall process length T

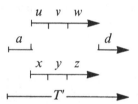

Due to the possibilities to decompose materials into metallic and non-metallic components the previously sequentially dependent states b and c now get substituted by strings of fabrication stages $u{\to}v{\to}w$ and $x{\to}y{\to}z$ which can now be arranged in parallel with substantial time saving ($T'<T$) in the process.

We might add that such decomposition of materials-in-process flows and hence in the transformation processes involved might not only lead to time saving as in the example described, but also to the possibility to use different types of fund factors (which, for example, are specialised in the handling of metallic and non-metallic materials respectively); hence there are repercussions on task specification and fund–task allocations; these, in turn, could lead both to strong cost reductions and improvements in qualitative performance (in this case the sequences $u{\to}v{\to}w$ and $x{\to}y{\to}z$ are not simply more detailed representations of the previous stages b and c but genuinely different transformation processes).

Improvements in material transformation processes from an organisational point of view might not only be the result of decomposition of previously 'merged' elements of materials in process, but sometimes due, on the contrary, to the *merger of previously distinct 'pipelines'*; in that case, previously distinct processes of transformation would be carried out jointly, for example, because a new type of machine might be able to do this. The efficiency improvement here would lie in the fact that what previously required careful organisational coordination of partial transformation processes in time and scale might now no longer be required. This points to the tradeoff between efficiency gains from a higher degree of specialisation of work processes which a higher degree of 'complexity' of a network of transformation processes might allow compared with the potential efficiency losses which the increased coordination problems linked with such increased complexity might entail.

To sum up, the organisation of the overall process of material transformation which can be represented as a system of pipelines denoting the timing and the sequential arrangement of the different stages in that transformation process, is strongly dependent on the state of knowledge of the constituent components of the materials being transformed, of the scope for changing the methods of transformation at the various stages and upon the capabilities/skills of fund factors which act upon the decomposed sequences of transformation processes.

6 Flexibilities and rigidities in the production process

In this section we want to summarise the organisational constraints and possibilities which are associated with the different dimensions of the production process outlined above.

We will deal with the following factors:

input indivisibilities and process indivisibilities: limitations in the bundling and unbundling of capabilities and limitations in the sizes of inputs and processes; this also includes limits to the decomposability of materials in process;

limited knowledge of the scope for task differentiation and task specification.

Let us discuss features of flexibility and rigidity linked to each of the three dimensions of our analysis of production processes in turn:

Fund inputs

Here flexibilities in the use of fund-input elements depend upon the capability structure of fund inputs which allows them to execute a narrower or wider range of tasks. As regards rigidities, the existing technological knowledge restricts the structure of capabilities that can at any point in time be embodied in particular types of fund inputs. Furthermore, there might be an important *scale dimension* linked to the embodiment of particular capability compositions (i.e., blast furnaces of different sizes have different properties as regards heating efficiency; the same is true for the material throughput to capacity ratio of pipes of any sort, etc.). This scale dimension, which we shall call *fund-input indivisibility*, plays an important role in considering the rationale for specific forms of production organisation. In addition, there is the rigidity related to the continuous availability of fund-input capacities over particular periods of time which poses the utilisation issue discussed earlier.

Materials in process and the transformation process

Here again the existing knowledge about materials and the set of feasible transformation processes of such materials constrains at any point in time sequencing possibilities of stages of fabrication and of the particular types of agents (flow and fund agents) required to initiate and carry through the different stages of these transformation processes. As discussed earlier, the possibilities of interrupting processes of transformation have consequences for the type of production arrangements (and consequent inventory dynamics) which could be implemented. If there are strict continuity requirements the required sequencing arrangements are more rigid. In addition there is also an important scale dimension linked to transformation processes which N. Georgescu-Roegen has pointed out:

Examples of processes that are not indifferent to size are so abundant in natural sciences that one can only wonder how their existence may ever be ignored by other disciplines. At the microscale, organic chemistry offers innumerable examples where new qualities emerge after polymerization, i.e. after a certain scale has been reached. . . . At the macroscale, in the theory of structures it is almost impossible to find a linear relation between homogenous and perfectibly divisible materials – iron, cement, insulation, etc. – and variables expressing measures of some quality – resistance to strain, elasticity, radiation, and so on.

. . . All individual processes whether in biology or technology follow exactly the same pattern: beyond a certain scale some collapse, others explode, or melt, or freeze. In a word, they cease to work at all. Below another scale, they do not even exist. (Georgescu-Roegen, 1976, p. 288)

This points to the fact that the set of feasible transformation processes is itself scale-dependent, i.e., at certain scale intervals certain transformation processes can take place, at other scale intervals, other transformation processes have to be adopted.

Task specification and task arrangement

Existing *process knowledge* defines the known 'task anatomy' of a productive process, i.e., the feasible set of task specifications and task arrangements. Advances in process knowledge increase the set of feasible task specifications and thus allow new patterns of task executions to be introduced.

We mentioned earlier that sequentiality and simultaneity requirements in the execution of different tasks result from the complementary nature of different primitive operations which belong to different tasks; however, this is not the only reason for a required sequencing of tasks; the other important reason is that tasks are formulated in response to the logic of particular transformation processes which require a sequence of tasks to be performed and, if there are some degrees of freedom available in such a sequencing, it could be the utilisation requirements of available fund elements which require a particular arrangement of tasks to be executed.

We can thus see that constraints with respect to a particular *time structuring* of a productive process can arise in all the three dimensions of a production process and, in addition, two of these dimensions (final input and process indivisibilities) might involve *scale requirements* with regard to the levels at which activities are to be executed. *Constraints with respect to the time structuring and with respect to scale are the two fundamental constraints on the internal organisational structure of a process* and these constraints are of course a function of the state of technological (or process) knowledge in all the three dimensions:

(a) knowledge about the possibilities of capabilities (skills) bundling in the development (or training) of fund-input elements and knowledge about potential utilisation patterns of given capability structures;
(b) knowledge about properties of existing materials and the development of new materials and the characteristics of feasible transformation processes of such materials;
(c) knowledge about the 'process anatomy' in terms of feasible task specifications and task arrangements.

In all these three dimensions learning processes (expansions of knowledge) affect each other; we will explore this issue further in section 8.3 and in chapter 9.

7 Dimensions of the problem of imperfect synchronisation in a production process

The aim of this section is to analyse the general problem of coordination across all the three distinct analytical dimensions of a productive process. It will be argued that *perfect synchronisation* of all the three levels of operation of production processes (i.e., of agents, tasks and materials) is a very special case and that, in general, agents are coordinated with each other according to a time pattern different from the one characterising the coordination of tasks, or the coordination of materials-in-process flows. This is to say that the coordination pattern which characterises overall production processes does not generally follow a perfectly synchronised pattern, and that different modes of coordination over time may be possible depending on which dimension of the production process is considered to be more important. Basically, there are two fundamental reasons why imperfect synchronisation would be the rule in actual production organisations: (a) the difficulty of matching the time sequencing requirements of the three distinct analytical dimensions of the production process, i.e., those of task interdependencies, agents' coordination and utilisation patterns and time sequences of material processes and material flows, and (b) the constraints which input and process indivisibilities impose quite distinctly on the three dimensions of the production process.

As discussed in section 3, a production process has inherent features of sequentiality, non-stationarity and boundedness along the time dimension (so that a process description should always include specifications of its initial and final stage). The coordination among productive elements (tasks, agents and materials) is essentially coordination among operational tasks, capabilities and agents' performances, and material transformation processes over time. As a result, the time structure of production emerges as a multilevel *network*, such that, for example, tasks are coordinated with each other according to a pattern that is distinct from that characterising the coordination over time of agents' capabilities and of stages in the material transformation processes. For example, tasks a, b, c and d could be arranged in such a way that a precedes b and c, while b and c are simultaneous and must both precede d; on the other hand, the 'bundling' of capabilities may be such that certain agents are capable of performing a and b while other agents are capable of performing c and d. Finally, the sequencing of material transformation stages may be such that the first stage requires tasks a and b, the second stage tasks b and c and the third (final) stage tasks c and d. In this case, the coordination over time of different productive elements is characterised by a problem of synchronisation. For the pattern of sequentiality or coincidence would be different depending on whether we consider execution of tasks, utilisation of capabilities or completion of transformation stages.

Figure 6.4 shows to what degree the distinction among three different levels of coordination (tasks, capabilities, transformation processes) complicates the time structure of a production process.

The precedence between tasks determines the *sequence* according to which tasks have to be executed, but leaves considerable freedom as to the continuity or discontinuity of task performance within the productive unit. In particular, the figure shows a time gap between the completion of the (simultaneous) tasks b and c, and the start of task d. The existing endowment of capabilities allows agents to be continuously active provided agent A_2 finds a task of type d which can be executed on completion of task c. (Note that, given the time gap between the execution of

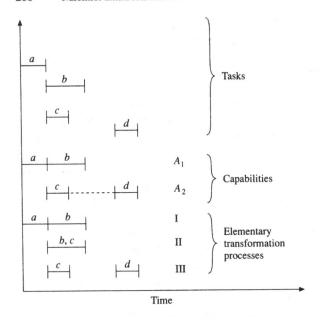

Figure 6.4   The time structure of production and the coordination of tasks, capabilities and transformation processes

simultaneous tasks (b, c) and the execution of d, the continuous utilisation of A_2 would require that a sufficient number of d-type tasks be executed in the productive unit.) Finally, the elementary transformation processes have to be sequenced in such a way that stage I starts before, and partially overlaps with, stage II, whereas stage II starts before, and partially overlaps with, stage III. The sequence of transformation stages may proceed in a continuous or intermittent way, depending on whether or not task d (necessary for completion of stage III) may be executed immediately on completion of task c. In addition, stage II may partially overlap with stage I provided agents A_1 and A_2 can operate alongside each other in executing tasks b and c respectively.

A production process may show a pattern of continuity along one particular dimension while showing patterns of discontinuity along other dimensions. For example, continuity of tasks execution is compatible with the intermittent utilisation of capabilities, or the intermittent completion of fabrication stages. The condition on the number of staggered processes that allows for the continuous execution of tasks is not necessarily coincident with the equivalent condition allowing for the uninterrupted utilisation of capabilities. In the case of figure 6.4, a sufficient number of staggered processes (as in the serial arrangement of figure 6.2) allows for the continuous execution of tasks at the level of the productive unit; however, such an outcome is not necessarily associated with the continuous execution of fabrication stages: stage II may only be simultaneous to stage I if a sufficient number of agents of type A_1 is available. For component b of stage II requires the use of this category of agents. Similarly, it is not difficult to imagine cases in which the continuous utilisation of capabilities is impossible.

The above distinction between three different layers of coordination within any given production unit highlights the multidimensional character of the time structure of production. Patterns of simultaneity or sequentiality may co-exist, depending on whether we consider tasks, capabilities or transformation processes. For example, tasks may (at least partially) be overlapping in time, even if the corresponding operations have to be performed in a sequence. Or, fabrication stages could be sequential even if the corresponding tasks are executed by agents operating at the same time. (This could be the case if a given raw material is processed through a sequence of stages which are executed in a (partially) overlapping way by workers and machines; in this way, stage II may be posterior to stage I but certain tasks pertaining to the execution of II could be performed at the same time as tasks pertaining to the execution of I.)

The above discussion has shown that the patterns of required sequentiality and/or simultaneity on each of the analytical dimensions of a production process (the level of task sequencing, of utilisation patterns on fund input elements, and of material transformation processes) poses, in the general case, formidable coordination problems which can usually *not* be solved in a manner such that perfect synchronisation (which implies perfect continuity of materials-in-process flows, no inventories and no underutilised capacities) at all the three levels could be assured. The constraints on the possible time structuring at the various levels constitute one major problem in the overall synchronisation in a productive process; the other problem results from *input and process indivisibilities* as mentioned above.

As we will see in greater detail in chapter 8 below, input and process indivisibilities are important factors causing changeovers between different forms of production organisation (i.e., in overall coordination patterns) as the overall scale of economic activity changes. In the current section we do not explore the relationship between scale and productive organisation in detail, but we would like to point out that each of the different analytical dimensions poses separate problems of indivisibility. Hence overall coordination across the three analytical dimensions will almost certainly lead to compromise arrangements in which some of the phenomena linked to imperfect synchronisation (i.e., temporary underutilisation of capacities, stop-go phases in transformation processes and inventories) will almost certainly appear.[13]

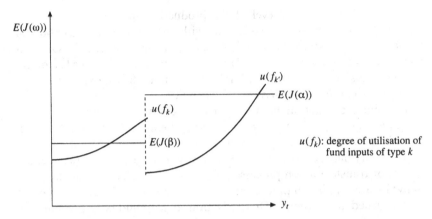

Figure 6.5   The tradeoff between task adequacy of different job specification programmes and degree of utilisation in the presence of fund-input indivisibilities

Take the case where the introduction of a particular job programme $J(\alpha)$ depends upon the use of particular fund-input elements which can only be installed/hired in indivisible units. Given the indivisibility of units, the level of output $\{y_t\}$ $t=1, ..., N$ might be such that continuous full utilisation of these funds cannot be assured. In that case, the choice exists to either have recourse to another job specification programme $J(\beta)$ which relies on another set of fund inputs where either indivisibilities do not exist or are not binding in the sense that they do not create problems of underutilisation at the given level of demand, or to stick to a job specification programme $J(\alpha)$ which in other respects is superior in terms of overall task performances.[14] The choice, which will lead to a switch between different job specification programmes as a function of the overall level of output is illustrated in figure 6.5 where $U(f_k)$ represents the degree of utilisation of fund inputs k. $E(J(\omega))$, $\omega=\alpha$, β, ...), represents an efficiency indicator which evaluates overall 'task adequacy' of different job specification programmes.)

A similar issue arises in the presence of process indivisibilities. Here again we might have an efficiency ranking of different processes $E[P(\alpha)]>E[P(\beta)]>...$ but there might be process indivisibilities in the sense that there are lower bounds on the activity levels by which these processes have to be operated. Again, if there is a lower bound on the activity level by which process $P(\alpha)$ has to be operated, a choice opens up between introducing the superior process $P(\alpha)$ at certain activity ranges but producing too much output over the period in which it is operated, giving rise to inventory accumulation and stop–go activation of different partial transformation processes, or using a less efficient process but avoiding

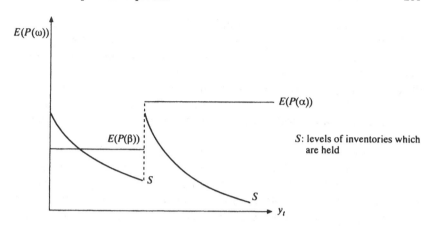

Figure 6.6   The tradeoff between process efficiency and necessary inventory accumulation in the presence of process indivisibilities

excess production and/or inventories. The choice and the scale-dependent switch between processes is demonstrated in figure 6.6. S refers to the levels of inventories which are held.

The above discussion should have made it clear that input and process indivisibilities not only cause important tradeoffs at each of the analytical levels of a process's organisational structure between technological efficiency and phenomena of imperfect synchronisation but that they can cause additional scale and organisational coordination problems across the different levels.

8 The evolutionary character of productive organisation

The previous section attempted to show that the actual 'functioning' of a production process requires the operation of a complex organisational structure, such that tasks, funds and transformation processes are coordinated with one another both in time and scale. Such a pattern of coordination is often the result of the emergence of a set of interlocking practices, as the ones associated with a workshop or an industrial district, but is not necessarily the outcome of deliberate planning by particular agents. As a result, time coordination takes an *evolutionary or historical dimension* that is not necessarily linked with a pattern of consistent intertemporal choices. Rather, coordination may often emerge as a result not only of adjustment but also of inertia in changing existing practices. Actually observable coordination is thus compatible with a considerable degree of imperfect synchronisation, and *perfect synchronisation* appears to be only a *special case* in which the utilisation patterns, task arrangements, and the continuity of materials-in-process flows are perfectly matched. In this particular case, the intertemporal working of production processes brings into existence a form of production organisation that may also be described by ignoring the time structure of production and by focusing on an organisational pattern of interacting tasks, capabilities and fabrication stages within a carefully chosen time interval; this organisational pattern then replicates itself from time interval to time interval.[15]

Not all forms of production organisation are similarly conducive to such an 'ideal type' description which ignores the 'time structure' aspect. The 'ideal type factory' (as discussed in section 4 of chapter 8) is best suited to the above descriptive simplification, due to the regular pattern of its operation. Other forms of organisation, however, would be insufficiently characterised by a description which ignores the 'time structure' aspect since this would overlook the compromise nature of the patterns of coordination of tasks, capabilities and fabrication stages which in most cases leads to *imperfect synchronisation*. For example, job-shop manufacturing (see section 2, chapter 8) is based upon a relatively loose organisation of tasks and capabilities and a precise arrangement of the transformation stages of materials in process up to the point of delivery.[16] A similar pattern is to be found in agricultural forms of production organisation, which generally show considerable flexibility of task arrangements and capabilities' utilisation but are otherwise constrained by fixed available times during which certain biological processes have to take place. On the other hand, the time structure of 'putting out' processes is remarkably different, for they are characterised by a more precise identification (and separation) of capabilities but also show a complex pattern of time coordination, relative to materials-in-process flows, which covers inventory adjustment and the carry over of stocks of semi-finished goods from one time period to another. For this reason, fully synchronised production can hardly be detected in actual production organisations, and a snapshot description of the production process (i.e., ignoring coordination patterns over time) cannot bring out the characterising features of most forms of production organisation.

9 Networks and subsystems in production organisation

9.1 The three dimensions of the analytical representation of the production process and production subsystems

The account of the production process that has been presented in the previous sections of this chapter shows that productive activity lends itself to descriptions in terms of distinct and interrelated dimensions, which are based respectively on the considerations of tasks, fund inputs and materials-in-process networks characterising each production process. This includes the identification of the coordination patterns among the 'active' elements of that process, the structuring and sequencing of tasks, and the analysis of the stocks and flows of materials in process moving from one stage of fabrication to another.

A heuristic representation of production activity should include all the above dimensions of the production process. However, any analytical investigation into the structure and workings of any production system may require, as a preliminary step, the selection of one of these dimensions in order to consider the network of interdependencies that may be identified on its basis. In this section we are going to use the analytical framework developed so far to discuss concepts of *'networks'* or *'subsystems'* as they could be identified along the three dimensions. In this way, a production system may be considered as a set of interrelated tasks to be performed, or as a network of productive agents that are coordinated in their operations with one another, or as a system of flows and inventory movements of different materials in process that are coordinated in time and quantity.

Production subsystems refer then to the bunching of production activities that are related to each other in terms of one or two or three of the analytical dimensions of the production process defined above. The identification of such subsystems allows a distinct treatment of different parts of the overall production system; the usefulness of such decomposition methods to consider issues of structural economic dynamics has been emphasised throughout the present volume (see also Landesmann and Scazzieri, 1990). The following three subsections will consider alternative subsystem specifications from the point of view of the production-analytical framework considered in this chapter. We will also return to the issue of subsystem specification in chapter 9 where we will see that such specification is an important component of the analysis of structural change processes.

9.2 Task differentiation and task arrangement

As pointed out in section 4 above, any production process may analytically be represented as a structured set of necessary operations, i.e., tasks. Viewing a production process from the point of view of tasks leads to a 'clustering' of productive processes either by the similarity of tasks or of those of the elementary operations which make up tasks.[17]

There is seldom a one-to-one correspondence between elementary

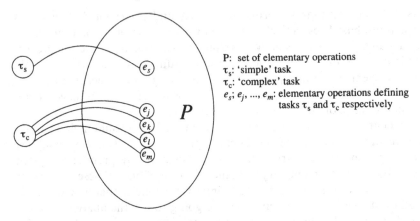

P: set of elementary operations
τ_s: 'simple' task
τ_c: 'complex' task
e_s; e_j, ..., e_m: elementary operations defining
tasks τ_s and τ_c respectively

Figure 6.7   Simple and complex task specifications

operations and tasks. In general, the same general operation may be executed in a number of different tasks and usually a given task is defined by a number of elementary operations which have to be performed. The fact that different types of tasks are often composed of the same or overlapping sets of elementary operations, even if these might have to be executed in different sequences or with different frequencies means that the same basic set of capabilities might be required to execute a differentiated range of tasks.[18]

Figure 6.7 shows two types of tasks: 'simple' and 'complex' ones; in the former only single or a very small set of elementary operations feature while in the latter a single task embodies a range of different types of elementary operations. It is clear that these two types of tasks give rise to different types of clustering or networking phenomena. If productive processes are made up of simple tasks it is more likely that the same type of fund-input element which can perform this type of elementary operation well could easily be involved in a number of productive processes which have this simple task specification. If, on the other hand, production processes define complex tasks which are themselves made up of a differentiated composition and sequence of elementary operations it is more likely that only very specific types of fund-input elements will be able to perform these tasks; only in the case where the very same 'complex' tasks would also feature in other productive processes could such (often purpose-built or specially trained) fund-input elements be involved in a number of such processes.

In the case where productive processes are defined as sets of 'simple tasks' therefore we would expect a clustering of productive processes around a pool of rather less sophisticated fund-input elements which are adequate with respect to such tasks and which would be rather easily substitutable in executing such tasks. Productive processes which contain rather 'complex tasks' will, on the other hand, be dependent upon rather specialised and sophisticated types of fund elements and there the problem of their maximum utilisation will be one of the dominating criteria of finding an appropriate form of work organisation. Such an organisation might be able to lead to a satisfactory degree of fund-input utilisation even within the same type of production unit or it will require a careful time arrangement of leasing with other production units in which the same types of tasks need to be performed. Thus, different types of task specifications give rise to different types of clustering phenomena.

As to the relationship between industrial development and task specification, one must say that technological advances (which, in a wider sense, includes new insights into forms of work organisation) are sometimes associated with a greater and sometimes with a lower degree of task complexity. An example in which tasks become simpler is Adam Smith's division of labour and, of course, Taylorist work organisation. By contrast, an example in which tasks might become more complex is the development of complex machinery that executes a large number of primitive operations with precision.[19]

9.3 Production subsystems and the coordination of productive agents

Some production subsystems are best identified through the pattern of agents' coordination which is suggested by the existence of fund elements in production processes. The particular pattern of utilisation of fund inputs and/or the pattern of coordination of their activities could lead to the grouping of particular productive activities into production subsystems. For example, the common utilisation of a shipyard or of the same assembly line by a number of different processes may be the reason for the grouping of such processes in the same subsystem.

The bundling of processes through the common utilisation of fund-input elements is often an outcome of attempts to solve the utilisation problem of indivisible fund inputs. Such a problem may arise with respect to individual fund-input elements as well as with respect to the interrelated use of a number of different fund inputs. The need to achieve a satisfactory coordination in the uses of a group of fund-input elements is one of the most important factors explaining the grouping of a set of productive processes into subsystems and even of the coordination of their activity levels.

There is a two-way system of grouping: on the one hand, the definitions of tasks within a process leads to the instalment/hiring/leasing of particular fund-input elements which can execute these tasks and thus to a grouping of fund-input elements; on the other hand, the problem of fund-input utilisation leads to a further process of grouping, namely to the bundling of productive processes and the coordination (in time and activity level) of their activities.

The interaction in the activities of different fund-input elements can also lead to *subsystems based on learning processes*. Four types of learning might emerge: one might learn about the possible uses of existing fund inputs' capabilities, or fund-input elements might expand their sets of capabilities either through their use in a variety of productive tasks ('learning by doing'), or develop new skills precisely from the interaction with other types of fund-input elements ('learning from each other'), and, finally, there is the learning of organisational possibilities which the coordination of different fund inputs' activities and fund-task allocations entails (expanding one's knowledge about the space of feasible 'job specification programmes').

The interactive network of fund-input elements in an *industrial district* is an example of a productive subsystem in which the pattern of interaction may yield significant learning processes.[20]

9.4 Subsystems, processes of material transformation and the common use of storage facilities

Traditionally, this is an area in which the economic literature has been most active so far in developing notions of subsystems (see, for example, Sraffa, 1961, Appendix; Leontief, 1953; Hicks, 1973; Pasinetti, 1973; Bharadwaj, 1966; Blin and Murphy, 1974).

The conception of a production process as a series of transformation stages of material in process is already prevalent in the classics (e.g., Rae, 1834, in Jevons, 1879), and was, of course, a characteristic feature of the Austrian approach to production and capital theory (see Böhm-Bawerk, 1989; Mayer, 1925; Hayek, 1941, and the revival of this approach by Hicks, 1970, 1973).

The consideration of materials-in-process flows has led to a variety of approaches to decompose a production system into subsystems.

The first is a decomposition by the linkages which directly or indirectly lead to the production of a final consumption (or export) good. This tradition goes back to the Austrian approach which starts from 'original' factors of production (such as labour and land) and follows the entire sequence of stages of transformation until the final consumption good emerges. This might be called a decomposition of a production system into *vertically integrated processes*. Leontief's inverse which focuses upon the direct and indirect interdependencies of different production processes (each of which are producing not only final but also intermediate commodities) is an extension of an approach of vertical integration in that it attempts to group together all the activities (or portions of those activities) which are directly or indirectly involved in producing particular final commodities. Luigi Pasinetti's (1973) notion of a 'vertically integrated sector' also falls into this category although in his case he not only keeps account of all those *flows* which are directly involved in producing final commodities but also of the portions of the different types of *stock* which participate directly or indirectly in the production of those commodities (see also Scazzieri, 1990).

The idea of defining subsystems by vertical integration of materials-in-process flows in the Austrian approach explicitly recognises the time structure of the stages of transformation. In the more recent techniques of vertical integration such as Leontief's inverse or Pasinetti's vertically integrated sectors, the time structure is being discarded and attention is focused upon the *horizontal integration of production processes*, i.e., upon the fact that different productive processes (identified by their techniques of production) are interdependent and thus each contribute to the production of a wide variety of final commodities. Once the time structure is discarded and the different commodities are all seen as being produced *within one accounting year* by a set of interdependent partial productive processes, one can speak of notions of horizontal interdependencies since the sequential nature of stages of fabrication in material transformation processes are no longer explicitly considered. This transition in the theoretical literature (the notion of the reproductive nature of a production system was developed in this way) has certain advantages for dealing with valuation and price theoretical issues but means a loss of information about the sequential nature of the production process and of organisational issues linked to the time interdependencies amongst partial productive processes. On the other hand, there have been a number of attempts (see particularly, Ando and Fisher, 1963, and Ando, Fisher and Simon, 1963) to introduce early formulations of a synergetic approach into input–output analysis which led to the specification of subsystems within a dynamical formulation of input–output interdependencies based on the relative strength of such interdependencies (see also Goodwin and Landesmann's contribution in this volume).

10 The analytical specification of subsystems and forms of production organisation

The production process is a complex system that cannot be adequately identified unless one is capable of distinguishing its different dimensions and the interrelationships among them. In this connection, the analytical specification of production subsystems, with its selective focus of attention upon particular features of the production process, is an essential logical prerequisite for the analysis of *historically specific forms of production organisation*. For it would be difficult to investigate the internal structure of any real process, or set of interrelated processes, unless the specific inter-relationships characterising the different analytical dimensions of the production process are identified and related to one another.

The discussion of different types of analytical specifications of production networks in section 9 has emphasised the possibility of identifying subsystems on each of the three analytical dimensions of a production process (task organisation, fund–factor interactions and stocks and flows of materials in process). However, we have also emphasised how the patterns of coordination which give rise to such subsystems on each of these levels interact across these levels. For example, it generally happens that, if the problem of task coordination is solved in a particular way, the coordination patterns among fund agents and materials in process will be affected. The notion of *form of productive organisation* attempts to reintegrate the three distinct dimensions of the analytical description of coordination patterns of productive processes. This reintegration gives rise to a typology of organisational forms which have historically emerged and characterised the way coordination problems have been resolved in particular circumstances, taking into account the state of technological knowledge, the evolution of patterns of demand, natural resource and environmental constraints, etc.

Another important feature of forms of production organisation is that they are not only defined by a certain degree of structural permanence, but they also experience such a permanence in historical time (see also the more detailed discussion in chapter 9, section 7). Such a *structural persistence* is responsible for the repetitiveness that characterises the sequence of movements, dynamic interactions and processes of transformation that occur within any given production system over considerable periods of time. Given this feature of persistence, production activity could be viewed as a sequence of 'nearly' repetitive cycles. In the course of each cycle, transformation processes with the by now well-known features of unidirectionality and sequentiality take place, materials in process get split up and others combine in different ways, fund elements may switch between different tasks and even undergo changes in their work capabilities, etc. However, in spite of all these changing patterns of coordination in the course of a productive process, it is nonetheless possible to recognise a certain degree of permanence in the patterns of dynamic interaction that get repeated from one production cycle to another. This will be the case as long as one form of production organisation does not get superseded by another form of production organisation.[21] In the next chapter we will characterise a number of forms of production organisation as they developed in the history of manufacturing processes.

To sum up: the coordination devices characterising any historically specific instance of production activity give shape to a repetitive pattern that identifies a particular form of production organisation. Such organisational forms tend to show a considerable degree of resilience over time. The reason for this is that any given set of coordination devices is a complicated system that is often difficult to install and may emerge only after transitional periods in which partial arrangements are successively tried out and integrated with one another. In addition, the adoption of particular coordination devices to deal with particular features of productive activity, such as those dealing with the coordination of materials-in-process flows, generally constrain in a significant way the use of other coordination devices that are introduced to deal with other classes of coordination problems (such as the utilisation of fund elements). The sheer complexity of coordination problems, together with other features such as the durability of fund agents, the irreversibility in the direction of learning processes, and the fact that work-in-process materials have definite characteristics which can only be changed with advances in the knowledge about materials and about the processes using such materials, makes any specific form of production organisation relatively difficult to introduce and explains its relative durability over time.

11 Production units and industrial networks

The final issue we want to raise in this chapter is whether our analytical framework can contribute to the definition and characterisation of a *production unit*. We believe that within the analytical framework we have outlined in the present chapter, the definition of a production unit is quite closely linked to the notion of a 'network'.

As will be discussed in detail in chapter 9, network relationships can be developed from the point of view of *neighbourhood relationships* in the task or materials-in-process organisation of a productive process and also of *compositional similarities* between tasks, fund-input elements and the materials involved in different parts of a productive system. The internal organisational structure of a productive process provides the basis for developing routines of coordination patterns amongst fund-input elements, fund-task allocations and materials-in-process flows which evolve over time as a range of production programmes develops and important problems of synchronisation in temporal patterns of coordination and of input and process indivisibilities get (imperfectly) resolved. The evolutionary character of productive organisation involving clusters of 'productive agents' and other assets (see below) is the main reason for the development of *production units* and also of persistent relationships between such units such as those named *industrial districts*.

In the recent literature on the theory of the firm, the firm has been characterised as a 'bundle of assets' (see, e.g., Mayhew and Seabright, 1992, for an overview). We concur with this characterisation but would like to specifically emphasise two types of assets that are involved:

(i) the set of fund-input elements with associated capability structures $\{c^{*}\}$ and
(ii) the know-how about feasible organisational and technological arrangements which the production unit could implement or upon which a group of such units could draw.

Let us explore (ii) a bit further since it involves a number of things. First it involves a knowledge about the capabilities of the fund-input elements; second it involves knowledge about the productive process itself, i.e., about the sets of feasible task specifications $\{\tau_j\}$ into which the process might be decomposed and also about the temporal sequencing arrangements which might be feasible and which would lead to an 'adequate' completion of the productive process; third comes the knowledge about feasible fund-task allocations or job programmes $J(\omega)$; and, fourth, know-how about the properties of materials m_i and materials-in-process arrangements $\{M_t(\omega), t=1, ..., N\}$. (i) and (ii) together allow a production unit to implement a variety of production programmes $P(\omega)$ which usually involve all the above production-analytical categories; the particular choice of such a production programme depends upon the composition and scale of final output required $[y(t)]$ and upon the nature of production linkages with other productive units, such as the temporal pattern and quality of inputs supplied by these other production units, possible material shortages, possible leasing arrangements of fund-input elements and of storage capacities.

Notes

1 Of course, even in a 'descriptive' account of productive operations, concepts are being used and associations among concepts established, but these concepts are not explicitly defined nor their relationship to each other analytically specified. The analytical structure underlying such 'description' remains thus amorphous. Nonetheless, we will see that the descriptive account of productive operations briefly introduced in this subsection will relate to the analytical structure developed in this chapter. The advantage of an initial descriptive account is that it allows us to introduce a rather 'holistic' picture of a set of relationships which later on need to be isolated in order to arrive at a more precise analytical insight.
2 The task specification of a production process is a feature that is largely

neglected in production theory. However, there are important insights into this dimension of production processes in authors such as Smith (1776), Storch (1815), Gioja (1815–17), Babbage (1832), Marx (1867), Martello (1890–1), Taylor (1911), Gantt (1912), Church (1912–13) and in a number of more recent writers in the production organisation literature such as Woodward (1956).

3 The view that the characteristics of productive agents may be associated with their capabilities may be found in the early literature on the division of labour (see Smith, 1776; Gioja, 1815–17; Rae, 1834; Babbage, 1832). Charles Babbage initiated the abstract treatment of the capabilities of tools and machines (Babbage, 1826; see also Babbage, 1832, and Ampère, 1834). Recently, the capability dimension has been emphasised in the management literature (see, for example, Bessant and Haywood, 1986) and in the analysis of the anthropological foundations of economic behaviour (see Sen, 1985; Dasgupta, 1993).

4 The importance of the raw material basis of productive activities has been emphasised by John Rae (1834). Subsequent contributions have considered the materials-in-process dimension of production processes when examining the relationship between production and time (see Menger, 1871; Böhm-Bawerk, 1889; Clark, 1899; Martello 1890–1; Mayer, 1925; Hayek, 1941; Hicks, 1973). Recently, the influence of materials-in-process flows in decisively shaping adjustment processes in an economy has been explored by Lowe, 1976, and Quadrio Curzio, 1986.

5 Our view of the constitutive elements of a production process has a number of features in common with the one developed in a number of important contributions by Nicholas Georgescu-Roegen (see Georgescu-Roegen, 1969, 1971), according to whom a critical distinction is that between 'fund elements' (inputs that enter a process under a certain description and also leave that process under 'essentially' the same description) and 'flow elements' (inputs that lose their identity in the course of the production process, for they enter the process with a certain description and leave the process under a different description). The above distinction between agents and materials keeps track of the difference between production elements that get transformed in the course of the production process and others that do not, in the sense that they may be identified by a set of characteristics which remains 'essentially' unchanged in the course of its utilisation over a particular time period. As we shall see below (section 5.2), this feature is a distinctive characteristic of fund elements.

6 However, we will later on distinguish productive processes which are not associated with sequences of transformations of materials. In such processes, such as education or health care, productive activity is associated with sequences of interactions among individuals which, of course, also require synchronisation amongst participating agents, but the process is not one primarily of material transformation (except in the form of an extreme physiological interpretation of human interaction).

7 We define *task specification* as the bundling of sets of primitive operations into tasks; this is distinguished from *task arrangement* which refers to the organisational arrangement of tasks in the overall productive process; it defines their

sequential and parallel ordering and thus the functional interrelationships of tasks in a productive process.

8 We will not use Georgescu-Roegen's notion of *process fund* since the analytical distinction between 'funds' which essentially maintain their characteristics in the course of a specified production process and a 'process fund' (materials-in-process) which undergoes qualitative change in the course of the process of transformation is too great. There might be capital-theoretic reasons to see a commonality between the two types of elements, but these do not concern us here.

9 An analysis of structural stability can be found in the engineering literature, see, e.g., Przemieniecki (1985).

10 For a general argument relevant in this connection, see Cartwright, 1989, pp. 141–82.

11 The example given here is somewhat special in that the time to execute the different types of tasks has been assumed to be the same, but the argument can be generalised to the case where the execution times of different tasks differ. In that case new processes have to be started at the smallest common denominator of the fractions $1/t(\tau_1)$, $1/t(\tau_2)$, $1/t(\tau_3)$ where $t(\tau_k)$, $k=1, 2, 3$, denotes the execution time of task τ_k. The number of fund-input elements hired in this (integer) case has to increase accordingly. For a discussion of the general case, see Landesmann (1986).

12 'If we confine our attention to some particular lot of raw materials, of rags, for instance, in paper manufacture, or of wire in needle manufacture, we perceive that it passes in succession through a series of stages in the hands of the detail workmen until completion. On the other hand, if we look at the workshop as a whole, we see the raw material in all the stages of its production at the same time. . . . The different detail processes, which were successive in time, have become simultaneous, go on side by side in space. Hence, production of a greater quantum of finished commodities in a given time' (Marx, 1972, p. 326).

13 E. A. G. Robinson pointed this out long ago in his study *The Structure of Competitive Industry*: 'Mechanical units do not arrange themselves easily into groups such that they give their best results with an output, one of one hundred units a day, another of two hundred, a third of four hundred, so that they can be fitted neatly into the industrial jig-saw. There will be several different mechanical bottlenecks in the firm, each requiring to be used, for greater efficiency, up to its fullest capacity, but each, requiring a daily output in order that it may be used. The escape from this difficulty may be a compromise, one machine being overdriven, so that it produces slightly more than it can with optimum efficiency, another producing slightly less' (Robinson, 1958, pp. 25–6, 1st edn 1931).

14 We can think here of the ranking of job specification programmes in terms of overall 'task adequacy' as $J(\alpha)>J(\beta)>J(\gamma)>\ldots$; see section 5.2.

15 See also Georgescu-Roegen (1970).

16 Abruzzi (1965, pp. 101–2) gives the following characterisation of the job-shop form of production organisation: 'the process is . . . segmented into linked organic work phases, each as functionally unified as is operationally

feasible. Also, each of these phases is decomposable into individual work cycles having the same characteristics, which vary in number and quality according to particular job orders. The organic work phases thus have variable contours, which means that they are mutable and elastic. With these properties, there is no necessity for defining separate connecting phases: successive phases, being organic and variable, have internal connecting operations with the quality of being fully sequential in the functional sense. In sum, then the organic work phases . . . are mutually interdependent to the point that their very structures are functionally linked. It follows that the production sequencing order is variable rather than fixed, with linkages based eventually on work content rather than work pace' (see also the detailed discussion in chapter 8).

17 The early literature on the analysis of machinery, i.e., kinematics, distinguishes between elementary operations and tasks. See, e.g., Babbage's paper in the *Philosophical Transactions* of the Royal Society (Babbage, 1826) and F. Reuleaux's *Theoretische Kinematik* (Reuleaux, 1875). In his treatise, Reuleaux introduces the distinction between 'elementary machines' and 'complex machines' and describes the latter as the result of combining a certain number of elementary machines into a single machine.

18 See, e.g., the following quote from Ferrara: 'if we consider [agricultural processes] from the point of view of final output, we shall certainly find great differences between what is needed to prepare the ground, to sow it, and to collect the harvest; and all such operations would greatly vary from one product to another. But *if we examine the aspect of human effort . . . we would hardly find ten different movements which are repeated all the time*' (Ferrara, 1860, p. 53, own italics).

19 Complex task specification (at least for the master craftsmen) was also characteristic of the medieval crafts workshop. However, the execution of operations, their sequencing in time and their exact durations could not be programmed in the same precise manner as in the case of complex machinery. We will return to this point in chapter 8.

We may conjecture that, before the Industrial Revolution, tasks tend to be 'complex' in terms of elementary operations – tasks both in agriculture as well as in the medieval craftshop may require the coordinated performance of a considerable number of distinct types of operations. The process of division of labour, as described by Adam Smith and later carried further with the time and motion studies of the Taylorist period of factory management, is instead characterised by the 'dissection' of the production process, first in its constituent tasks (*stage 1*) and then in its constituent elementary operations (*stage 2*). In stage 1, the production process is divided into its constituent elements (tasks) and each task is assigned to a special type of fund input which, in turn, has or develops a specialised set of capabilities in executing that particular task; this is the stage considered by Adam Smith. In stage 2, the production process is further dissected for its constituent elementary operations so that tasks which become assigned to individual workmen consist of a very small set of elementary operations. The abstract theory of machinery that was developed in the course of the nineteenth century by authors such as Charles Babbage (1832) and Franz Reuleaux (1875) may be seen as an attempt to analyse existing machines in order to discover their constituent elementary operations and thus make the construction of more complex machinery possible (complex machinery may be seen as the result of combining in different ways a limited number of elementary machines).

The notion that division of labour, rather than being opposed to the combination of operations executed by machinery (see, for instance, Lauderdale, 1804) is in fact a necessary condition for the construction of complex machines, was explicitly formulated in the course of the nineteenth century by authors such as Dunoyer (1845) and Leroy-Beaulieu (1896). It is at this stage that machinery (as distinct from tools) becomes an important element in the production process, not only for the production of power but also for the actual execution of tasks. For it is a special feature of machinery that in it motions can be performed and combined in the most efficient way by establishing a direct connection between the utilisation of power and the particular types of motion that have to be performed. As a result, the analysis of the production process in terms of elementary operations (rather than in terms of tasks) and the development of the pure theory of machinery (*kinematics*) makes it possible to reach a very precise definition of tasks and a highly synchronised system of task arrangement and task execution which was impossible to achieve in non-mechanised forms of production organisation. In this way, it is either the single machine which performs in a highly synchronised manner a particular sequence of elementary operations or, in further extension, a system of coordinated machinery.

20 Alfred Marshall points out: '[W]hen large masses of men in the same locality are engaged in similar tasks, it is found that, by associating with one another, they educate one another. To use a mode of speaking which workmen themselves use, the skill required for their work is "in the air, and the children breathe it as they grow up"' (Marshall, 1930, 1st edn, 1879, pp. 8–9).

Marshall also called attention to the relationship between interactive patterns of learning and inventive activity: 'if the total number of firms engaged in a particular industry is small, there are but few men in a position to make improvements in the processes of manufacture, to invent new machines and new methods. But when the total number of men interested in the matter is very large there are to be found among them many who, by their intellect and temper, are fitted to originate new ideas. Each new idea is canvassed and improved upon by many minds; each new accidental experience and each deliberate experiment will afford food for reflection and for new suggestions, not a few persons but to many. Thus in a large localised industry new ideas are likely to be started rapidly; and each new idea is likely to be fertile of practical improvements' (ibid.).

21 The notion of a repetitive cycle emerges from the fact that individual productive processes are bounded in time (see section 3), so that the productive process of the entire productive system consisting of interdependent productive processes must be bounded in time.

References

Abruzzi, A. (1965) 'The Production Process: Operating Characteristics', *Management Science*, 11 (6, April): B98–B118.

Ampère, A.-M. (1834) *Essai sur la philosophie des sciences*, Paris, Bachelier.

Ando, A. and Fisher, F. M. (1963) 'Near Decomposability, Partition and Aggregation, and the Relevance of Stability Discussions', *International Economic Review*, 4, (1, January): 53–67.

Ando, A., Fisher, F. M. and Simon, M. A. (1963) *Essays on the Structure of Social Science Models*, Cambridge, Mass., The MIT Press.

Babbage, C. (1826) 'On a Method of Expressing by Signs the Action of Machinery', in *Philosophical Transactions* (Royal Society), pp. 250–65.
(1832) *On the Economy of Machinery and Manufacturers*, London, Charles Knight.

Bessant, J. and Haywood, B. (1986) 'Flexibility in Manufacturing Systems', *Omega: The International Journal of Management Science*, 14 (6): 465–73.

Bharadwaj, K. (1966) 'A Note on Structural Interdependence and the Concept of "Key" Sector', *Kyklos. International Review for Social Sciences*, 19 (2): 315–19.

Blin, J. M. and F. Murphy (1974) 'On Measuring Economic Interrelatedness', *Review of Economic Studies*, 41 (3): 437–40.

Böhm-Bawerk, E. von (1889) *Positive Theorie des Kapitales*, Innsbruck, Wagner (translated as *The Positive Theory of Capital*, London, Macmillan, 1981).

Burchardt, F. A. (1931–2) 'Die Schemata des Stationären Kreislaufs bei Böhm-Bawerk und Marx', *Weltwirtschaftliches Archiv*, 34: 525–64, and 35: 116–76.

Cartwright, N. (1989) *Nature's Capacities and their Measurement*, Oxford, Clarendon Press.

Church, A. H. (1912–1913) 'Practical Principles of Rational Management', *Engineering Magazine*, 44 (1912): 487–94, 673–80, 894–903, and 45 (1913): 24–33, 166–73, 405–11.

Clark, J. B. (1899) *The Distribution of Wealth*, New York, Macmillan.

Cohendet, P., Ledoux, M. and Zuskovitch, E. (eds.) (1988) *New Advanced Materials. Economic Dynamics and European Strategy*, Berlin–Heidelberg–New York, Springer-Verlag.

Dasgupta, P. (1993) *An Inquiry into Well-Being and Destitution*, Oxford, Clarendon Press.

Dunoyer, C. (1845) *De la liberté de travail: ou, simple exposé des conditions dans lesquelles les forces humaines s'exercent avec le plus de puissance*, Paris, Guillaumin.

Ferrara, F. (1860) Introduction to vol. II, 2nd series of the *Biblioteca dell'Economista*, Turin, UTET, pp. v–lxxii.

Gantt, H. L. (1912) 'The Task and the Day's Work', in *Addresses and Discussions at the Conference on Scientific Management held October 12–13–14 1911*. The Amos Tuck School of Administration and Finance, Dartmouth College, Hanover, New Haven.

Georgescu-Roegen, N. (1969) 'Process in Farming versus Process in Manufacturing: A Problem of Balanced Development', in G. U. Papi and C. Nunn (eds.) *Economic Problems of Agriculture in Industrial Societies*, New York, St. Martins Press, pp. 497–528.

(1970) 'The Economics of Production', *American Economic Review*, 60 (May): 1–9.

(1971) *The Entropy Law and the Economic Process*, Cambridge, Mass., Harvard University Press.

(1976) *Energy and Economic Myths: Institutional and Analytical Economic Essays*, New York and Oxford, Pergamon Press.

(1986) 'Man and Production', in M. Baranzini and R. Scazzieri (eds.), *Foundations of Economics. Structures of Inquiry and Economic Theory*, Oxford and New York, Basil Blackwell, pp. 247–80.

(1990) 'The Production Process and Economic Dynamics', in M. Baranzini and R. Scazzieri (eds.), *The Economic Theory of Structure and Change*, Cambridge, Cambridge University Press, pp. 198–226.

Gioja, M. (1815–17) *Nuovo Prospetto dello Scienze Economiche*, Milan, Pirotta.

Hayek, F. A. von (1941) *The Pure Theory of Capital*, London, Routledge.

Hermann, F. B. W. (1932) *Staatswirthschaftliche Untersuchungen*, Munich, A. Weber.

Hicks, J. (1970) 'A Neo-Austrian Growth Theory', *Economic Journal*, 80 (June): 257–81.

(1973) *Capital and Time, A Neo-Austrian Theory*, Oxford, Clarendon Press.

(1977) 'An Addendum to "Capital and Time"', in J. Hicks, *Economic Perspectives. Further Essays on Money and Growth*, Oxford, Clarendon Press, pp. 190–5.

Jevons, W. S. (1879) *A Theory of Political Economy*, London, Macmillan, 2nd edition.

Landesmann, M. (1986) 'Conceptions of Technology and the Production Process', in M. Baranzini and R. Scazzieri (eds.), *Foundations of Economics. Structures of Inquiry and Economic Theory*, Oxford and New York, Basil Blackwell, pp. 281–310.

Landesmann, M. and R. Scazzieri (1990) 'Specification of Structure and Economic Dynamics', in M. Baranzini and R. Scazzieri (eds.), *The Economic Theory of Structure and Change*, Cambridge, Cambridge University Press, pp. 95–121.

Lauderdale, J. (1804) *An Inquiry into the Nature and Origin of Public Wealth, and into the Means and Causes of its Increase*, Edinburgh, A. Constable and Co., London, T. N. Longman and O. Rees.

Leontief, W. (1991) 'The Economy as a Circular Flow', *Structural Change and Economic Dynamics*, 2 (1): 181–212 (German original published in 1928).

Leontief, W. et al. (1953) *Studies in the Structure of the American Economy. Theoretical and Empirical Explorations in Input-Output Analysis*, New York–Oxford, Oxford University Press.

Leroy-Beaulieu, P. (1896) *Traité théorique et practique d'économie politique*, Paris, Guillaumin.

Lowe, A. (1976) *The Path of Economic Growth*, Cambridge, Cambridge University Press.

Marshall, A. (1930) *The Pure Theory of Foreign Trade. The Pure Theory of Domestic Values*, The London School of Economics and Political Science, London.

Martello, T. (1890–1) *Appunti di economia politica*, University of Bologna, Lecture notes for the academic year 1890–1.

Marx, K. (1867) *Das Kapital*, Hamburg, O. Meissner, vol. I.

(1972) *Capital. A Critique of Political Economy*. Book One: *The Process of Production of Capital* (1st edn. 1867), London, Lawrence and Wishart.

Masci, G. (1934) *Alcuni aspetti odierni dell'organizzazione e delle trasformazioni industriali*, in G. Masci (ed.), *Organizzazione industriale*, Turin, UTET.

Mayer, H. (1925) *Produktion*, in L. Elster and A. Weber (eds.), *Handworterbuch der Staatswissenschaften*, Jena, Gustav Fischer, vol. VI, pp. 1108–22.

Mayhew, K. and Seabright, P. (1992) 'Incentives and the Management of Enterprises in Economic Transition: Capital Markets are not Enough', *Oxford Review of Economic Policy*, 8 (1): 105–29.

McGilvray, J. W. (1977) 'Linkage, Key Sectors and Development Strategy', in W. Leontief (ed.), *Structures, System and Economic Policy*, Cambridge, Cambridge University Press.

Menger, C. (1871) *Grundsästze der Volkswirtschaftslehre*, Vienna, Braumüller.

Mill, J. S. (1848) *Principles of Political Economy with some of their Applications to Social Philosophy*, London, J. W. Parker.

(1965) *Principles of Political Economy with some of their Applications to Social Philosophy* (1st edn. 1848), Introduction by W. Bladen; textual editor J. M. Robson, Toronto, University of Toronto Press; London, Routledge and Kegan Paul.

Pasinetti, L. L. (1973) 'The Notion of Vertical Integration in Economic Analysis', *Metroeconomica*, 25 (January–April): 1–29.

(1981) *Structural Change and Economic Growth. A Theoretical Essay on the Dynamics of the Wealth of Nations*, Cambridge, Cambridge University Press.

(1988) 'Growing Subsystems, Vertically Hyper-integrated Sectors and the Labour Theory of Value', *Cambridge Journal of Economics*, 12: 125–34.

Passy, H. P. (1846) *Des systèmes de culture et de leur influence sur l'économic sociale*, Paris, Guillaumin.

Przemieniecki, J. S. (1985) *Theory of Matrix Structural Analysis*, New York, Dover, London, Constable.

Quadrio Curzio, A. (1986) 'Technological Scarcity: an Essay on Production and Structural Change', in M. Baranzini and R. Scazzieri (eds.), *Foundations of Economics. Structures of Inquiry and Economic Theory*, Oxford and New York, Basil Blackwell, pp. 311–38.

(with an Appendix by C. F. Manara and M. Faliva) (1996) 'Production and Efficiency with Global Technologies', in this volume.

Quadrio Curzio, A. and Pellizzari, F. (1991) 'The Structural Rigidities and Dynamic Choice of Technologies', *Rivista internazionale di scienze economiche e commerciali*, 38 (6–7, June–July): 481–517.

Rae, J. (1834) *Statement of Some New Principles on the Subject of Political Economy, Exposing the Fallacies of the System of the Free Trade and of Some Other Doctrines Maintained in the Wealth of Nations*, Boston, Hilliard, Gray.

Reuleaux, F. (1875) *Theoretische Kinematik: Grundzüge einer Theorie des Maschinenwesens*, Braunschweig, F. Vieger and Son.

(1876) *The Kinematics of Machinery. Outlines of a Theory of Machines*, translated and edited by A. B. W. Kennedy, London, Macmillan.

Robinson, E. A. G. (1958) *The Structure of Competitive Industry*, Digswell Place, Nisbet; Cambridge University Press.

Rosenberg, N. (1969) 'The Direction of Technological Change: Inducement Mechanisms and Focusing Devices', *Economic Development and Cultural Change*, 18: 1–24.

Scazzieri, R. (1990) 'Vertical Integration in Economic Theory', *Journal of Postkeynesian Economics*, 13 (1, Fall): 20–46.

(1993) *A Theory of Production. Tasks, Processes and Technical Practices*, Oxford, Clarendon Press.

Sen, A. (1985) *Commodities and Capabilities*, Amsterdam, North Holland.

Smith, A. (1776) *An Inquiry into the Nature and Causes of the Wealth of Nations*, London, Strahan and Cadell.

Sraffa, P. (1960) *Production of Commodities by Means of Commodities*, Cambridge, Cambridge University Press.

Storch, H. F. (1815) *Cours d'économie politique, ou exposition des principes qui déterminent la prospérité des nations*, St. Petersbourg, Pluchart.

Strassman, W. P. (1959–60) 'Interrelated Industries and the Rate of Technological Change', *The Review of Economic Studies*, 27 (72): 16–22.

Strigl, R. (1928) 'Die Produktion unter dem Einflusse einer Kreditexpansion', in *Schriften des Vereins für Socialpolitik*, vol. 173: *Beiträge zur Wirtschaftstheorie*: Part Two: *Konjunkturforschung und Konjunkturtheorie*, pp. 187–211.

Taylor, F. W. (1911) *The Principles of Scientific Management*, Harper, New York and London.

White, R. N. et al. (1976) *Structural Engineering*, vol. 1: *Introduction to Design Concepts and Analysis*, Books on demand UMI.

Woodward, J. (1965) *Industrial Organisation: Theory and Practice*, London, New York, Toronto, Oxford University Press.

7   Agricultural forms of production organisation

ALESSANDRO ROMAGNOLI

1 Introduction

The description of agricultural activities involves a number of different disciplines, so that the representation of an actual agricultural process results from the consideration of different dimensions. The most important among them are the following (see Kostrowicki, 1977; De Walt, 1985; Spedding, 1988):

(i)   the *'social'* dimension, represented by features such as population structure, tenure, farming family organisation, farmer attitude to innovation, and so on;
(ii) the *'economic'* dimension, which is related to the enterprise structure, the market structure, the interrelationships between farms and markets, the business policy, and so on;
(iii) the *'biological'* dimension, which concerns technical and productive conditions.

Any type of agricultural process may be conceived as a *system*, that is, as 'a group of interacting components, operating together for a common purpose, capable of reacting as a whole to external stimuli: it is not directly affected by its own output and has a specified boundary based on the inclusion of all significant feedbacks' (Spedding, 1988, p. 18). And for special purposes a subsystem may be identified and extracted from the general system if the subsystem presents a degree of integrity and independence of the whole, and has the same output as the main system. As a result, in any real type of agricultural process, we may distinguish the family farm subsystem, the spatial subsystem of agricultural activities, the agricultural markets subsystem, the production subsystem (describable in terms of major components, different combinations of crop, cultivation method, fertiliser input, sowing date), and so on.

Each subsystem may be represented analytically by its 'morphological conception', which is a weighted combination of different images associated with the isolation of certain analytical concepts. From an economic standpoint the morphological conception of any agricultural production subsystem is determined by the following analytical concepts:

  (i) the nature of physical elements of production;
 (ii) the structure of productive operations;
(iii) the pattern of technological progress;
 (iv) the forms of organisation of the production process (that is the task organisation, the arrangement of productive elements and the network of transformation stages), which arise from the interaction between previous analytical concepts.

As a result the forms of production organisation which take place in actual types of agriculture may be synthetically represented by the *productive operating system*, that is 'a configuration of resources combined for the function of manufacturing an agricultural product by means of a management operation, concerned with the design and the operation of the system' (see Wild, 1985, pp. 4 and 8). The above functions are mainly related to the design specification of the process, the determination of capacity, the design of works and jobs and the planning and scheduling of activities (Wild, 1985, p. 13).

2 General features of the farm productive operating system

If we consider the nature of agricultural production processes, we may discover features which are peculiar to that sector. As a matter of fact there are some differences between agriculture and manufacturing that concern not only the *productive arrangement*, but also the *primitive elements* which make up the production process, the *factors* which influence the output and the *coordination problems* of the farm productive operating system. The nature of agricultural productive elements is significant in determining the specification and structure of *agricultural works*, whereas the factors affecting the output and the economic problems related to farm organisation determine *coordination of works and agents*.

2.1 The productive arrangement

In general, the production process of a farm is planned to produce more than one product for technical and economic reasons, which impose some constraints on the choice of a set of crops. From the agronomic point of view the crops may be classified as:

  (i) *impoverishing*, when at the end of the production process land is less fertile than at the beginning. This is the case, among others, of wheat, barley and rice;

(ii) *improving*, when the conditions of land are better after cultivation. This effect is brought about by graminaceous and by leguminous crops;

(iii) *getting ready*, when the crops give a good condition of fertility because of their operations related to cultivation (such as deep ploughing). Among others this grove includes beets, potatoes, tobacco, tomatoes, maize.

Because of the above agronomic properties of crops the productive arrangement of a farm must be planned in such a way that, on each plot of land, an 'improving' or 'getting ready' crop is cultivated after an 'impoverishing' one, to maintain fertility. As a result, there is a particular time sequence of crops on the same plot, as well as a rigid set of species of crops produced each year. The latter set depends on the chosen rotation, that is on the number of years which characterises any given crop sequence. Several rotations have been used, but the one which contributed to the first revolution of commercialised agriculture is a four-year rotation (called a Norfolk rotation) which by the second half of the eighteenth century had spread throughout England and then Europe. Nowadays economic conditions and chemical progress push agriculture to adopt free sequences, but, in spite of that tendency, the rotation method is still valid (Giardini, 1986, p. 532).

From a technical viewpoint, the *farm arrangement* is thus a multicrop production with a certain degree of rigidity in the choice of the set of goods to be produced. This is also due to economic reasons. As a matter of fact, among the advantages brought about by the rotation system, we can mention:

(i) the attainment of output more than once a year (see figure 7.1a);

(ii) a well-balanced share of 'agricultural works' during the year (see below).

In the first case, the farmer can reduce the risk of null output that arises, because of climatic conditions, when he cultivates one crop only; in the second case he can avoid the idleness of productive elements.

But a farm arrangement, settled according to a certain rotation, sometimes may present 'inserted crops' and 'associated crops' in order to achieve the above goals. The 'inserted crops', cultivated on a plot which is idle between one production period and the next in the same rotation, allow full utilisation of the land (see figure 7.1b), while the 'associated crops' (see figure 7.1c), which presents two partially overlapping production periods, allow a full utilisation of the other fund elements.

Another feature of the farm in some forms of agricultural production organisation is that the productive arrangement includes the restoring of

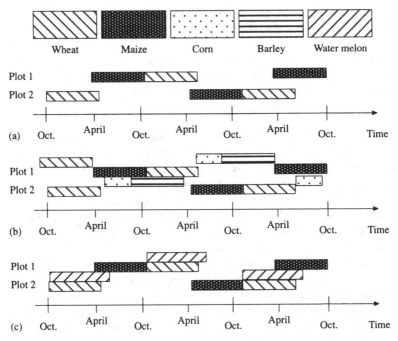

Figure 7.1 Simple two-year rotation (a); two-year rotation with 'inserted crops' (b); with 'associated crops' (c)

fund elements. The *agricultural restoring process* is a real productive process that, by means of its output, enables some fund elements to improve crop production. As we mentioned above, the grasses in the rotation 'bring about a profitable effect on land that benefits, for several years, the crops cultivated after the grass' (Giardini, 1986, p. 516). In the Norfolk rotation, for example, fodder cropping, turnip and clover productions supply forage for the livestock. Thus some crops have a twofold function: they restore fertility and serve to feed the livestock.

Such restoring processes are essential in non-industrialised agriculture, whose inputs come mostly from the farm, since they 'increase the livestock which can be nourished in a farm, and as a consequence, the availability of dung; . . . this improved amount of dung raises the output of cereal crops' (Grigg, 1985, p. 235). As a result the restoring processes reproduce what Ruttan calls 'the conservation model' of agricultural development (Hayami and Ruttan, 1971, p. 28). In this context, marketable crops may be seen as the result of the integration of the 'restoring productive processes' in the productive processes for the market.

Finally, we must remember that there is another important restoring process: it is poultry breeding whose output is used, sometimes to a great extent, as food for the farmer and his family.

2.2 The nature of productive elements

With regard to productive elements, agriculture utilises three different kinds of fund elements (see Georgescu-Roegen, 1969): land, labour and 'cooperating instruments'. The last ones may be represented by animals or engines which increase the results of human effort either by giving more power to the work, or by performing more than one task at the same time. But the agricultural implements also belong to the third kind of fund elements: they perform more accurately an operation and reduce the time necessary to do it. As a result, both power sources and machines employed in farming cooperate with labour to increase the speed of productive operations: their aim is to improve the productivity of labour. This was also the opinion of Ricardo who argued that 'improvements in agriculture are of two kinds: those which increase the productive power of the land and those which enable us, by improving our machinery, to obtain its produce with less labour' (Ricardo, 1951, p. 80).[1]

The dependence on labour that characterises the third element is due to the type of agricultural mechanisation: farm machinery and implements try 'to reproduce mechanically the job carried out by the farmer, thus strengthening its effect' (Pellizzi, 1984, p. 270). This is the reason why each 'cooperating element' operates under the control of one or more workers (according to a fixed ratio that is peculiar to each instrument), and why the time of its utilisation always corresponds, for each individual engaged in it, to an equal time of work.

As a result we may say that in agricultural production two fund elements (land and labour) are critical, while the third one ('the cooperating element') is functional to labour. Since the farmer applies the 'cooperating instruments' only if there is a shortage of manpower to carry out farm work, their presence depends on the labour/land ratio (that is the ratio between farm availability of labour and land to be cultivated). If in the farm:

Q_1 is the labour requirement per acre cultivated according to a certain technique;

A_1 the farm availability of labour per acre;

X is the output per acre,

we may define

$$q_1 = Q_1/X$$

as the 'labour coefficient' (labour used per unit of output) and

$$a_1 = A_1/X$$

as the available labour per each unit of output. If

$$Q_1 < A_1$$

the farmer introduces 'cooperating elements' in order to reduce the coefficient of labour per unit of output, that is to adopt a technique whose labour/land ratio is closer to the farm's labour/land ratio. As a result he increases the capital/labour ratio and the 'degree of mechanisation' (see Pasinetti, 1981, p. 182) when the introduced cooperating instrument is a machine. On the other hand, a reduction of that ratio occurs when $Q_1 > A_1$ and the farmer applies process innovations such as new agronomic and genetic technologies in order to increase the output per acre. Since such innovations generally involve a growth in labour needs A_1 (see Grigg, 1985, p. 141) as well as an increased output/land ratio, the capital/labour ratio decreases. If a low yield/land ratio characterised extensive cropping and a high ratio an intensive one (see Cochrane, 1984, p. 184), we may say that any movement from the first to the second corresponds to an approach of A_1 to Q_1.

Land is a special fund element because it is always present in the process, whereas the other funds are present only when required by the specific needs of the working process that are, for the most part, connected to the various moments of the land's action. But land presents a special relation with flow elements too, because in farm processes a lot of flow elements serve to *restore* the land. Both *organic fertilisation* (which is an artificial contribution of organic materials to land for the purpose of improving its fertility (see Giardini, 1986, p. 366)) and *manuring* (which is the distribution of nutrients to the plants, put into effect through the land (Giardini, 1986, p. 399)) improve the performance of that element by restoring its fertility.

2.3 The structure of 'agricultural works'

In agricultural analysis the tasks being performed are generally described not only from the point of view of the work to be done, but also with regard to the nature of the 'unit operation' which gives a productive effect.

Attention to 'works to be done' is due to the fact that agricultural production is a process which can be controlled by human beings only partially because it consists of a sequence of operations whose *order*, *duration* and *respective distances* are significantly dependent on weather conditions.

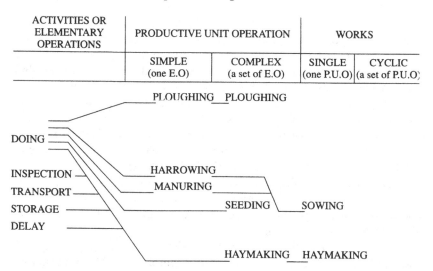

Figure 7.2   The structure of agricultural works

This general feature has not been influenced by mechanisation, that in agriculture takes the form of a 'spectacular change in the implements of production, whereas in industry it is a further revolution in the sequence (order) in which men use their implements' (Brewster, 1950, p. 70): in industry, the machine directly transforms the raw materials into goods, whereas in agriculture machinery 'has only the task of creating the more suitable environment for the life of the cells, during the production process, and of picking up the result of their work, at the end' (Bolli and Scotton, 1987, pp. 19–20). In this context the farm operation is itself defining the organisational phenomenon: thus it has a strong effect on the other factors of the agricultural process.

In agricultural process analysis the 'productive unit operation' is a unit of homogeneous productive action (whose main features are the degree of complexity and the pattern of coordination), which 'processes a material and produces and delivers other material(s)' (Van Elderen, 1980, p. 2) by combining some 'activities' (such as inspection, transport, storage, delay, 'doing' – see Buckett, 1988, p. 189), which are called 'elementary operations', within a given period of historical time (see figure 7.2).

Because of this time dimension, it is impossible to perform activities which comprise a particular unit operation separately and in different periods. Though machines tend to simplify each operation, the complexity remains in spite of technological advances. As a matter of fact agricultural mechanisation is constrained by an essential feature of agriculture, the presence of land. Since 'farming deals with living things, fixed in the soil', 'transport and processing functions are inseparable aspects of any operation involving land, the job of transport being to carry operations to their materials. Hence farm mechanisation results in independent (moment-by-moment) machines insomuch as each machine (doing operations involving land) must embody both these functions and is therefore able to provide itself with its own materials' (Brewster, 1950, p. 70).

As a consequence of the complexity and of the coordination requirement, a unit operation is often performed by a team of workers, or 'gang': in silage making, for example, a worker drives the tractor and the forage harvester directly coupled to the trailer, another worker drives the tractor and the trailer, exchanges empty for full trailers in the field and drives to and from the pit, and a third worker is at the pit, fills the pit with the buck-rake, hand spreads and rolls.

The chain of reasoning presented below shows not only that the agricultural unit operation is an independent and complex variable, but also that it is a particular primitive element inducing technological advances. In addition, having no influence at all on the order of operations, agricultural mechanisation embodies other features due to the nature of the agricultural processes and operations:

(i)   as opposed to the case of industrial mechanisation, mechanisation in agriculture doesn't increase the number of concurrent operations which must be carried out at the same time: for biological reasons, agricultural machines cannot introduce the simultaneous performance of many operations in a production process.

(ii) hence the input–output rate and quality of an operation is not controlled by the moment-by-moment flow of materials between operations: their connection and control has to be, in general, *goal oriented* rather than *mechanical*.

(iii) the farmer is the 'director of production', being in possession of the old artisan's creative satisfaction. It is possible to identify the worker with the product, since the same worker is generally associated with most of the productive operations.

(iv) 'since farm mechanisation in no way increases the number of things which must be done at the same time, it provides no new bases whatever for either the functional or task form of specialisation' (Brewster, 1950, p. 75).

The specialisation of the agricultural unit operation is an important issue because it is always mentioned to show the inferiority of agricultural production with respect to industry.[2] The traditional definition of division of labour as the division of a process into parts, each of which is carried out by a separate person (see Groenewegen, 1987, p. 901), is ineffectual in order to show the degree of specialisation of agricultural unit operations, because their decomposition into different activities gives evidence of the technical possibility of this sort of division in agricultural processes. And if we consider that sometimes agricultural mechanisation tends to introduce machines which perform all unit operations embodied in a task (replacing, for example, the three workers engaged in the silage making by a yard with only one man – see Casati, Garibaldi and Cavalchini, 1979), we realise that the problem is more complex and that it must be approached from the point of view of the relation between labour and cooperating instruments, given the constraints due to land.

The starting point must then be that the division of labour 'is a function from the set of tasks to the set of skills, so that any skill must be associated with one or more tasks and any task with only a single skill' (Scazzieri, 1987, p. 239). As a result each production process may be divided into elementary components consisting of the abstract function performed (*functional division of labour*), or of the specific task independent of the general abilities required (*content-specific division of labour*) (see Scazzieri, 1987, p. 78; see also Scazzieri, 1993, chapter 4). Agricultural production, which as a rule presents a 'personal division of labour', shows either the first kind of 'technical division of labour' or the second as well.

When the farm production process is the result of elementary processes that allow a uniform utilisation of workers throughout the year (so that, in each operation's available period, labour need is equal to labour availability), there is a 'personal division of labour': 'in the share cropper family or in the tenant family there is a specific distribution of functions. The direction of the farm belongs to one of the men, on the contrary the direction of the household office is attributed to a woman, who sometimes is not the wife of the farm director. The livestock is entrusted particularly to a breeder who is helped by some stable-boys. . . . The tasks performed by adult men are different from those performed by women, when they work on field. Children are utilised in some other ways' (Valenti, 1918, vol. II, pp. 49–50 ff.).

We may think of a 'functional division of labour' when a worker performs many operations of the same kind, so that it is a special worker who prunes or seeds. On the other hand, Valenti and Serpieri agree that there is a 'content-specific division of labour' in agricultural activities in the case of continuous operations within the same farm (these are operations lasting most of the year), or in the case of adjoining operations in different farms ('so that it is possible for the worker to find a job in the same operation during a great part of the year, if he moves from one farm to the other' – Serpieri, 1946, p. 72). Livestock breeding, irrigation and the driving of special machines belong to the first kind of operations, whereas harvesting and industrial cropping belong to the second.

If the impossibility of continuous utilisation of a worker on the same agricultural operation is a constraint for the diffusion of the technical division of labour, on the other hand, the contemporary cultivation of 'competing crops' (which are 'crops that require attention at the same time of year' – see Taylor, 1925, p. 37) tends to increase the 'content-specific division of labour'. This is because of the concurrence of the 'available periods', which are the time intervals within which operations must be performed. But the most important push towards a 'content-specific division of labour' is due to the 'degree of relative intensity' for a fund service, which characterises each agricultural job. Given the need for a fund service j to perform a particular operation i on each acre according to a certain technique, and given the available time for that operation, we may define the 'fund service need per unit of time' x_{ij}. If the 'work capacity per unit of time' of the fund j available for the operation i is α_{ij}, the 'degree of relative intensity' of j in i is the ratio

$$\epsilon_{ij} = \frac{x_{ij}}{\alpha_{ij}}$$

Given a 'degree of mechanisation', the more ϵ_{ij} is >1, the greater will be the push towards technical specialisation (a trend which is found in the cases of hay or silage making mentioned above).

3 The coordination problems of the farm productive operating system

From the agronomic point of view, vegetable production is a process which enables the running of a 'photosynthetic machine' (Meynard and Sebillotte, 1989, p. 35) producing fruits. If we consider animal production too, we may say that farm production is a rearing process whose output is affected by:

(i) the features of the living organism that is bred;
(ii) the physical environment in which the process takes place, that is land and the climate;
(iii) the arrangement of production.

There are thus biological, environmental and economic factors that influence the quantity and quality of output.

The first group of factors determines both the majority of the flow elements of an elementary process and the technical formalities necessary to obtain the output, because time sequence, quantity of flow inputs and their administration depend on the needs of every living organism during its growth process. The second group (physical environment) includes some risk factors that may be avoided by investment activities such as land reclamation on one side, and protective structures (greenhouses) on the other. As a matter of fact, such investments lead to the constitution or restoration of productivity to fertile land, or to its improvement. They are the economic activities which determine, from a qualitative (or technical) point of view, the 'plant' of the farm.

The third group of factors affecting output determines the economic features of the productive operating system, since it determines the number of products obtained by the farm process, the scale of production, the adopted technique, the 'productive functions' for the various crops and hence the total operative costs (prime costs plus operation overheads) by means of the coordination of fund elements such as labour and the cooperating instruments.

In the agricultural production processes, the presence of previous factors has a twofold influence: on the output and on production organisation. As opposed to manufacturing, in agriculture the relation between a set of productive elements (combined according to a technological pattern) and the output is never qualitatively and quantitatively determined. Biological (related to the growing process) and climatic risks introduce a probability element in the issue of agricultural production processes. In order to avoid such risks, agronomy specifies the task sequence, whereas mechanics and economics specify the arrangement of productive agents, whose definition is due to technological patterns too.

In agriculture, technological advance, that is, 'a situation wherein resources are combined in a new form, or a new configuration, such that . . . a lesser volume of resources measured in value terms yields the same output' (Cochrane, 1984, p. 201), is an adjusting process tending to achieve the full utilisation of the 'excess' fund element: 'The historic path of technological advance in agriculture is determined by the amount of labour and land availability. This is the reason why in the USA plentiful land and scarce labour pushed the farmers to the maximisation of output per worker' (Grigg, 1985, p. 145). This was obtained by means of mechanisation, which reduced the labour coefficient per acre with the technique employed, thus allowing the full and optimal utilisation of land by available labour. In Japan, the scarcity of land induced the introduction of techniques characterised by a lower land coefficient in order to use labour fully: this was achieved through the adoption of commercial fertilisers, irrigation water, herbicides and pesticides (see Grigg, 1985, p. 145).

As a result, the dynamics of fund elements which characterise the technological advance is, together with the biological and environmental constraints, an important factor in the specification of task network and of agent coordination within the farm.

3.1 The biological constraint on task-process organisation: the crop-growing technique

If vegetable production is, like animal production, a rearing process settled on a certain plot of fertile land, the productive operating system of each crop is subject to organisational constraints associated with the needs of the living organism and with environmental conditions. Such constraints impose qualitative restrictions on the character of operations, the order which must be followed in performing tasks, the length of the production period and the scheduling of flow elements. This is the reason why agronomists identify clear principles that must be followed in order to cultivate crops and obtain the maximum yield, and provide a 'crop-growing technique' for each vegetable.

'The crop-growing technique is an agricultural method (that is a set of arranged and connected operations) that may be considered, by scientific and applied knowledge, the most suitable to obtain the optimal yield of the crop, that is the maximum output per plot' (Polidori and Romagnoli, 1987, p. 338). Each crop-growing technique is identified by taking into account the features of the land and the elements needed in each moment of the life of the plant. As a result it prescribes rotations, fertilisations and irrigations in order to have in the fertile soil, at every moment of the production period, the amounts of the productive elements that are requested by the crop. A crop-growing technique provides, for the set of ordered operations, also the conditions to be followed in their performance. Finally, it identifies the 'useful period' within which each operation must be carried out (see table 7.1). Such a useful period reflects not only the length of time available to perform a certain productive unit operation, but also the historical starting point at which it must begin.

The sequence of useful periods shows the production period of an elementary process as the result of the span between the beginning of the useful period of the first productive unit operation and the end of the useful period of the last one. But it also shows '*the number of stages*, i.e., the number of production stages in the whole process, and . . . *the stage interval*, i.e., the way in which the various stages are distributed over the total production period' (Frisch, 1965, pp. 33–4).[3] Such intervals are the consequence of a special feature of agricultural production, that is the fact that land is a fund element that is all the time present in the process, and that human operations must facilitate the growing process carried out on land.

Table 7.1. *Crop-growing technique for wheat*

Cycles (or stages)	Useful periods	Productive unit operations		Flow-input amounts on each hectare
Land dressing	1–15/9	ploughing	0_1	30 cm
	20–30/10	manuring	0_2	400 phosphate
		harrowing	0_3	
Sowing	1–15/11	seed curing	0_4	150 seed
	1–15/11	seeding	0_5	150 seed
Growing works	20–30/1	manuring	0_6	
	20–3/30–4	rearing	0_7	
Harvesting	10–20/6	reaping	0_8	25.000 grain and 20.000 straw
	10–20/6	transport	0_9	
	20–30/6	threshing	0_{10}	
	20–30/6	storing	0_{11}	

Hence the crop growing technique is a real recipe, which may be conceived:

(i) as an *ex ante* technique;
(ii) as a set of input/output coefficients for flow elements;
(iii) as a time sequence (see figure 7.3).

Each crop-growing technique is the result of experiments carried out on a certain quality of land, planned on the basis of agronomic knowledge, whose aim is to obtain the maximum yield. Thus it provides a technically efficient relation between inputs and output. Since for every crop to be cultivated on soil of given qualities there are different genotypes available, and since each of these yields a different quantity of output, we may say that there is a range of efficient crop-growing techniques (see Scazzieri, 1981, p. 9) for any crop to be cultivated.

Another important feature of the agronomic recipe is that the quantities of flow elements (but also the quantities of output) are determined in relation to the unit of measurement of land: this leads to a set of input/input coefficients (or of flow elements per quantity of fund service) (see table 7.1). This is a natural consequence of the fact that, from the agronomic point of view, land is the 'container' of the elements requested by the vegetable at every moment of its life. It is also a consequence of the 'Law of

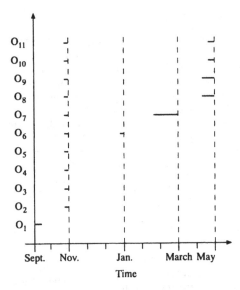

Figure 7.3   Time sequence in the wheat crop-growing technique

the minimum' which governs the quantitative relations between nutrients in the growing process (see Frisch, 1965, chapter 12; Paris, 1981; Polidori and Romagnoli, 1987, pp. 345–7). The complementarity between inputs, the presence of limitational factors, and the identification of a set of fixed coefficients of production are all involved in the crop-growing technique.

With regard to the time structure of production, we may add that the intervals between the periods of cultivation cannot be modified, as they depend on the growing process of the plants: 'in such cases we say that the entire process is *time-rigid*' (or a 'fixed chronology' process, according to the terminology introduced in Frisch, 1965, p. 35), not only in the sense that it consists of sequentially dependent works (see above) performed by fund elements such as labour and cooperating instruments, but also because there is a sequential dependence between the activity of land (whose 'work' lasts just one 'interval') and the agricultural works carried out by other fund elements.

3.2 Task processes, fund endowment and agent coordination: the work calendar

The crop-growing technique provides the technical coefficients for the flow elements, their scheduling, the sequence of useful periods and some features of each productive unit operation within an elementary process. The rules of execution of works are determined by the characteristics of cooperating elements, which cannot modify either the rigid time sequence of the agricultural works, or their complexity (represented by the number and kind of productive unit operations that must be performed in a single useful period). As the *farm productive process* is a multiproduct process, the task network is a set of unconnected sequences of jobs, whose pattern is mostly out of human control. The *farm productive operating system*, on the other hand, shows some 'networks of execution features' representing the sequence of utilisation of the same fund element in more productive processes, wherein it performs similar productive unit operations in the same way.

Among the elements influencing the 'fund-task allocation' (or 'job specification': see above), we may mention:

(i) the scale of production;
(ii) the farm endowment of fund elements;
(iii) the technological pattern.

The scale of each process is obtained by multiplying the flow-input co-efficients, provided for every crop-growing technique, by the extent of cultivation, whose determination is related to decisions about the productive arrangement of the farm. And the productive arrangement is carried out by taking into account:

(i) the extent of the farm and the crop constraints coming from the accepted rotation;
(ii) the relations of complementarity or competition between different crops, and between crop production and animal breeding, in the request for fund services during the duration of the farm production process;
(iii) the opportunity of including the production processes necessary to restore the fund elements in the productive arrangement;
(iv) the technology of production of each crop, that is, the way of carrying out operations by means of labour and/or cooperating instruments ('the farm practice');
(v) the consistency of the fund services of farm equipment with the needs of the crop arrangement or, alternatively, the market prices of services supplied by fund inputs external to the farm.

A trading farm has a specific quality and quantity of productive land divided into plots where, once the rotation has been fixed, the same crop is reintroduced after a given number of years. In general the farmer cultivates all crops of a given rotation every year and the plots have the same extent, so that the decision regarding which crop to produce and its amount is made when the rotation is established. However, the farmer can choose every year the kind of crop within each class (renewal crops, impoverishing crops, meadow crops) in order to 'have a chance of performing a specific operation better', 'to have more time available to arrange land', 'to have a chance of a better utilisation of the equipment or of a higher employment of the available workers during the year' (Giardini, 1986, pp. 514–15) and in order to adapt to the variations of market demand.

But the choice of crops must take into account the technology available to the farm, that is the farm endowment. This results from previous investments in implements and motive power in order to introduce new cooperating instruments (or to renew the existing ones), thus changing the performance of one kind (or class) of operations. Hence the choice of technology too is a *long-term decision* with effects on the farmer's short-term performance.

The aim in managing production from one year to another will then be the choice (within the possibilities shown above) of the productive mix that allows for a more efficient utilisation of the fund elements within the farm, that is, minimum idleness or downtime. To determine the yearly productive mix in this context, the farmer must calculate the quantity of services that each fund element supplies per day and per year, and the amount of each service that is needed for each arrangement which the farmer may choose. The former quantities correspond to the maximum work capacity of machines and farm workers, whereas the latter is determined by the particular 'work calendar' adopted by the farm.

The *work calendar* is a table that shows, given the technology employed, the load of man hours and equipment hours necessary to each crop daily and monthly according to the farm's statistical trends (see Adams, 1921, pp. 142 ss.; Brizi, 1942, para. 51; Duckham, 1963, chapter 14). The work calendar identifies the periods (corresponding to works) of great intensity in the demand for fund services during the production period of a given crop (figure 7.4) and hence, once the area of every crop is determined, the scheduling of services of fund inputs necessary for each farm production. It is the result of economic decisions adopted by the farmer in accordance with biological factors and the structural features of the farm. It is in this way that the problem of 'fund-task allocation' is solved in actual forms of agricultural production organisation.

4 Agricultural forms of production organisation

In previous sections we have pointed out that in agricultural production the sequence and the features of transformation stages form a rigid set of elements beyond human control, while the coordination of agents is a complex process which allows different patterns of organisation. The task sequence and the fund-task allocation cannot be separated because in agriculture it is impossible to identify the 'materials-in-process' (see above), that is materials coming from one 'work' to another which may be

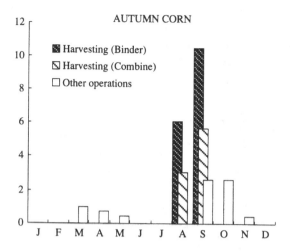

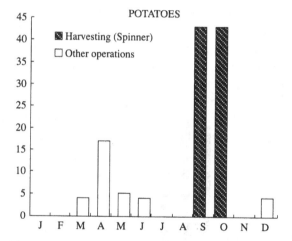

Figure 7.4   Work calendar for the production of a given crop
Source: Duckham, A. N., *The Farming Year*, London, Chatto and Windus, 1963,
p. 402. (Personal communication from Lloyd, P. H., Reading University, 1960)

decomposed at each stage of transformation and rearranged according to
other sequences. This is due to the fact that agricultural production processes are characterised by the continuous activity of the land, which may
be stopped only at the end of the process. In effect, the little trees of the
breeding-ground too are a product (*not* a partly finished product) of an
agricultural production process which is feasible from the biological point
of view.

In this context we may say that agriculture presents a specific form of
production organisation, whose main features are:

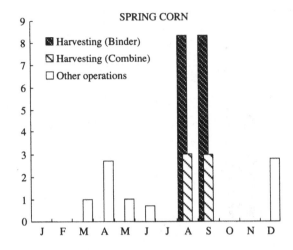

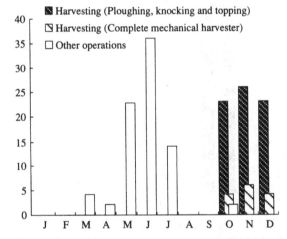

Figure 7.4   (*cont.*)

(i)   the rigidity in the sequential ordering of the works;
(ii) the impossibility of identifying the material in process;
(iii) the versatility of, at least, two fund elements in each technological
      pattern (land and labour, land and cooperating instruments), so that
      there is, in each case, either multiskilled labour or multiskilled
      machinery operating on the land;
(iv) the solution of the coordination problem between demand and pro-
      duction and technological advances.

The last two features are the only ones that in the history of agricultural technology produced different patterns of production organisation: as a result, we may distinguish the *peasant farming organisation* from the *mechanised farming organisation*.

4.1 The 'peasant' farming organisation

The main problems of commercialised agriculture derive from the need for arranging the productive mix in order to obtain the output with maximum utilisation of the fund elements whose amounts are fixed and intransferable in the short run, and from the relation between market demand and supply of agricultural products. In the peasant farming organisation, which consists of 'a family that does not hire outside labour, has a certain area of land available to it, has its own means of production, and is sometimes obliged to expend some of its labour force on nonagricultural crafts and trades' (Chayanov, 1966, p. 51), the first kind of problem is solved 'on the principle of the lowest production overheads and according to rules which follow from [peasant production] technology' (ibid., p. 71).

In organising the production process, the farmer must choose crops 'that would give the most convenient distribution of labour throughout the year, i.e., a smooth distribution without excessive bunching in critical periods and without obligatory unemployment in other seasons' (Chayanov, 1966, p. 134). As a result, he must try to cultivate *complementary crops* that allow farm production to be carried out in accordance with an economic utilisation of the farm endowment. This is a very difficult task, both because the consistency between the farm supply of fund services and their needs cannot be economically conceived in terms of the equality between the needs during the critical periods and the work capacity within the same period, or because for specialised agricultural implements and workers (for example the mowing machine) the critical period and the available period occur at the same time, thus determining long periods of idleness. As a matter of fact, the market price of a fund service is sometimes less than its farm cost, because of the high level of idleness of funds during the year. Such a situation may occur when there is a difference between needs during the critical period and average yearly needs of a cooperating instrument or labour, or if such fund inputs are used only for one job, and the farm has a work capacity equal to demand in the period of utilisation.

Under these conditions, the farmer wishing to introduce the best arrangement with the best technology, has to attempt the full utilisation of the most important fund element he possesses, while having recourse to the market for the fund inputs whose service has a request lower than yearly capacity, or a pattern of utilisation that causes excessive idleness.

Otherwise, 'If an organizer lacks sufficient land, capital, or work hands to develop his farm on the optimal scale, the undertaking will be built on a smaller scale in accordance with the minimum available factor' (Chayanov, 1966, p. 91). 'Then, it is natural that the production element, the availability of which is less than the norm demanded by technical harmony, becomes to a considerable extent a determining factor for the agricultural undertaking' (ibid., p. 93).

But the farmer arranging production in order to avoid the idleness of fund inputs may also decide to use a technique intensive in the fund element that prevails on the farm, without taking into account the fact that this technique is obsolete because of technological progress.

The problem of best utilisation presents itself also in the case of land. If the cropper fallow and the change of motive power raised the amount of productive land on the farm (see Grigg, 1985, p. 166), the 'inserted' and the 'associated crops' would increase its time of utilisation and its output. As previously pointed out, the inserted crops are short-productive-cycle vegetables which are cultivated on a plot between the two main crops of the rotation in order to utilise land which would be idle for a long time (for example, nine months between wheat and beet; see Giardini, 1986, p. 533). The associated crops, on the contrary, are more than one type of vegetable cultivated on the same land at partially overlapping time periods in order to obtain the maximum output on a given plot.

The aim of avoiding labour and land idleness also constitutes the solution of the market problem in the peasant farming organisation. As a matter of fact, in this form of production organisation the best utilisation of workers and land tends to increase the farm output and, as a consequence, the surplus, with respect to the family's subsistence, which may be supplied. But it also provides a low cost of production. Nevertheless, there is not an interrelationship between agricultural supply and market demand, because farm output arrives on the market only once or twice a year, in particular periods: therefore there is a certain degree of independence between farm output and market demand.

In the peasant farming organisation, the labour force and land are multiskilled fund elements because they perform different operations, whereas the cooperating elements (both animals or implements) are specialised: the animals provide power, the implements are associated with a given productive unit operation.

4.2 The mechanised farming organisation

By mechanised agriculture we do not mean the use of a given machine to perform a unit operation, but a general change in the rules of execution of works jointly, due to mechanical, biological and agronomic advances. If in the peasant farming organisation there is only 'the possibility of mechanisation for some unit operations, because the aim is to create the best agronomic conditions to sowing and growing plants' (Bolli and Scotton, 1987, p. 21), in mechanised agriculture the aim is 'to modify not only the shape and arrangement of plants, but even the features of products in order to mechanise the harvesting' (ibid.) in addition to other operations. This technological advance is a way to manage both the problem of maximum utilisation of fund elements and the production–market relationship problem.

From the point of view of the task–process network, mechanisation allows the contemporary performance of two unit operations, which may also be carried out in a sequence. As previously pointed out, sometimes a work is the result of two or more unit operations that may be performed in sequence; if the machine can 'perform, with a single passage on the field, all the unit operations of the cycle (see figure 1), . . . we say that the work is carried out by a connected-functional machine' (Bolli and Scotton, 1987, p. 7). As a result, the machine tends to be specialised in a single job, while the labour force controlling its action is generally multiskilled.

In this context the fund element whose utilisation must be maximised is the cooperating element, because it represents the most expensive asset within the farm. In order to achieve this aim, mechanics tries to increase the work-speed of machines, while genetics selects species which present a wider useful period in the crop-growing technique. As a result, the machine may be switched from one production process to another, so that the managing task of the farmer is to arrange crops in order to obtain the minimum idleness of those cooperating elements.

In carrying out this task, the farmer also provides a solution to the other problem of agricultural production: output–market coordination. The mechanised farm does not share the aim of farm family subsistence, so it is market dependent. In order to ensure a continuous flow of output towards the market, mechanics and biology try to avoid climatic and genetic risks (see, for example, 'protected crops', or 'climate-resistant crops') in such a way that it is possible to have more production processes in a year and also supply out-of-season output.

Notes

1 Ricardo also notes that: '[t]he improvements which increase the productive power of the land, are such as the more skilful rotation of crops, or the better choice of manure' (Ricardo, 1951, p. 80).

2 'Among economists the discussion had chiefly dealt with farm organisation, where, it was argued, division of labour and machines are applied to a less extent, with the consequences of an inferiority of agriculture compared with the industries' (Valenti, 1918, p. 44).

3 The meaning of stage in Frisch's *Theory of Production* is the same as cyclic work employed in table 7.1, that is a set of productive unit operations that must be performed in a single useful period.

References

Adams, R. L. (1921) *Farm Management*, New York, McGraw-Hill.

Bolli, P. and Scotton, M. (1987) *Lineamenti di tecnica della meccanizzazione agricola*, Bologna, Edagricole.

Brewster, J. M. (1950) 'The Machine Process in Agriculture and Industry', *Journal of Farm Economics*, 32(1): 69–81.

Brizi, A. S. (1942) *Economia agraria*, Casa Editrice L. Macrì, Città di Castello.

Buckett, M. (1988) *An Introduction to Farm Organization and Management*, Oxford, Pergamon Press.

Casati, D., Garibaldi, A. and Cavalchini, A. G. (1979) 'Meccanizzazione della raccolta dei foraggi affienati', *Terra e Vita*, 442: 478–519.

Chayanov, A. V. (1966) *The Theory of Peasant Economy*, The University of Wisconsin Press, Madison (1st edition 1925).

Cochrane, W. W. (1979) *The Development of American Agriculture*, Minneapolis, University of Minnesota Press.

(1984) *The Development of American Agriculture. An Historical Analysis*, Minneapolis, University of Minnesota Press.

DeWalt, B. R. (1985) 'Farming Systems Research', *Human Organization*, 44(2): 106–14.

Duckham, A.N. (1963) *The Farming Year*, London, Chatto Windus.

Frisch, R. (1965) *Theory of Production*, Dordrecht, D. Reidel Publishing Company.

Georgescu-Roegen, N. (1969) 'Process in Farming versus Process in Manufacturing: a Problem of Balanced Development', in G. U. Papi and C. Nunn (eds.), *Economic Problems of Agriculture in Industrial Societies*, New York, St. Martin's Press, pp. 497–528.

Giardini, L. (1986) *Agronomia generale*, Bologna, Patron Editore.

Grigg, D. (1985) *La dinamica del mutamento in agricoltura*, Bologna, Il Mulino.

Groenewegen, P. (1987) 'Division of Labour', in *The New Palgrave. A Dictionary of Economics*, London, Macmillan Press, vol. I, pp. 901–7.

Hayami, H. and Ruttan, V. W. (1971) *Agricultural Development. An International Perspective*, Baltimore, Johns Hopkins Press.

Kostrowicki, J. (1977) 'Agricultural Typology Concept and Method', *Agricultural Systems*, 2(1): 33–45.

Meynard, J. M. and Sebillotte, M. (1979) 'La conduite des cultures: vers une ingénierie agronomique', *Economie Rurale*, n. 192–3, pp. 35–41.

Paris, Q. (1981) 'Alcune recenti innovazioni nei metodi di analisi quantitativa in economia della produzione', in M. De Benedictis and R. Fanfani (eds.),

Economia della produzione agricola e metodi quantitativi, Milano, Franco Angeli, pp. 17–54.

Pasinetti, L. (1981) *Structural Change and Economic Growth. A Theoretical Essay on the Dynamics of the Wealth of Nations*, Cambridge, Cambridge University Press.

Pellizzi, G. (1984) 'Le macchine per l'agricoltura: situazione attuale e prospettive dell'innovazione tecnologica', in G. Antonelli (ed.), *Innovazioni tecnologiche e struttura produttiva: la posizione dell'Italia*, Bologna, Il Mulino, pp. 262–79.

Polidori, R. and Romagnoli A. (1987) 'Tecniche e processo produttivo: analisi a – fondi e flussi – della produzione nel settore agricolo', *Rivista di economia agraria*, 42(3): 335–72.

Ricardo, D. (1951) *On The Principles of Political Economy and Taxation*, in *The Works and Correspondence of David Ricardo*, ed. P. Sraffa, Cambridge, Cambridge University Press, vol. I.

Romagnoli, A. (1989) 'Teoria del processo produttivo: il caso dell'azienda agraria', in S. Zamagni (ed.), *Le teorie economiche della produzione*, Bologna, Il Mulino, pp. 195–217.

Scazzieri, R. (1987) ''Tasks, Processes and Technical Practices: A Contribution to the Theory of the Scale of Production', D.Phil. Thesis, University of Oxford.

(1993) *A Theory of Production. Tasks, Processes and Technical Practices*, Oxford, Clarendon Press.

Serpieri, A. (1946) *Istituzioni di economia agraria*, Bologna, Edizioni Agricole.

Spedding, C. R. W. (1988) *An Introduction to Agricultural Systems*, London, Elsevier Applied Science.

Taylor, H. C. (1925) *Outlines of Agricultural Economics*, New York, The Macmillan Company.

Valenti, G. (1918) *Principi di scienza economica*, Barbera, Firenze, 2 vols., 3rd edition.

Van Elderen, E. (1980) 'Models and Techniques for Scheduling Farm Operations: A Comparison', *Agricultural Systems*, 5(1): 1–17.

Wild, R. (1985) *Essentials of Production and Operations Management*, London, Holt Rinehart and Winston.

8 Forms of production organisation: the case of manufacturing processes

MICHAEL LANDESMANN AND ROBERTO SCAZZIERI

1 Introduction

The persistence of particular coordination patterns characterises any given form of production organisation (see chapter 6 above). Manufacturing activities provide what is perhaps the most important example of a type of production process in which the structuring of tasks may generally be distinguished from the coordination of fund agents and the integration among flows of work-in-process materials. Following standard practice, we may identify manufacturing activities as those transformation processes associated with '[t]he conversion of raw materials into useful products' (Kazanas, Barker and Gregor, 1981, preface). In this case, it is generally possible to separately identify the raw materials undergoing the various fabrication stages, the productive agents performing an active role at each stage and the particular operations that must be executed in order to obtain a finished product.

Manufacturing processes provide an example of productive transformations in which the three fundamental coordination patterns (that is, task coordination, agents' coordination and materials-in-process coordination) may be separated from each other. Other types of production processes do not lend themselves to the identification of separate components in the same way. For example, agricultural processes (and, more generally, processes associated with the control of biological transformation) are characterised by a close interaction between fund agents and the material in process, particularly if one is considering the operation of natural funds (such as land). Here, the transformation of the material in process often depends in a critical way on the internal transformation of certain funds (such as the soil) according to a pattern that may be changed by technical intervention only up to a certain degree. A similar difficulty with the identification of a clear-cut internal structure of the production process may be found in the case of 'immaterial production', of which service activities could provide examples. For in this case materials in process cannot be identified, at least in the usual sense, and the production process generally takes the form of a close interaction among fund agents, in the course of which some of the characteristics of such agents (and sometimes their capabilities as well) may get transformed. (An example could be the interaction between teacher and pupil in the educational process.)

In this chapter, we shall discuss the most important forms of production organisation that have evolved in the case of manufacturing processes. More specifically, we shall consider the institutional arrangements that have historically provided the standard practice by which the following three features of manufacturing activity are dealt with, that is, (i) the regulation of the timing, and the coordination, of the different flows and stocks of material in process; (ii) the specification of tasks and of the *technological ordering* of fabrication stages; (iii) the determination of the *sequential ordering* by which fund agents (such as workers or machines) have to execute these tasks.

In general, the technological ordering of fabrication stages required to carry out a given productive transformation is not coincident with the sequence followed by fund agents in working upon the materials in process. The reason for the difference is that the actual pattern of execution of tasks is dependent not only upon the technological requirements that determine a certain sequencing of tasks (for example, cutting has to be executed before assembling in cabinet making), but also upon the ways in which fund-input elements can be utilised and coordinated in a given production process. Thus technological requirements only act as constraints but not as fully determining factors of the actual pattern of execution of tasks within the production process.

This chapter is organised as follows. Section 2 examines the job-shop form of production organisation, which provides the classical pattern of a flexible arrangement of tasks and productive agents. Section 3 considers the 'putting out' organisation of production activities, which is centred upon a flexible arrangement of the flows of materials in process, whereas section 4 examines the factory forms of production organisation, in which a precise and rigid pattern of coordination among elementary components of production activity may be discovered. Finally, section 5 considers certain new forms of production organisation, such as the flexible manufacturing system and just-in-time production, and examines the ways in which the complex problem of coordination is being approached in a flexible system of production.

2 The 'job-shop' form of production organisation

2.1 The 'job-shop' production process

The 'job-shop' form of production organisation is the characteristic way of dealing with the coordination of input flows and with the utilisation of fund inputs when manufacturing activity is based upon the craft system. However, instances of job-shop production may also be found in technologically advanced fields of manufacturing activity, particularly when production follows the 'manufacturing-to-order' pattern. Indeed, certain features (even if not the whole organisational pattern) of the job shop also characterise modern forms of manufacturing organisation, such as 'just-in-time' production and the flexible manufacturing system (see section 5 below).

Characteristic features of the job shop are (i) the 'satisfactory' speed with which the turnover of material in process takes place (in spite of low, and often discontinuous, demand for specific products, the variety of goods produced within each workshop and the relatively homogeneous materials required for the different goods make a reasonable overall speed of materials' turnover compatible with stop-and-go phases of the materials in particular fabrication processes); (ii) the versatility of fund-input elements, which are normally capable of performing a wide range of tasks in a variety of processes; (iii) the flexibility of task arrangements, which makes it possible to have different combinations of tasks in different sequences within the same workshop (see also Scazzieri, 1993, for the analysis of the organisational and functional characteristics of the job shop).

The 'turnover' feature of the job-shop form of manufacturing is associated with the fact that here instruments of production such as tools are generally few and relatively inexpensive: 'the turnover of . . . materials was the centre of [the artisan's] business . . . the artisan has his tools, but they are not a major part of the capital employed' (Hicks, 1969, p. 142). In this case, the degree of differentiation of the material in process within any given workshop should be low, in order to permit quick adjustment to changes of demand from one product specification to another within a fixed range of commodities.[1] It is possible to show that the job-shop form of production organisation is a coherent arrangement that deals with the three fundamental dimensions of coordination within the production process (coordination of material flows, productive tasks and fund elements) and that it allows for a satisfactory solution to the above coordination problems under specific historical circumstances. A situation favourable to the introduction of the job shop is the one in which manufacturing activities are carried out by craftsmen. In this case, technical capabilities are associated with workers rather than with tools, and those capabilities that are critical to the successful transformation of the material in process are concentrated in multiskilled workers (the master craftsmen). As a result, 'the boundary between firms in a process was apt to be the boundary between kinds of labour' (Ames and Rosenberg, 1965, p. 354).[2] An essential feature of craft production is the relative independence of constraints due to the supply of raw materials or to the availability of equipment that would normally be too expensive for the individual craftsman. Indeed, the guild organisation of craftsmen undertaking the same type of activity (a characteristic feature of craft production in different historical periods and parts of the world) could be considered as an institutional device by which the organisation of the production process remained 'capabilities oriented', in spite of objective difficulties that could otherwise lead to the concentration of production activities according to criteria (such as economies of scale) independent of the technical skills identifying craft production. For example, craft guilds in medieval Europe had to ensure a stable and cheap supply of raw materials, and often took up the establishment of expensive equipment and the supervision of certain critical stages of the production process: 'the corporation, if not the corporate town itself, sets up those establishments that require great expenses and cannot be founded by the individual craftsman; such facilities would then be used by guild members in common, just as grazing land and woods in a village community. . . . Well known examples are establishments for washing raw wool and those for combing it; oil presses . . . sharpening establishments, woollen-manufactures, dye-houses, rooms where fabric could dry; courtyards for bleaching; storage space for building materials (brick-fields), shops where fabrics could be sold. In a word, whenever a common work or the collective utilisation of production facilities is necessary . . . the guild takes up the role of a collective entrepreneur' (Sombart, 1916, book I, chapter 12).

Guild organisation provides an institutional set-up in which the different dimensions of productive coordination can be dealt with by a form of organisation that is built around the master craftsman's capabilities.

2.2 The 'job-shop' principle

In the job shop, the coordination of the flows of material in process is achieved externally by means of guild control of the raw materials' supply and of facilities by which 'equipment-intensive' or especially time-consuming stages of production could be carried out. Within each workshop, flows of material in process are coordinated by means of the 'waiting system' that characterises the relationship between the craft workshop and its customers. Such a relationship is another expression of the critical role of capabilities within craft organisations, for that relationship is based on the assumption that capabilities are available, by which a given product may eventually be made, rather than the principle that customers should be able to find a ready-made product whenever they

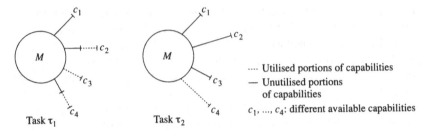

Figure 8.1   Bundles of capabilities and their patterns of utilisation

want. The coordination of tasks within each 'production line' is achieved by allowing waiting times between consecutive stages of the productive process, whereas the coordination of the operations performed by workers and tools is achieved by maintaining within each workshop a 'loose bundle' of capabilities, that is, a set of available skills that could be used when necessary but often remained underutilised or completely idle for considerable time periods. This situation is represented in figure 8.1, which shows how different tasks (τ_1 and τ_2) could be associated with different patterns of utilisation of the available capabilities of a multi-skilled fund input, such as the master craftsman of a medieval workshop.

The figure describes a situation in which a 'master craftsman' (M) has capabilities $c_1, ..., c_n$, which are unevenly utilised for performing either task τ_1 or task τ_2. (Continuous lines show utilised capabilities, dotted lines idle capabilities.) The structural pattern characterising the job-shop form of production organisation (of which medieval craft production is an example) may be described as follows:

(i) the elementary processes (or 'jobs') completed within each establishment may have different technological orderings. (For example, 'wood cutting' precedes 'wood assembling' in job 1, whereas 'wood assembling' precedes 'wood cutting' in job 2.)

(ii) Not all sequence orderings are feasible. (Workers and tools must 'recognise' the technological identity of each job, as is determined by the corresponding technological ordering, and then process the different jobs in a sequence compatible with the stage structure of each.)

(iii) Each job (elementary process) is carried out in an interlocking way with other jobs characterised by different technological orderings. As a result, the material in process of each job undergoes many stop-and-go phases before reaching completion. (Notice that such an organisational feature is instrumental in the quick turnover of the material in process, provided the different types of elementary process use the same pool of materials.)

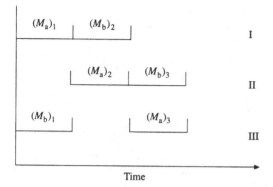

Figure 8.2   Utilisation of complex fund inputs in a job-shop production process

Figure 8.2 shows the 'job structure' of a workshop in which two master craftsmen (M_a and M_b) are employed, and three different jobs (I, II, III) are carried out. We assume that jobs I and II must be processed first by M_a then by M_b. (Thus, jobs I and II have the same technological ordering, whereas the technological ordering of III is different.)

Both master craftsmen are continuously active if the following sequences of operations are adopted:

(i) M_a processes first job I, then job II, and finally job III;
(ii) M_b processes first job III, then job I, and finally job II.

This situation is represented in figure 8.2, in which each interval $(M_a)_i$ and $(M_b)_i$, $i=1, 2, 3$, shows the periods for which master craftsman M_a, or M_b, is processing job i. The index i denotes that this is the ith use of M_a or M_b. (For instance, the interval $(M_b)_1$ of line III indicates the period for which M_b is processing job III, and the index 1 shows that this is the first job that M_b is processing.) A necessary condition for the continuous operation of the two master craftsmen is that jobs with different technological order-ings be carried out within the same workshop. In our example, M_b can be active since the beginning of the working day due to the fact that job III requires the intervention first of M_b then of M_a (the technological ordering of tasks in job III is the reverse of the technological ordering of tasks in jobs I and II).

Another necessary condition for the continuous operation of both master craftsmen is the possibility of performing the tasks of each job within 'available times' that leave scope for the shortening or lengthening of tasks according to the needs of fund-input utilisation within the work-shop. As a result, each master craftsman is allocated to a particular job for a certain available time, which reflects the 'urgency' of that job (that is, the maximum waiting that the customer is prepared to accept), as well as the need to accomplish 'on time' certain stages of transformation of the material in process. For example, M_b cannot operate in job III beyond time t, for otherwise the material in process of job I cannot successfully be transformed into a finished product (say, hot iron in a blacksmith's workshop cannot wait more than a certain time if iron has to be moulded into a knife). Similarly, M_a cannot operate job II beyond t', for the maximum waiting interval of the material in process of job III is $[t, t']$. On the other hand, there may be great flexibility of operating times within each available interval. This often allows for the fitting of additional jobs (additional customers), by taking advantage of the flexibility of real-task durations within the limits set by available times, and also of the multidimensional character of each master's skill. (New jobs can be taken in as long as they are compatible with the available times of previously accepted jobs, and with the available skills of the master craftsmen employed in the workshop.)

A third important prerequisite of job-shop production is that, for at least some of the jobs taken in, the material in process can wait on the production line for some time. In our example, if M_a has to process job III immediately after M_b, job III cannot be taken in; for M_a cannot process job III immediately after M_b if the workshop has already committed itself to job II. (Obviously, this is true as long as the processing of job I by M_a stops at t; but even in the abstract case in which processing times may be infinitesimally reduced, it is impossible for M_a to process jobs II and III after completing its task in I unless waiting intervals are introduced for the material in process in one or the other of the two former jobs.)

The job-shop form of production organisation allows for the fabrication of manufactures under historical circumstances in which multiskilled fund inputs transform a relatively homogeneous material in process (such as wood, wool, etc.) into small batches of finished products that can be significantly different from the technological point of view (in particular, it may differ in the technological ordering of the corresponding jobs).

The above argument shows that a minimum degree of technological differentiation is a necessary condition for the continuous utilisation of the fund inputs available in the workshop. (It is easy to see from figure 8.2 that a certain waiting time for M_b cannot be avoided if only jobs I and II are carried out.) It is also possible to show that the number of jobs of any given type may be changed, within certain limits, without changing the basic pattern of utilisation of 'master craftsmen' M_a and M_b. For example, it is possible for there to be a small increase (or decrease) in the number of jobs of type I simultaneously processed in the workshop provided that there is also a decrease (or, respectively, an increase) in the number of jobs of type II. The reason is that jobs of types I and II have the same technological ordering, so that it is possible to substitute the operation of M_a or M_b in jobs of type I for the operation of the same master craftsmen in jobs of type II (and vice versa) without changing the periods of utilisation of such complex fund inputs. (However, it is likely that the fine pattern of capabilities' utilisation will be changed, for different jobs are likely to utilise the different capabilities of the master craftsmen to different degrees.)

On the other hand, the possibility to change the 'job mix' within each workshop is limited by the requirement that a certain degree of technological differentiation be maintained. (For example, it will be impossible to substitute job III with another job of types I or II without also changing the number of master craftsmen in the workshop.)

As the overall number of jobs that are 'taken in' is increased, the number of multiskilled masters will also be increased, but their continuous utilisation will still be constrained by the requirement that a minimum number of jobs be carried out and that a certain technological variety be maintained among them.

2.3 Versatility of fund inputs and 'just-in-time' coordination of the job structure

The combination of a relatively homogeneous material in process with a flexible arrangement of tasks and productive processes (see below) makes craft production (and job-shop organisations in general) especially useful in reducing the storage problem. Goods are made 'to order' and finished products pile up in traders' warehouses rather than stopping within the producer's workshop.[3] The versatility of fund inputs in the job shop is related to the requirements of a form of manufacturing organisation in which the variability of tasks to be executed makes it necessary that fund inputs be capable both of switching to different types of operation and of changing the durations of tasks in order to deliver a different product mix. In traditional craft production the versatility of fund inputs results from two distinct but complementary features, that is, the existence of workers (the master craftsmen) capable of performing a variety of tasks in processes leading to different types of finished product, and the availability of tools designed to execute a rather wide class of mechanical operations (such as cutting, turning, etc.). Workers' and tools' capabilities are such that each 'task' may be identified by a *range* of possible operations rather than by a particular operation, or arrangement of operations, which may be described by a specific 'time and motion' pattern. In this situation, the actual content of production activity critically depends on the learning processes by means of which the craftsman acquires the skills that make him capable of 'reacting' in the appropriate way to the changing requirements of a flexible production programme.[4]

The versatility of fund inputs is a critical feature of job-shop manufacturing, in which productive organisation is structured so as to face a high degree of uncertainty and the essential skills required are related to the capability of solving problems rather than to the effectiveness by which plans are carried out.

The job shop integrates versatile fund inputs with a flexible arrangement of tasks and processes. The latter type of arrangement is obtained by taking advantage of the co-existence within the same workshop of productive processes associated with *different* (technologically required) sequences of tasks (that is, with different sequences according to which the various 'jobs' must be processed by the different fund-input elements).

The execution of 'jobs' characterised by different technological orderings has one important implication. This may be seen by considering the actual sequences according to which the fund-input elements may execute the different 'jobs'. If all processes or jobs have the same (technologically required) sequence of tasks, it may be shown that existing fund inputs can 'process' the different jobs according to a variety of sequences. (see Bakshi and Arora, 1969, p. B250). In this case, all jobs are structurally identical to one another, so that the allocation of jobs to fund inputs is only constrained by the 'sequence requirement' that any fund input cannot execute a new job until the old job is finished. On the other hand, if productive processes have different technological orderings (as in the job shop) the fund inputs are not 'free' to choose the job to be processed at any given time. In this case, the structuring of the productive process is a more complex issue, and the satisfactory utilisation of working capabilities and tools requires a precise scheduling of the different jobs on the various work stations. Once a given work station has processed a certain job, the fund-input elements constituting that station cannot be maintained busy by processing a new job chosen at random, for that job may not be feasible on that work station owing to its stage structure.

The latter feature of job-shop manufacturing makes it especially sensitive to the time structure of the different jobs and to the 'job structure' of the productive process. However, the critical time element here is related to the precedence pattern of different jobs on the various work stations rather than to the precise duration of each task. It is essential that the material in process appears *at the right moment* (in terms of its own sequence of transformations) at the work station that must process it, even if task durations can often be stretched or shortened depending on the need for job coordination. As a result, '[t]ime was a discipline which structured the artisan's life to an enormous extent. He or she worked within the limits of set delivery times of raw materials, availability of assistants who might have a different time economy, set dates for markets and fairs, and the time patterns of other social and income-earning activities' (Berg, 1985, p. 88).

3 The 'putting out' form of production organisation

3.1 The 'putting out' production process

The flexible structure of task arrangements within the job-shop form of productive organisation is based upon the interlocking operation of different types of productive processes and a 'stop and go' pattern of transformation of the material in process (see above). This pattern of tasks and processes organisation is particularly suitable when demand for specific products is uncertain or low, since the job-shop workshop may approximate the continuous utilisation of fund inputs while at the same time capabilities' underutilisation may be avoided and the synchronisation of the different material flows is made easier by the physical homogeneity of the raw materials processed in each workshop.

However, such advantages of the job shop become serious drawbacks if demand for specific products increases to a considerable extent, if the productive process requires great skill in the performance of single tasks (or combination of tasks) or if the technical characteristics of certain stages of the transformation process make the material in process especially sensitive to the speed at which tasks follow one another along a particular fabrication sequence.

The above factors have been responsible for the differentiation of the forms of (manufacturing) productive organisation from an early stage in the development of technology and of the social division of labour. For example, medieval manufacturing processes already present a rich picture of distinct forms of production, which sometimes interact with one another at different stages of the same productive process. The differentiation of tasks and the specialisation of capabilities is the most characteristic feature in the transition from the job shop to other forms of productive organisation. In this connection, we also find cases in which early forms of factory production coexist with the differentiation of tasks among small-scale workshops and the utilisation of cottage industry to carry out certain stages of the productive process according to the 'putting out' system.

The specialisation of tasks is a common feature of the forms of productive organisation that tend to be substituted for the job shop when output levels of *specific* commodities are increasing, or when technical devices reducing the time required to perform particular tasks are introduced, which would lead to an excessive degree of waste within the job shop.

We may say that the disappearance of the job shop as the dominant form of production organisation coincides with the transition from a technology based upon the *social* division of labour to one in which a form of the *technical* division of labour (the division of labour by stages of the transformation process) becomes the critical element relating productive activities to one another. The splitting of the productive process into subgroups of constituent tasks is a common feature of the various forms of production organisation that may be substituted for the job shop once the waste associated with craft organisations becomes excessive. However, such forms of production organisation may be sharply different from one another due to different ways of dealing with the 'interface' between different stages of any given transformation process.

From this point of view, we may say that the 'putting out' system is a simple way of organising the production process by having the distinct stages of the process carried out in separate workshops or establishments, while the general supervision and coordination of the whole process is exerted by one particular workshop (for example, the workshop responsible for the finishing stage) or by some independent agent. The latter could be the merchant who undertakes selling the finished product and who sometimes also provides the raw material necessary to the whole process. (This latter arrangement characterises the 'Verlagssystem' widespread in early modern Europe and analysed by a number of authors, from Marx (1867) and Bücher (1901, 1st edn. 1893), to Unwin (1904) and Usher (1921).)

3.2 The 'putting out' principle: materials in process and the role of inventory adjustment

The relationship among stages of a productive process organised according to the putting out system is based upon the separate execution of stages requiring different capacities, skills, etc. or simply requiring the performance of operations that can be separately arranged. In this way, various drawbacks of craft production may be overcome, such as the need to simultaneously operate different production lines in an intermittent and interlocking way (with associated 'stop and go' phases of the material in process), the limited capability of coping with a specialised demand, and the difficulty of incorporating technical innovations affecting single stages of the productive process. As a matter of fact, the different stages may be carried out by different productive units, and may indeed provide scope to

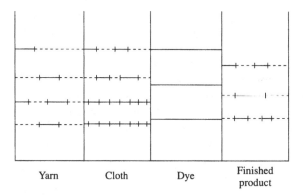

Figure 8.3   The time structure of textile production in the putting out system

different types of productive organisation. The structure of early textile industrial districts in medieval Europe provides evidence of the way in which the putting out system was used to split the traditional craft process into a number of separate stages:

The woollen industry was divided into four primary occupations: the preparation of the yarn which was chiefly concerned with spinning, the weaving of the cloth, the physical manipulation of the cloth, shrinking, picking of burrs, shearing, stretching, and pressing; the dyeing. Each of these primary tasks was ultimately sub-divided, but these sub-divisions were slow to appear . . . The work necessary to prepare wool for spinning required proportionately few hands, so that specialisation of these tasks was not usual until the industry came to be organised on a large scale. The tasks subordinate to weaving were probably fairly well specialised at an early date though we hear little of them as distinct occupations. Much of such work could be done by children and was undoubtedly done by the apprentices or the children of the weaver. The processes associated with fulling were by necessity the work of adults. Fulling, rowing and shearing was men's work, burling-picking knots and burrs out of the cloth was done by women as soon as it became a separate occupation. These various finishing operations became distinguished at an early date. (Usher, 1921, pp. 202–3)

The organisation of an early putting out system may be illustrated by figure 8.3 above.

Each stage of the process from spinning to finishing could be carried out in separate workshops. However, there would generally be a minimum coordination requirement concerning the different stages of the productive process. In particular, such stages would have to be performed within specific 'available times'. The figure above describes a putting out 'industrial district', in which spinning is carried out within peasant households in an interlocking way with traditional peasant activities such as crop production and cattle raising. (Here, the continuous lines represent time intervals in which the raw material is actually processed within the household, whereas dotted lines represent the idle times of the material in process). The weaving stage, on the other hand, is compatible with different forms of production organisation, since the yarn received from the spinning stage may be processed either in a continuous way within workshops specialising in a single operation, or in an intermittent way within 'flexible' workshops, which are capable of dealing differently with different batches of raw material and to produce a wide range of cloth types. The weaving stage is compatible with the existence of specialised workshops making the same type of cloth throughout the working day, or of 'versatile' workshops, which could possibly be arranged according to the job-shop principle and deliver different types of cloth according to customers' requirements. Dyeing operations, owing to the 'continuous' character of chemical processes, are most efficiently carried out within specialised workshops, which can process relatively large batches of product during each time interval. Finally, the finishing tasks would normally be carried out within small flexible workshops organised according to the job-shop principle and capable of processing in an intermittent way different batches of material during the working day.

In the putting out case considered above, the coordination among stages of the productive process is obtained by having recourse to different forms of production organisation that cope differently with the utilisation of fund inputs and the carry over of stocks of semi-finished goods from one time period to another. In the above example, spinning activities may take place within a relatively wide 'available time' interval. This shows that the dyeing workshops are able to operate continuously (this is a technical requirement of the corresponding chemical transformation) even if the 'spinning households' are only intermittently employed.[5]

A different pattern of coordination may be identified if one looks at the relationship between dyeing workshops and weaving workshops. Here, the raw material is continuously delivered to a variety of weaving shops that deal with it in different ways, depending on the type of demand they cater for and on their organisational structure. Workshops specialising in a single type of cloth will provide the most important and stable outlet for each dye workshop. However, the versatile type of cloth workshop is also essential, for the internal structure of such workshops allows for the carry over of semi-processed stocks and provides a buffer between the dyeing stage and the finishing stage. Finally, the mechanism of inventory adjustment within the job-shop framework is the way in which the finishing stage transmits the relatively differentiated, and possibly volatile, demand by the final consumers to the supply of cloth delivered by the dyeing shops.

3.3 Capabilities and craft differentiation in the putting out system

In the putting out system the productive process is separated into stages corresponding to the transformation stages of the material in process. For example, yarn making is separated from cloth making, but spinning and weaving maintain the character of relatively 'complex' tasks, that is, of tasks consisting of a simple arrangement of a number of distinct primitive operations.

The putting out form of productive organisation leads to a process of *craft differentiation*, in the sense that, ultimately, 'each phase of the transformation of the primary raw material becomes the basis of a separate craft' (Usher, 1921, p. 12). However, craft differentiation was not generally associated with any increase in *task differentiation*: each task was still identified by the corresponding transformation stage of the material in process and there was no attempt to split the tasks themselves into constituent operations that could be performed by different fund-input elements on account of the different degrees of skill, strength, speed, etc. required in each operation.

The organisation of the putting out system is 'job-oriented' rather than 'task-oriented': the coordination among different stages of any given productive process is governed by the traditional sequence of transformation stages of the material in process and is only indirectly related to the physical characteristics of the operations that must be performed. As a result, the differentiation among fund-input capabilities is only a loose one (it is often based upon differences in strength rather than skill) and the degree to which each fund-input capability is actually used depends on the stage of production in which such a fund input is employed. In a number of cases, the existence of relatively undifferentiated capabilities may still be an essential condition for the execution of particular tasks, which may be performed in an interlocking way with other tasks, as in the case of job-shop production. In other cases, however, craft differentiation makes the interlocking utilisation of capabilities more difficult and leads to the permanent underutilisation of capabilities no longer called for to perform the productive stage which a particular fund input was allocated to.

In a craft workshop of the traditional type, different capabilities may be bundled in different ways in order to perform productive tasks identified by particular stages in the transformation process rather than by the technical characteristics of the operations to be performed. As a result, combined capabilities that are distant from one another in the space of

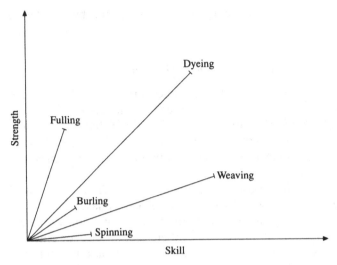

Figure 8.4   The capability structure of tasks in the traditional wool industry

elementary capabilities (see figure 8.3 above) may be lumped together in the same workshop if they are all employed in the same transformation stage of the raw material into a finished product.

For example, in the case of woollen crafts, we may describe all productive tasks as combinations of two primitive capabilities, such as skill and strength. In this case, the degree to which the different tasks draw upon primitive capabilities may be shown in figure 8.4 above.

The pooling together of tasks into individual workshops was traditionally carried out according to the stage structure of the transformation process. As a result, spinning was for a long time carried out in peasant or urban households, which provided the bulk of the yarn necessary to the subsequent stage; weaving was often carried out in combination with fulling and burling within the same productive unit, regardless of the fact that they require distant capabilities; finally, dyeing required a considerable degree of both skill and 'strength' (in the sense of the capability to produce a given result by means of concentrated utilisation of resources) and was often carried out within specialised establishments.

It is clear from the above example that the separation of crafts was traditionally made without necessarily pooling together tasks requiring similar primitive capabilities. As a result, dyeing led to specialisation at an early stage, but weaving was for a long time carried out together with subordinate tasks such as burling and fulling within the same weaving shop, regardless of the fact that such tasks could all be considered as relatively distant from one another.

This organisational background could sometimes lead to a further disintegration of the productive process into independent crafts, or even to the utilisation of wage labourers in order to carry out productive stages requiring only a limited degree of skill. For example, between the thirteenth and the fourteenth century '[t]he trade in finished cloth expanded much less rapidly than the trade in crude cloth. The industry as a whole grew much more rapidly . . . than the finishing departments' (Usher, 1921, pp. 2 and 4). As a result, finishing tasks such as fulling and burling emerged as distinct occupations, which first led to the employment of unskilled labourers and subsequently to the introduction of machinery (see Usher, 1921, pp. 205–6).

In this case, the splitting of cloth making into independent activities (weaving, fulling, burling) was the result of a particular evolution of market demand. This made it difficult to coordinate, within the same workshop, the making of crude cloth and the fabrication of finished cloth, the demand for which was expanding at a lower rate. In other words, craft differentiation here followed the traditional pattern by which a complex process was split according to its different transformation stages, regardless of the distance between the capabilities required in the different tasks. (For example, burling came to be performed by the fullers themselves, who 'went over the cloth with weaver's teasels to raise the nap' (Usher, 1921, p. 205), in spite of the distance between fulling and burling within the capability space.) The putting out system made it possible to rearrange productive processes by lifting some of the scale constraints operating upon the traditional job-shop arrangement of craft activities. However, it did so by overlooking, to a large extent, the technical characteristics of productive tasks and of the corresponding capabilities. The result was a considerable degree of scale and product flexibility, but also a significant increase of fund-input waste at certain stages of the productive process. For multiskilled fund inputs could specialise in the execution of tasks that maintained, in general, the traditional technological characteristics. Traditional capabilities were still called for, and the potential for the development of new capabilities was ordinarily checked by the survival of the traditional pattern of division of labour, which was based upon the stage structure of productive activity rather than upon the 'unbundling' of traditional capabilities according to the technical requirements of each task.

3.4 Subcontracting, technical imbalances and the problem of 'just-in-time' coordination

The existence of *flexible linkages* among different phases of the productive process is a characteristic feature of the putting out form of productive organisation. To achieve this pattern of coordination, certain stages of the process may be carried out within a relatively wide *available time*, rather than spanning a time interval of definite length. In addition, certain stages of the process are executed in workshops in which considerable inventories of unprocessed materials may be carried over from one time period to another.

Historical circumstances in which the 'just-in-time' delivery of finished (or semi-finished) commodities is required, or in which technical change is rapidly transforming the characteristics of individual productive stages (by also requiring a more precise coordination of the activities carried out at each stage) bring to the fore the constraints upon further organisational improvements within the putting out framework.

This situation is at the root of the transformation of the putting out system into different forms of productive organisation, such as the manufacture and the classical factory.

As a matter of fact,

Especially in the eighteenth century . . . we see the putter out, the *Verleger*, developing a new character as a centre about which craftsmen-producers begin to associate themselves in somewhat higher and more complex forms, and as an influence upon the quantitative and qualitative production of the workman. The Sieur Dartalongue, master and merchant tailor at Paris, for example, announced that he was '*able to satisfy the wants of his customers almost without delay, because of the number of workers he employed*'. The putter out was also the source of new standards. Here he had to fight against the custom and statute-sanctioned standards of the old industry, as when the French hat-makers' gild prevented the introduction of hats made of a mixture of beaver and wool. (Nussbaum, 1933, pp. 210–11)

The putting out system may be described as a way to organise the productive process by having its different transformation stages performed in different productive units. Such an organisational pattern allowed for greater flexibility than the job-shop pattern with respect to the capability to process different materials, and also to satisfy orders of widely different sizes. (Both small batch and large batch production are compatible with the putting out system, as a result of the inventory adjustment mechanisms, that may operate at the 'interfaces' of different stages of the productive process.)

The loose pattern of coordination among stages of the productive process made '[t]he putting out system . . . by nature highly elastic, admitting many gradations of capitalistic control of the process of production, and corresponding variety in the degree to which the disintegration of industry into separate crafts is remedied by centralised direction' (Usher, 1921, p. 14). However, the need to concentrate resources in the organisation of the fabrication stages that had to be carried out within the shortest available times (such as the finishing stage of tailoring in the case of businesses operating in a competitive environment) made it clear that the putting out also had serious drawbacks, such as the need for the parallel operation of a considerable number of workers performing similar (or only slightly different) tasks upon a relatively homogeneous batch of material in process. This need exposed a failure of the putting out system in achieving a closer integration among stages of any given process.[6] Such an integration could be achieved, for example, by 'shifting backwards' the differentiation of the material in process, so that intermediate stages could deliver the required amounts of 'just-in-time' and 'just-in-quality' materials to the finishing stage. Such a vertical integration of the productive process would reduce the amount of circulating capital maintained as a buffer stock at the different stages; it would also reduce the number of finishing operations to be simultaneously performed at the last stage. (In this case, materials could reach the finishing stage in a shape that could lead to the final product with a smaller number of finishing operations.)

A closer attention to the forms of waste inherent in the putting out system also led to the splitting of traditional capabilities. Here, for the first time, a widespread reorganisation of productive activities was started that was rooted in the unbundling of tasks and the differentiation of capabilities, rather than in the separation of stages of transformation from one another. This is shown, for example, by the technical transformation that took place in the English weaving industry in the course of the eighteenth century:

[w]eaving, as practised by the craftsmen of the old school, comprised three distinct operations or tasks: preparation of the warp; the placing of the warp on the beam of the loom; and the throwing of the shuttle through the warp. The preparation of the warp and the setting-up of the loom required much skill, though neither task required as much time as the throwing of the shuttle. Concentration of skilled workmen on the preparatory tasks would thus make it possible to delegate the laborious work with the shuttle to inferior workmen, or even to unskilled beginners. A considerable dilution of skilled workers was thus possible. (Usher, 1921, p. 15)

The above situation is illustrated by figure 8.5 below.

In the above case, a major restructuring of the technological basis of textile activity was achieved with the transition from a division of labour based upon the fabrication stages of the material in process to one reflecting the distinct tasks to be performed. For the coordination among fabrication stages may ordinarily be much looser than the coordination among the distinct operations required to achieve a single, complex type of motion. In particular, the synchronisation of distinct operations had to be achieved by using organisational devices which were unnecessary, from a

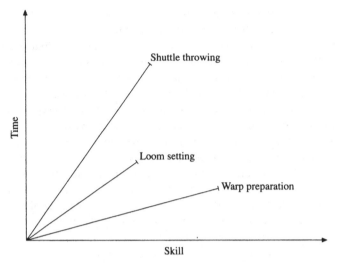

Figure 8.5   The 'fine' capability structure of weaving

technological point of view, when the production process was organised on the basis of independent transformation stages. The splitting of traditional tasks into a precise arrangement of operations and capabilities was an important element in the transition 'to a new system of organisation in which the workshops were to be more than mere aggregations of units. The increased subdivision of processes of production made it more necessary than in the past to work out carefully the correlation between the various groups of workmen' (Usher, 1921, p. 15).

Such a technological reorganisation, together with the advantages associated with the introduction of a closer linkage among different transformation stages of the material in process, is at the root of the concentration of workers and equipment in the same physical location that characterises the manufacturing pattern of production organisation (see below).

4 Manufacturing operations and the factory form of production organisation

The transition from job-shop and early putting out systems to modern forms of manufacturing organisation was based upon the identification of three fundamental sources by which productive efficiency may be increased, that is, (i) increasing the degree of task differentiation and task specialisation; (ii) emphasising the continuity and linkages between the different stages of the fabrication process; and (iii) resolving problems of utilisation of indivisible fund-input elements and processes.

The evolution of modern forms of organisation of manufacturing processes is not only linked to the recognition of the potential to be derived from task differentiation and fund-input specialisation – as the early literature on division of labour had stressed[7] – but also to a careful consideration of the different fabrication stages involved in any given productive process. In particular, issues related to the utilisation of fund-input elements and to the continuity of the material transformation process received careful consideration.

The early analysts of division of labour – such as Petty (1671, 1683), Tucker (1755, 1775), Beccaria (1771), Smith (1776) – did not explicitly discuss the important role which the arrangement of partial processes played in assuring the continuity of the material transformation processes and the utilisation of capacities, but rather emphasised the gains that could be made from allocating workmen to a narrower range of tasks and from reducing the changeover times among tasks to be performed.

The latter point implicitly recognised the importance of the way in which partial processes are arranged, and also of the *scale* required for particular arrangements to be possible. However, it is only with subsequent authors that the arrangement of partial processes became a central focus of attention. This shift of emphasis occurred when manufacturing processes became more heavily mechanised and the continuous utilisation of rather expensive pieces of specialised equipment was seen as a major problem to be solved. At this point, insightful analysis of the *'factory system'* was undertaken by writers such as Charles Babbage and Karl Marx. These authors identified important principles that were geared to deal not only with the critical issue of the continuous utilisation of indivisible fund-input elements, but also with a dramatic reduction of inventory holdings and maximum continuity of material-in-process flows, thus leading to a dramatic increase in production throughout.

In the following we shall outline an analytical formulation of the principles of manufacturing production organisation developed in the above authors' writings. We shall also attempt a generalisation of their analyses in some respects.

We may start with Babbage's statement of what later became known as the *'Babbage Principle'*:

By dividing the work to be executed into different processes of skill or of force . . . the master manufacturer . . . can purchase exactly that precise quantity of both which is necessary for each process; whereas, if the whole work were executed by one workman, that person must possess sufficient skill to perform the most difficult, and sufficient strength to execute the most laborious, of the operations into which the art is divided. (Babbage, 1832, pp. 175–6).

Figure 8.6   Time profile of a production process P

Specialisation in manufacturing production is thus a two-fold process: (i) on the one hand, it involves the splitting up of manufacturing processes into work steps (or 'detail processes' as Marx called them); (ii) on the other hand, it means a decomposition of 'capabilities' previously embodied in general-purpose fund inputs (such as the 'master craftsmen' in the early job-shop form of production organisation) into more specialised skills or capabilities associated with fund inputs that concentrate on a narrower set of tasks. This pattern of specialisation allows fund inputs more scope to develop their 'dexterity' (Smith) in executing these tasks more efficiently and also to develop their capabilities (and specialised skills) further.

The next important point that emerges from these authors' writings is that the implementation of more specialised work patterns is associated with important *scale* requirements.

As a matter of fact, a prerequisite for more specialised work arrangements, and also for the development of more specialised skills, is that workmen are able to 'constantly adhere to the execution of the same process' (Babbage, 1832, p. 172). For this to be possible, it is necessary that an arrangement of partial processes is found that allows for the *continuous* application of a specialised workman's skills to the same specialised task or set of tasks. Such an arrangement has been described by Marx in what he called *serial manufacture*.[8] In such a system:

The different detail processes, which were successive in time, have become simultaneous, go on side by side in space. Hence, the production of a greater quantum of finished commodities in a given time. (Marx, 1972, p. 326, 1st edn. 1867)[9]

How is the continuous side-by-side operation of different processes, which are both simultaneously and consecutively performed, possible? To consider this issue, it may be useful to examine a relatively simple production process consisting of three stages of fabrication (see figure 8.6 above).

Let us assume that we may identify the 'capability' of a particular fund input k (for instance, a worker) in just one dimension ('time available' in the worker's case), and that the utilisation profile of that fund input, when it is engaged in the three fabrication stages of production process P, may be characterised as in figure 8.7.

Let us now find an arrangement of fabrication stages (or 'partial processes') that could lead to the continuous and full utilisation of fund-input elements of type k. The solution of this problem is relatively simple if

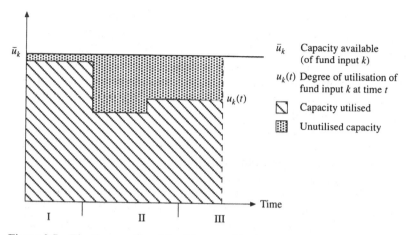

Figure 8.7   The time profile of fund-input utilisation in process P

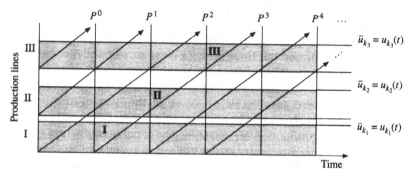

Figure 8.8   Full utilisation of a fund input through the splitting of a production process into fabrication stages

we consider only one type of fund-input element and the utilisation profile shown in figure 8.7 above.

Take first the case where there is no fund-input indivisibility at the point of instalment, so that fund-input elements of type k of *any unit size* may be installed in the productive system. In this case, full utilisation may be achieved by splitting the production process P into its three fabrication stages I, II, III (which in our particular example are of equal length) and install a fund-input element of type k in each *production line*, which consists of fabrication stages I, II and III.

As may be seen from figure 8.8, under the conditions set out above, full utilisation of fund-input elements of type k may be achieved by the *simultaneous* and *continuous* execution of each of the fabrication stages of production process P. We may also see that full and continuous utilisation may only be achieved if *a sufficient number of processes is staggered* over time; in other words, processes P_1, P_2, P_3, ... have to be started at intervals (in our case equal in length to the time duration of each individual fabrication stage) such that the fund elements installed in each production line can switch immediately, after completing the fabrication stage of one process, towards executing the same fabrication stage in the next process. In this case, each of the fund-input elements (they are all of type k, but 'installed' in different production lines) can 'constantly adhere to the execution of the same process' (see Babbage's quotation above). The staggering of processes at the right intervals amounts to an important *scale requirement* for the productive system as a whole.[10]

As we may see from figure 8.8, the splitting up of a production process into fabrication stages, and the continuous employment of fund-input elements in the specific tasks associated with such detailed work steps, also implies a particular arrangement insofar as the *material in process* is concerned. As stated in Marx's quotation, in such an arrangement one can 'see the raw material in all the stages of its production *at the same time*'. Thus not only are all the work steps being simultaneously and continuously performed but there is also a clear correspondence between the division of labour (the splitting up of the overall productive process into distinct work steps and allocating these to particular fund-input elements) and the corresponding organisation of the 'system of pipelines' which regulates the flows of the material in process. Differently from a job-shop form of production organisation, the serial manufacture system emphasises not only continuity in the utilisation pattern of the capabilities of fund-input elements but also *continuity of material in process flows*. In a perfectly synchronised factory system, no inventory should accumulate at any stage of the overall production process (a possible exception may be at the point of completion of the finished commodity, when the pattern of final demand might require the accumulation of inventories). We shall come back to a discussion of material-in-process flows, and to the question of inventory holdings at intermediate stages of the fabrication process, in section 5 below.

Let us now consider in which way the previous analysis of the utilisation question in the factory system may be generalised by dropping some of the simplifying assumptions made in the presentation above.

First consider dropping the assumption that at the point of installation fund-input elements of type k *of any unit size* can be installed, and consider the situation in which only fund-input elements of a particular size can be utilised. In that case, to assure that fund-input elements can be both continuously utilised *and* adhere to the execution of the same partial process, a sufficiently large batch of processes must be started *at the same*

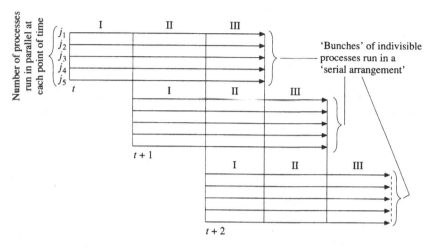

Figure 8.9   Production arrangement involving both the *parallel* and *in series* operation of productive processes

point of time; and this is in addition to having batches of such processes started at regular time intervals, that is, staggered over time. Figure 8.9 shows a combination of the arrangement *in parallel* of the productive processes and of their arrangement *in series*[11] for bunches of parallel processes which are started at regular time intervals.[12]

The combined operation of processes in parallel and in series may resolve the question of utilisation for the case in which fund-input elements of only particular unit sizes are available because it is always possible to find a multiple of unit processes that can fully utilise the capacities of an equally determinable number of fund-input elements installed in a particular production line.

Consider three specialised fund-input elements, *j*, *k* and *m*. Assume that *j* is specialised in stage I, *k* in stage II and *m* in stage III. Denote the partial processes associated with these stages by P(I), P(II) and P(III) respectively. The fund-input elements *j*, *k* and *m* in our example are available in unit sizes such that, if the overall process is operated at a chosen unit intensity level (producing, for example, one unit of the finished commodity in a specified time interval), one unit of *j* would be utilised at one-third of its capacity in stage I, one unit of *k* would be fully utilised in stage II, and one unit of *m* would be utilised at two-thirds of its capacity in stage III. To achieve full utilisation of all fund-input elements engaged in their respective fabrication stages, P(I) would have to be run at three times the unit intensity level (or an integer multiple thereof), and one would have to install a minimum of two units of fund input of type m and operate P(III) at twice the unit intensity level (or an integer multiple thereof).

Given the requirements of the overall production process P (of which P(I), P(II) and P(III) are only stages, or partial processes), it would be impossible to operate P(I) at three times the unit intensity level and P(III) at twice the unit intensity level. We would have to find the minimum common integer multiple (in this case of 2 and 3, that is 6) such that the stage requirements of the overall production process and, at the same time, the full utilisation requirements of all the indivisible input elements engaged in that process are satisfied. The end result, in this example, would be to operate the overall process P at (a minimum of) six times the unit intensity level (that is, to produce a minimum of six units of finished commodities within the same specified time interval), and to install (or hire) two units of fund-input element j, six units of k and four units of m.

The above example shows that the 'Law of Integer Multiples' has to be employed a number of times to allow for the full utilisation of fund-input elements in the presence of fund-input indivisibilities. The above law has first been employed to determine the activity levels by which individual stages of fabrication have to be operated, so that the indivisible units of the fund-input elements employed in that stage are fully utilised. Arithmetically, we are dealing here with finding the smallest integer mult-iple of the fractions β_k (these are the fractions of an indivisible fund-input element of type k utilised in a process P) such that if these fractions are multiplied by that scale factor they would become integers themselves. The same law has then been brought in to determine the activity levels of the partial processes that have to be arranged in series with other partial pro-cesses where each partial process represents a fabrication stage of the overall process P. If, in the first application of the Law, we have deter-mined the activity levels n_1, n_2 and n_3 for the different partial processes, we are dealing here with finding an integer multiple of the numbers n_i (where n_i refers to the number of stages that have been identified).

The first step of the above analysis is formulated in such a manner that it may easily be extended to the case where a number of fund elements $k = 1, 2, \ldots, K$ are involved in one particular stage of fabrication installed in production line i. In this case, the first step of scale determination brings out the need to find the smallest common integer multiple of the fraction β_{ki} of capacities utilised in fabrication stage i of all the indivisible fund-input elements of type $k = 1, 2, \ldots, K$.

It is easy to see that the above applications of the Law of Integer Multiples may entail a formidable *scale requirement* for the production system as a whole if the full utilisation of indivisible fund-input elements is to be achieved.[13] The relationship between the full-utilisation requirement, the determinants of an appropriate degree of task specialisation of fund elements, and the overall scale requirement linked to such an arrangement, has been recognised early on in the economic literature.[14] In particular, awareness of such a relationship is a critical feature of subsequent attempts to achieve the full and continuous utilisation of fund-input elements at lower scales of production (see also section 5 below).

Let us now summarise the distinct features of the factory system as discussed by classical authors such as Babbage and Marx. These authors not only emphasised the correct quantitative combination and allocation of fund-input elements to the different stages of a fabrication process, but also the continuity of the material fabrication process that allows the material in process to move through the entire sequence of fabrication stages *without any interruption*. The factory system was in their view not only an example of a perfect *just-in-place* production system, in which all fund-input elements are continuously *fully utilised* (and utilised to perform the same set of tasks throughout), but it was also a *just-in-time* production system, in which the material fabrication process never gets interrupted and no inventories are ever building up at any intermediate stage of fabrication. It was an example of a perfectly synchronised form of production organisation.

The advanced form of factory is characterised by what Marx called a 'complex system of machinery', in which:

the subject of labour goes through a connected series of detail processes that are carried out by a chain of machines of various kinds, the one supplementing the other. Here we have again the co-operation by division of labour that characterises Manufacture; only now, it is a combination of detail machines. . . . Each detail machine supplies raw material to the machine next in order; and since they are all working at the same time, the product is always going through the various stages of its fabrication, and is also constantly in a state of transition, from one phase to another.

Just as in Manufacture, the direct co-operation of the detail labourers establishes a numerical proportion between the special groups, so in an organised system of machinery, where one detail machine is constantly kept employed by another, a fixed relationship is established between their number, their size, and their speed. The collective machine, now an organised system of various kinds of single machines, and of groups of single machines, becomes more and more perfect, the more the process as a whole becomes a continuous one, i.e., the less the raw material is interrupted in its passage from its first phase to its last; in other words, the more its passage from one phase to another is effected, not by the hand of man, but by the machinery itself. In Manufacture the isolation of each detail process is a condition imposed by the nature of division of labour, but in the fully developed factory the continuity of those processes is, on the contrary, imperative. (Marx, 1972, pp. 358–60)

However, the picture which emerges from the above analysis is also one embodying a high degree of rigidity. As a matter of fact, the splitting up of the productive process into stages or partial processes, the allocation of fund inputs to tasks, and the organisation of the system of 'pipelines' through which the material in process flows, is entirely dominated by the full and continuous utilisation requirement of indivisible units of fund-input elements. As a result, a very complex and highly integrated system emerges which allows little flexibility to adjust to changing requirements (such as changes in the output mix or learning both by individual workers as well as teams of workers) without violating the full-utilisation condition.

This feature of rigidity is reinforced by another well-known principle of Babbage, which we shall call Babbage's *Factory Principle*.[15] In this principle, Babbage asserts that, once a particular integrated pattern of utilisation of fund-input elements has been established, then any change in the overall scale of production has to be accomplished by a complete replication of that unit of production and its form of organisation:

When [from the peculiar nature of the produce of each manufactory] the number of processes into which it is most advantageous to divide it is ascertained, as well as the number of individuals to be employed, then all other manufactories which do not employ a direct multiple of this number, will produce the article at a greater cost. (Babbage, 1832, pp. 172–3)[16]

The factory principle follows directly from the above analysis, in which full and continuous utilisation of indivisible fund-input elements in the same types of *jobs* (sets of tasks) over time is made possible by a precise and unique pattern of stage differentiation and of activity levels of the different partial processes, as well as by a particular arrangement of such processes over time. Once the minimum process scale permitting the *full* and *continuous* utilisation of fund inputs has been identified, any change in the overall scale of production above or below that scale (or an integer multiple of it) would violate the *full* utilisation condition, due to the indivisibilities of fund-input natural units.

From Babbage's Factory Principle we obtain a picture of the industrial organisation of individual industries according to which any given industry, given the nature of fund-input indivisibilities, would be characterised by the same distribution of plant sizes, with the same degree of task differentiation and the same pattern of fund-task allocations within each plant. If different distributions of sizes, or different plant organisations were adopted, such plants would become uncompetitive (they would 'produce an article at a greater cost').[17]

The descriptive power of the above analysis was rightly criticised on account of the fact that different distributions of plant sizes and different plant organisations are a persistent feature of most industries. As new forms of production organisation emerged, such as the flexible manufacturing system (FMS), new forms of putting out, just-in-time production and so on, the focus of industrial analysis switched back to allow for the co-existence of heterogeneous distributions of sizes in the same industries. (We shall come back to this issue in section 5 below.)

In many respects, the classical authors made division of labour central to their analysis of manufacturing forms of production organisation. However, they were unable to actually determine appropriate degrees of fund-input specialisation, apart from emphasising that this degree should be highly sensitive to the overall scale of production and thus suggesting a link to the question of utilisation of indivisible fund-input elements.[18]

It will be clear from our analysis in the following section that if attention is focused upon the utilisation of fund-input elements as an overriding principle in organising a productive system, then there will be a strong tendency to reduce the multiplicity of skills embodied in the individual fund-input elements involved in a productive process. We shall explore this question further with the view of extending our analysis to forms of manufacturing production organisation in which there was a move away from strict skill specification and rigid fund-to-task allocations. A discussion of this topic requires an examination of the patterns of *bundling* and *unbundling* of capabilities that are either embodied in particular fund-input elements or that develop over time as a result of skill acquisition. It is well known that the evolution of the factory system, especially as it developed towards its Taylorist and Fordist forms, was associated with a move towards an extreme form of task specialisation and task differentiation.[19] The factory form of production organisation attempted to reduce the multiplicity of skills by identifying *jobs* (sets of tasks) that were themselves 'simple' (they included only a small set of primitive operations) and were carried out in a repetitive manner. In this way, operators such as workers and machines could adhere to the same set and sequence of operations over time. Characteristic features of the factory system were the attempt to minimise the time in which productive operations were executed, and attention to the detail and precision by which such operations were performed. Such features, together with the minimisation of change-overs among different jobs, were considered as the most important advantages to be derived from increasing the degree of task specialisation in any given productive system.

5 New forms of manufacturing production organisation

5.1 Introduction

The factory form of production organisation came under severe criticism almost from its inception and such criticisms were furthermore substantiated when this form of organisation had to adjust to a number of demands arising in modern industrial systems. In this section, we shall deal with a number of such criticisms and examine the various more recent forms of production organisation that have evolved as responses to those demands:

(i) objection against a too high degree of fund-input specialisation and the reemergence of the need for versatile, multiskilled fund inputs;
(ii) recognition of a tradeoff between achieving a high degree of synchronisation with a system of rigidly defined job allocation patterns and more flexible task arrangements within the productive processes;
(iii) recognition of a continuous tension between fund-input utilisation (in a multicapability space) and continuity of material flows in flexible forms of production arrangements.

The evolution from a traditional factory form of production organisation to more flexible forms is well described in a detailed account by Raju and Karlson:[20]

The [traditional] transfer line systems are designed to be used for a single type of product with high volume production. They are also highly efficient and are known for their high utilization of machines. Production in small quantities is uneconomical with those systems. Unfortunately, since the fifties, the demand structure for the products in the metal manufacturing industry which accounts for more than 30% of the GNP in most of the industrialized countries has changed to more diversified products creating the need to produce a variety of products in smaller quantities. The answer to this problem came with the invention of the computer numerical control (CNC) machines. These machines are capable of providing middle to low volume production capacity and high flexibility, making them suitable for small batch manufacturing. However, these systems involve some drawbacks of their own, viz. longer set-up times, high work-in-progress inventory, low machine utilizations and high manning levels. The FMS evolved in the 1960's from the idea of combining the best features of the transfer line system with those of the CNC machines. . . . FMS . . . can be defined as a process facility under total computer control with an automated work flow system to produce a variety of parts in small batches within the stated capability and to a predetermined schedule. In simple terms, it can be defined as a system providing mass production economies in a batch production environment. (Raju and Karlson, 1985, p. 166)

At the heart of modern forms of manufacturing production systems lie various compromises and also important new developments which attempt to deal with the tensions which arise between the principles underlying the older job-shop form of production organisation and the factory system (see also Scazzieri, 1993). In the following subsection we shall consider a number of classic criticisms of the factory system. Subsections 5.3 and 5.4 examine two aspects of the flexible coordination devices that have recently emerged within the framework of new forms of production organisation (the flexible manufacturing system and just-in-time production). Finally, subsection 5.5 calls attention to the features of industrial organisation that may result from the introduction of new forms of production organisation as compared with those in which productive units are organised according to the traditional job shop, putting out or factory patterns.

5.2 Coordination failures and the factory system

As pointed out above (see section 4 above), the identification of the principles underlying the factory system may be considered as the outcome of an historical process in the course of which any given production activity came to be seen as a particular combination of elementary tasks, fabrication stages and job assignments for workers and tools. As a result of this process, the organisational pattern of a factory came to be associated with the precise subdivision of the production process into constituent tasks and the coordination of interdependent fabrication stages, so that the time structure of job assignments would be compatible with the continuous utilisation of fund inputs (primarily workers, tools and machines).

However, since a relatively early stage it was recognised that the effective working of the factory system was dependent upon a number of particular conditions, and that their absence could lead to significant coordination failures. A first problem to be recognised was that the splitting of any given process into more elementary tasks could make it more difficult, rather than easier, to identify jobs (that is, combinations of tasks) that could be executed by multipurpose fund inputs. This point of view was clearly expressed in Lauderdale's criticism of Smith: '[t]he division of labour tends to confine the attention, and of course the knowledge of the workman, to the performing of one single operation; whereas, the perfection of manufacturing machinery is to combine and embrace the execution of the greatest possible *variety of operations* in the formation of a commodity, by the use of one machine' (Lauderdale, 1804, p. 204; our italics). Later on, a similar problem came to be identified with the fact that the subdivision of a complex job into more specific assignments would make it more difficult to adapt existing capabilities (of workers or machinery) to a changing economic environment. In this connection, Nikolay Chernyshevskij pointed out that, in a textile industry in which silk and wool weaving may be executed by specialised workers only, 'it would clearly be necessary to set up two different factories, one for wool and one for silk fabrics, and it would be necessary to have a market large enough to permit the purchase of the yearly output of both' (Chernyshevskij, 1860). However, a type of production technology that would permit 'the utilisation of the same worker in a number of alternative tasks' (ibid.) makes it possible to achieve a relatively continuous pattern of fund-input utilisation even at lower levels of process scale. A similar point was made by Francesco Ferrara, who argued that the subdivision of a complex job into its component operations is not necessarily an advantage if the job consists of operations that are 'simple and similar to one another', as in the case of agricultural processes (Ferrara, 1860, p. 53). In particular, Ferrara insists that a distinction must be made between *tasks* and *jobs*. The former may vary considerably depending on which fabrication stage or product specification is taken into account. The latter, on the other hand, may be quite similar to one another across different fabrication stages and product specifications.[21] As a result, the subdivision of jobs (that is, their assignment to different and specialised types of fund inputs) may not be an advantage if tasks require the execution of a limited number of operations repeated from one job to another. In this case, the requirements of the Law of Multiples (see section 4 above) may be satisfied at lower process scales if tasks are assigned to multipurpose fund inputs that may be switched from one type of job to another.

A third type of criticism against the Smith–Babbage view of production organisation was raised in the context of the discussion about the principles of 'scientific management' that took place in the United States at the turn of this century. In particular, it was pointed out that the splitting of production processes into constituent tasks, and of complex jobs into elementary operations, was bound to lead to considerable problems of coordination requiring the introduction of *ad hoc* administrative functions. As Alexander Hamilton Church noted in this connection,

[t]he necessity for co-ordination . . . is an inevitable result of the evolution of the factory, no one mind can grasp and hold all the details. The object of modern administrative organisation is to readjust the balance of responsibilities disturbed by the expansion of industrial operations, and enable the central control to be restored in its essential features. (Church, 1900, p. 395)

More generally, Church argued that '[c]oordination is the keynote of modern industry . . . The necessity for coordination . . . is an inevitable result of the evolution of the factory' (Church, 1900, pp. 393–5).

As a matter of fact, the factory system that could be based upon implementation of time and motion studies was still exposed to the possibility of failures in the coordination of flows of materials in process, since

the possibility of *retaining* the advantage which quicker process time gives is dependent on keeping up a flow of work past the delivery point. If, for example, in an 8 hr. day we have a series of jobs that each take 1 hr. to process and if, by improved methods of handling, we cut 15 min. of each job, a total saving of $8 \times 15 = 2$ hr. will be effected. But unless we have at hand jobs which will utilise the 120 min. thus saved, it is evident that the drip will fall into the pool of waste. This waste may be sufficient to neutralise the gain due to time reduction on the jobs, or at any rate to diminish it considerably. (Church, 1930, pp. 94–5)

In other words, time and motion studies bring to the fore the advantages associated with Smith's economies of speed (reduction in the time taken by any given fund input to switch from one job to another), and with the reduction in the fund inputs' periods of idleness within each workshop. However, the 'liberation of production capacity' (Church, 1930, p. 98) obtained in that way was dependent upon implementation of a coordinated pattern of work-in-process materials. As a result, it has been argued that the economies of 'modern mass production' derive 'more from the ability to integrate and coordinate the flow of materials through the plant than from greater specialisation and subdivision of the work within the plant. Even in the metal-working industries, where increasing subdivision was possible, the primary impact such subdivisions had on factory organisation was to intensify the need for coordination and control' (Chandler, 1977, p. 251).

Finally, it may be argued that the coordination failures to which the factory organisation is exposed ultimately derives from the relatively rigid pattern according to which jobs must be executed by the various fund inputs and work-in-process materials have to be coordinated with each other. As a matter of fact, the more precise is the pattern of job-fund allocation, the more difficult the adaptation to a changed environment tends to be. In particular, learning and reshaping may only take place at considerable cost, and the transformation of the productive structure often requires the substitution of complete productive networks, rather than being compatible with smooth processes of adaptive change within the existing structure.[22]

5.3 The flexible manufacturing system (FMS)

FMS is an interrelated system of machinery (as was the factory system) but it is a system that is composed of a number of multiskilled fund inputs which are flexibly allocated to different sets of tasks as the production

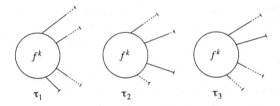

—— Utilised portions of the capabilities of fund k
······ Unutilised portions of the capabilities of fund k

Figure 8.11   Multiskilled fund inputs and utilisation of capabilities with a flexible manufacturing system

programme (or job specification programme) changes over time. Thus, just as in the old job-shop form of production organisation, a particular multiskilled fund-input element f^k could undertake a sequence of tasks, τ_1, τ_2, τ_3, in which its capabilities (skills) are utilised to different degrees and in different compositions. (See section 5 of chapter 6 for a preliminary discussion of capabilities, tasks, and job specification programme.)

For example, a multiskilled fund input f^k may execute a sequence of different tasks (see figure 8.11). Algebraically, we may describe the utilised and unutilised portions of the capabilities of a particular type of fund element as a function of the tasks it performs in the following way: let $\bar{c}^k \equiv \{\bar{c}_i^k\}$ be the vector of capabilities which a fund input of type k embodies, and $c^k(\tau_j)$ be the vector of capabilities/skills actually used when executing task τ_j. Then $uc^k(t) = \bar{c}^k(t) - c^k(\tau_j(t))$ represents the portions of unutilised capabilities of fund element f^k when executing a sequence of tasks τ_j ($j=1$, 2, 3, ...) over a time interval t. The problem faced both in the old job-shop form of production organisation as well as in modern flexible manufacturing systems is to assure, through a proper sequencing and bundling of tasks in an environment of changing production programmes, that multiskilled fund-input elements are relatively well utilised in all their capability dimensions.

The difference between the flexible manufacturing system and the old job-shop form of production organisation consists in the efforts put in the former upon the synchronisation of a *number* of multiskilled fund-input elements, while in the old job shop the typical feature was that of *one* master using a number of relatively simple tools and interacting with less skilled apprentices. In that sense, one has to see the FMS as an integrated 'system of machinery' (as in Marx's description of the factory system) but one that has to flexibly adjust to changing production programmes. On the other hand, the FMS is – differently from the ideal factory system but in common with the job shop – an imperfectly synchronised system for reasons that will be explored below.

The emphasis upon the integrated use of machinery and the difference between newer forms of the job-shop production organisation and the FMS is well expressed in the following quotation from Ranky in his discussion of scheduling:

the order in which [the] parts are manufactured is given by a list, or schedule. The schedule defines for a period of time which operations shall be performed, on which parts, by which machines. . . . The scheduling algorithm used in job shop systems is off-line because it is applied at the beginning of a scheduling period, and the results are valid for the entire shift, or longer. If an unexpected event happens, such as tool break, machine or robot breakdown, because of the deterministic scheduling methods used, production is disrupted. (Ranky, 1983, pp. 3–4)

Let us first explore the problem of the flexibility of use of multiskilled fund-input elements.

The factory form of production organisation was characterised by the singular attention paid to the continuous utilisation of fund elements in the same (set of) tasks. This was achieved through the continuous (in line) operation of partial processes (processes that focus on particular detailed stages of the overall fabrication process) such that there was a non-fluctuating need for precisely the same capacities of the same fund elements through time. It involved the design (where possible) and installation of fund elements on production lines such that their (combined) capacities at each point of time would precisely equal the input requirements on the different production lines. We also showed that, due to the existence of fund-input and process indivisibilities, a certain *scale* of operation of the productive system was required to assure the full utilisation of fund elements. The degree of task specialisation – and hence the degree to which fund inputs could concentrate on a narrower range of tasks – which the system would adopt was strictly related to these scale requirements.

The shift towards a flexible manufacturing system has to do with two demands made upon a productive system in an advanced market environment:

(i) a continuously changing product programme in the form of changes in the composition of goods (or component parts) to be produced; and

(ii) changes in the levels of demand (overall or for individual products; which, of course, would imply a change of type (i)).

There are two more elements which originate directly from the productive system which make it very difficult – and inefficient – to adhere to a strict factory form of production organisation:

(iii) the near impossibility to aim at full utilisation of fund-input elements when their multicapability dimension is recognised; and

(iv) the understanding of a production environment as a 'learning' environment which continuously changes the identities of fund-input elements in the multicapability space and also develops a new and deeper understanding of the nature and internal structures of fabrication processes (both of tasks and material transformation processes involved in these).

It should be clear that features (i) to (iv) above make it very difficult to adhere to a strict factory organisation principle.

As we noted before, the factory form of production organisation is based on a strict pattern of synchronisation of different fund inputs' activities such that they can constantly adhere to the same tasks and be continuously utilised to the same degree. Fluctuations in the overall level of activity and/or changes in the composition of output would mean that such fund elements (whose 'capacities' are by definition durable; see the definition of fund elements in chapter 6 above) will be partially underutilised and that, furthermore, some capabilities will be underutilised, others overutilised as the production programme changes over time.

As to point (iii) above, we have made it clear in our discussion of indivisibility phenomena that indivisibilities inherent in fund elements may, in principle, be defined with respect to any dimension of the capability space. Thus, there may be particular scale requirements that have to be satisfied to achieve a certain degree of accuracy, or of speed, or a particular ability to withstand shocks, and so on. The bundling of capabilities in particular fund-input elements has to deal with both 'upper' as well as 'lower bound' threshold phenomena. For example, a machine might need a certain minimum weight to achieve a certain degree of resistance to shocks while, on the other hand, a certain speed requirement might imply an upper bound on weight. The 'upper' and 'lower' thresholds on the design of particular components of a fund-input element and of their interaction thus involves a consideration of indivisibility phenomena in all the dimensions of the capability space that define a particular fund input. Just as the factory system dealt with the problem of putting together units of different types of fund-input elements and coped with the problem of utilisation by regulating the overall level of activity such that an integrated system of machinery would be fully utilised, so the construction of individual units of multicapability fund inputs has to deal with the various 'upper' and 'lower' thresholds associated with the different capability dimensions embodied within it. However, while in the factory system specialised fund-input elements were designed to fit the precise capability requirements of the specific tasks they were meant to continuously execute, fund-input elements in the newer flexible forms of manufacturing organisation have to be equipped with a capability structure that allows them to execute a variety of different types of task sequences as the job specification adjusts to the requirements of different production programmes. The scale of production activity may, in these new forms of production organisation, not be seen as an endogenously determined variable allowing the continuous utilisation of fund-input elements. Rather, job specification programmes have to adjust to exogenously given changes in the levels and composition of demand. The capability structure of a productive system (the sum total of capabilities available in a productive system) has to be such as to cope with the input requirements which varying batch sizes of different types of outputs imply and flexibly define task sequences and 'jobs' for the different fund inputs so as to deal with the utilisation problem of multicapable fund-input elements. In numerical examples one can show that, while an effective programme of job redefinition and task coordination may attempt to exploit the relative task adequacies of different types of funds, it cannot assure that fund-input elements will be utilised in all their capability dimensions. Furthermore, as different production programmes are adopted, the 'efficiency' of a flexible manufacturing system will not solely be judged by the pattern of utilisation of fund elements, but also by a number of additional elements, such as (i) the costs involved in designing and implementing a system of flexible job specification and task coordination, (ii) the building up of inventories at intermediate stages in the fabrication process due to gaps in the time structure of productive operations, and (iii) the potential 'learning' and 'improvement' in a production environment due to the experiences accumulated from changing job specifications and fund-input interactions.

An important aspect of the flexible manufacturing system is its relative decomposability into 'cells' or 'modules' of interacting fund-input elements.[23]

One important reason for such a relative decomposition of a productive system is that it is much easier to achieve renewed synchronisation of a number of interacting (multiskilled) fund-input elements if that group of elements is not too large. The design of a whole set of job specification programmes to deal with a number of varying output demands is easier to resolve if the number of immediately interacting fund-input elements is not too large. Secondly, relative decomposition allows some degree of independence among the different work units or work stations, so that failures in the operation of one such module would not immediately impede the operation of other modules.

Of course, once a certain degree of independence among the different work stations (the 'modules' of the flexible manufacturing system) is achieved, the question of inventories at the interface between the activities of these modules reemerges. It goes without saying that the ideal type, perfectly synchronised factory (transfer line) system had no need for such buffers. J. Lenz, in a review of job shop, transfer line and FMS, discusses the role of buffer stocks in making work stations relatively independent of each other:

[I]n the job shop, inventory is raised until the operation of one station is isolated from what might happen to any other station. That is, each station is surrounded by inventory so that its operation is independent of all other stations. This creates a situation where production is tied to inventory level. If the inventory level were to drop, stations would become less independent so their dependency will cause some interruption in service. These are termed *integration effects*. In the job shop, integration effects are eliminated by maintaining longer inventories around each station. The penalty for increasing these inventories is in extending the flow time of parts. But since inventory can accumulate without creating serious trafficking problems, the flow time has no effect upon station usage (production). However, flow time does have a critical relationship to production in *transfer line* manufacturing. . . . The objective of the transfer line is to obtain perfect balance. In this situation, no inventory is needed to smooth over integration effects because all parts spend exactly the same amount of time at each station. As a result, changes to the flow time have direct relation to production and, as well, station usage. . . . *Flexible manufacturing systems* are any manufacturing environments where low inventory exists with unbalanced operations. The degree of automation in this environment has very little impact on these characteristics. Therefore, the characteristics of FMS can be applied to any job shop with low inventory, unbalanced transfer line or any other type of integrated manufacturing system. (Lenz, 1986, pp. 257–8)

As Lenz remarks, a distinctive feature of the flexible manufacturing system is its ability to reduce inventory levels in an imperfectly synchronised manufacturing production system. This leads to the discussion of another feature of new forms of production organisation, that is, the just-in-time (JIT) system, which will raise issues such as 'batch continuity', product versus process organisation and the role of learning in a modern production environment.

In conclusion, we would like to emphasise that the picture which emerges from the above discussion is that the FMS is an imperfectly synchronised system of production organisation (just as was the old job shop, but not the factory system) and that the relative effectiveness with which the FMS deals with the problem of a changing production programme (both in levels and in composition) is by searching for optimal solutions in the variety of tradeoffs which the existence of various forms of imperfect synchronisation impose.

For example, a higher and continuous degree of utilisation of fund inputs making up a particular 'cell' or 'module' may be achieved by allowing inventories to build up at the interfaces between the different modules; or, more continuity in the productive operations of fund inputs may reduce changeover costs but allow less adaptability to adjust the production programmes to changing demand conditions; or, while the implementation of a new programme of job specification and task coordination may increase the overall degree of synchronisation, it may also require substantial adjustments and a learning period during which the efficiency of the productive system may be substantially reduced.

5.4 'Just-in-time' (JIT) manufacturing

While the discussion of flexible manufacturing systems has concentrated on the fund-task allocation within modern forms of production organisation, we shall now focus on the material flow features of such forms, in particular with respect to the 'just-in-time' mode of organisation. We will also touch upon the emphasis put in modern forms of production organisation upon 'learning'.

A short but rather narrow definition of the JIT technique is given by Schonberger:

> The JIT idea is simple: Produce and deliver goods just in time to be sold, subassemblies just in time to be assembled into finished goods, fabricated parts just in time to go into subassemblies, and purchased materials just in time to be transformed into fabricated parts.[24] (Schonberger, 1986, p. 16)

The above definition emphasises changes in the way in which material in process moves through a production system. Some authors have described that change by referring to the transition from a 'push' to a 'pull' production system:

> Just-in-time manufacturing is a pull production system in that it supplies product only on demand. The goal of the pull system is to pull the material requirements without the intervention of inventory and with minimum advance notice of production requirements from the customer (whether it be a workstation, function, or company). [A] pull production system only allows for a minimum amount of material to be at any given point in the manufacturing process, and additional material cannot be ordered until needed. This has the net effect of maintaining low inventory levels. (Lubben, 1988, pp. 37 and 13)

The feature which the JIT system has in common with the factory system is that the production arrangement should be such as to allow the *continuity* of the flow of material in process through its various stages of fabrication. However, differently from the factory system, in which the volume of production and the product programme remains the same for long periods of time, the type of continuity of the material in process relevant for JIT is *batch continuity*.

The difference between the type of continuity of work in process which leads to the continuous replicability of the material in process in any of its stages through time typical for the factory system[25], and the *batch continuity* relevant for modern flexible forms of production organisation is of course due to the changing character of the production programme (in the scale and composition of output) in the latter case.

Each change in the production programme causes, in flexible forms of production organisation, a change in the fund-task allocations (that is, a change of the 'job specification programme') which in turn changes the organisation and sequencing of tasks and consequently the features of the transformation process. These features refer to the characteristics of work in process which moves through the 'pipelines' of the productive system, the various transformations it undergoes from stage to stage and the timing of the stop and go sequences of that process. Each stop involves some degree of inventory accumulation and a subsequent 'go phase' leads to the decumulation of such inventories. Flexible manufacturing systems will try to find a definition and sequencing of transformation stages that assures as much as possible the *continuity* of the transformation process and hence reduces the need for inventories. In other words, while just-in-time production is based on the principle that the right quantity of material will reach the right station at just the right time, it will nonetheless attempt to minimise stop phases once a production programme has been specified. It is the 'pull production system' which starts the ordering of the right quantities of work in process, materials and so on, from the final stages back to the initial stages and thus assures that maximum batch continuity can be achieved. It will thereby draw upon those work stations/cells which have either inventories or free capacity to meet increased demand. Of course, it is advances in the field of information transmission and numerical control technology that greatly facilitate quick changeovers in fund-task allocations and in the sequencing and the characteristics of the transformation process. Closely linked to the success of a pull production system is the adequacy of plant layout (the location of fund-input elements relative to each other), adequate material handling systems, and the changeover from a *process*-based to a *product*-based production organisation:[26]

In a JIT system, the lay-out of the factory is designed to minimise the amount of material in work-in-process (WIP), the amount of material and handling involved, and the total cycle time of the process, and to improve information feedback. To accomplish this, it is preferable to have all the processes involved in the production of a product as close as possible to each other and in the proper sequence. . . .

[H]aving equipment arranged in order of production, reduces the amount of material handling involved, allows for smaller lots to be moved between machines, reduces the need for expensive and complex material-handling systems, and allows for a better flow of information and employees in the production area. (Lubben, 1988, pp. 119–120)

An adequate material handling system is also an essential prerequisite to assure the continuous flow of material in process through the 'pipelines' of a production system:

A well-designed materials system will minimise accounting for products, reduce shipping damage, reduce handling costs, and improve the efficiency of the user working with the material. The design of the material-handling system will also greatly influence the case of implementing a JIT system. . . . The objective of JIT manufacturing is to move products constantly forward like so many branches of a river. As the individual branches of the material flow merge, the product becomes more complete until the last operations are completed. The design of the material-handling system maintains the integrity of this process by making sure that materials will arrive in a serviceable condition and by minimising the involvement of overhead systems. (Lubben, 1988, p. 125)

It is interesting to note that the emphasis in recent forms of production organisation has shifted from maximising the quantity of throughput at any particular workstation (this was one of the traditional factors relevant for achieving economies of scale and allowing a higher degree of specialisation) to minimising the costs of transporting materials in process flows, reducing the costs of handling such flows and assuring their continuity and quality.[27]

While classical authors acknowledged the importance of costs of materials handling and tool changes as an important drawback of the job shop, their emphasis on division of labour and large-scale production was precisely intended to call attention to organisational features that could solve the problems of inventory and materials handling costs, changeover costs, and so on. With the advent of flexible manufacturing systems in response to the need for an ever changing production programme, the emphasis on materials handling and inventory control reemerged, but this time it gave rise to new concepts such as product organisation, group technology, etc. as discussed above.

However, as most authors who examine the just-in-time system repeatedly emphasise, it would be wrong to think of JIT as primarily an inventory control technique. As a matter of fact the emphasis on inventory minimisation serves rather as a 'focusing device' (Rosenberg, 1969), as a means to bring out clearly which other aspects of the production organisation could be improved. The recognition of *flexible* manufacturing as being an imperfectly synchronised system of production organisation whose different components (fund-task allocation, task structuring and sequencing, material flow organisation) need to be continuously calibrated with respect to each other as the production organisation has to be adapted to the requirements of a changing production programme, brings the 'learning' aspect to the forefront of modern forms of production organisation:

In general explanations of the JIT system, there is a tendency to put excessive emphasis on the aspect of stock control and the minimisation of inventory. . . . The reduction of the amount of inventory to an extreme if not absolute minimum . . . plays an important role in uncovering waste of time and material, usage of defective parts and components, and inappropriate machinery movements. In order to reduce inventory to a minimum it is necessary to eliminate any wasteful use of raw materials as well as defective operations and unnecessary work time, and to have every one of the workers directly involved in trying to discover problems and come up with creative ideas and means to correct them. Under this system, when an aberration in either quality or equipment occurs, an automatic device installed in every work station stops the line. As a result, there is no chance of accumulating defective parts or rectification operations. The system thereby generates unavoidable pressures to maximise uptime, or effective operation time, and to minimise defective parts or products. Such pressure not only requires excellent maintenance of machinery but has to be reflected in the relationship with parts and component suppliers and in the standard operational practices on the production lines. Suppliers, in this system, have no choice but to try to maintain and meet high quality standards. The workers directly involved at a work station that is installed with an automatic line stop device, on the other hand, are also compelled to try to thoroughly eliminate waste and solve problems. (Shimokawa, 1986, pp. 229–34)[28]

The process of learning and improvement in which all the different organisational features of the productive system (task definition and task sequencing, fund-task allocations, capability development, and material flow coordination) interact point to a continuous sequence of mutual impulses for further improvements.[29] In other words, learning and innovations take place on all the three levels of analysis of productive systems thus bringing about (i) explorations of new combinations of capabilities in the development of new employments of old types of fund inputs; (ii) further analysis and understanding of the consistent characteristics of production processes, in the tasks to be performed and in their sequencing possibilities; and (iii) learning about the characteristics of materials which can be used and the transformation processes undergone by such materials.

5.5 Industrial networks and forms of production organisation

The various forms of production organisation bring to the fore a number of alternative patterns according to which different productive units may interact with one another within any given network of productive activities.

The traditional job shop may originally be associated with a type of network in which individual workshops provide 'finished products' to each other. For example, butchers may provide hide to tanners and tanners deliver leather to shoemakers. In a putting out network, linkages among different workshops are also based upon the flows of materials going over from one fabrication stage to another.

On the other hand, the factory system brings to the fore the possibility of splitting the production process not only by fabrication stages but also by tasks assigned to specific fund inputs (workers or machines). In this case, we may distinguish within any given production process the flows of work-in-process materials that get worked upon by different sequences of fund inputs. Such a distinction does not arise in the case of the job shop, where the same multipurpose fund input may execute all the tasks required at the various fabrication stages of the material in process, nor is it relevant in a manufacture where parallel work stations do not interact with each other. On the other hand, the above distinction is a critical one when the factory system is considered. For the interlocking processing of different material flows by fund inputs, which characterises the factory system, brings to the fore an important application of Babbage's *Law of Multiples*. This is the fact that the full and continuous utilisation of fund-input elements requires a *minimum number* of interlocking flows of material in process. However, this scale requirement may be different for different fabrication stages. As a result, the factory principle may lead to the formation of industrial networks in which different productive units operate distinct fabrication stages depending on the mode of operation of the Law of Multiples in each particular case. For example, fabrication stages requiring large equipment may be executed in establishments of the factory type, whereas other fabrication stages may be carried out in small workshops or even in private households (see, for example, Robinson, 1935, pp. 14–35).

The new forms of production organisation considered in the previous subsections may also lead to the formation of *industrial networks*. However, the specific characteristics of the flexible manufacturing system and of just-in-time production make it possible to have networks different from those considered above. In particular, Babbage's assumption of a given pool of capabilities existing in each establishment is no longer satisfied, nor may productive organisation be based upon the one-to-one correspondence between fund-input elements and capability types. This implies that the industrial networks based on new forms of manufacturing must exploit the advantages associated with pooling criteria different from those considered above. For example, industrial networks could be based upon the pooling of process types that allow for the full utilisation of different capabilities at different times, or for effective learning (discovery of new capabilities) over a wide product range, or for the combination of a large number of different flows of materials in process. A general characteristic of such industrial networks would be the relative independence of networking processes from the size of productive establishments, since large productive units may be participating in networks in which they contribute a 'low scale' capability, that is, a capability whose effective practice is compatible with the processing of a small quantity of materials per unit of time. On the other hand, small workshops may contribute a 'high scale' capability (defined as above) to networks of the same type.

Notes

1 For example, many medieval artisans 'specialised in one or more of the odds and ends of semi-luxury articles that women in particular shopped for in towns – buckles and belts, little carved images, silk hairnets and so on. . . . Demand in these trades as a whole had . . . long been expanding but could never have been very great for any single item, and in fact its growth depended on the craftsman's response to customers' desire for individuality within fashion trends that throve on innovation' (S. L. Thrupp, 1972, p. 250).

2 This situation may be contrasted with that characteristic of modern factory production, in which 'the boundaries between firms in a process are apt to be at the boundaries between the activities of different machines' (Ames and Rosenberg, 1965, p. 372).

3 This feature of medieval craft production has been noted by Cipolla: 'as one can still see in Florence and Venice, the mansions of the merchants included in their structure large rooms intended solely for the storage of the raw materials and the finished goods' (Cipolla, 1981, p. 115). Cipolla also notes that, with this form of production organisation, 'fluctuations in the level of stocks kept in warehouses were both a most evident sign and a determining factor of the dynamics of the economic cycle at that time' (Cipolla, 1974, p. 157).

4 As pointed out by Sombart, in craft production technical knowledge is of an 'empirical' kind, since 'it is solely based upon personal experience, it is independent of rules other than those that are considered to be right from a subjective point of view, rules which the "master" learns in the real course of his own activity and passes on to the "apprentice" as rules of the craft, just as a personal endowment. However, anybody who has learnt a craft only knows the details of the technical practice but ignores why it works that way' (Sombart, 1916, book I, chapter 13).

5 Of course, there are cases in which the high level of demand leads to the execution of spinning within specialised workshops processing a large quantity of

raw material per unit of time. For example, the silk-throwing industry of Bologna was transformed in the course of the fourteenth century by the utilisation of a machine driven by water power and throwing hundreds of threads at once (see Nussbaum, 1933, p. 212; see also Poni, 1976, for a detailed appraisal of the productive organisation of the silk-throwing industry in early modern Bologna). An opposite development characterised textile cottage industry in China. There, 'a dispersed but extensive rural industry [producing] cotton textiles was established during the fourteenth century. . . . [However] [t]his immense, nationwide cottage industry was not based on a putting-out system. Rather it operated through the market. A woman with no money at all could get credit on cotton bought one day which she returned to sell as thread the following day' (Goody, 1982, pp. 31–2; see also Chao, 1977).

6 As was noted by E. P. Thompson, '[t]he putting-out system demanded much fetching, carrying, waiting for materials. Bad weather could disrupt not only agriculture, building and transport, but also weaving, where the finished pieces had to be stretched on the tenters to dry' (Thompson, 1967, p. 71). This loose pattern of coordination among the different stages of the material in process could be a reason for the flexible pattern of utilisation of capabilities that characterises putting out workshops: '[a]s we get closer to each task, we are surprised to find the multiplicity of subsidiary tasks which the same worker or family group must do in one cottage or workshop. Even in larger workshops men sometimes continued to work at *distinct tasks* at their own benches or looms, and except where the fear of embezzlement of materials imposed stricter supervision – could show some flexibility in coming and going' (ibid.).

7 As William Petty emphasised: 'each *Manufacture* will be divided into as many parts as possible, whereby the Work of each *Artisan* will be simple and easy: As for Example. In the making of a *Watch* if one Man shall make the *Wheels*, another the *Spring*, another shall Engrave the *Dial-plate*, and another shall make the *Cases*, then the *Watch* will be better and cheaper, than if the whole work be put upon any one man' (Petty, 1683, pp. 471–2).

8 Marx develops this idea of the simultaneous operation of partial processes when he contrasts the 'factory' with earlier forms of manufacturing: 'In Manufacture, the isolation of each detail process is a condition imposed by the nature of division of labour, but in the fully developed factory the continuity of those processes is, on the contrary, imperative' (Marx, 1972, p. 360; 1st edn. 1867).

9 The implications for the scale of industrial production of such an arrangement of partial processes had early on been recognised by Dugald Stewart: 'It [the division of labour] produces also an economy of time, by separating the work into its different branches, all of which may be carried on into execution at the same moment. . . . By carrying on all the different processes at once, which an individual must have executed separately, it becomes possible to produce a multitude of pins for instance completely finished in the same time as a single pin might have been either cut or pointed' (Stewart, 1855–6, p. 319).

10 Figure 8.8 illustrates Marx's description of 'serial manufacture' (see also sub-section 5.2 of chapter 6)

11 In the present treatment, the arrangement *in series* corresponds to the arrangement of processes in Marx's 'serial manufacture'. It also corresponds to the 'arrangement in line' recently discussed by Georgescu-Roegen (see Georgescu-Roegen, 1969).

12 There are two ways of thinking of an arrangement of unit processes in line: the first is when processes themselves have an inherent feature of 'process indivisibility' such that they can only be operated at a particular intensity level (or within a range of intensity levels) without changing their characteristics (see Landesmann, 1986, for a discussion of 'strict' versus 'weak' forms of process indivisibilities); in that case an arrangement in parallel means determining the number (n) of unit processes which are to be operated side-by-side having started at the same points of time. Alternatively, if we are not faced with process indivisibility, then it is appropriate to think of n as the activity level at which a process P has to be operated to achieve full utilisation of those fund-input elements which embody indivisibility properties (such as blast furnaces, workers, etc.). (For the original statement of 'process' and 'input indivisibilities', see Georgescu-Roegen, 1971.)

13 A further application of the Law of Multiples could be found if we drop our assumption of simplicity of a utilisation profile of fund inputs as in figure 8.10. Consider, for example, the utilisation profile of fund inputs k and m of the following type

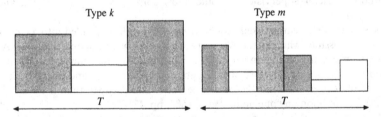

Figure 8.10   Utilisation profile of two funds in process P.

The consideration of such differentiated time profiles of the utilisation patterns of different fund-input elements in the course of a production process P is important for the determination of the number of distinct fabrication stages or 'production lines' which have to be distinguished in order to achieve full utilisation of all the (indivisible) types of fund inputs involved in a production system.
If T is the total length of process P and τ_{ki} are the time periods over which distinguishable utilisation requirements of fund inputs of type k ($k=1,2,\ldots,K$) can be identified, then the number of fabrication stages ('production lines') that will have to be distinguished in order to achieve the full utilisation of all the (indivisible) fund-input elements engaged in a production system will be the *largest common denominator* of the fractions T/τ_{ki}.

14 See, for example, the following remarks by John Rae: 'The exercise of the arts of

the weaver, the blacksmith, the carpenter, the farmer, implies the existence of a great variety of tools with which they may be carried on. But, as a man can only do one thing at once, if any man had all the tools which these several occupations require, at least three-fourths of them would constantly lie idle and useless. It were clearly then better . . . that the members of [the society] should if possible divide them amongst them, each restricting himself to some particular employment . . . [In the early stage of a human settlement] every man is at first probably obliged to be his own carpenter, glazier, tanner, cobbler, and perhaps to a great extent his own blacksmith. As the settlement fills up, and the population becomes sufficiently dense, he gives up this multifarious industry, and takes to some particular branch' (Rae, 1905, pp. 102–3; 1st edn. 1834).

 A concise statement of this point of view may be found in Young: 'It would be wasteful to furnish a factory with an elaborate equipment of specially constructed jigs, gauges, lathes, drills, presses and conveyors to build a hundred automobiles; it would be better to rely mostly on tools and machines of standard types. . . . Mr Ford's methods would be absurdly uneconomical if this output were very small, and would be unprofitable even if his output were what many other manufacturers of automobiles would call large' (Young, 1928, p. 530).

15 Babbage states this principle at the beginning of chapter XXI, entitled 'On the Causes and Consequences of Large Factories'.

16 Marx reiterates this principle when he writes: 'When once the most fitting proportion has been experimentally established for the numbers of the detail labourers in the various groups when producing on a given scale, that scale can be extended only by employing a multiple of each particular group' (Marx, 1972, p. 327; 1st edn. 1867).

17 It can be shown (see Landesmann, 1986) that Babbage's Factory Principle gets strongly modified if instead of 'strict' process and input indivisibilities, we are dealing with 'weak' indivisibilities, i.e., processes maintain their characteristics over a *range* of activity levels or fund-input elements of the same type exist for a class of sizes rather than for unique sizes.

18 For example, Babbage clearly emphasised that the hiring of a specialised repair workman would be worthwhile only once a certain scale of production was attained: 'since the good performance and the duration of machines depend to a very great extent upon correcting, as soon as it appears, every shake or imperfection in their parts, it will soon become apparent that a workman resident on the spot will reduce the expenditure arising from wear and tear of the machinery. But in the case of a single lace-frame, or a single loom, this would be too expensive a plan. Here then arises another circumstance which tends to enlarge the extent of a factory. It ought to consist of such a number of machines as shall occupy the whole time of one workman in keeping them in order, and in making any casual repairs: if it is extended beyond this, the same principle of economy would point out the necessity of doubling or tripling the number of machines in order to employ the whole time of two or three skilful workmen' (Babbage, 1832, p. 175).

19 The Fordist system, or 'transfer line' system, as it was also called, is described by Kazanas and his associates as follows:

Line production derives its name from the assembly line of parts moving past work stations. Henry Ford pioneered this concept. . . . By moving the parts to the worker time for assembly was greatly reduced simply because no time was lost by assemblers moving back and forth. Further time savings were made by studies that found ways of reducing reaching, lifting, sorting and positioning actions by workers. The time taken to reach for a wrench can be very costly when repeated thousands of time. Thus, moving the wrench closer can reduce costs and increase production rates. . . .

Several factors are important to both profitable and successful operations. The areas include *interchangeability of similar parts, division of labour and processes* into tiny elements that can be quickly performed at one pace, *movement of the materials to the work station*, efficient use of time and the placement of the work station . . . lowering material cost by purchasing in large quantities, reducing the amount of labour through efficiency studies to the lowest possible amount; reducing the cost of labour by reducing the need for highly skilled crafts people in the assembly line and the utilisation of specialised tools to increase the rate of work performance. Automated and semi-automated machines are also used to eliminate reproductive time and to increase the speed of assembly. However, the more specialised the equipment, the more critical certain essential factors become. These include the need for a mass market to consume vast quantities of the product, increasing cost of labour skills, and the need for redesign to minimise assembly processes. (Kazanas, Barker and Gregor, 1981, p. 329)

20 The demands imposed upon a modern manufacturing system are also well expressed by Warnecke and Steinhilper: 'As a result of the worldwide trend to decreasing batch sizes, together with an increasing variety of the part spectrum, the demand for a minimisation of throughput times and a simultaneous maximisation of machine utilisation is increasingly gaining importance. Today this conflict of objectives may be solved with the application of newly designed manufacturing and material-flow devices with *a high degree of flexibility regarding batch size variations and differing operation sequences*' (our italics) (Warnecke and Steinhilper, 1985, p. 3).

21 See the passage by Ferrara quoted in chapter 6, subsection 9.2 above.

22 The association of learning with the existence of relatively complex bundles of capabilities, rather than with the single-minded practice of a specialised skill, had been recognised long ago by Lauderdale who maintained that 'the simplest and most efficacious machines for supplanting labour . . . are introduced, at an early period of society, when the division of labour is comparatively unpractised and unknown, for the purpose of supplanting the personal labour of man in the conduct of agricultural industry' (Lauderdale, 1804, pp. 291–2). On the other hand, Lauderdale also maintained that 'the habits of thinking which the division of labour tends to generate in the manufacturer must be determined; as they are destructive of that train of thought which leads to the perfection of machinery' (Lauderdale, 1804, pp. 294–5). In both cases the introduction of machinery is related to learning processes

requiring the existence of multipurpose operators, and the economies of speed associated with the operation of machinery are considered to be unrelated to increases in the division of labour.

23 For example, it has been pointed out that 'The FMS consists of a number of flexible cells which achieve computer integration' (Moodie and Ben Arieh, 1986, p. 236), so that 'complementary fund inputs (generally, machine tools) may be linked together by a common "stock" of tools and materials'.

24 In addition, Schonberger considers the just-in-time system: 'as a quality and scrap control tool, as a streamlined plant configuration that raises process yield, as a production line balancing approach, and as an employee involvement and motivational mechanism' (Schonberger, 1982, pp. 17–18).

25 We refer here to the description of the factory system as one where 'we see the raw material in all the stages of its production at the same time' (Marx, 1972, p. 326) with the same picture being repeated from time interval to time interval as long as the production programme does not change. (See our discussion of the factory system in section 4 above.)

26 The changeover from process to product organisation is well described by Burbridge who emphasises both the different grouping and fund elements of the different material flow systems typical for these two forms:

> Production flow analysis (PFA) is a technique used to plan the change in a factory from process organisation to product organisation and also to plan the change from process layout to product layout. These two changes so simplify the 'material flow system', or system of routes along which materials flow between work places in a factory, that PFA can also be defined as a technique for planning the simplification of material flow systems in factories. In batch and jobbing production the term 'group technology' (GT) is a synonym for production organisation and PFA can again be defined, therefore, as a technique for finding the 'families' (sets of parts) and 'groups' (related sets of machines and other facilities) for group technology. By these definitions, process organisation is a type in which units specialise in the completion of particular sets of assembled products, or particular sets of families of components. (Burbridge, 1989, p. 1)

27 Kazanas, Barker and Gregor, for instance, have argued that: 'About 80 per cent of production time is spent in transferring the materials from one place to another on the production floor, and less than 20 per cent is spent on the actual processing. In most cases it takes more handling than processing operations to produce a part' (Kazanas, Barker and Gregor, 1981, p. 19).

28 It is interesting to note that Japanese 'just-in-time' techniques exploit the feature of imperfect synchronisation inherent in modern forms of production organisation explicitly as a 'learning device':

> [t]he Japanese no longer accept the buffer principle [to counter irregularities in production through the holding of buffer stocks]. Instead of adding buffer stocks at the point of irregularity, Japanese production managers deliberately

expose the workforce to the consequences. The response is that workers and foremen rally to root out the causes of irregularity . . . the Japanese principle of exposing the workers to the consequences of production irregularities is not applied passively. In the Toyota Kanban system, for example, each time that workers succeed in correcting the causes of recent irregularity (machine jamming, cantankerous holding devices, etc.), the managers remove still more buffer stock. The workers are never allowed to settle into a comfortable pattern; or rather, the pattern becomes one of continually perfecting the production process. (Schonberger, 1982, p. 32)

29 See Rosenberg (1969) who emphasises the role of disequilibria in production systems as 'focusing devices' for technological innovation.

References

Ames, E. and Rosenberg, N. (1965) 'The Progressive Division and Specialisation of Industries', *Journal of Development Studies*, 1 (July): 363–83.

Babbage, C. (1832) *On the Economy of Machinery and Manufactures*, London, Charles Knight.

Bakshi, M. S. and Arora, S. R. (1969) 'The Sequencing Problem', *Management Science*, 16, (4, December): B247–B263.

Beccaria, C. (1771) *Elementi di economia publica*, in S. Romagnoli (ed.) *Opere*, Florence, Sansoni.

Berg, M. (1985) *The Age of Manufactures: Industry, Innovation and Work in Britain 1700–1820*, London, Fontana.

Bücher, C. (1901) *Industrial Evolution*, New York, H. Holt and Company (German original 1893).

Burbridge, J. L. (1989) *Production Flow Analysis for Planning Group Technology*, Oxford, Clarendon Press.

Carrie, A. (1988) *Simulation of Manufacturing Systems*, Chichester–New York, John Wiley and Sons.

Chandler, A. D. (1977) *The Visible Hand. The Managerial Revolution in American Business*, Cambridge, Mass., The Belknap Press of Harvard University Press.

Chao, K. (1977) *The Development of Cotton Textile Production in China*, Cambridge, Mass., Harvard University Press.

Chernyshevskij, N. G. (1860) 'Trud i Kapital kak elementi proĭsvodstva', *Sovremennik* (St Petersburg), n.s., vol. lxxxii, n. 8, August, pp. 209–22 of the Supplement.

Church, A. H. (1930) *Overhead Expense in relation to Costs, Sales and Profits*, New York, McGraw-Hill Book Company.

(1900) 'The Meaning of Commercial Organization', *Engineering Magazine*, 20: 391–8.

Cipolla, C. (1974) *Storia economica dell'Europa preindustriale*, Bologna, Il Mulino.

(1981) *Before the Industrial Revolution. European Society and Economy, 1000–1700*, London, Methuen, 2nd edition.

Ferrara, F. (1860) Introduction to vol. II, 2nd series of the *Biblioteca dell'Economista*, Torino, Unione tipografico-editrice torinese, pp. v–lxxii.

French, S. (1982) *Sequencing and Scheduling: an Introduction to the Mathematics of the Job-Shop*, Chichester, Ellis Horwood Ltd.

Georgescu-Roegen, N. (1969) 'Process in Farming versus Process in Manufacturing; A Problem of Balanced Development', in G. U. Papi and C. Nunn (eds.), *Economic Problems of Agriculture in Industrial Societies*, New York, St. Martin's Press, pp. 427–528.

(1971) *Entropy Law and the Economic Process*, Cambridge, Mass., Harvard University Press.

Goody, E. N. (1982) 'Introduction', in E. N. Goody (ed.), *From Craft to Industry: the Ethnography of Proto-industrial Cloth Production*, Cambridge, Cambridge University Press, pp. 1–37.

Hay, E. J. (1988) *The Just-in-Time Breakthrough. Implementing the New Manufacturing Basics*, New York, John Wiley and Sons.

Hicks, J. R. (1969) *A Theory of Economic History*, Oxford, Clarendon Press.

Kazanas, H. C., Barker, G. E. and Gregor, T. (1981) *Basic Manufacturing Processes*, New York, Atlanta, Gregg Division McGraw-Hill Book Company.

Landesmann, M. (1986) 'Conceptions of Technology and the Production Process', in M. Baranzini and R. Scazzieri (eds.), *Foundations of Economics. Structures of Inquiry and Economic Theory*, Oxford, Basil Blackwell, pp. 281–310.

Lauderdale, J. (1804) *An Inquiry into the Nature and Origin of Public Wealth and into the Means and Causes of its Increase*, Edinburgh, Constable and Co.; London, Longman, Hurst, Rees.

Leijonhuvfud, A. (1986) 'Capitalism and the Factory System', in R. N. Langlois (ed.), *Economics as a Process. Essays in the New Institutional Economics*, Cambridge, Cambridge University Press, pp. 203–23.

Lenz, J. E. (1986) 'General Theories of Flexible Integration', in K. Rathmill, pp. 255–64.

Litterer, J. A. (1961) 'Systematic Management: the Search for Order and Integration', *Business History Review*, 35 (4, Winter): 461–76.

Lubben, R. T. (1988) *Just-in-Time Manufacturing*, New York, McGraw Hill.

Marx, K. (1867) *Das Kapital*, Hamburg, O. Meissner, vol. I.

(1972) *Capital, a Critical Analysis of Capitalist Production* (1st edition 1867), London, Lawrence and Wishart, vol. I.

Moodie, C. C. and Ben Arieh D. (1986) 'Strategies for Material Transportation in a Computer Integrated Manufacturing Environment', in K. Rathmill, pp. 235–45.

Nussbaum, F. L. (1933) *A History of the Economic Institutions of Modern Europe: an Introduction to Der Moderne Kapitalismus of W. Sombart*, New York, F. S. Crofts.

Petty, W. (1671) *Political Arithmetick, or A Discourse concerning the . . . Value of Lands, People, Buildings . . .*, London, R. Clavel.

(1683) *Another Essay on Political Arithmetic Concerning the Growth of the City of London*, London, Mark Pardoe; also available in *Economic Writings of Sir William Petty*, ed. C. H. Hull, reissued New York, A. M. Kelley, 1963.

302   Michael Landesmann and Roberto Scazzieri

(1690) *Political Arithmetick*, London, R. Clavel; also available in *Economic Writings of Sir William Petty*, ed. C. H. Hull, reissued New York, A. M. Kelly, 1963.

Poni, C. (1972) 'Archéologie de la fabrique: la diffusion des moulins à soie "alla bolognese" dans les Etats Vénitiens du XVIᵉ au XVIIIᵉ siècle', *Annales Économies, Sociétés, Civilisation*, 27: 1475–96.

(1976) 'All'origine del sistema di fabbrica: tecnologia e organizzazione produttiva dei mulini da seta nell'Italia settentrionale' (sec xvii–xviii), *Rivista Storica Italiana*, n. 3, pp. 444–97.

Rae, J. (1905) *The Sociological Theory of Capital*, New York, Macmillan; originally published as *Statement of Some New Principles on the Subject of Political Economy* (1st edition 1834), New York, Augustus M. Kelley.

Raju, V. and Karlson, T. J. (1985) 'Flexible Manufacturing Cells with Robots', in H.-J. Warnecke (ed.), *Proceedings of the 3rd International Conference on Flexible Manufacturing Systems*, Bedford, IFS Publications; Amsterdam, North-Holland, pp. 165–73.

Ranky, P. (1983) *The Design and Operation of FMS. Flexible Manufacturing Systems*, Bedford, IFS Publications Ltd, Amsterdam, New York, Oxford, North-Holland.

Rathmill, K. (ed.) (1986) *Proceedings of the 5th International Conference on Flexible Manufacturing Systems*, Bedford, IFS Publications.

Robinson, E. A. G. (1931) *The Structure of Competitive Industry*, with an Introduction by J. M. Keynes, London, Nisbet and Co.; Cambridge, Cambridge University Press.

(1935) *The Structure of Competitive Industry*, with an Introduction by J. M. Keynes, London, Nisbet and Co.; Cambridge, Cambridge University Press.

Rosenberg, N. (1969) 'The Direction of Technological Change: Inducement Mechanisms and Focusing Devices', *Economic Development and Cultural Change*, 18: 1–24.

Scazzieri, R. (1993) *A Theory of Production. Tasks, Processes, and Technical Practices*, Oxford, Clarendon Press.

Schonberger, R. J. (1982) *Japanese Manufacturing Techniques. Nine Hidden Lessons in Simplicity*, New York, The Free Press; London, Collier Macmillan.

(1986) *World Class Manufacturing. The Lessons of Simplicity Applied*, New York, The Free Press; London, Collier Macmillan.

(1987) *World Class Manufacturing Casebook*, New York, The Free Press; London, Collier Macmillan.

Shimokawa, K. (1986) 'Product and Labour Strategies in Japan', in S. Tolliday and J. Zeitlin.

Smith, A. (1776) *An Inquiry into the Nature and Causes of the Wealth of Nations*, London, Strahan and Cadell.

Sombart, W. (1916) *Der moderne Kapitalismus*, Munich and Leipzig, Dunker & Humblot.

Stewart, D. (1855–6) *Lectures on Political Economy*, volumes 8 and 9 of *The Collected Works by Dugald Stewart*, edited by Sir William Hamilton, Edinburgh, T. Constable and Co.

Thompson, E. P. (1967) 'Time, Work-Discipline, and Industrial Capitalism', *Past and Present*, 38 (December): 56–97.

Thrupp, S. L. (1972) 'Medieval Industry 1000–1500', in C. M. Cipolla (ed.), *The Fontana Economic History of Europe*, vol. I: *The Middle Ages*, London, Fontana, pp. 221–73.

Tolliday, S. and Zeitlin, J. (eds.) (1986) *The Automobile Industry and its Workers: Between Fordism and Flexibility*, Oxford, Polity Press.

Tucker, J. (1755) *The Elements of Commerce and Theory of Taxes*, Bristol.

(1774) *Four Tracts on Political and Commercial Subjects*, Gloucester, R. Raikes.

Unwin, G. (1904) *Industrial Organisation in the Sixteenth and Seventeenth Centuries*, Oxford, Clarendon Press.

Usher, A. P. (1921) *An Introduction to the Industrial History of England*, London, G. C. Harrap and Co. Ltd.

Warnecke, H. J. and Steinhilper, R. (eds.) (1985) *Flexible Manufacturing Systems*, Bedford, IFS Publications; Berlin, Heidelberg, New York, Tokyo, Springer-Verlag.

White, R. N. *et al.* (1976) *Structural Engineering*, vol. I: *Introduction to Design Concepts and Analysis*, Books on Demand UMI.

Young, A. (1928) 'Increasing Returns and Economic Progress', *Economic Journal*, 38 (December): 527–42.

9 Coordination of production processes, subsystem dynamics and structural change

MICHAEL LANDESMANN AND ROBERTO SCAZZIERI

1 Introduction

The contributions in part I of this volume considered different approaches to the theory of production dynamics within a simplified set-up, which relies upon the description of production systems in terms of input–output flows between processes. In these contributions we have seen that advances which have been made in analysing economic dynamics in the context of disaggregated representations of the productive structure of an economy relied heavily on various *methods of decomposition*. In the succeeding chapters of part II we examined instead the dynamics of production by looking at the complex internal structure of individual processes, and at the pattern of interdependence among such processes. The aim of this chapter is to explore the implications of the more detailed representation of production processes presented in chapters 6–8 for the analysis of the dynamics of the economic system as a whole. Again, we will see that the decomposition of the productive system as implied by the explicit analysis of 'networks' or subsystems' in chapter 6 will provide the basis for the analysis of economic dynamics at the level of the economic system as a whole. In particular, the identification of various types of 'networks' facilitates the identification of the factors ('impulses') which initiate patterns of structural change and they also contribute to the explicit analysis of structural change in the wake of such initial impulses.

The following section 2 examines the way in which the time structure of production activities (along the three previously identified dimensions) may influence the *time phasing of structural change*, and thus its characteristics as a *process* with particular features through historical time. Section 3 explores the impact of various forms of technological change within our analytical framework and how an initial 'impulse' may give rise to 'chain effects' due to the interrelatedness of the different dimensions of the production process. Section 4 considers changes in the consumption structure and how these may influence the organisational structure of the economic system by changing the scale and ways of producing commodities, and changing the weights of different subsystems within the economic system. Section 5 analyses the way in which dynamic impulses, originating either at the level of the microstructure of production or at that of the economic system as a whole, may start processes of structural change that work themselves out through the formation of networks and the generation of 'local' dynamics that may or may not spread through the whole system. Section 6 considers the relationship between local and general patterns of economic dynamics, and highlights the critical role of decomposition techniques in the formulation of adequate analytical frameworks. Section 7 with its various subsections sets up a framework to study 'decomposable dynamics' in economic systems. The concept of 'networks' of productive relationships is developed in more detail linked to the study of similarity and neighbourhood relationships. The study of structural change involves a detailed discussion of the formation of 'dynamic networks' following the impact of an impulse and the role of 'rigidities' and of 'buffers' (un-/under-utilised capacities and inventories) is discussed to identify a circumscribed area of production relationships which absorbs within a particular time horizon the impact of a given impulse. Relative structural rigidities and buffers are a function of, both, longer-term organisational designs and of conjunctural factors; these both influence the way a productive system responds to a particular shock, i.e., evolves new organisational patterns and hence makes the process of structural adaptation path dependent. Finally, we deal in this section with the distinction between adjustment versus innovation and attempt in a limited way an endogenisation of organisational and technological innovation within our analytical framework. Section 8 concludes this chapter by outlining the complementarity between the 'macro-to-micro' (or system-to-subsystem) and the 'micro-to-macro' (subsystem- to-system) approaches to studying structural change in economic systems.

2 Patterns of coordination in the wake of economic change

The analysis of production processes introduced in part II suggests the identification of three distinct levels of coordination among elements of production, which are associated respectively with tasks, agents and materials in process. The actual organisational structure of any given process, however, cannot be fully described unless one is capable of determining in which way the three levels are related to each other so as to specify a relatively stable form of production organization. The latter may be considered as the *repetitive pattern of coordination* among tasks, agents and materials that gives shape to a particular production process as it operates through time (see section 6 of chapter 6). It follows that the actual operational structure of a production process has to do not so much with the specific agents, tasks and material flows interacting with one another, nor with the specific outputs delivered by that process, but with the set of feasible transformations within a given organisational set-up.

Production processes have to be observed and analysed over a considerable time to detect the complex patterns of coordination amongst tasks, agents and materials in process which characterise its mode of operation. In the following two sections we are going to discuss two types of factors which can affect gradually or discretely the mode of operation and internal organisational structure of production processes. The first group of factors refers to *changes in technology* which can affect all three dimensions of productive processes, that is, task definitions and task arrangements, the embodiment of new 'capabilities' in productive agents allowing new feasible fund-task allocations and changes in the definition and composition of materials. All these three features of technological change can and – in most cases – will have strong implications for process organisation, that is, for the way in which the coordination problems involving all the three analytical levels of process organisation are solved. In section 4 we shall focus upon the other factor affecting process organisation, that is, *changes in the level and structure of demand*. These changes will, even without a widening of the set of technologically feasible options, affect the choice of technological practices and of the coordination mechanisms characterising a particular form of production organisation. A third factor which similarly affects the choice of technological practices and might restrict the ability of the productive system to respond to changes in the level and structure of demand are *constraints* which result from the restricted (temporary or permanent) supply of particular types of inputs, in particular *natural resources.*

3 Production organisation and the process of technological and organisational change

The analysis of production activities as complex patterns of time-related task definitions and task arrangements, patterns of utilisation of capabilities and of processes of material transformation suggests the consideration of structural change as a *process*, that is, as a phenomenon that may be described in terms of its *directionality, stage structure* (or phases) and *irreversibility*. Directionality implies that it is possible to describe a particular pattern of structural change in a teleological manner: an initial state is disturbed by an 'impulse' (such as technological change, demand shifts, environmental constraints) which gives rise to a process of adjustment involving all the three levels of production coordination; finally, an end-point in the adjustment process may be identified. Of course, a 'new impulse' might affect the process of transition before a 'final stage' has been reached. The stage structure implies that the set of transformations leading from the initial to a final state must take place according to a particular sequence, or a finite number of sequences, depending upon the initial arrangements and interdependencies of productive elements and their relative persistence over time. Finally, the irreversibility of a process is related to the fact that certain transformations cannot be undone, due to objective properties of materials in process and, in a somewhat weaker form, that patterns of coordination become 'interlocked' in such a way that 'organisational rigidities' emerge.

The transformation of productive structures may be considered as the changeover from one quasi-repetitive pattern[1] of operations to another, such that the existing time structure of production is replaced by a new arrangement of productive elements over time. It follows that the change of any productive set-up may be described as a transition from one relatively stable mode of operation of a productive process to another, and that the transformation itself is a process in the course of which different elements of the production system adjust to the new mode of operation.

We now come to discuss more specifically the impact of *technological change* upon production activities. Within our analytical framework, technological change can occur on all the three levels which define productive operations:

(i) the level of task specification and task arrangements;
(ii) the level of the embodiment of new sets of capabilities in fund elements, either through the construction of new fund inputs or through learning;
(iii) the development and introduction of new materials with new characteristics.

We shall see that technological change in each of these dimensions acts, in the first instance, as a 'disturbance' to a given pattern of production coordination. It opens up a range of new technologically feasible options but, by doing so, disturbs the 'stability' of the existing production arrangements. Of course, not all technological changes will automatically upset the stability of existing production arrangements since, under certain internal or external conditions,[2] new technological options will not be activated; but such conditions can change.

In the following we shall deal with situations in which new technological options are indeed adopted, and we shall analyse the range of coordination problems which such an adoption will open up and the adjustment processes which a decision for adoption will initiate.

Take the case of an *invention of a new machine*; that machine embodies capabilities or combinations of capabilities which did not exist within the range of previously available machines. In principle, the embodiment of new capabilities will open up fund-task allocations which were not feasible before, even if the sets of tasks (themselves bundles of 'primitive operations') would not change. However, the existing set of 'tasks' was influenced by the availability of particular fund elements, as there was no point in combining a particular set of primitive operations into new tasks which could not be executed by any of the available fund elements. Thus, once the invention of a new machine (or a new 'skill' acquired by a worker) gives rise to a new set of available fund elements, there is scope for a *new task specification*, i.e., a bundling of primitive operations into new tasks.

Hence, technological expansion in one dimension of the productive system (the level of productive agents) gives rise to innovations in another dimension (new task specifications). Once a new set of task specifications has emerged to allow a fuller utilisation of the new capability structure of fund elements, the way is open to attempt a new solution of the specific coordination problem which allocates tasks to funds. The invention of a new fund element will thus give rise to new task definitions and to a new solution of the coordination problem defined by fund-task allocations ('job specification'). The new job specification gives rise to a new time structure of the production process itself, with a new sequencing of productive operations and hence also a new system of materials-in-process flows. The latter describes the stages of transformation which the materials in process undergo from the point(s) of entry into the productive process up to the point(s) of exit. As the timing and sequencing of productive operations on the materials-in-process change, the coordination of materials-in-process flows will change as well. Hence, we can observe a clear chain of events, starting from an invention in one sphere of the productive system (in this case, at the level of fund factors) leading to adjustments, new specifications and new solutions of coordination problems in the other spheres.

We would like to draw attention to a further feature of such an adjustment process: the implementation of technological innovations which take place at one level of the productive process (the invention of a new machine) is always constrained by the technological feasibilities at the other levels. For example, new task definition which would allow a better utilisation of the capability structure of a new fund element, requires itself a *knowledge of the internal (task) structure of the productive process* (of the range of primitive operations which make up these tasks and the possibilities of the bundling or unbundling of such sets of primitive operations).[3] Knowledge of the internal characteristics of productive processes (in terms of the tasks and primitive operations which constitute them) is itself a reflection of the state of technological knowledge (*'process knowledge'*). Hence the ability to respond to fund innovation by devising new task specifications and task arrangements is a function of the state of technological knowledge, and hence constrains the ability to respond to the technological possibilities opened up by the invention of the new machine.

Similarly, the change in the time structure, sequencing and even definition of stages of transformation of materials in process is a function of the state of *knowledge about the transformation process*, of the precise chemical and mechanical changes which materials undergo in the course of that process. Progress in *materials science* which allows, for example, stages of the transformation process to be differently sequenced or allows separate components of the material in process to be handled separately or in a combined manner, also allows the set of feasible fund-task allocation patterns to be increased, and may lead to better utilisation profiles of existing fund-input elements.

The above discussion singled out one example which shows that technological innovations at one level of the productive process leads to responses at other levels. In the course of such adjustment processes, the inherited patterns of task definitions, fund-task allocations, materials-in-process coordinations will all be scrutinised in order to check whether adjustments would allow an exploitation of the potential of the innovation and will set in operation a chain of adjustment processes. As these new coordination problems are scrutinised and their interdependencies realised, the constraints on technological options at each of the different levels of productive operations will set limits to the exploitation of the new technological opportunities in the productive process. As Nathan Rosenberg realised in the course of his historical research, the unevenness of technological change at the different levels and the emergence of new coordination problems act as a powerful 'focusing device' for complementary technological innovations at other levels (see, in particular, Rosenberg, 1969).

4 Changes in the level and structure of demand

The other factor, besides technological change, which poses continuously new challenges to devise new coordination patterns in productive organisations is represented by changes in the level and structure of demand.

The relation between scale and organisation of productive activity has been a recurring theme in economic analysis even before Adam Smith (see

Scazzieri 1993, pp. 34–79 for a review of this theme). In Adam Smith's writings, in particular, the relationship between the overall scale of production, as determined by the level of demand ('the extent of the market'), and the detailed specification of productive processes, tasks and the development of skills (summarised as 'division of labour') is a focus of his analysis of overall growth.

We shall take up in this section some of Smith's analytical insights which considered the impact of changes in the *overall level of demand* upon productive organisation.

In contrast to Smith's focus on the overall level of demand, later writers emphasised the impact of changes in the *structure of demand* upon the organisation of production activity.[4] In particular, in the recent writings of Pasinetti (1981, 1993) 'Engel's Law' – i.e., the differential impact of the rise in real incomes upon the demand for different types of products – plays a crucial role in the uneven dynamics of a multisectoral economic model. In addition to Engel's Law, one might also mention the impact of the *degree of product differentiation* as a factor exerting a major influence upon the way production activity is organised.

In the following, we will explore (building both upon the analytical framework introduced in chapter 6, and the discussion of stylised historical forms of production organisation in chapters 7 and 8) the impact of these three factors – *scale, composition* and *degree of product differentiation* – upon the organisational features and coordination patterns of productive activity.

Scale In chapter 8 above we have already explored a number of relationships between scale and the organisation of productive activity. Stress was laid on the importance of 'process' and 'input indivisibilities' determining the degree of 'splitting up' of production activity into partial processes and the utilisation of specialised fund-input elements. An increase in the overall scale of economic activity allows the splitting up of productive processes into a larger number of partial processes (overcoming 'process indivisibilities'), the utilisation of more specialised fund-input elements which would be too much underutilised at a lower level of production, and – related to both the above factors – the introduction of a higher degree of task differentiation.

Furthermore, a change in the overall scale of production might induce a shift to a different pattern of time coordination of partial processes (for example, from an arrangement in sequence to an arrangement in line or in series) thus creating a marked change in the overall organisation of production (say, from a job-shop workshop to a putting out or factory system). Changes in partial process differentiation, task differentiation and task sequencing has, of course, direct implications for materials-in-process flows and their coordination in time and space. Hence if a higher overall level of production allows a higher degree of process differentiation, a higher degree of fund-input specialisation and, consequently, of task differentiation, the productive system as a whole gains in complexity on all the three levels which constitute the coordination patterns in a productive system.

We have seen that, as the degree of complexity of a productive system increases, different overall forms of productive organisation will be adopted (at times shifting from a craft organisation to an early putting out system, then moving towards a perfectly synchronised system such as the factory organisation; then again to new forms of putting out systems if the coordination problems in a changing environment become too complex, and so on). Increases in the overall level of demand thus pose continuous challenges to the ways in which these coordination problems are being solved, giving rise to different forms of productive organisation being adopted over time and, at times, to the co-existence of such forms alongside each other.

Changes in the composition of demand One aspect of the impact of a change in the composition of demand can be well understood in traditional input–output based multisectoral or multiprocess models. These models emphasise how changes in the composition of demand affect the activity levels of different productive activities at uneven rates since they are directly or indirectly involved to differing degrees in the production of different final commodities. Hence, a change in the level of demand for commodity 1 as compared with commodity 2 will also change the relative activity levels of production activity A as compared to production activity B if the two activities are related to different degrees – directly and indirectly – to the production of commodities 1 and 2 respectively. Not only are activity levels affected but, as a consequence, also the relative flows of materials in process which characterise the interdependence between production activities in such a model. And, since in an imperfectly synchronised productive system, the impact of activity level will – in part – be mediated by inventory movements, this, in turn, has implications for storage movements and required storage capacities.

If the model takes explicit account of the time structure of the interdependence between production activities, two consequences may be observed:

(i) changes in the levels of activity of different but interrelated processes will change the mass of materials in process which will be located at the different work stations at different points of time; and

(ii) changes in the levels of activity imply changes in the work loads for the productive agents involved at the different work stations and hence upon their utilisation patterns over time.

Thus changes in the relative activity levels of different productive activities which were initiated by a change in the composition of demand, have implications for the mass of materials-in-process flows at different points of the productive system and for the work loads of different (groups of) fund elements operating at different work stations.

The consequence is that adjustment processes will take place at each of our analytical levels of productive activity:

(i) materials-in-process flows will be affected by changes in the relative activity levels of different interdependent processes;
(ii) task-fund allocation patterns will be adjusted and different types of fund-input elements may be used as input indivisibility threshold levels are reached;
(iii) process and task differentiation and task sequencing may be varied, as changes in activity levels may imply that threshold levels of process indivisibilities are transcended.

Changes in the degree of product differentiation Changes in the degree of product differentiation may modify the degree of 'complexity' of a productive system in all its dimensions:

(i) the network of interrelated partial processes increases 'in scope', as new fabrication stages necessary for the production of an increasing number of products are introduced;
(ii) an increase in the 'network complexity' of fabrication stages implies an increase in the complexity of materials-in-process flows, for 'new branches' of materials-in-process flows have to be introduced at least in the final stages of fabrication;[5]
(iii) as the network of partial processes gets more varied, there is scope for increased task differentiation and fund-input specialisation.[6]

It may be noted that demand for increased product differentiation *without* an overall increase in the scale of production creates a demand for increased differentiation (on all analytical levels) of a productive system and thus makes coordination more difficult. However, product differentiation usually does increase the overall level of demand, since consumers (final and industrial) obtain goods more particularly geared in their specification towards their particular needs. (For an analysis of how scale and dispersion of demand structures may interact to determine the number of variants of a product, see Gabszewicz and Thisse, 1986, and Shaked and Sutton, 1982.)

This brings us to a particular issue of compositional change in demand structures in market economies: the features which are related to the provision of immaterial goods, and thus to the evolution of *tertiary activities*, particularly in the area of person-to-person services.

This has been a particularly lively field of research recently (see, for example, Gershunyi, 1987 and Gershunyi and Robinson, 1988). Some of this analysis has emphasised, in particular, the constraint which activities requiring intensive person-to-person contact (such as education, health, social work, artistic interaction, and so on) put upon overall productivity and output growth in an economic system. It may be argued that product differentiation, and particularly the continuously changing character of product differentiation, affects the nature of work organisation in these areas particularly strongly. It leads to a situation where a bulk of tertiary service activities have to be provided in a form that strongly resembles the old job-shop form of production organisation (with the modern equivalent of the 'master manufacturer' playing a central role).[7]

As Baumol and others have shown, a sector which has intrinsic limitations in generating productivity growth attracts more and more resources in a growing economy (for a fuller analysis of this issue, see Baumol, 1967). If this is the case with person-to-person services, and product differentiation is a determining feature of the type of work organisation adopted in that sector, then we may expect a renewed and increasing importance of the 'job-shop' principle in the most advanced economies.

5 Networks, subsystems and economic change

Changes arising from the microstructure of production will influence, at the level of 'intermediate structures', the formation of networks and subsystems within the economy (see the discussion of 'networks' and 'subsystems' in sections 8 and 9 of chapter 6). Such an influence will take different forms depending on which dimension of the production process is mainly affected. Thus, for example, the diffusion of a new material across different productive branches may be associated with the emergence of patterns of complementarity or substitutability among new and old materials, which may in turn speed up or slow down the growth of activity levels in the corresponding sectors (see Cohendet *et al.*, 1988). A complementarity pattern would normally reinforce the existing dynamic, thus speeding up sectors that are already on an expanding path, and slowing down sectors that are already contracting; a substitutability pattern, on the other hand, would have an opposite effect, by speeding up contracting sectors and slowing down the expanding ones. As a result, the existence of complementarity or substitutability relationships among different new materials may induce the formation of '*dynamic networks*', that is, subsystems of productive activities related to each other through the emergence and diffusion of a new impulse. In turn, the local dynamic emerging at one particular level of the productive system (at the level of materials-in-process in our case) may influence dynamic patterns at other levels as well. For example, the speeding up of a subsystem of interrelated sectors, due to complementarity relationships among new materials, may favour the introduction of new patterns of division of labour (increased specialisation) at the task-process level, and the emergence of a new pattern of utilisation of capabilities as far as productive agents are concerned.

The formation of dynamic networks may also result from a *change in the structure of available capabilities*, as could be associated with the invention of a new machine, or the employment of workers having new and better qualifications, skills and know-how. The new capabilities are likely to affect the ways in which tasks are allocated to fund elements. For even with given task durations, we may have fund elements better equipped for the simultaneous execution of different tasks, or for the switch from one type of task to another. If this is the case, then it is likely that some new pattern of division of labour among fund elements with associated capabilities will emerge: funds whose capabilities have expanded will be able to execute more tasks of a similar type (simultaneous execution) or will shift more rapidly from one task type to another; on the other hand, fund elements of a traditional type will probably 'lose' tasks that may more effectively be carried out by the new funds. The superior capabilities of new funds are likely to attract tasks and processes away from traditional funds; at the same time, the latter may continue to execute a certain number of tasks provided there are tasks that the advanced fund elements are unable to execute or for which they may be too expensive.

As a result, the initial impulse (refinement of certain capabilities) initiates structural changes by affecting the fund-task allocations within a neighbourhood of the capabilities initially affected. The form of the process of structural change (the depth of the restructuring that takes place over time, its time-phasing, the overall speed of transformation) depends upon the way in which capabilities of distinct fund elements are initially related to one another, and upon the rigid or loose pattern of utilisation of these capabilities within each productive unit. For example, the introduction of flexible machinery involves the pooling of previously distinct capabilities and the improvement of the 'capability to shift' from one type of task to another. The process of structural change that may then be initiated can take different forms depending, for instance, on the different degrees of adaptiveness of the utilisation structure of existing fund inputs to local dynamic impulses. If the preexisting pattern of utilisation (fund-task assignment) is loose enough, then flexible machinery may be compatible with a rearrangement of traditional capabilities and widespread acceleration of processes of material transformation. On the other hand, if the utilisation pattern of preexisting capabilities are very rigidly defined, then the introduction of flexible machinery could be the origin of a major disruption: most 'traditional' fund elements will be discarded and structural change will be associated with underutilisation phenomena analogous to technological unemployment.

6 Local and general patterns of economic dynamics

The fact that productive processes are seldom 'perfectly synchronised' means that *'buffers'* (unutilised capacities and inventories) will be a general feature of productive organisations; these, on the one hand, ease the adaptation process of existing productive structures to 'dynamic impulses'; on the other hand, imperfect synchronisation also implies that there will often be options in the pattern of adjustment to given impulses. Furthermore, imperfect synchronisation and associated buffers also provide the possibility of identifying 'local dynamics' emanating from given impulses which can segment the overall process of adjustment to given impulses into *sequences of relatively independent local chain patterns of change*. However, these local chain patterns might again interact over a particular time horizon (short-, medium- or longer-run interactions). Let us examine these issues in more detail.

A process of structural change may originate in one particular dimension of productive activity and then spread to other dimensions of the same or other activities. In general, structural change will initially be 'local', for it will influence, both in a temporal and in a material sense, only a neighbourhood of the productive elements that are first affected. Subsequently, such a local process may either develop into a widespread transformation of the productive system, or come to a standstill. The diffusion pattern initiated by a given impulse may reflect not only the strength of the impulse but also the degree of persistence ('inertia') of existing coordination patterns in a given process or across a set of interconnected processes.

It may happen that a particular local dynamic brings about a generalised process of structural change if a transformation affecting a specific dimension of productive activity provides opportunities for advantageous change in other dimensions. But it may also happen that the local dynamic becomes a positive hindrance to generalised structural change, if the need to adapt to the local factor of transformation induces organisational adjustments that make it more difficult to induce changes in and to establish positive feedbacks with more distant parts of the economic system; in this case, a *process of decoupling* takes place.

Hence, structural change, as a process occurring in historical time, would generally manifest itself in the formation of the *dynamic networks* mentioned above, that is, of networks whose pattern of connectedness is gradually revealed over time. On a first approximation, such networks may be identified by certain common dynamic features (for example, the clustering of different productive activities around a diffusion pattern of particular new technological devices), but a further structural cohesion may generally be detected, which is related to emergent patterns of complementarity among the activities being considered. For example, technological and ensuing organisational change could bring about a shift from a pattern of connectedness based on material flows to one based on the complementarity of different capabilities or tasks. In this case, the analysis of structural change requires first the identification of the dimension of productive activity that is primarily affected, then the investigation of the interaction between processes of transformation taking place at the different levels of production activities, and of the temporal sequence of transformation stages at such levels.

A generalised process of structural change often originates at one particular point on one dimension of the productive system, and then spreads to the other dimensions and other subsystems. This process may be such that the dimension that is originally influenced remains the dominant one throughout the whole sequence of transformations; or it may happen that changes in one dimension (say, a sequence of changes in the capability structure) propagate themselves by inducing changes in other dimensions (say, changes in the composition of material-in-process flows throughout the system). The *identification of subsystems* is thus an essential step in the analysis of structural change: subsystem specification isolates complementary movements within the economic system and makes it possible to explain such movements in a sequence of steps. The identification of different subsystems in an economy undergoing structural change allows for the decomposition of the overall dynamic of the economic system.

We have seen that an economic system may be split into different subsystems depending on whether tasks, capabilities or materials are considered (see, in particular, chapter 6 above). A technical innovation affecting certain 'nodes' within the capability network may induce a dynamic reshuffling of human and mechanical skills whose initial result, in terms of incentive to growth, may be only loosely connected with changes in the specification of tasks or in patterns of interindustry trade (see, for instance, some of the cases of technological innovation considered in Rosenberg, 1963, where emphasis is placed on the role of machine tools as diffusion devices in a process of technological change). In a subsequent stage, also tasks and material flows could be affected, and the pattern of structural dynamics may be different depending on which sequence of transformations is followed. If task specifications are relatively rigid, the change in the capability structure may lead first to a change in the composition of material flows between sectors, and only subsequently to the introduction of new tasks and task arrangements. In this case, the distinction between different dimensions of the production process is a condition for decomposing the overall dynamic into separate sources of dynamism influencing the movement of the economy in a sequence of steps.

7 Decomposable dynamics

Decomposition of an economic system into subsystems may be useful to explain a given sequential process of structural change. In particular, the identification of distinct sources of dynamism is related to the appearance of different dynamic networks (or 'subsystems') as any given impulse makes itself felt within a complex structure. As a result, a process of structural change may be decomposed into a sequence of phases associated with different sources of dynamism and patterns of structural adaptation. The analytical device of decomposing a complex system into 'coherent' subsystems is thus a flexible tool permitting greater realism in the representation of an evolving structure and in the identification of the causal relationships explaining the observed pattern of structural change. The utilisation of decomposition techniques makes it possible to differentiate between slow- and fast-moving parts of the economic system. It also makes it possible to identify a variety of structural specifications based on different decomposition techniques, so that the structural impact of a given impulse can be analysed by considering different subsystem specifications depending on the time scale adopted. This may be especially useful if an overall historical process of structural change results from the combination of subprocesses taking place at different time scales and requiring different representations of economic structure for each scale.

Decomposition techniques also allow for a more realistic analysis of the sources of dynamism. For any given 'impulse' or 'dynamic force' (such as technical progress, capital accumulation or population growth) may be associated with a definite sequence of transformation stages, such that the motion of the economic system is influenced by previous changes of structure and is itself influencing the subsequent pattern of structural change. The actual impact of any given dynamic impulse is thus inherently related to 'complementarities over time' (Hicks, 1939) and to the historical linkage between subsequent periods. The decomposition of economic structure, by permitting the separate treatment of processes of structural change influencing different parts or 'layers' of the same economic system, also suggests the decomposition of dynamic impulses into a number of distinct sources of transformations. The final result (the actual course of structural change) depends on the historical blend of subprocesses occurring at different time scales, on their particular sequencing, and on the way in which bottlenecks appear and are eventually overcome (see also Chakravarty, 1987).

Decomposition techniques are thus essential in the analysis of structural change, both if emphasis is laid upon the changing composition of aggregates and if dynamics of the structural adaptation process of a system is considered. Indeed, the dynamic properties of a system are closely related to its composition (in terms of subsystems), while compositional changes may be influenced by dynamic factors operating in different parts of the system (determining the 'dynamics' of such subsystems).

7.1 Structural invariance and the dynamics of decomposable systems

The aim of this subsection is to refer to some existing contributions in order to extend our analytical apparatus to the consideration of *nearly decomposable dynamics* (the dynamics of nearly decomposable economic systems) when the distinction between the three dimensions of productive activities (tasks, agents, materials in process) is introduced. A few words are in order to explain what is meant here by 'decomposable dynamics'. As is known from the theory of linear economic models (see, for example, Gale, 1960) a decomposable system is one in which input–output flows may be arranged so as to form a number of self-contained subsystems. '*Nearly decomposable systems*' are ones in which the relationships between the different subsystems are not non-existent but weak (see, e.g., Ando and Fisher, 1963). Interesting implications of the concept of decomposable systems have been identified when dynamic behaviour is considered. In particular, it has been pointed out that decomposability helps stability, whereas a non-decomposable system may be highly unstable (see Simon and Ando, 1961; Ando and Fisher, 1963; Simon, 1969; Fisher and Ando, 1971; see also Loasby, 1976).

A decomposable economic system lends itself to the analysis of dynamics mainly as a result of the fact that decomposition introduces a hierarchical description of the different dynamic processes operating within the economic system. In particular, the economic system under consideration may be decomposed into a certain number of subsystems, each associated with a particular time horizon (such as the short-short, short and long period discussed in Marshall's *Principles*). Each time horizon may be associated with the length of certain adjustment processes, and the resulting dynamics will be characterised by the simultaneous operation of distinct patterns of motion hierarchically related to one another. Thus decomposition of economic structure entails decomposition of economic dynamics not only in the sense that certain processes are stationary (they represent themselves without variation from one time period to another) and others are in a state of changeover to a different dynamic pattern, but also in the sense that a given sequence may be introduced in the *timing* of structural change as it affects the different component parts of the economic system.[8] As noted above, such a sequence may reflect 'contingent' constraints (historical, institutional or other), and may be an important factor in shaping a path of endogenous structural change.

If such a perspective is adopted, it may turn out that *relative structural invariance* (an essential prerequisite of decomposability in the dynamic sense) is one important factor in determining the persistence of an economic system in the midst of structural changes that often appear to be of a disruptive kind (see also Landesmann and Scazzieri, 1990). The dynamic decomposability of an economic system would thus be on a par with other factors connected with forms of rigidity and responsible for relative stability over time.[9] It may be argued that relative structural invariance and complementarities over time are features of the same fundamental dynamic property of an economic system, that is, of the fact that an economic system is normally built upon a hierarchical set of arrangements, so that a perturbation affecting certain parts of the system (units or subsystems) is unlikely to exert an immediate influence upon the economic system as a whole.

This may be seen by considering a process of structural change in which instantaneous adjustment to exogenous impulses (or forces) is impossible because of the *different speeds* at which the various parts of the system may change, and also because of the *order* in which such component parts are changing.

For example, the introduction of a new energy-saving device may entail reactions on a variety of levels: new materials have to be used, a different stage-structure of the relevant manufacturing process has to be implemented, new skills have to be developed. In different historical circumstances (initial conditions) the transformation of the economic structure may be constrained by differences in the speed of change at one or another level. And the sequence according to which changes may be introduced could be different depending on institutional, geographical or other constraints. It follows that the original perturbation may produce, in principle, a variety of dynamic paths on which structural change takes place. It is worth noting that such a variety of structural change processes reflects the hierarchical structure of feasible motions, and the complementarities over time (path dependencies) related with it.

7.2 Microstructures and the pattern of structural change

The sources of structural change are manifold and a realistic investigation of these is likely to have an essential descriptive component. However, the process by which structural change originating within a particular unit or subsystem propagates to other units and eventually to the whole economic system is conducive to investigation at a more general level. In characterising such a process we shall discuss the following issues: firstly, we shall return to the description of interdependencies (*networks*) which allows a determination of the location and then diffusion of an initial impulse which generates structural change; secondly, we shall discuss the role of *rigidities* in existing coordination patterns and of *buffers*; thirdly, we shall illustrate how the ingredients above can give rise to an *endogenous analysis of the process of structural change*.

7.2.1 Network identification

The starting point for analysing patterns of structural change are the specifications of networks at the three analytical levels of process description; the network description allows a determination of the location and the level(s) on which structural change is first initiated and then diffused. As we will see, there are two basic principles by which networks can be constructed: The first principle refers to *neighbourhood relations* of different components or activities within the time (and locational) structure of the productive system. The second principle refers to *similarity relationships* of different components and activities in terms of their respective contents or internal structures.

(i) *At the level of tasks*, the immediate network relationship which comes to mind are the dependency relationships which require the simultaneous or sequential execution of tasks; hence the clustering in time of groups of tasks can be described by the 'neighbourhood' of such tasks in their necessary arrangement in time; e.g., $N(\tau_j, \tau_k)=0$ would indicate that the two tasks τ_j and τ_k have to be executed in the same subperiod; similarly $N(\tau_j, \tau_k)=(0,1)$ means that the two tasks have to be performed either simultaneously or in subsequent periods, etc. In general, $N(\tau_j, \tau_k)=(a,b)$ where a and b give the shortest and the longest time intervals respectively, within which tasks j and k have to be performed; they show the dependency relationship of tasks upon each other given a particular task structuring of a production process. The notation could be extended to express dependency relationships of groups of tasks upon each other, such as $N(\{\tau_j, \tau_k\}; \{\tau_m\})=(c, d)$ which expresses the time dependency requirements in the execution of that task j and k upon another task m. As we will see, the technological requirement of the structuring of tasks in time thus gives rise to one type of network relationship which is of relevance for the propagation of structural change processes. The other network relationship has to do with the similarity of different tasks in terms of their composition (as sets of primitive operations). We specify such relationships in the form of a distance measure which compares the compositional difference of two tasks in terms of the primitive operations which they are composed of; we use $s^\tau_{jk}=s(\tau_j, \tau_k)$ as a scalar measure for this compositional similarity.[10] As we will see later on, dynamic network relationships, following the invention of a new type of fund element, could be based on the similarity of tasks to be performed in different parts of an economic system; similarity indicators s^τ_{jk} are an important informational input into diffusion analysis.

(ii) Next, network relationships at the *level of fund-input elements*: As we know, fund inputs are characterised by the capabilities they embody, which are measurable and limited in scale. $\bar{C}\equiv[\bar{c}_{kc}]$ represents the available capability structure of an economic system. Each row of matrix $\bar{C}$ specifies a separate fund-input element ($k=1, ..., m$) and each column represents a different kind of capability ($c=1, ..., n$). For our analysis of diffusion processes it will be useful to define a distance measure to represent the similarity between two different types of fund-input elements in terms of their respective capability structures. We use $s^f_{kl}=s(\bar{c}_k, \bar{c}_l)$ to specify a measure of the distance of two types of fund inputs k and l in terms of their capability structures.[11]

In addition, we will again be interested in the neighbourhood of two types of fund-input elements in terms of their current employment in a productive system. For this we use matrix T which contains all the information about fund-task allocations (jobs) which are being performed in a productive system and also the levels at which these tasks are being performed; an element t_{kj} of matrix T shows the performance level of fund input of type k when performing task of type j. Across the rows of matrix T we show all the tasks which a particular type of fund-input element is engaged in, and along the columns we show which types of fund-input elements are engaged in the same types of tasks. This information is again useful when analysing propagation patterns of particular types of impulses. However, we can go further, and use a more continuous distance measure for the job assignments of different fund-input elements in a productive system. $s_{kl}^t=(t_k, t_l)$ is a measure[12] of the 'closeness' of different types of fund elements' activities ('jobs') in the productive system, whereby a 'job' is defined by the vector t_k, i.e., the set of tasks which a particular type of fund input k is performing in a productive system and the levels of its task performances in this job. The similarity of jobs as shown by the matrix $S^T \equiv [s_{kl}^t]^{13}$ will be another important piece of information in analysing the responses of a productive system to a given impulse: e.g., if two types of fund elements are already performing similar types of jobs, a change in job specification between them might be relatively easy.

Let us still add another dimension of fund-task allocations which is relevant for network specification: task performances occur in the course of the entire duration of a productive process, i.e., we have a whole sequence of matrices $T_t(t=1, ..., N$ where N is the duration of the productive process) which describe the task performances which take place in the course of a productive process. Of course, task performances have to be organised in such a way that time dependencies across task executions are taken care of; these time constraints which have to be satisfied in any chosen job specification pattern T_t were described by the dependency relationships $N=(\tau_j, \tau_k)$ above. The choice of a particular sequence of task performances, i.e., a choice of $T_t(t=1, ...,N)$, gives rise to a particular utilisation pattern of the existing structure of funds. Using $u_k(t)$ as the notation for the utilisation pattern of a particular fund-input element k over the periods $t=1, ..., N$ then $\bar{u}_k(t)=\bar{c}_k(t)-u_k(t)$ shows its pattern of underutilisation.[14]

This utilisation pattern through interdependent task performances is, of course, the other important dimension which generates network relationships between fund-input elements, in that changes in the utilisation of particular fund-input elements change the options of how to use other fund-input elements in a productive system. The reason for this interdependence is that job specification programmes have to be 'complete' (see chapter 7, section 5), i.e., all the essential tasks which constitute a particular production process have to be performed at certain minimum task performance levels. In this case, whenever elements in matrices T_t are changed below (above) certain lower (upper) bounds, compensating adjustments in other elements of the sequence of matrices T_t will have to (can) take place as well so that the job specification programme remains 'complete'. One can think of a set of feasible job specification patterns $T_t(\omega) \equiv [T_t(\alpha), T_t(\beta), ...]$ which all have the characteristic of fulfilling the 'essential tasks' at (least at) minimum task performance levels so that the overall production process gets successfully completed at a particular scale.[15] Once minimum task performances by some fund elements in some periods are not carried out, then compensating changes in the task performances by other fund-input elements in the same period or by the same or other fund-input elements in other periods have to take place such that the overall process gets completed at the scale specified. These changes have, furthermore, to take place within the boundaries of temporal complementarities required by the task neighbourhood requirements $N(\tau_j, \tau_k)$ discussed above. Changes in job specification patterns (say, from $T_t(\alpha)$ to $T_t(\beta)$) imply, in the general case, changes in utilisation patterns of given fund-input elements, say from $U_t(\alpha) \equiv [u_{kt}(\alpha)]$ to $U_t(\beta) \equiv [u_{kt}(\beta)]$ and, correspondingly, in patterns of underutilisation (i.e., in the structure of excess capacities/capabilities). The above defines interdependencies in the patterns of task definition and task arrangements and of fund-input utilisations across time and work stations.[16]

(iii) Thirdly, we come to network relationships defined by the *structure of material transformation processes* and by the actual materials involved in such processes.

Just as in the case of network specifications with tasks, the time interdependencies amongst stages of fabrication of materials in process can be described by neighbourhood relations of the type $N(m_{ij}, m_{jk}) = [a]$ which, for instance, shows that a transformation process which transforms input i into material in process j has to be followed, sequentially, by another transformation process which transforms material j to k within a time interval a. Neighbourhood relationship of types $N^m = 1$, $N^m = 2$, etc. thus show stages of transformation which are one, two, etc. stages removed from each other, with $N^m = 0$ describing transformation processes which take place alongside each other. Alternatively, N^m can represent *local neighbourhood* relationships: If we interpret m_{ij} as a material which undergoes a stage of fabrication at a work station i and then moves to a work station j, then the neighbourhood relationships described by the relations N^m define the network of pipelines which characterise the movements of work in process across different nodes/work stations in the overall transformation process.

Just as in the case of the distinction between neighbourhood relationships between different tasks $N(\tau_j, \tau_k)$ and actual task execution T_t, in the case of material transformation interdependencies also, we differentiate between the interval or locational constraints defined by the neighbourhood relationships N^M and the actual flows of input–output interdependencies $M_t = [m_{ij}(t)]$ which reflect a particular (actual) pattern of material transformations given a particular process structure. In both cases, T_t and M_t reflect *scale* (levels of task performances and quantities of materials undergoing transformations) as well as *type* (of tasks, materials). As the process structure changes, new tasks being specified, new materials or fund-input elements introduced, etc., neighbourhood constraints and scale characteristics of material transformation processes are both likely to be affected. Scale, time and locational dependencies of different stages in the overall transformation process will give rise to a *network impact* (i.e., upon a particular region of the M_t matrices) of any exogenous impulse.

Finally, we come to *network interdependencies across the three analytical dimensions of our production process analysis.* This brings up again the issue discussed shortly in chapter 6 (section 7) concerning the overall 'synchronisation' of a productive process across the three analytical dimensions but this time we refer to 'dynamic network' specifications, i.e., networks which get activated in the course of the propagation impact on a particular impulse. We will, in the following, give some examples of constraints which new network specifications on one dimension impose on the feasibility of network specifications on other dimensions: take the case of a change in task specification and task arrangement, i.e., from $\{\tau(\alpha)\}$ to $\{\tau(\beta)\}$.[17] Such a change will entail a change, say from a set $T_t(\alpha)$ to a set $T_t(\beta)$. While such job specification programmes might be compatible with the change in task specification and temporal constraints on task executions, they might not be compatible with either the capacity constraints available to the system in terms of existing capability structures $\bar{C}_t$ or in terms of a feasible pattern of coordination of materials-in-process flows and inventory movements. Hence, the actual shift from a job specification programme $T_t(\alpha)$ to a job specification programme $T_t(\beta)$ depends on the feasibility of these job programmes in terms of capability constraints, and the availability of compatible arrangements of material-in-process flows (with their own sequencing and continuity as well as scale requirements); the latter includes available stocks s and storage facilities $\bar{s}_t$. There are thus clear relationships between the feasibilities of coordination patterns across the different analytical dimensions of a production organisation. A shift in organisational patterns in any one dimension depends upon (i) the existence of compatible feasible coordination patterns in the other two dimensions and upon (ii) the feasibility of the introduction of new coordination patterns given the capacity and inventory constraints.

This completes our analysis of network interdependencies; these network interdependencies provide us with a basis for *potential feasibility analysis of structural change.* Next we come to the other two concepts which allows us to move from the *potential* to the *actual* process of structural reorganisation: buffers and rigidities.

7.2.2 The role of buffers

Buffers play a role in the impulse-propagation mechanism because they allow a relatively independent absorption of an initial shock by a subsystem within an overall productive system. In a perfectly synchronised productive organisation in which there are no excess capacities, in which fund elements' activities are perfectly coordinated in time and in which materials in process flow continuously through their various stages of fabrication and thus no need for inventories exists, the impact of an impulse would in general affect all the components of a non-decomposable productive system. In an imperfectly synchronised system, on the other hand, stocks of inventories and un- or underutilised capacities act as buffers which allow the absorption of that shock (at least over a certain time horizon) within a certain specified region of a productive system.[18] Buffers in the strict sense are *non-utilised capacities* (in an m-dimensional capability space) and *unused inventories*.

As mentioned above, matrices U_t show the degrees of utilisation of the different fund-input elements along the different capability dimensions as they are engaged in a variety of tasks; i.e., $u_{kc}(t_{kj})$ $j=1, ..., n$ shows the degree of utilisation of capability c of fund input k when that fund input is involved in a set of tasks $j=1, ..., n$. In turn $\bar{c}_{km}(t) - u_{kc}(t)$ which we denote as $\bar{u}(t)$, describes the pattern of underutilisation of fund-input element k with respect to the various capability dimensions c for the entire duration $t=1, ..., T$ of the productive process. Matrices $\bar{U}(t)$ give a complete picture of the available excess capacities of the fund elements engaged in a particular productive system. Any change in the capacities installed, i.e., the $\bar{C}(t)$, or in the structure of fund-task allocations and levels of task performances T_t will change the utilisation pattern and hence the available excess capacities in the course of time.

Similarly *stock matrices* $S(t)[\equiv s_{ij}(t)]$ show the stocks of material inputs $i=1, ..., n$ available at different work stations/production lines $j=1, ..., n$ and vectors $\hat{s}_j(t)$ show the overall accumulation or decumulation of these inventories in the course of a time interval at a work station j. Alternatively, vectors $\hat{s}_i(t)$ refer to the decumulation or accumulation of a particular stock i in the course of a time interval across all work stations/production lines. The above two series of matrices $\bar{U}(t)$ and $S(t)$ determine the *buffers* which exist in the productive system. As we will see in subsection 7.2.4. below, buffers play an important role in circumscribing specific regions or subsystems in a productive organisation which absorb (temporarily or permanently) the impact of a particular impulse.

7.2.3 *Relative rigidities*

Next, we come to the element of *persistence* inherent in production relationships: We are unable at this stage to provide any theoretical ideas which could constitute an endogenous explanation of why particular production patterns are more rigid than others and, instead, will assume that certain measures of the relative rigidity of different production relationships are given and can be represented by the following matrices:

$R(\bar{C})$ expresses rigidities in the existing capability bundling which characterises the available structure of fund-input elements (in the short, medium, and longer run; see below);

$R(T)$ expresses the constraints in devising new task specifications and new task sequencing, which requires a rather complex re-think of a synchronised pattern of agent coordination and task assignment;

$R(M)$ or $R(N(M))$[19] reflects the difficulties in changing a system of materials-in-process flows once it is in place; the 'resistance to change' here is a function of the difficulty of disrupting an old and installing a new synchronised system of fabrication processes with its interdependent flows of materials in process, inventory movements and structure of storage capacities.

To illustrate, an element $r(t_{kj})$ of matrix $R(T)$, for example, represents a measure of the rigidity ('resistance to change') of the allocation of fund of type k to task j. Similarly, elements $r(m_{ij}, m_{jk})$ of matrix $R(M)$[20] represent measures of the rigidity of particular materials-in-process flows (of work-in-process flows in and out of work station j). In the case of fund-input rigidities, we might be particularly interested in the difficulty to adjust the capability structure of given fund-input elements, for example, the difficulty of equipping a particular fund-input element k with a new type of skill/capability m', for which we use a measure $r(c_{m'k})$.

Let us spend a bit more time in discussing the issues of relative rigidity (*relative structural invariance*) of different production relationships. Such rigidities are not absolute but depend, firstly, on the type of impulse to which certain production arrangements are exposed to and, secondly, on the time horizon over which one attempts to specify the relative rigidities of different production networks in the face of structural change. Hence rigidities should in principle be defined with respect to a particular time horizon and also with respect to particular types of impulses (or sequences of such impulses) to which production arrangements are exposed.[21] To simplify the analysis, however, we will assume in the following a particular time horizon and analyse the impact of a particular impulse upon the productive structure of an economic system; for such a situation we then take particular matrices $R(C)$, $R(T)$ and $R(M)$ as given. Later on we will relax the assumption of a given time horizon and analyse the sequences which characterise structural change over time periods of varying lengths (such as Marshall's short-short, short and long run).

The other issue which needs to be mentioned is that, in many cases, the issue of rigidity is not simply defined on one particular component of a productive system, such as job specifications for one type of fund-input element (represented by one row of matrix $R(T)$), but that such rigidities affect a particular region/network of specified production relations (e.g., the job specification of a number of fund-input elements and hence a number of rows of matrix $R(T)$). Hence, given that the specification of structural rigidities is impulse and time-horizon dependent, there are often relationships between the rigidity measures of the different elements of the matrices $R(T)$ and $R(M)$. In other words, *rigidities are most often a feature of networks rather than of individual components in an economic system.* Hence, rigidities should in principle be defined on networks of job coordination patterns $\{t_{kj}\}$, where k and j are the subsets of fund elements and tasks involved in that network, or on networks of materials-in-process flows $\{m_{ij}\}$ where m_{ij} refers to the subset of materials-in-process flows belonging to that network (see note 21 for the more general definition of *rigidities of networks* rather than individual components of matrices T and M).

We are now ready to bring our three elements together which allow us to describe the factors involved in shaping the particular pattern of structural change following the incidence of a particular impulse (such as learning or the availability of a new technology). The three components are *networks specifications, buffers and rigidities.*

In the following we will claim that these three components can be used to explain important features of the specific paths of structural change adopted by productive systems when changing from one organisational structure to another.

7.2.4 Endogenous 'dynamic subsystem specification'

As mentioned earlier, endogenous structural change analysis has to start from the identification of the particular *impulse* which initiates a *process of structural adaptation* and possibly, further endogenous *innovation*. Given our specification of production processes on the three analytical levels (i.e., tasks, funds and materials in process) the first incidence of such an impulse could appear on any one of these levels. If it is a learning process it would affect the capability structure of a particular fund element; if it is a shortage of a particular material it will affect in the first instance particular materials-in-process flows and/or inventories; if it is a new organisational scheme of task specification or task arrangement, it will affect the specification of specific tasks τ_j and also the constraints $N(\tau_j, \tau_k)$ on the time structuring of tasks. Once the initial incidence of the impulse is known, we can use the information about existing networks to analyse its *potential pattern of propagation* (*diffusion potential*). We distinguish between potential and actual patterns of diffusion, since network relationships are only one factor which have to be taken into account when analysing diffusion patterns; the others are, as mentioned above, buffers and relative rigidities. Only when all the three determining factors are combined could one speak of an endogenous analysis of *actual patterns of propagation*. The network relationships which we discussed under subsection 7.2.1 above, are of two types: dependency relationships in a time structure of the production setting described by the neighbourhood relationships $N(\tau_j, \tau_k)$ and $N(m_{ij}, m_{jk})$ and similarity relationships of the type $s^{\tau}_{jk} = s(\tau_j, \tau_k)$, $s^t_{kl} = t_k$, t_l), $s^f_{kl} = s(\bar{c}_k, \bar{c}_l)$. Once neighbourhood and similarity relationships are ordered by the quantitative measures $N(...)$ and $S(...)$ in descending order from the point of initial incidence of the impulse (i.e., the tasks, work-in-process flows and fund factors immediately affected), we can define network relationships around the point of initial impact. This defines, in descending order of strength, the region which would *potentially* be most affected through the *first round impact of a particular impulse*.[22] Which region within the structure of production interdependencies would actually be affected will also be a function of the two other moments in our endogenous analysis of impulse-propagation patterns: buffers and rigidities.

Buffers allow the temporary or even long-run definition of a particular region or subsystem of production interdependencies which can isolate the impact of an initial impulse so that only coordination patterns within that subsystem or partial network of a productive system are affected. The reason for this is that buffers, i.e., un- or underutilised capacities and inventories, allow a reorganisation of existing coordination patterns (fund-task allocations, materials-in-process flows) which need not affect any production relations outside the specified network or subsystem.

We can describe the role of buffers in the dynamics of impulse absorption in the following way

$$\Delta B_i \equiv (\Delta U\{k\}, \Delta S\{i\})_{\bar{i}} \geq \Delta P(\{k, j, ij\}; I_i)_t$$
$$\equiv (\Delta T\{k, j\}, \Delta M\{ij\}; I_i)_t \qquad (1)$$

Here $\Delta P(\{k, j, ij\}; I_i)_t$ refers to a production rearrangement within a specified subsystem composed of a certain subset of fund factors $\{k\}$, of tasks $\{j\}$ and of materials-in-process flows $\{ij\}$. Such a reorganisation consists of respecification and reassignment of tasks (i.e., changes in 'job programmes') $\Delta T\{k, j\}$ and a readjustment of materials-in-process flows (transformation processes) $\Delta M\{i, j\}$ within that subset. Condition (1) states that the impact of a given impulse I_i can potentially be contained within a specific subset of transformation processes, utilising the capability structures of a specific subset of fund-input elements and respecifying a specific subset of tasks if the required changes in production arrangements are:

(i) within the set of technologically and organisationally known arrangements (we will return to this condition later on in subsection 7.2.6) and
(ii) the existing buffers B consisting of unutilised capacities available to the subsystem, $\bar{u}\{k\}$ and of stocks $s\{i\}$ would be sufficient to facilitate the required reorganisation of production within the specified time horizon $\bar{t}$.

If the condition (1) above is not fulfilled, i.e., if the inequality $\geq$ were to be violated, then the buffers contained within that network would be insufficient to deal with the required production rearrangements. There could be three responses to such a situation: (a) production rearrangements within the specified network $\{k, j, ij\}$ are constrained by the available buffers and hence only a more limited type of production rearrangement can take place, say $\Delta P'$, while the adjustment processes within the time horizon $\bar{t}$ would still be confined to the previously specified subsystem or (b) the network has to be widened or changed in one or more dimensions, say to $\{k, j, ij'\}$ or to $\{k', j', ij\}$,[23] so that the condition (1) could be fulfilled, or (c) condition (1) can be fulfilled within the specified network but the time horizon has to be longer, i.e, $\bar{t}' > \bar{t}$.

We can see that buffers contribute substantially to dynamic network specification: while the potential network relationship N and S define a continuous set of neighbourhood and similarity relationships (arranged in descending orders) which *might* give rise to propagation patterns, buffers indicate why such propagation might (temporarily or permanently) only take place within the borders of a clearly defined region within a productive system. The reason why the subsystem defined in this way might only be of a temporary nature is that while excess capacities and inventories might in the short run be used to 'buffer' the adjustment patterns taking place within a particular region of the productive system from its surrounding relationships, in the longer run adaptation processes which include further potential network relationships outside the initial region might take place. These second- (third-, etc.) order adjustment processes will take place in further subsystems (networks) which are involved at the different stages of a structural adjustment process. In this way, buffers contribute to an analysis of the sequencing of network activation in that the reaction to a specific impulse might be contained within a particular subsystem due to the temporal availability of buffers to that subsystem; over a longer time horizon the propagation of a particular impulse (including a wider network of similarity and neighbourhood relationships) might draw on the buffers of a wider network, etc.

The other factor which determines the sequence by which different networks of production interdependencies get involved in an overall adjustment process following the impact of a given impulse I_i are relative rigidities. *Relative rigidities* of different network relationships are a further important factor in defining the scope and temporal sequence of adjustment processes within a productive system. We may recall that relative rigidities could be defined on individual components (e.g., specific fund-input elements, in specific fabrication stages, etc.) but are more often defined on particular networks of task specifications, fund-factor utilisations, job patterns and materials-in-process flows. The $R(\Delta T\{k, j\}; I_i; \bar{t})$ specifies, for example, the rigidity which an impulse I_i encounters with respect to achieving a particular required respecification of job programmes within a network of fund-input elements $\{k\}$ executing a particular set of tasks $\{j\}$ within an adjustment period $\bar{t}$. Similarly, $R(\Delta M\{i, j\}; I_i; \bar{t})$ specifies the rigidity of a particular network of materials-in-process flows $M\{i, j\}$ when exposed to the demands of change within an adjustment period $\bar{t}$ following the impact of an impulse I_i. We know, furthermore, that such rigidities can be further decomposed in the case of $\Delta T\{k, j\}$ into resistances to changing a particular utilisation pattern of a set of fund-input elements $\Delta U\{k\}$ and to rigidities in changing task specifications and task arrangements $\Delta\tau\{j\}$. Similarly, resistances to changes in materials-in-process flows might be a function of rigidities of changing the sequencing of fabrication stages and of materials-in-process flows associated with these, i.e., $R(\Delta M\{i, j\})$, or of rigidities in inventory management $R(\Delta s\{i\})$.

Let us now proceed to discuss the role which rigidities may play in the propagation and sequencing of production reorganisation. If we return to formula (1) above we can see that production rearrangements within a subsystem of production relationships are made up of the two components $\Delta T\{k, j\}$ and $\Delta M\{i, j\}$. Hence the requirement for changes in productive arrangements following the impact of a particular impulse may encounter resistance on the various levels which define productive relationships, and the degree of rigidities which are encountered on these various levels. In principle, we can compare the rigidities which would be encountered in different subsystems/networks if they were to absorb the impact of a particular impulse within a particular time horizon $\bar{t}$. Such comparisons allow us to determine (endogenously) the likelihood of the sequence by which and the types of networks which will respond to the impact of a particular impulse. We can formulate this idea with the two conditions (2) and (3) below

$$R(\{k, j, ij\}; I_i; \bar{t}) \equiv R(\Delta T\{k, j\}; \Delta M\{i, j\}; I_i; \bar{t}) \le$$
$$\Delta P(\{k, j, ij\}; I_i; \bar{t}) \equiv (\Delta T\{k, j\}; \Delta M\{i, j\}; I_i; \bar{t}) \qquad (2)$$

What condition (2) expresses is the following. If the required production rearrangements, following the impact of an impulse I_i within a particular network $\{k, j, ij\}$,[24] are to be feasible to take place within a particular time horizon $\bar{\imath}$ then the above condition must hold, i.e., the resistances to such changes cannot exceed certain levels. If resistance is greater than that then again a number of alternatives might exist: (a) resistances within the specified subsystem $\{k, j, ij\}$ are too great and hence they constrain the production rearrangements which can take place, i.e., $\Delta P' < \Delta P$ or (b) the adjustment process will have to occur within a differently specified subsystem (i.e., for example, involving a different or wider set of fund-input elements or materials-in-process flows) or (c) the resistances can be overcome within the specified subsystem but only over a longer time period $\bar{\imath}'$.

Once condition (2) is satisfied, we know that resistance encountered to a particular rearrangement of production conditions within a particular subsystem is sufficiently weak to allow such a rearrangement within the specified time horizon. However, once this condition is satisfied by a number of subsystems or for a number of alternative production rearrangements within the same subsystem, then it is presumably the ranking of the relative strengths of resistances put up by different subsystems or *vis-à-vis* alternative production rearrangements which will determine the probabilities by which different subsystems will be activated to react to a given shock and in which way.

$$\text{Prob}\,(\Delta P(\{k, j, ij\}; I_j; \bar{\imath})) \geq \text{Prob}(\Delta P(\{k', j', ij'\}; I_j; \bar{\imath}))$$
$$\text{if } R(\Delta P(\{k, j, ij\}; I_j; \bar{\imath})) \leq R(\Delta P(\{k', j', ij'\}; I_j; \bar{\imath})) \tag{3}$$

Of course, as the time horizon changes, the rankings of different subsystems in terms of their ease with which they would adjust to a given impulse might change. Consequently, the probabilities of different dynamic subsystem responses to a given impulse are a function of the time horizon within which such an adjustment is to take place. This aspect of the analysis thus points again to a time horizon dependent pattern of dynamic subsystem activation.

We should remember that conditions (2) and (3) do not reveal the full details of which particular resistances are responsible for the degrees of resistance encountered within a particular network $\{k, j, ij\}$ when it is exposed to a particular impulse. Such networks are themselves composed of a number of levels, i.e., utilisation patterns, task specifications and task arrangements, stocks of inventories and materials-in-process flows, and the detailed analysis of which dimension(s) is (are) the binding one(s) if condition (2) is not fulfilled requires careful attention to these various levels. Such an analysis reflects also the managerial search procedure to find adequate responses to the impact of impulses such that these can be absorbed by particular regions within the overall productive system or by a sequence of such regions over the stage structure of an overall adjustment process.

It is clear that both conditions (1) and (2) have to be satisfied for a particular subsystem of production interdependencies to fully absorb the impact of a particular impulse I_i within a specified time period.

In order to complete our analysis of adjustment patterns in a productive system, we should mention that there are second, third, etc. order effects of an original impulse. Once a particular impulse affects particular networks of production relationships, such changes in existing production arrangements can be seen as further rounds of impulses, which – as before – are clearly definable in character and location within our production analytical representation of a productive process. The impact of such further rounds of (induced) impulses can in principle be analysed in the same way as the impact of the first impulse, i.e., through the endogenous specification of 'dynamic subsystems' based on the location of the (endogenous) new impulse, through the analysis of potential networks and propagation patterns and the explicit analyses of relative rigidities and buffers which allow one to analyse actual propagation patterns within different time horizons. We thus obtain a representation of a sequential process of structural adjustment or, as we set out to demonstrate, a *theory of structural change as a process*. We discuss this in more detail in the next subsection.

7.3 Pervasiveness and structural change as a process in historical time

The above analysis allows one to approach the process of structural change as a process which shows clear features of *path dependence*, that is, *historical specificity* in the way in which a particular productive system responds to the impact of a particular impulse. We have seen that the three components of structural adjustment analysis, i.e., the definition of potential network interrelationships and the adequate accounting for buffers and rigidities have to be combined to show the sequential patterns by which different subsystems respond to a given impulse. We now want to emphasise the elements of the analysis which makes the responses of a particular productive system to a given impulse historically specific, i.e., dependent upon the particular *organisational features* of that system and also upon the more *conjunctural features*.

Let us start with organisational features. We have seen that buffers are an important ingredient in our analysis of endogenous subsystem specification in that they allow the circumscription of a particular 'region' of network relationships which can fully absorb the initial impact of a particular type of impulse. Buffers are, by definition, not determined technologically in the strict sense since they refer to capacities and inventories which are un- or underutilised and hence are not in the strict sense (technologically) necessary in the course of the current productive process. They are a feature of a particular organisational rather than strictly technological arrangement of a productive system. However, we have shown that precisely these organisational features have an important function to play in the way a productive system absorbs the impact of particular impulses. Hence productive systems which have different structures of un- or underutilised capacities and/or inventories available and/or have these located at different points in the productive system will respond differently to the impact of a particular impulse.

The availability of unutilised capacities and inventories is not only a function of longer-term organisational arrangements in a productive system but also of shorter-run changes in the overall level of activity (which we denote by vectors y_t, the vectors of final output over the duration of a particular production process). The dependence of buffers upon changes in the scale of productive activity, such as at different points in a business cycle, creates a dependence upon *conjunctural conditions* mentioned above. Hence a productive system at a high point of industrial activity, when it uses its capacities and inventories more fully, will respond to the impact of an impulse with the formation of different 'dynamic' subsystems more readily than a system which operates at a low level of activity and with high un- or underutilised capacities and inventories. A similar point can be made with respect to network rigidities. It could very well be that the rigidities (resistance to change) which have so far been defined for different network relationships as conditional upon (i) the time horizon $\bar{t}$ over which such a change is to take place and (ii) the particular impulse I_i which affects the system, may also be conditional upon (iii) the particular conjunctural conditions in which the productive system finds itself. Hence, in principle, the rigidity relationships should be defined as

$$\Delta R(\{k, j, ij\} I_i; \bar{t}; y_t)$$

where y_t refers again to the vectors indicating overall activity levels. The idea here is that rigidities (resistance to change) will be different at high/low levels of economic activity. For example, resistance to adopt a new fund-task allocation (job programme) might be less when the level of overall activity is low; similarly, rearrangements of the system of material flows might be easier when the pressure of demand is lower. As a result, 'dynamic subsystem' specification in the course of a system's response to a particular impulse will be dependent also in this respect upon conjunctural conditions.

The picture which emerges is that not only does the particular technology and organisational arrangement which is in place and which defines the potential network relationships $N(...)$ and $S(...)$ shape a productive system's response to a particular impulse, but so do the available buffers and rigidities which are partly conjuncturally determined. And, of course, if particular organisational and technological rearrangements are a function of conjunctural conditions then the organisational and technological arrangements in place at any one point in time will also be a function of past conjunctural conditions; we here have a path dependency of existing organisational arrangements and organisational responses to new impulses upon the sequence of previous conjunctural conditions and previous organisational structures.

7.4 Adjustment versus innovation

The final issue we want to address in this subsection is whether it is useful to distinguish in our analytical framework between two types of adjustment patterns: *adjustment with and without innovation*. In other words, whether our analysis yields anything useful in the direction of a partial *endogenisation of innovation* in a productive system.

Technological and organisational knowledge in our framework refers to sets of production elements and organisational arrangements on the three analytical levels of our production process analysis:

The set of technologically and organisationally known task specifications and task arrangements within a productive system

$$\{\tau_j\}, \{N\{\tau_j, \tau_m\}(\omega)\} \text{ where } \omega \subset \Omega^\tau.$$

The set of known fund-input elements and their (organisationally) conceivable utilisation patterns

$$\{\bar{c}_k\}, \{T_i(\omega)\} \text{ where } \omega \subset \Omega^T.$$

The set of available materials and conceivable material-in-process arrangements

$$\{m_i\} \text{ and } \{M_i(\omega)\} \text{ where } \omega \subset \Omega^M.$$

Out of these sets of organisational arrangements Ω^T and Ω^M, particular choices will have been made at any point of time, say a combination $[T_i(\alpha), M_i(\beta)]$ which refer respectively to particular organisational structures of fund-task allocations and performances and materials-in-process flows.[25]

From a purely definitional point of view, it is easy to distinguish whether the impact of a particular impulse leads to an adjustment with or without innovation. It depends whether any additions to any of the above defined sets of productive elements and organisational arrangements occur, i.e., whether any of the Ω's become Ω^*'s and whether the sets of input elements expand, say, from $\{\bar{c}_k\}$ to $\{\bar{c}_{k*}\}$ and/or from $\{m_i\}$ to $\{m_{i*}\}$.

However, the more interesting issue is whether our analysis provides a handle to partially contribute to the question of when it may be more likely that innovations (of an organisational or technological nature) may occur and of which kind such innovations may be. We will try to address this issue now.

An endogenous theory of innovations (and here we follow N. Rosenberg; see, e.g., Rosenberg, 1969, 1976) should perceive of innovation as the successful outcome of a search procedure to solve particular problems which have arisen. In our particular context, this means that a contribution to a theory of innovation could be made by specifying in a relatively precise way the nature of the problem which has arisen in a particular productive system and the relative ease with which such problems might be solved. In our production analytical framework, the following problems arise:

(a) Problems of synchronisation between the organisational structures at the different production-analytical levels;
(b) Problems in the adjustment processes to given exogenous impulses;
(c) New disequilibria emerging as a result of endogenous changes (including innovations).

Let us discuss each of these in turn:

(a) Synchronisation issues have already been discussed in chapter 6. The problem of synchronisation basically arises because the three organisational levels have to be coordinated in the overall production process and such coordination often means that improvements in the 'organisational efficiency' on one level can only be achieved by adopting suboptimal solutions at another level. For example, it could be that the adoption of a new programme and/or the hiring of new fund-input elements could improve the efficiency of fund-task allocations by the criteria of that level of organisational analysis: prominent amongst the efficiency criteria of that level would be the attainment of high levels of capability utilisation and of high task performance levels. Rearrangements in the light of these criteria might lead to a move from an inferior fund-task allocation and performance pattern $T(\beta)$ to a superior one, say $T^*(\alpha)$. However, at another organisational level, such a shift might require a rearrangement of materials-in-process flows, say from $M(\alpha)$ to $M(\beta)$; the efficiency criteria used to arrive at a particular efficiency ranking of the different materials-in-process flow arrangements would, of course, be those that are suitable for the evaluation of that level of organisational analysis (such as, for example, minimising interruptions of material-in-process flows and of inventory space). Because of the multiplicity of criteria operating at the different levels of organisational analysis, it is clear that any solution of the overall coordination problem across all the three levels will usually entail a compromise, such that efficiency gains at one level may entail efficiency losses at another level.

One aspect of innovation analysis is hence to point to the fact that problem-solving activities will be motivated by the potential efficiency gains which could be made if *new solutions* could be found to organisational structures which are at the source of *efficiency compromises* in particular organisational arrangements.

(b) This refers to the shake-up which a particular impulse causes in existing organisational set-ups. In the previous subsections we have described an approach of how to endogenise the process of structural adjustment in a productive system following the impact of a particular type of impulse. We have shown that there are basically three ingredients in such an endogenous analysis of structural change processes: the analysis of potential network/propagation patterns by keeping track of the $N(...)$ and $S(...)$ relationships, the analysis of relative rigidities and of buffers, all of which channel the impact of a particular impulse in particular directions and affect the timing and the pervasiveness of a particular process of structural adjustment. As discussed above, structural adjustment means a change in organisational patterns at the various analytical levels: e.g., a shortage of particular materials could lead to a situation such that an inferior arrangement of materials-in-process flows has to be adopted (shifting, e.g., to the use of inferior materials) and also the pattern of utilisation of fund elements might deteriorate. There could thus be a move from a process organisational structure $[T_t(\alpha), M_t(\beta)]$ to an inferior one, say, $[T_t(\beta), M_t(\gamma)]$. This obviously implies a clear efficiency loss on two analytical dimensions and might start a search process to find a better solution. If a better solution could not be found within the realm of existing knowledge of available materials, fund-input elements and organisational alternatives, then a search might develop to find a better solution outside the realm of technologically and organisationally known production elements and organisational arrangements.

(c) This refers to the importance of secondary (endogenous) innovations when the '*potential*' impact of an impulse is recognised within the constraints of existing technological and organisational knowledge. Here it is quite possible that the efficiency impact of the original impulse could be less detrimental (if it was negative in the first place) or much more positive (if it was already positive) if further complementary innovations would take place. The potential network relationships of the $S(...)$ type are particularly important here.[26] The similarity relationships $S(...)$ show whether there are particular similarities in the compositional structures of tasks, funds, jobs, etc. For interdependent learning processes such similarity relationships are very important. However, also the $N(\ldots)$ network relationships are important since they show the degree of temporal and locational interdependencies between different production elements as they are involved in the production process. A change in one such element or an organisational change in one (temporally and/or locationally defined) area will affect components which are particularly 'close' in either the $S(\ldots)$ or the $N(\ldots)$ sense.

8 Macrodynamics and microstructures (on the relationships between the contributions of parts I and II of this volume)

There is an agreement amongst economists that technical change is an issue which occurs at a microeconomic level. We also know from both old and new growth theory and their empirical implementation at a macroeconomic level that technical and organisational change accounts for a major part of economic growth (as measured by GDP per head). We face here a basic dilemma. The most important factor behind macroeconomic growth is of a microeconomic nature and hence we have no choice but to combine two distinct levels of analysis: the macro- and the microeconomic levels. This book has attempted a two-pronged attack on linking these two levels of analysis.

The contributions of part I of this book have attempted (following previous work by Hicks, Goodwin, Pasinetti and Simon) to break macroeconomic phenomena of growth and fluctuations down into the behaviour of the disaggregated components of a productive system employing a variety of methods of decomposition of an overall economy (such as vertically integrated processes and sectors, eigensectors, synergetic approaches, etc.). We refer to these approaches which link the vital issues of structural change and macroeconomic dynamics as 'top–down' or 'macro-to-micro' approaches.

The contributions of part II of the book adopt a different but complementary route to link microeconomic analysis and macroeconomic issues. These contributions developed a detailed picture of the microeconomic components of productive processes and of organisational structures. These ingredients were then used to provide insights into the endogenous formation of 'networks' and 'subsystems' which are activated by and shape the process of structural change in economic systems. This approach, starting from a detailed analysis of microeconomic production linkages and then formulating a (partially) endogenous analysis of structural adaptation and even innovation could be called 'bottom–up' or 'micro-to-macro'.

In both the top–down and the bottom–up approaches there is a shared perspective: the detailed examination of differentiated developments across the different components of an economic system is an absolutely vital component of the analysis of economic dynamics and hence continued work on *subsystem–system dynamics* with due attention paid to appropriate decomposition techniques and the endogenous specification of networks (or subsystems) provides the best hope to comprehend the difficult issues of structural economic dynamics.

Notes

1 We use the notion of 'quasi-repetitive' here because a particular production organisation might, at any point in time, be able to cope with a number of different production cycles (out of a discrete, and finite set) and thus not be strictly repetitive in its operation. However, a given production organisation will be defined by the set of 'feasible' production cycles it might be able to operate.

2 New technological options can be 'blocked' from implementation as a result of a number of factors, such as the following:

   (a) particular production units may not be aware of such options;
   (b) internal factors may block their adoption: internal evaluation criteria may be such that they are not preferred to existing technological options;
   (c) according to external performance criteria (market or non-market criteria, the latter could for example be of a legislative nature) the technological options would not be deemed superior.

3 This of course was the focus of the Scientific Management school in the first quarter of this century (see, e.g., Gantt, 1912).

4 Smith did of course also consider changes in the structure of demand, for example, when discussing the difficult adjustment processes which activities using fixed capital have to undergo when faced with changes in the composition of demand (for an exploration of the issue in Smith, see Scazzieri, 1996).

5 Of course, if the increase in the number of end products involves also an increase in the overall level of production, some rationalisation of materials-in-process flows might also occur; by 'rationalisation' we mean here that fabrication stages and materials-in-process flows which were previously distinct now get combined. Recent experience of industrial developments in advanced economies suggests that productive systems react to consumers' pressure for increased product differentiation by differentiating final fabrication stages (final design, colour, shape, additions, etc.) while rationalising earlier fabrication stages.

6 However, the qualification made in the previous footnote applies here as well: increasing product-specific task differentiation at the final fabrication stages to develop a multitude of designs/models is costly and might – if the level of demand and scale of overall activity permits – lead to task integration and the rationalisation of fund-input uses at earlier fabrication stages.

7 The analogy with 'master manufacturers' in person-to-person services needs

one important qualification. While the 'master' producing material goods (such as the carpenter, blacksmith, baker) can achieve efficiency improvements by producing ranges of *homogeneous* products (thus exploiting the discreteness of the set of products he is willing to supply to his customers), the supplier of person-to-person services (the doctor, the teacher, the social worker, etc.) works on a '*continuum*' of product/service variants that he is supposed to supply. Each patient at each visit demands a slightly different and specific care, each child receiving lessons has some specific needs, and so on. An attempt to exploit economies of homogenisation, that is to provide the same uniform service to a class of patients, pupils, etc., although their needs are somewhat differentiated, leads to a loss in the 'quality' of the service provided. This difference in the need for and the potential ability to supply a continuous spectrum of differentiated services does differentiate the 'craft' principle as applied to person-to-person services, from its application to the production of material goods (although even here there are exceptions such as custom-made clothes or furniture).

8 Such an *order of change* may recall the relationship between different price levels in Wicksell's cumulative process. For, as Myrdal describes it, such a process entails 'a race of different "price levels"': of prices for real capital, factors of production, and consumption goods', which is supposed to take place in order to make good for any given discrepancy between the 'natural rate of interest' and the money rate of interest (see Myrdal, 1939, p. 27).

9 In *Value and Capital*, Hicks examined the role of complementarities over time in dampening fluctuations and ensuring the persistence of certain fundamental economic structures in spite of remarkable sources of perturbation (see Hicks, 1939, pp. 258–302).

10 Given that measure s^τ_{jk} refers to a comparison of two compositional structures this requires a vector comparison so that the distance measure could itself be a vector; alternatively, a weighting scheme would be employed to obtain a scalar representation. In the following we shall adopt a specification which will employ a scalar representation of the distance between two types of tasks.

11 See previous note which also applies in this case.

12 See again note 10.

13 This matrix is a matrix containing symmetric information along the diagonal (just as in the case of S^τ). Hence all the information could be contained in a triangular representation of that matrix. However, for diffusion analysis we might be interested in analysing the measures of similarity from the point of view of each type of fund element so that, for example, the funds closest to that type of fund element in terms of job structure and job performance could be arranged in descending order.

14 The pattern of utilisation of a fund-input element k can be described by a vector if all the dimensions of that fund factor's capabilities are to be represented, in which case $u_k(t)t = 1, \ldots, N$ represents a series of vectors of utilisation; alternatively, it can be a scalar representation of utilisation if only one 'capacity' dimension is considered.

15 While the overall scale requirements and the successful completion of the overall productive process would be assured, the '*quality of performance*' of

some of the task performances will differ across the different job specification programmes and an overall aggregate measure of the quality of the overall process fulfilment might be constructed allowing us to rank the different programmes by such an aggregate quality indicator, i.e., $T_t(\alpha) \geq T_t(\beta) \geq \ldots$.

16 The notion of work station refers to an additional locational definition of fund-input elements, i.e., where they are located physically in the coordination patterns within a production process; this would supplement the analysis of task performances in time as specified by the time subscripts on the T_t's. The reference to locational patterns will be found again below when defining different neighbourhood relationships amongst materials-in-process flows. We will not, in general, work out the full implications of neighbourhood relations in space which seem to us to be analogous to neighbourhood relations in time, except, of course, for the unidirectionality of dependency relationships in the case of the latter. The neighbourhood specifications $N(\tau_j, \tau_k) = (0,1)$ could here refer to constraints concerning the locational distances in the performances of different tasks.

17 $\{\tau(\alpha)\}$ defines both a particular set of tasks $[\tau_k(\alpha)]$ to be performed as well as the temporal constraints on the execution of these tasks, i.e., the $N^\alpha(\tau_j, \tau_k)$.

18 A 'region' can be defined in terms of the various network relationships defined above: a particular group of interacting fund factors executing a specific set of circumscribed tasks, a particular subset of materials-in-process flows or of transformation stages carried out in the productive system.

19 As the M_t show the quantitative structures of work-in-process interdependencies and the $N(m_{ij}, m_{jk})$ show the time structure of materials-in-process flows, $R(M)$ and $R(N(M))$ define the relative rigidities of the currently installed time and quantity scheduling of materials-in-process flows.

20 We use here a shorthand for $r(n(m_{ij}, m_{jk}))$ and for $R(N(M))$. See previous note.

21 To express the above dependence of rigidities upon the time horizon and the nature of the impulse impacting upon a particular productive component or a network of such components, we can use the following notation: $R(\{t_j\}; \bar{t}; I_l)$ or $R(\{m_{ij}\}; \bar{t}; I_l)$ where $\{t_j\}$ and $\{m_{ij}\}$ refer respectively to particular subsets of tasks or materials-in-process flows, $\bar{t}$ refers to a particular time horizon, I_l to a particular type of impulse with respect to which the 'rigidities' of particular structures of capabilities $\{\bar{c}_k\}$, job arrangements $\{t_j\}$ or materials-in-process flows $\{m_{ij}\}$ are respectively defined.

22 Notice that the two types of network relationships, specified as N and S relationships respectively, are of very different types. While the N relationships define the temporal and locational networks in a productive system, the S relationships define similarity relationships which, in the first instance, ignore locational or temporal proximities. Both these types of network relationships could, in principle, give rise to propagation processes independently of one another. That is, if fund-input elements are similar in their capacity structures and learning processes occur in one part of the economic system, this could affect learning processes in (locationally and within the existing time arrangement) other quite distant regions of the system as long as there are the similarity relationships $S\{t_k, t_l\}$ or $S\{\bar{c}_k, \bar{c}_l\}$. On the other hand, fund-input elements which are

engaged in quite different sets of tasks or jobs which, however, are complementary in the time structure of the production process and have hence quite high $N\{\tau_j, \tau_k\}$ values could similarly be affected. Of course, there are also instances in which the two types of network relationships reinforce each other. For example, fund-input elements which are both similar in their capability structures and are close to each other locationally or within the time structure of fabrication processes will more likely affect each other through learning processes than fund elements which are situated more distantly from each other in the productive system.

23 In the first case $\{k, j, ij'\}$, the network is changed in that more, $\{ij'\} > \{ij\}$, or different materials-in-process flows/fabrication stages are involved without any change in the specified set of fund elements, while in the second case, $\{k', j', ij\}$, the same network of materials-in-process flows is involved as before but the set of fund-input elements involved has been changed or widened (in which case $k' > k$) involving a respecification and reassignment of tasks.

24 This is a shorthand notation for defining a specific subsystem on all the three analytical dimensions so that $\{k\}$ stands for a subset of fund-input $k \subset K$, $\{j\}$ specifies a subset of tasks $j \subset J$, $\{ij\}$ defines a subset of materials-in-process flows with $i, j \subset N$. Notice that in order to avoid proliferation of subscripts, we have used the same subscripts for identifying tasks and for the output from a particular fabrication stage/work station, namely j. For many purposes this identification will not create any difficulties.

25 The combination $[T_t(\alpha), M_t(\beta)]$ expresses the idea that actual synchronisation requirements often require that organisational arrangements have to be found that are not optimal if the efficiency criteria of different analytical dimensions of a production process (tasks, funds, materials in process) are applied in isolation. The $T(\alpha), T(\beta), T(\gamma), \dots$ and $M(\alpha), M(\beta), M(\gamma), \dots$ represent particular organisational structures at the level of task performances and materials-in-process flows respectively, and the indices $\omega = \alpha, \beta, \gamma, \dots$ also indicate rankings of these organisational arrangements by efficiency criteria appropriate for these levels. These efficiency criteria are differentiated across the different analytical dimensions and hence not 'global'. Thus the efficiency criteria relevant for the ordering of the $T(\omega)$ might refer to the degree of utilisation of fund-input elements and the degrees of task adequacy of the different job specification programmes, while the efficiency criteria underlying the ordering of the $M(\omega)$ might refer to throughput times of materials-in-process flows and the needs for storage capacities under the different organisational arrangements. For more details, see the discussion in section 7 of chapter 6.

26 See also note 22 above where the qualitative difference between $N(\dots)$ and $S(\dots)$ network relationships is discussed.

References

Ando, A. and Fisher, F. M. (1963) 'Near Decomposability, Partition and Aggregation, and the Relevance of Stability Discussions', *International Economic Review*, 4 (1, January): 53–67.

Baumol, W. J. (1967) 'Macroeconomics of Unbalanced Growth: the Anatomy of Urban Crisis', *American Economic Review*, 57 (3, June): 415–26.

Chakravarty, S. (1987) *Development Planning: the Indian Experience*, Oxford, Clarendon Press.

Cohendet, P., Ledoux, M. and Zuskovitch, E. (eds.) (1988) *New Advanced Materials. Economic Dynamics and European Strategy*, Berlin, Heidelberg; New York, Springer-Verlag.

Fisher, F. M. and Ando, A. (1971) 'Two Theorems on *Ceteris Paribus* in the Analysis of Dynamic Systems', in H. M. Blalock, Jr. (ed.), *Causal Models in the Social Sciences*, London and Basingstoke, Macmillan, pp. 190–9.

Gabszewicz, J. J. and Thisse, J. F. (1986) 'On the Nature of Competition with Differentiated Products', *The Economic Journal* (March): 160–7.

Gale, D. (1960) *The Theory of Linear Economic Models*, New York, McGraw Hill.

Gantt, H. L. (1912) 'The Task and the Day's Work', in *Addresses and Discussions at the Conference on Scientific Management held October 12–13–14, 1911*. The Amos Tuck School of Administration and Finance, Dartmouth College, Hanover, New Haven.

Georgescu-Roegen, N. (1990) 'Production Process and Dynamic Economics', in M. Baranzini and R. Scazzieri (eds.), *The Economic Theory of Structure and Change*, Cambridge, Cambridge University Press, pp. 198–226.

Gershunyi, J. I. (1987) 'Time Use and the Dynamics of the Service Sector', in G. Akehurst and J. Gadrei (eds.), *The Economics of Services*, London, Cass, pp. 56–71.

Gershunyi, J. I. and Robinson, J. P. (1988) 'Historical Changes in the Household Division of Labour', *Demography*, 25 (4, November): 537–52.

Hicks, J. R. (1939) *Value and Capital. An Inquiry into Some Fundamental Principles of Economic Theory*, Oxford, Clarendon Press.

Landesmann, M. and Scazzieri, R. (1990) 'Specification of Structure and Economic Dynamics', in M. Baranzini and R. Scazzieri (eds.), *The Economic Theory of Structure and Change*, Cambridge, Cambridge University Press, pp. 95–121.

Loasby, B. J. (1976) *Choice, Complexity and Ignorance. An Enquiry into Economic Theory and the Practice of Decision-Making*, Cambridge, Cambridge University Press.

Myrdal, G. (1939) *Monetary Equilibrium*, London, William Hodge.

Pasinetti, L. L. (1981) *Structural Change and Economic Growth. A Theory of the Economic Consequences of Human Learning*, Cambridge, Cambridge University Press.

  (1993) *Structural Economic Dynamics. A Theory of the Economic Consequences of Human Learning*, Cambridge, Cambridge University Press.

Rosenberg, N. (1963) 'Technological Change in the Machine Tool Industry, 1840–1910', *The Journal of Economic History*, 23 (3, September): 414–43.

  (1969) 'The Direction of Technological Change: Inducement Mechanisms and Focusing Devices', *Economic Development and Cultural Change*, 18 (October): 1–24.

  (1976) *Perspectives on Technology*, Cambridge, Cambridge University Press.

Scazzieri, R. (1993) *A Theory of Production. Tasks, Processes and Technical Practices*, Oxford, Clarendon Press.

(1996) 'Classical Traverse Analysis', forthcoming in M. Landesmann and R. Rowthorn (eds.), *Structural Dynamics of Market Economies*, London, Macmillan.

Shaked, A. and Sutton, J. (1982) 'Relaxing Price Competition Through Product Differentiation', *Review of Economic Studies*, pp. 3–13.

Simon, H. A. (1969) *The Sciences of the Artificial*, Cambridge, Mass., MIT Press.

Simon, H. A. and Ando, A. (1961) 'Aggregation of Variables in Dynamic Systems', *Econometrica*, 29 (2, April): 111–38.

Name index

Abramovitz, M., 138
Abruzzi, A., 222n, 225
Adams, R.L., 244, 250
Aftalion, A., 167
Akehurst, G., 342
Allais, M., 77n, 79n
Amendola, M., 100n, 103, 158–60, 162n, 163, 163n
Ames, E., 254, 294n, 300
Ampère, A.-M., 221n, 225
Anderson, P.W., 27
Ando, A., 174, 184n, 185, 187, 217, 225, 318, 341–3
Antonelli, G., 251
Arora, S.R., 260, 300
Arrow, K.J., 27–30, 77n, 79n
Arthur, B., 7, 27

Babbage, C., 2, 27, 221n, 223n, 224n, 225, 271–2, 274, 277–8, 282, 293, 297n, 300
Bakshi, M.S., 260, 300
Baldone, S., xiv, 10, 17, 81, 101n, 103, 159, 164n
Baranzini, M., 15, 27–30, 139, 164–5, 226–7, 301, 342
Barker, G.E., 252, 298n, 299n, 301
Batey Blackman, S.A., 28
Batten, D., 186
Bauer, O., 167
Baumol, W.J., 2, 5, 27–30, 313, 342
Beccaria, C., 27–8, 271, 300
Bellman, R., 78n, 79n
Belloc, B., xiv, 10, 15–16, 33, 76n, 77n, 79n, 82, 88, 100n, 102n, 103, 159, 163n, 164
Ben Arieh, D., 299n, 301
Benassy, J.P., 78n, 79n
Benhabib, J., 185
Berg, M., 261, 300
Bernoulli, D., 169
Bessant, J., 221n, 225
Bharadwaj, K., 216, 225

Bladen, W., 227
Blalock, H.M., 342
Blin, J.M., 225
Böhm-Bawerk, E. von, 2, 28, 81, 103, 143, 145, 216, 221n, 225
Boldrin, M., 185
Bolli, P., 235, 249–50
Bouniatian, M., 167
Brewster, J.M., 235–6, 250
Brizi, A.S., 244, 250
Bücher, C., 262, 300
Buckett, M., 235, 250
Burbridge, J.L., 299n, 300
Burchardt, F.A., 143, 145, 158, 160n, 161n, 164, 225
Burmeister, E., 41–2, 76n, 79n, 101n, 103, 163n, 164

Capelli, A., 132
Carrie, A., 300
Cartwright, N., 222n, 225
Casati, D., 237, 250
Casti, J., 186
Cavalchini, A.G., 237, 250
Chakravarty, S., 28n, 163n, 164, 318, 342
Chaloner, W.H., 28
Chandler, A.D., 283, 300
Chao, K., 295n, 300
Chayanov, A.V., 247, 250
Chernyshevskij, N.G., 282, 300
Chipman, J.S., 168, 185
Chng, M.K., 163n, 164
Church, A.H., 221n, 225, 282–3, 300
Cipolla C., 294n, 300, 303
Clark, J.B., 221n, 225
Cochrane, W.W., 234, 239, 250
Cohendet, P., 194, 225, 313, 342
Cole, W.A., 5, 28
Collard, D.A., 165–6
Cooke, K.L., 78n, 79n
Craven, J., 76n, 80n

344

Subject index